AN INTRODUCTION TO POLITICAL SCIENCE
THE MANAGEMENT OF CONFLICT

MARK R. AMSTUTZ
Wheaton College

SCOTT, FORESMAN AND COMPANY
Glenview, Illinois
Dallas, Tex.   Oakland, N.J.   Palo Alto, Cal.   Tucker, Ga.   London, England

To my daughters,
Anne and Caroline,
with the hope that their world
will remain peaceful and free.

Library of Congress Cataloging in Publication Data

Amstutz, Mark R.
  An Introduction to political science.

  Includes index.
  1. Consensus (Social sciences)   2. State, The.
3. Political science.   4. Comparative government.
I. Title.
JC328.2.A46   320   81-18342
ISBN 0-673-16053-X   AACR2

Production Editor: Laurie Greenstein
Text Design: Linda Robertson
Cover Design: Matt Pomaski
Illustrations: Etc. Graphics
Composition: Hightower Typesetting

ISBN: 0-673-16053-X

CONTENTS

PREFACE

The aim of this introductory text is to present some of the major elements of political science to the beginning college student. The primary challenge in writing such a text is to describe the significant concepts and issues of the discipline with clarity and simplicity. Every discipline has its distinctive jargon, technical concepts, and specialized terminology, and political science is no exception. But while such terminology may be important to the professional researcher or advanced student, it can be a barrier to learning for the beginning student. In preparing this text, the author has therefore sought to minimize the use of technical terms and to express the major elements of politics and government with maximum simplicity.

The preparation of this book is a direct outgrowth of my teaching experience at a small (2,000 students) liberal arts college. During the past eight years I have regularly taught an introductory political science course and have used a variety of approaches and methods. In one term, I used an eclectic perspective, taking different approaches to examine different aspects of the discipline. A normative perspective was used during another term, when the major concern was the problem of justice in political communities. In still another term I used a behavioral approach, in which contemporary research on political behavior of individuals and groups was emphasized.

From my teaching experience, I discovered that student learning in the introductory course could be facilitated when two dimensions were emphasized —unity among various parts of the discipline and relevance of the material. Since political science, like other academic fields, has numerous subfields, relating the different parts to a common perspective helped students understand the essential elements of politics and how the subfields of political science relate to each other. Second, greater interest and learning result when politics is related to the common experiences of life, i.e., to familiar events in neighborhoods, schools, churches and towns.

The perspective that I have developed and used in recent years in my introductory course allows these two dimensions to be emphasized. The focus is on social and political conflict, and seeks to develop awareness of the methods and processes involved in managing and resolving conflict. The conflict-management approach helps ensure coherence in covering the various aspects of the discipline and, most importantly, helps provide a bridge from the known to the unknown—from students' understanding of social and political tensions in their communities to their limited knowledge of national and international political conflicts.

Politics can be viewed either as a quest for justice or a quest for peace. Justice and peace, however, are interdependent — no community can remain peaceful very long without justice, and no society can be just without substantial harmony among individuals and groups. Nonetheless, most political scientists tend to emphasize one element over the other rather than both. This is not because either peace or justice is recognized as more important but because of sheer difficulties in defining and implementing either element in society. Indeed, the task of defining justice is so difficult that it could become the all-consuming concern in politics.

This text focuses on the search for peace in human society. Peace is more easily defined than justice and thus provides a less cumbersome framework for examining the nature of politics and the role of governmental institutions in society. The conflict-management approach can be easily integrated into the various elements of political science. Another advantage of the conflict-management perspective is that it provides a medium through which students can build on their knowledge of human tensions and conflicts in their homes, schools, neighborhoods, and towns.

In this text politics is defined as the search for a peaceful and orderly community where people's individual rights and needs are protected. The search for peace and harmony is a universal quest, for the natural outcome of all interpersonal relations is some human conflict. Although some conflict is desirable for a vigorous and creative society, when conflict becomes too frequent or too intense it can become destructive to society. What is needed in human communities is not only order and peace but also a stable environment where legitimate conflicts among individuals and groups can be managed and resolved openly and effectively.

Since no society can be creative and dynamic without some degree of interpersonal and intergroup tension and conflict, the goal of politics is to protect human rights by maintaining community order through the management of conflict. This means that government seeks to control some behaviors but never extends its control to inhibit creative and productive energies of people. Thus, it is possible to develop harmonious and stable communities that also protect diverse and conflicting interests within society.

Three major sections comprise the text. The first part deals with conceptual and theoretical perspectives about conflict and its regulation. Chapter one examines the nature and role of conflict in human communities, and chapters two and three analyze the nature of politics and government with reference to the task of managing human incompatibilities. Chapter four describes four classic theories of building a political community and of maintaining social harmony.

The second part looks at some of the major governmental institutions for managing conflict within the state. Chapter five is concerned with the nature of the nation-state, the most important political community in our contemporary world. The subject of chapter six is the major institutions for making and implementing binding rules. Chapters seven, eight, and nine are concerned with less formal political processes and institutions in building social harmony and political consensus, i.e., political culture, political socialization, public opinion, interest groups, and political parties.

The third part, the practice of conflict management, concentrates on some of the key institutions and political processes involved in building social unity and resolving community conflicts in selected modern states. The United States, Great Britain, the Soviet Union and the developing nations illustrate significant patterns and institutions found in other political systems. Chapters fourteen and fifteen analyze the nature of international politics and some of the methods used in managing and resolving international disputes.

ACKNOWLEDGEMENTS

In preparing this text, I have benefited from the assistance and support of many people. Writing is a lonely enterprise and without outside support this text would not have been written.

Firstly, I want to thank the students of Political Science 10. They were the first ones who thought I had something to say and encouraged me to put into writing some of my ideas on politics and conflict management. I am also grateful to the Wheaton College Alumni Association which supported financially a fall quarter leave in 1977. It was during this time that I prepared materials that served as the foundation for this text.

I have benefited from the suggestions and comments of numerous persons who read different parts of the manuscript. In particular I am grateful to the following persons for their incisive suggestions: Arthur Holmes, Wheaton College; W. Lance Bennett, University of Washington; Mark Blitz, University of Pennsylvania; and Peter F. Cowhey, University of California at San Diego. Their comments have made this book better than it would have been otherwise.

The staff at Scott, Foresman has been most helpful. I am particularly grateful to Jim Boyd, who provided direction and encouragement during the writing phase, and to Laurie Greenstein, who guided the project through the various production phases.

Finally, I want to thank Steve Smith, Donna Reifsnyder, and Dave Bourne, my student assistants over the past several years, who helped directly and indirectly with different aspects of this book.

PART I
THE THEORY
OF CONFLICT
MANAGEMENT

1 / CONFLICT IN HUMAN COMMUNITIES

One of the inescapable facts of life is human conflict. Daily events remind us of the persistent and widespread nature of human discord and of the inability of people to live harmoniously with others. Interpersonal, intergroup, and international conflicts are part of human existence. A natural byproduct of the nature of interpersonal relations, most conflict has a beneficial impact on people and their communities. Conflict is the source of a vigorous and dynamic society. An environment without tensions, disagreements, and disputes would be uncreative and unproductive.

When individuals and groups are unable to reconcile incompatible goals peacefully, conflict can become destructive. The inability to reconcile interests betweeen husbands and wives can lead to separation or divorce. The incompatible aims of labor and management can lead to costly strikes. Ethnic or social groups unable or unwilling to achieve their goals within the established norms of society may resort to force in an attempt to alter governmental policies. Most significantly, states unable to achieve foreign-policy aims peacefully may resort to aggressive war to obtain their goals.

Of the many social conflicts, the most visible are those public tensions affecting whole societies. Daily news events are based on the most dramatic social and political tensions within and between countries. A review of the major headlines at the beginning of 1980 revealed the following major domestic and international disputes:

1. American-Iranian relations were deeply strained by the unwillingness of the Iranian government to return U.S. hostages seized from its embassy in Tehran. Moslem radicals had overtaken the embassy in an effort to force the United States to return the Shah and to admit publicly its unjust and erroneous policies in supporting the Shah's regime.

2. Following the Soviet invasion of Afghanistan at the beginning of 1980, Soviet-American relations became increasingly strained. In response to Soviet expansionist actions, President Carter ordered a trade embargo on high technology and major cutbacks in grain exports, and recommended a boycott of the Moscow Summer Olympics.

3. A deep cleavage continued to exist between China and Vietnam. Although both countries consider themselves Marxist-Leninist, deep ethnic, ideological, and political differences between the two states exploded into armed conflict in 1979. The Chinese invasion of Vietnam in February 1979 was precipitated by the Vietnamese invasion of Cambodia a month earlier. A truce was subsequently established along the border, but armed clashes between the two states continued to threaten the peace in Southeast Asia.

4. Domestic armed conflict continued in Kampuchea (Cambodia) between Vietnamese forces and Khmer Rouge guerillas. The Khmer Rouge, the pro-Chinese communist forces that ruled Cambodia from 1975 to 1979, were defeated by the Vietnamese early in 1979 but continued armed opposition in the countryside.

5. Zimbabwe (Rhodesia) remained a politically divided state between the moderate forces of Abel Muzorewa and the more radical forces of the Patriotic Front led by Joshua Nkomo and Robert Mugabe. The British Foreign Ministry established a cease-fire between the two opposing groups and set up a transitional government to oversee new elections in February 1980.

6. Guerilla activity from both rightist and leftist groups continued to threaten the civilian-military junta governing El Salvador. The junta deposed the civilian government in October 1979 but had been unable to establish control over the state. The inability to reconcile the political and economic interests of major social groups threatened the country with a major civil war not unlike that which had occurred in Nicaragua a year earlier.

Besides major political disputes such as these, every province, city, village, school district, or other form of political or social association was similarly faced with conflicts and tensions, although their intensity or magnitude may not have been as great or significant. A review of the local news of several midwestern towns revealed the following disputes:

a conflict in a school district between the teacher's union and the school board;

a dispute between land developers who wanted to alter zoning regulations and village members who opposed such a change;

a disagreement between local government officials and villagers over the proposed enlargement of a two-lane road to a four-lane highway;

tension among community members over the creation of a low-income housing project;

a political dispute within members of city government over ways to attract new business to the community; and

a disagreement among village members over the site of a new fire station.

The list could be expanded indefinitely. Wherever people seek to work in community with others, the inevitable result is some form of tension, rivalry, and conflict.

The fundamental problem in political science is how to build and maintain stable and orderly communities in which individuals are free to develop their own abilities and pursue their particular interests. Order is required to facilitate human interaction, but freedom is also required if individuals are to develop their own creative skills and abilities. Too much order can result in an uncreative and stifling environment, yet too much freedom can result in a disorderly community. What is needed is a balance between the general concerns of the community expressed in terms of the social and political order and the particular concerns of individuals expressed in terms of the specific aims of people.

Establishing and maintaining peaceful, creative and dynamic communities is not an automatic byproduct of human interaction. The natural tendency of human associations large or small, complex or simple, is to have too much freedom and therefore too much conflict. The creation of viable communities requires the establishment of certain norms and rules that help to guide behavior and facilitate the management and reconciliation of conflict.

The easiest way to cure excessive conflict is to eliminate and suppress conflict altogether. But as will be made plain throughout this text, the elimination of conflict is neither an effective nor a desirable response to human tensions. Because conflict is a direct outcome of all salutary interpersonal and intergroup activity, the elimination of conflict is impossible. Authoritarian regimes like those in Cuba and the Soviet Union may be able to establish a high level of external order and harmony but are unable to regulate the motives, drives, and spirit of their citizens. Conflict can be momentarily suppressed but not eliminated.

This text presents politics and government from the perspective of conflict management. It begins with an examination of the nature and role of conflict in society. Our concern is not limited to political tensions and incompatibilities but extends to other forms of human conflict. The intent is to show the organic connection between politics and other dimensions of human activity. A fundamental assumption is that it is impossible to understand the resolution of political conflict within and between states before comprehending the nature of conflict within those communities with which we are most familiar — our homes, schools, churches, businesses, and school districts. This chapter discusses the nature of social conflict; subsequent chapters show how political activity arises out of human tensions and incompatibilities found at all levels of human association.

THE PROBLEM OF COMMUNITY

The fundamental problem of politics is finding an appropriate balance between community order and individual freedom. This basic concern is called the *problem of community*. There are two fundamental assumptions on which the problem of community is based: (1) people need people; and (2) people can't get along with others. The first assumption affirms the social nature of the person; the second affirms the conflictual nature of interpersonal relations. The first assumption affirms that community life is essential, while the second affirms that the creation and maintenance of human communities is impaired by incompatible and competitive aims of individuals.

Some political thinkers, notably Thomas Hobbes, John Locke, and Jean Jacques Rousseau, have popularized the atomistic conception of man. But the view that people exist, or have ever existed, as isolated entities, separate from society, is pure fiction. From the moment of birth through childhood and adult life, human beings are constantly in touch with other people as they seek to survive, procreate, and find meaning in life. The very humanity of a person depends upon his ability to live, work, play, and worship with others. Psychologically, human beings need the acceptance, approval, and affection of others. When a person is unable to relate to others effectively, he or she tends to develop psychological problems that impede normal functioning in society.

People are generally involved in human associations at various levels simultaneously. At the fundamental level, most persons are part of a family structure. In some cultures, the extended family pattern provides a strong psychological and social bond among the many family relatives. At the next higher level, people participate in their neighborhoods. Friendships are established among families and individuals living in geographical proximity, and common interests are developed that affect schools, zoning codes, and other local concerns. People also become attached to larger political communities like the city, province, nation-state, and even the world system itself. Clearly, the pervasive nature of the family, the town, the city, and the nation provides unmistakable evidence of the social nature of people.

It is equally clear, however, that people often can't get along with others. Whenever and wherever individuals seek to live, work, and associate with others, the result is not only peace and harmony but also tension, discord, and conflict. Such conflict is found both in simple communities like homes, churches, and neighborhoods and in more complex communities like cities, nation-states, and the world system itself. Moreover, since the cause of conflict is rooted in the competitive and selfish nature of human beings, conflict results whenever individuals or groups seek to maximize their particular interests while disregarding the interests of other community members.

It is easy to overemphasize the conflictual nature of interpersonal and intergroup relations, since harmony and cooperation are generally assumed to be the normal and expected form of human interaction. The news media provide daily accounts of human conflict worldwide: rising divorce rates, homicides, robberies, hijackings, strikes, domestic political disturbances, guerilla activity, international tensions, and war. Media emphasis of dramatic expressions of human conflict makes it easy to assume that all human relationships are basically conflictual. But human conflict is noticeable only because the vast majority of human activity is harmonious and peaceful.

Human communities are much like icebergs, with the visible one-ninth representing conflictual interrelationships and the submerged eight-ninths representing cooperative and harmonious relationships (Figure 1.1). Obviously, if cooperation and harmony did not exist among people, it would be impossible to establish and maintain human communities of any size or form.

Figure 1.1   The Nature of Community Relations

The existence of communities at all levels demonstrates not only the social nature of human beings but also the ability of people to live and work cooperatively. Conflict results in all human interrelationships, but such tension and conflict is the exception, not the dominant feature of community life.

Besides the overemphasis on conflict, our culture tends to give it a negative bias. When interpersonal conflict develops, often the first reaction is to eliminate it or at least to minimize its effects. Similarly, when one thinks of family disputes, racial tensions, industrial conflicts, or political revolts, the first reaction to all these phenomena is negative. Human concern with conflictual situations generally focuses on controlling, eliminating, or resolving conflict. Kenneth Boulding has stated the bias against conflict as follows:

Conflict is discord, and the opposite of conflict is harmony; the words reveal the valuational bias in the language and in the common experience. Discord may be necessary to make music interesting and to give it drama, but its significance lies in the ability of the composer to resolve discord into some meaningful harmony, however subtle. The essence of the drama of conflict is likewise its resolution; it is not the conflict as such that makes the drama but the resolution of the conflict as a meaningful process through time. A conflict that went on and on without end and without resolution would lose even dramatic interest; it would eventually become mere noise and confusion. It is the process of conflict toward some kind of resolution which gives it meaning and which makes it good. This is true even in sports and games; a game that went on interminably without any resolution would be intolerable.[1]

Although conflict is the major source of the problem of community, we must resist the assumption that a world without conflict would be meaningful and enjoyable. Despite the commonly accepted negative bias of conflict, it is particularly important to emphasize the value of human disputes and to recognize that vigorous and dynamic community life depends on the management, not the elimination, of conflict.

THE NATURE OF SOCIAL CONFLICT

Conflict occurs whenever a real or perceived incompatibility exists between people. Incompatibilities may occur between individuals, between individuals and groups, or between groups themselves. They arise because two or more parties seek to get or do something that can only be realized by one party. Conflicts may involve occupying the same space, pursuing the same incompatible goals or rewards, or using mutually incompatible means to achieve objectives. From the standpoint of game theory, conflict relationships are those in which an increase in one group's welfare diminishes the welfare of another.

Some scholars have stressed the role of direct opposition between parties in conflict. Coser, for example, defines conflict as "a struggle over values and claims to scarce status, power, and resources in which the aims of the opponents are to neutralize, injure, or eliminate their rivals."[2] This view of conflict must include a high degree of involvement among the parties, since they seek to limit each other's capacity to fulfill their aims, even if it means injuring or eliminating the opposing party. But not all conflicts involve important issues in which parties may wish to oppose each other directly. Some incompatibilities may involve relatively unimportant issues, and parties may be unwilling to use destructive efforts to achieve their aims.

It may be useful to view conflicts along a continuum from relatively insignificant differences and incompatibilities that occur between individuals and groups to major ones in which every effort is made to realize an objective. As one moves along the continuum (Figure 1.2) from left to right, the intensity between opposing parties tends to rise. Disagreements, for example, involve incompatibilities that parties may wish to leave unresolved. But as issues become more important, parties become involved in competitive actions, although their behaviors are generally guided by accepted norms or rules of conflict resolution. Significant incompatibilities lead not only to competitive action, but also result in violent action.

Figure 1.2   A Continuum of Conflicts

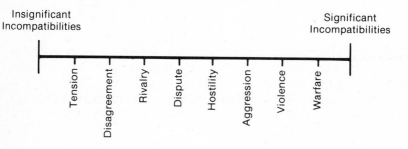

All social conflict presupposes some degree of community among competing parties. If individuals and groups were not interested in the same aims and goals or were not in the same community or association, there would be no conflict. Conflict requires interaction. A football game, for example, is a conflict between two different athletic teams. The conflict, however, presupposes a general acceptance of football rules and certain accepted norms in playing such a sport. Similarly, an election is a competition between two opposing political groups or parties, each of which has accepted the legitimacy of the electoral rules governing the election. A war is a violent conflict between two states; it presupposes general acceptance of the international community of nations and the values and standards associated with it. In short, conflict always occurs within the context of some human community.

Elements of Conflict

Social scientists have generally disagreed on the exact nature of conflict. One study that summarizes some of the essential elements of social, political, and psychological conflict was carried out by Mack and Snyder. According to them, a conflict requires the following elements:[3]

"That's my cousin's place. I want you to go up there and flatten it!"

Drawing by W. Miller; © 1980 The New Yorker Magazine, Inc.

1. Social conflict requires at least two distinct parties that interact with each other. Just as harmony develops from group interaction, so, too, is conflict a byproduct of human interdependence. The distinction between cooperative and conflictual relationships, however, is often difficult to ascertain. For example, a nation may sign a peace treaty and may outwardly demonstrate peaceful and cooperative behavior but may secretly be preparing for war. Such a relationship could be considered either cooperative or conflictual.

2. Conflict is generally the result of either position scarcity or resource scarcity. Position scarcity involves a situation in which only one party can enjoy a particular responsibility or a business or governmental position. For example, only one congressman can be elected from a congressional district, and only two senators can be elected from each state. Similarly, only one governor can be elected in each state, and only one person can be chief justice of the Supreme Court. Those individuals who view politics as a struggle for power and influence tend to view politics in terms of position scarcity. Resource scarcity, on the other hand, is a situation in which the demand for economic resources exceeds the supply. People always want more than they have, and conflict thus emerges over ways to use and distribute society's resources. Those who view politics as class conflict, as did Karl Marx, tend to view politics in terms of resource scarcity.

3. Conflict involves behavior that seeks to destroy, injure, thwart, or otherwise control another person or group. Since gain in a conflict relationship can only come at the expense of another person or group, conflictual behavior generally seeks to limit the gains for another party or to maximize one's own gains or both.

4. Conflict requires mutually opposing actions between participants. A conflict relationship is a dynamic situation in which parties to a conflict carry out actions and reactions in the pursuit of mutually exclusive goals. During the 1962 Cuban missile crisis, for example, the United States and the Soviet Union had mutually exclusive goals (The United States wanted to eradicate all intermediate Soviet ICBMs from Cuba, and the Soviet Union wanted to withdraw them only on condition that the United States would withdraw its missiles from Turkey). Consequently, the actions they pursued were mutually opposed. Studies of major political conflicts have shown that misperception of the action-reaction sequence of behaviors in a conflictual situation often compounds and aggravates intergroup and interstate relations. When misperception increases, it then becomes possible for erroneous perceptions themselves to become a major source of hostility and tension.

5. Conflict relations generally involve attempts to influence the behavior of each party to the conflict. Influence involves the effort by one party to get the other to do something it would not do otherwise. Trying to alter behavior, however it might be accomplished, is the goal of influence. Since a large portion of all social and political conflicts involve redistribution of scarce resources and positions, most conflictual relationships involve attempts to control the dispositions of resources and positions. The continued ability to determine the outcome of the distribution of scarce resources and positions of influence signifies that one party has developed greater power than another.

Power in this context may be defined as the ability to control the disposition of scarce resources and positions. It is thus an outward manifestation of continued influence. The United States and the Soviet Union, for example, have been considered powerful countries because they have been able to achieve a large number of their foreign-policy goals. Similarly, political leaders like Joseph Stalin, Mao Tse-tung, Fidel Castro, and Charles de Gaulle have been considered powerful leaders because of their ability to direct historical events. When Congressman Wilbur Mills was chairman of the House Ways and Means Committee, he was considered one of the most powerful members of Congress. This perception was based largely on Mills's ability to influence and direct the outcome of tax legislation.

Types of Social Conflict

Social and political conflicts can be distinguished in terms of their scope, level of violence, level of institutionalization, and substance.

Scope   Conflicts between individuals or groups are called *interpersonal* or *intergroup*. Of these two types of social conflict, the latter is more significant because it involves tensions and incompatibilities within major groups and large communities. Although interpersonal conflict affects the manner in which the problem of community is resolved, students of politics are generally concerned with conflict resolution within communities (intracommunity) and between them (intercommunity). Thus, presidential campaigns, civil disturbances and international disputes are generally considered more significant than incompatibilities between individuals.

Levels of Violence   Social conflicts also differ in terms of their level of destructiveness. *Violent conflicts* are those in which mutually exclusive goals of participants are resolved through destructive, forceful means. Violence may be carried out directly against the opposing party or against the whole community.

Nonviolent conflicts are disputes in which parties seek to resolve incompatible aims peacefully. By far, the most common forms of peaceful conflict resolution are discussion and persuasion. The nonviolent approach to conflict resolution was popularized by Mahatma Gandhi, who used peaceful protests to mobilize public opinion in India and ultimately to win the nation's independence from Britain. Martin Luther King, Jr., the American civil rights leader, also dramatized the nonviolent approach to conflict resolution during the 1960s as he sought to pressure national and state governmental institutions to alter their discriminatory racial policies.

Social conflicts cannot be easily divided into those that are destructive and those that are not. Indeed, most tensions are located along a spectrum between peaceful, relatively unimportant tensions and intense, destructive conflicts. For example, the following conflicts are listed in order of increasing level of intensity and human destructiveness:

1. family quarrel
2. parliamentary debate
3. labor-management tension
4. presidential election
5. strike
6. riot
7. major civil disturbances
8. civil war
9. conventional war
10. nuclear war

Level of Institutionalization   Conflicts can be distinguished in terms of the degree to which they follow predetermined patterns and rules. The level of institutionalization does not refer to the extent to which the actors are formal political institutions but rather to the extent to which the conflict behavior is guided by particular norms. *Institutionalized conflict* is the discord or incompatibility expressed in terms of certain accepted fundamental principles or explicit rules. Since such conflict is carried out within a commonly accepted framework, the behavior of the parties in conflict tends to be somewhat predictable. Examples of institutionalized conflict include labor-management negotiations, parliamentary debate, and congressional elections. Wars could also be included in this type of conflict, for nations have generally accepted rules and principles of international law that inhibit certain inhumane actions and practices during combat.

Noninstitutionalized conflict, by contrast, is characterized by an absence of principles or rules. Unlike institutionalized conflict, which is organized and carried out to achieve a particular objective, noninstitutionalized conflict is most often the result of frustration expressed in spontaneous and uncontrolled anger. Examples of this type of conflict include the spontaneous eruption of civil violence in the United States in the late 1960s and the racial tensions in Southern Africa in the late 1970s.

Substance Another distinction must be made between realistic and nonrealistic conflicts. *Realistic conflicts* arise when individuals or groups clash over specific interests or goals. This form of conflict involves a real incompatibility involving resources, prestige, or some other tangible or intangible resource. Realistic conflicts can, in turn, be classified as either true or latent based on the extent to which the parties recognize the incompatibility of interests.

A *true conflict* is one where an objective incompatibility exists and where the parties become involved in hostile actions because they have accurately recognized their irreconcilable aims and interests. An example of this type of conflict surfaced in the 1970s between Chile and Argentina over three small islands of the Beagel Channel in the Straits of Magellan.

Latent conflict involves the existence of an objective incompatibility but the failure of the participants to carry out opposing behavior. Latent conflict, in other words, is based on a real problem but because parties suppress, displace, or misperceive reality they do not carry out hostile actions. The acceptance by blacks of policies and practices of racial discrimination throughout many decades represents a type of latent dispute. Although an objective incompatibility existed between the interests of whites and blacks, the latter failed to express their opposition until the mid-twentieth century.

Nonrealistic conflict is a dispute without any objective basis. Such conflicts occur not because of real incompatibilities between parties but because of subjective misperceptions or personal, aggressive impulses. The cause of such conflicts is thus in the subjective feelings of individuals and communities. For example, the foreign-policy objectives of Nazi Germany, which led to the Second World War, were largely caused by the aggressive Nazi drive for additional territory. Similarly, the tensions between the Soviet Union and the United States have been exacerbated by frequent misperceptions of each other's aims and motives.

FUNCTIONS OF CONFLICT

The problem of community has its source in the inability of people to live with others. Harmony is not a natural outcome of community life but must be created. Obviously, the easiest way to establish a peaceful and harmonious community is to minimize or eliminate all conflict. But such a solution would be intolerable. To create such harmony, most freedom and liberty would be lost, and the consequence would be a peaceful society of dwarfed and incomplete persons. To understand why some conflict is desirable, it is necessary to review some of the major positive and negative functions of conflict.

Positive Functions

1. *Conflict tends to diffuse more serious conflict.* Social scientists have found that groups and societies that have frequent conflicts tend to avoid major violence and destruction.[4] A reason for this is that frequent small disputes prepare the community to resolve disagreements through institutionalized procedures. Since all human interaction is prone to conflict, the avoidance or suppression of conflict only serves to build up pressure within a community and ultimately to express itself in unmanageable terms. The 1979 revolution in Iran, which led to the overthrow of the Shah's regime and the establishment of an Islamic government headed by Ayatollah Khomeini, occurred in part because of the government's authoritarian policies. The Shah achieved relative peace and stability by suppressing dissidents and eliminating all political opposition, but the masses were to have the last word.

2. *Conflict tends to encourage human creativity and innovation.* When individuals are free to express their ideas, perceptions, and views, the resulting dialogue helps to clarify issues and encourages the search for better solutions. A major source of innovation is the creative competition and conflict that occurs within a free society. When Western democratic nations are compared with communist totalitarian states, clearly the Western democratic states have a higher level of political and social conflict. But it is also evident that the disharmony and tension of the democratic societies has led to greater vitality, dynamism, and creativity. Democratic decision making is slower and less efficient, but higher conflict levels in these societies can lead to better decisions and higher productivity because of broader community involvement. Conflict is thus beneficial to relationships, groups, and communities because it prevents the ossification of relationships and encourages the continuing search for new patterns and procedures. A vigorous and dynamic community can be maintained only through some tension and disharmony.

3. *Conflict is beneficial because it encourages community cohesion.* Such unity can be encouraged both internally and externally. When two groups or nations are in conflict with each other, the members of each community forget their own tensions and focus on the external issues. When this occurs, members of a group are drawn together. When external conflicts occur, members' perceptions of their own group generally become more positive; their perceptions of the opposing group tend to decline. Eventually, the perceptions of each of the disputing parties become increasingly distorted. External conflict, in other words, tends to have a positive and stimulating effect within a community but tends to produce adverse results in the community's external relations. The unifying effect of a community's conflict is perhaps most easily demonstrated

in time of war, when people forget domestic problems and rally to defend the nation. Smaller, less significant adversities tend to bring about a high level of community cohesion. One study, for example, shows that community conflict declines and harmony increases after natural disasters, particularly in the early phases following the event.[5]

Intragroup or intracommunity conflict can also encourage unity and cohesion although not as much as can external conflict. Frequent conflict requires (besides participant interaction) a high degree of interdependence. But whether or not the high level of interaction leads to unity or disorder depends on the type and quality of conflict. Hostile, destructive conflicts tends to be dysfunctional and impair group cohesion. Conflicts dealing with relatively small, substantive issues, however, tend to strengthen community or group unity. For example, a marriage relationship that has a low level of tension and conflict may suggest a high level of compatibility; such a condition may also represent a relationship in which the partners have a low level of interaction. Similarly, a democratic state like the United States has a high degree of open conflict, while the People's Republic of China or Cuba has a much lower level of visible tension. Yet, the continuing conflict in the United States has tended to strengthen the pluralistic unity among the many social and political groups within the nation; the lack of open conflict in China and Cuba has tended to obscure the differences among its groups. The value of conflict, then, is that it increases the frequency of interaction among parties and tends to clarify positions and interests of community members. However paradoxical it may appear, an open, conflictual society encourages a more mature and stable community.

4. *Conflict is useful because it provides a means of measuring the relative strength of competing parties.* Knowledge of the power capabilities of each community member is an important aid in managing conflict. Those individuals or groups that have won a reputation for dominance and influence are more likely to pursue their own interests; those that have a reputation for limited influence tend to pursue their own interests less aggressively. Thus, conflict tends to develop an informal hierarchy of influence among community members. Such a hierarchy tends to inhibit and regulate more serious conflict.

Negative Functions

1. *Conflict is detrimental when it leads to disorder and instability.* Disorder results either from an overabundance of conflict or from highly intense conflicts. When a community is unable to provide the peace and order its members desire, individuals seek to maximize their well-being through individualistic rather than communitarian means. Maximizing individual

interests in an unstable and uncertain environment can be costly and inefficient. In the international system, there is no fundamental order; and therefore, each country must depend upon its own resources to find security and economic well-being. As a result, the 150 nations of the world annually spend more than 400 billion dollars for military defense. The irony of military defense is that the very security that states are trying to achieve through major defense programs becomes more elusive with the increasing destructive power of states.

Too much conflict within smaller communities can also have detrimental effects. When a business organization, college, town, or county is governed through decentralized institutions, frequent tensions tend to arise between centers of decision making, leading to ineffective community management. When governmental institutions are permitted to promote their specific interests at the expense of community concerns, the interplay of the various groups' interests may not benefit the total community. Competition is desirable to ensure efficient operations, but an overabundance of institutional conflict can inhibit central planning and impair decision making.

The American governmental structure provides for three separate centers of power, each carrying out its separate responsibilities. Although the separation of powers has helped to ensure the continuation of a limited, democratic government, the prolonged tension between the executive and the legislative branches has at times been a major barrier to developing much needed legislation.

2. *Conflict is detrimental when it becomes violent and destructive.* As noted earlier, conflicts can be peaceful or violent. When tensions become destructive, the human and economic costs of conflict can be enormous. For example, the inability to resolve labor-management disputes can lead to major economic loss both to companies and workers. Similarly, when nations are unable to resolve their international incompatibilities, states may consider military force to resolve the dispute. (In this century more than 90 million persons have died as a result of international wars.)

Violent conflict is not only costly but also can lead to community disintegration. When parties seek to gain their interests at all costs, conflicts become destructive and ultimately lead to community dissolution. For example, when a husband and wife are unable to resolve their incompatibilities, continuing tensions may lead either to separation or divorce. Similarly, the intransigence of business and labor groups can lead to the closing of a business firm. The inability to resolve a political dispute between two major political groups can threaten the continued viability of a state. For instance, increasing tensions in Canada between French-speaking citizens of Québec and English-speaking citizens from other provinces are seriously threatening the unity and cohesion of the nation.

3. *Conflict leads to slow and inefficient decision making.* When communities do not have a well-established hierarchy of decision making, the process of managing and governing communities is slow and cumbersome, and the implementation of programs and policies is difficult. In highly orderly military regimes, government leaders can make policy decisions quickly and can implement them by using the authority of military institutions. Totalitarian communist regimes also enjoy efficient decision making processes, since the communist party controls all major governmental institutions. In countries like the United States and Great Britain, however, decision making is generally carried out by a multitude of organizations, and the procedures for enacting and implementing laws are often inefficient. In the late 1970s, for example, American society needed a general energy policy that would help curb the use of oil while simultaneously increasing production of alternative energy sources. But the inability to reconcile different group interests made it impossible to establish a comprehensive energy policy.

Since conflict can have either positive or negative effects on a community, it is intrinsically neither good nor bad. Whether conflict is beneficial to a relationship, group, or community depends upon such factors as type, frequency, and intensity. Obviously, a major international war in which thousands of persons are killed is a destructive form of conflict that should be avoided. But it is equally evident that continued conflict among branches of government, or competition for political influence among interest groups can have major beneficial results on a political community. Some conflict is constructive and integrative to a community, while other conflict can be destructive and dysfunctional. The dividing line between constructive and destructive conflict, however, is difficult to ascertain and can only be determined by individual case. Some conflict may be destructive for some groups and communities, yet for others it may be helpful and integrative. On the other hand, some conflict beneficial to some relationships and groups may be counterproductive for others. The positive and negative functions of conflict are so closely interrelated that they may be viewed as opposite sides of the same coin.

SUMMARY

The fundamental task of politics is to create and maintain stable, harmonious communities where the claims of freedom and order are balanced. This problem of community arises from the social nature of people, which leads them into cooperative activity, and from their selfish human nature, which leads them into competitive and conflictual behavior. All communities experience conflict. Since it is more visible than peaceful, harmonious, and cooperative relationships among individuals and groups, the fundamental nature of community life is assumed to be conflictual. This is not so. The foundation of all community life lies in peaceful, cooperative relationships among society's members. Conflictual relations represent only a small fraction of the totality of human experience.

Conflicts vary in scope and nature. Some incompatibilities may be significant, and others may not be. Some may involve violence; others may be peaceful. Some conflicts may be expressed through institutionalized practices, while others may result from spontaneous, uncontrolled anger. Some conflicts may be based on objective incompatibilities; others may have no factual basis but may arise from subjective feelings of inadequacy and frustration.

Human conflicts can impair the development of creative, dynamic societies. When conflicts arise, the easiest solution is to suppress or eliminate them. But such a solution is not only inadequate but also detrimental. The reason for this is simple: some conflict is essential for all human creative activity.

Conflicts perform many functions, some positive and some negative. Some of the main positive functions include: the diffusion of more serious conflict, the facilitation of creativity, the development of community cohesion, and the measurement of power among individuals and groups. Some of the major negative functions include: the creation of unstable and disorderly relationships, the encouragement of violent and aggressive behavior, and the impediment to quick and efficient decision making.

Given the positive role of conflict, human communities need to regulate conflict, not suppress or eliminate it. Only when societies practice conflict management can they be assured of a reasonable balance between freedom and order. Only then can their members realize their full productive potential.

KEY TERMS

problem of community
conflict
interpersonal vs. intercommunity
 conflict
violent vs. nonviolent conflict

institutional vs. noninstitutional
 conflict
realistic vs. nonrealistic conflict
true conflict
latent conflict

NOTES

1. Kenneth Boulding, *Conflict and Defense: A General Theory* (New York: Harper & Brothers, 1962), p. 307.
2. Lewis Coser, *The Functions of Social Conflict* (New York: The Free Press, 1956), p. 8.
3. Raymond W. Mack and Richard C. Snyder, "The Analysis of Social Conflict — Toward an Overview and Synthesis" in *Conflict Resolution: Contributions of the Behavioral Sciences,* ed. Clagett G. Smith (Notre Dame, Ind.: University of Notre Dame, 1971), pp. 8-9.

4. Coser, *The Functions of Social Conflict;* and Alan C. Filley, *Interpersonal Conflict Resolution* (Glenview, Ill.: Scott, Foresman & Co., 1975), pp. 4–7.

5. Russell R. Dynes and E. L. Quarantelli, "The Absence of Community Conflict in the Early Phases of Natural Disasters" in *Conflict Resolution: Contributions of the Behavioral Sciences,* ed. Clagett G. Smith (Notre Dame, Ind.: University of Notre Dame, 1971), pp. 200–204.

SUGGESTED READING

BOULDING, KENNETH E. *Conflict and Defense: A General Theory.* New York: Harper & Brothers, 1962. An advanced theoretical analysis of social conflict. Chapters 14 and 15 on ideological and ethical conflict and approaches to conflict resolution will be of particular interest to the beginning student.

COSER, LEWIS A. *The Functions of Social Conflict.* New York: The Free Press, 1956. A discussion of 16 major functions of social conflict based on the theories of Georg Simmel, an early 20th-century sociologist.

DAHRENDORF, RALF. *Class and Class Conflict in Industrial Society.* Stanford: Stanford University Press, 1959. Argues that the dominant expression of social conflict in advanced societies is in terms of social classes. But whereas Marx suggested that class conflict was based on economic considerations, Dahrendorf believes that the basic cause is political.

DEUTSCH, MORTON. *The Resolution of Conflict: Constructive and Destructive Processes.* New Haven: Yale University Press, 1973. An analysis of the nature and resolution of interpersonal conflict from a psychological perspective.

FILLEY, ALAN C. *Interpersonal Conflict Resolution.* Glenview, Ill.: Scott Foresman and Co., 1975. An invaluable introductory study of the nature, functions, management and resolution of interpersonal conflict.

GURR, TED ROBERT. *Why Men Rebel.* Princeton: Princeton University Press, 1970. A prize-winning study of the nature, conditions and results of political violence. Argues that rebellion is caused by the perception of relative deprivation.

MCNEIL, ELTON B., ed. *The Nature of Human Conflict.* Englewood Cliffs, N.J.: Prentice-Hall, 1965. An interdisciplinary collection of studies on the nature of interpersonal, intergroup, and intercommunity conflict by leading social scientists.

OBERSCHALL, ANTHONY. *Social Conflict and Social Movements.* Englewood Cliffs, N.J.: Prentice-Hall, 1973. An introductory study of the sources, structure, and manifestations of human conflict from a sociological perspective.

SMITH, CLAGETT G., ed. *Conflict Resolution: Contributions of the Behavioral Sciences.* Notre Dame, Ind.: University of Notre Dame Press, 1971. An outstanding collection of readings on the nature, management, and resolution of social conflict.

2 / POLITICS AND HUMAN CONFLICT

The problem of community, as observed in Chapter 1, occurs because communities experience too much conflict. Since no automatic method exists for limiting or regulating human conflict, establishing and maintaining effective social and political communities requires the management of interpersonal and intergroup conflict. Peaceful and harmonious human communities are not an automatic byproduct of human interaction but the result of deliberate human action.

The purpose of this chapter is to analyze the nature and purpose of politics and to focus on the quest for order. First, we shall examine possible alternative responses to human conflict; we then shall review some common approaches to politics. Second, we shall examine the nature of politics from the conflict-management perspective, highlighting a number of concepts essential to an understanding of political activity. Finally, we shall review a variety of methods available for managing and resolving social conflict.

ALTERNATIVE RESPONSES TO HUMAN CONFLICT

Essentially, there are three different ways in which people cope with conflict; they can suppress or avoid it; they can minimize or eliminate it; or they can manage it.

The Avoidance of Conflict

The avoidance or suppression of conflict is practiced by those who believe that all expressed forms of human incompatibilities are detrimental. This approach assumes that no interaction is preferable to conflictual inter-relationships. Since a community is a web of human interdependencies, the

20

avoidance of conflict is impossible within a community, except as individuals withdraw momentarily into isolation. Similarly, the avoidance of conflict can be practiced between two persons, but any continued use of this approach would inevitably harm, if not destroy, the relationship between them. To repeat a generalization made in Chapter 1, conflict and consensus are two sides of the same coin. It is impossible to avoid conflictual relationships without also avoiding harmonious ties. Clearly, then, avoidance of conflict cannot serve as an effective means of dealing with the problem of community.

The Minimization of Conflict

The second method by which communities seek to cope with conflict is by minimizing or eliminating it. This approach, in contrast to the avoidance of conflict, assumes that community health is achieved by maintaining a minimum amount of tension and disorder. The problem with this approach, however, is that minimization of conflict not only eliminates destructive tensions and conflicts but also positive interrelationships as well. The reduction of some conflict is generally a requirement of all social and political communities. But any attempt to eradicate completely the disharmony and disorder that naturally results from human interchange leads to a stale, unproductive society. Since the minimization of conflict is an efficient means of creating and maintaining community order, totalitarian and authoritarian regimes commonly use it.

The weakness of the first two approaches is perhaps best articulated by the American statesman James Madison (1751–1829). In the tenth *Federalist,* Madison argues that the fundamental problem of political communities is "faction," which he defines as group conflict. There are two ways by which communities can deal with such conflict: they can reduce or remove its causes, or they can control its negative effects. Madison suggests that removal of the causes of faction can be accomplished, either by destroying liberty (which is essential to its existence) or by giving every citizen the same opinions, desires, and interests. Neither method is desirable, however. These solutions would be worse than the problem they hope to cure. Of the elimination of liberty, Madison observes: "Liberty is to faction what air is to fire, an aliment without which it instantly expires. But it could not be less folly to abolish liberty, which is essential to political life, because it nourishes faction, than it would be to wish the annihilation of air, which is essential to animal life, because it imparts to fire its destructive agency."[1] The development of common interests and values, Madison continues, is similarly foolish. It would be impossible to create a completely homogeneous society where human factions are eliminated.

Conflictual relationships, Madison argues, are based on human nature; thus, whenever and wherever people live in association with others the potential for faction arises. Since eliminating conflict is not an effective means of dealing with faction, Madison concludes that the only adequate means of developing a peaceful political community is by controlling its effects. In other words, conflict should not be eliminated or minimized at all costs but should be regulated through various political and governmental means.

The Management of Conflict

The third and preferable method of dealing with community conflict is to manage it. The management approach assumes that conflict, which is a natural outcome of all human interrelationships, can play either a positive or negative function. Whether conflict is beneficial or not depends on its quality and quantity. Since the type and frequency of constructive conflict varies among different types of human communities, the determination of what is constructive and destructive conflict can only be determined individually for each community. For example, the management of conflict is different within a town, school board, nation, or the international system. In each case regulation of the different types and levels of conflict requires different approaches and institutions. (This text is based on the assumption that the only adequate response to human conflict is to manage it. Politics and government will therefore be defined in terms of management and regulation of community conflict.)

APPROACHES TO POLITICS

Before examining politics from the perspective of conflict management, it will be useful to analyze some of the fundamental approaches to politics. Historically, politics has been defined in three ways: first, in terms of moral norms; second, in terms of activities of the state; and third, in terms of establishment of authority relations through the struggle for influence and power. The first approach represents *normative politics;* the second, *institutional politics;* and the third, *interpersonal politics.* The normative approach is primarily concerned with the application of ideal norms to the political process, while the institutional and interpersonal approaches focus on the means to politics. Each of these three perspectives shall be examined.

Normative Politics

This approach assumes that the fundamental purpose of a community is to realize specific ends. These ends have generally been defined in terms of moral standards (such as natural law or justice) or some general norm (such as the public interest or the common good) that is established apart from private interests within the community. Historically, most political thinkers up until the time of Niccolò Machiavelli (1469-1529) approached politics from the normative perspective. In *The Republic* Plato argued that the basic task of politics was to establish justice. Aristotle, Plato's pupil, also approached politics from a normative perspective by defining the state as a community that aims at the highest good, or what he called the "good life." Thomas Aquinas and the medieval Catholic theorists who followed him further refined this approach by searching for Christian principles that could provide guidance in the political realm. In addition to the principles that God revealed in nature (eternal law) and Scriptures (divine law), Aquinas believed that there were moral principles that could be apprehended by reason (natural law). It was the duty of rulers to ensure that political communities were governed in accordance with these standards. When these normative standards were applied to politics, Aquinas assumed that the result would be justice and order.

The normative approach to politics has been repeatedly demonstrated in the life of the American republic. The founding of the United States was based on normative standards set forth by Thomas Jefferson in the Declaration of Independence of July 4, 1776. That statement suggests that "self-evident truths" can guide the establishment and maintenance of the new country. The purpose of government, according to Jefferson's Declaration, was to protect the inalienable human rights of "life, liberty, and the pursuit of happiness." When a government is unable or unwilling to secure these rights, Jefferson believed that it was the right of people to establish a new government.

Since the early days of the American republic, presidents, statesmen, and political leaders have continually applied moral norms to the formulation and implementation of domestic and foreign policies of the United States. For example, early in the twentieth century President Woodrow Wilson pursued foreign policies that were guided by moral democratic norms. Similarly, Martin Luther King, Jr., the civil-rights leader of the 1960s, repeatedly called for elimination of racial injustice by applying moral values to the political process. His moral approach is perhaps best expressed in the famous speech given in Washington, D. C., on August 28, 1963, when he said:

> *I have a dream that one day this nation will rise up and live out the true meaning of its creed: We hold these truths to be self-evident, that all men are created equal. I have a dream that one day on the red hills of Georgia the sons of former slaves and the sons of former slaveowners will be able to sit down together at the table of brotherhood. I have a dream that one day even the state of Mississippi, a state sweltering with the heat of oppression, will be transformed into an oasis of freedom and justice. I have a dream that my four little children one day will live in a nation where they will not be judged by the color of their skin, but by the content of their character.*[2]

More recently, President Jimmy Carter reawakened American idealism by applying moral values to both domestic and, particularly, international politics. In foreign affairs the idealistic perspective has been vigorously articulated in terms of human rights by publicly criticizing governments that violate minimum standards of human dignity and by refusing military and economic assistance to those nations that fail to protect individual rights.

The normative approach has both strengths and weaknesses. One advantage is that it encourages the search for and application of standards by which political communities are judged. The development of such standards helps give direction and purpose to a community and raises community concerns from self-interest to common concerns. But a major disadvantage of the approach is the lack of certainty that norms espoused by political thinkers or leaders are universal moral principles.

Historically, each age has defined its standards from a cultural perspective. While this has resulted in many noble acts, occasions have arisen when such principles were not the expression of disinterested, noble aspirations but the articulation of self-interest cloathed in abstract, moral words. It is important to know what the ends of a political community are. We also need to be careful that the articulation of such standards is not the product of a dominant interest group.

Institutional Politics

The inability to differentiate the private good from the common good has led some political thinkers to view politics as all those activities that relate to the governance of a political community. One of the first thinkers to popularize this approach was the German sociologist Max Weber (1864–1920). He argued that because it is impossible to define a political community in terms of its ends, it should be defined in terms of the means used to achieve those ends. According to Weber, the distinctive feature of the state was that it could use force to ensure compliance. "A state," he observed, "is a human community that (successfully) claims the monopoly of legitimate use of physical force within a given territory. The state is considered the sole source of the 'right' to use violence."[3] Politics thus involves all those activities associated with government institutions whose decisions can ultimately be implemented by the use, or threat of use, of force.

One of the major shortcomings of Weber's approach is that it limits politics to well-established political communities, i.e., those having a government that can successfully gain the obedience of its citizens through the use of violence. But politics is a process that takes place in undeveloped communities as well. Indeed, politics is the process by which communities are established. The international system of some 150 nation-states is a community where there is much politics among the various states. Yet that activity occurs in a nebulous and uncertain world environment where no single administrative unit can command allegiance from its subjects.

Some contemporary political scientists have sought to deemphasize the territorial boundaries of the state and to focus on the authority of the government. David Easton, for example, has defined politics as the process of making authoritative decisions for an entire society.[4] According to this widely accepted definition, the essence of politics lies in the two dimensions emphasized by Weber — its compulsory quality of decision making and its scope within a society. The difference between Easton and Weber, however, is that Easton is far less concerned with the use of coercion as a means to achieve a binding decision. He seeks to define a political community in more flexible terms.

Another political scientist who uses this approach is Austin Ranney. In his introductory text *The Governing of Men,* he describes, politics as "the process of making government policies."[5] Karl Deutsch, another contemporary political scientist, defines politics in a slightly different way—as the "making of decisions by public means."[6] Although both Ranney and Deutsch are far more flexible in defining the environment in which politics occurs, both assume that a rather clear distinction exists between the public and private realms and between the arenas for government and private actions. Decision-making activities that occur within the public sector and are recognized as binding are thus political in nature.

Interpersonal Politics

This approach, the most contemporary and the broadest in scope, defines politics as a form of behavior that can be found in all types of communities. In his *Politics: Who Gets What, When, How,* Harold Lasswell defines politics as follows: "The study of politics is the study of influence and the influential. . . The influential are those who get the most of what there is to get. Available values may be classified as deference, income, safety. Those who get the most are elite; the rest are mass."[7] Following after Lasswell, Robert Dahl defines politics as human relationships that involve, to a significant extent, "control, influence, power, or authority."[8] Since these qualities are found at all levels of human interaction, politics is not confined to a state or a public sector but is an activity found in neighborhoods, schools, business organizations, civic groups, primitive tribes, and even families.

Another political scientist who defines politics from this perspective, but in slightly different terms, is Hans Morgenthau. In *Politics Among Nations* Morgenthau defines politics, both domestic and international, as a struggle for power. By power, he means "man's control over the minds and actions of other men."[9] Politics is thus concerned with the interpersonal, intergroup, and interstate conflict and with competition for positions of power. Although people may define their goals in economic, philosophic, religious, or social terms, they ultimately seek a position of influence over others so that they are able to obtain whatever resources they wish. Whatever the long-term objective of individuals, groups, and states, the immediate goal is always the same—power.

This concern with power and influence has the advantage in that it recognizes political activity in all forms of human association. This broader scope is illustrated in Figure 2.1. Whereas all normative politics occurs within a state or political system, politics defined as influence or power is found both within and outside the structures of the state. Thus, the most limited approach to politics is normative, while the broadest is the pragmatic struggle for power.

A major weakness of Lasswell's and Morgenthau's approaches is that the concern is with means and not ends. Since the focus is on the process of acquiring power, it obscures the common aims of communities. The competition for influence and power is of course a significant aspect of interpersonal behavior. We should not, however, lose sight of the fact that competition is carried out ultimately for the general interests of a community. Politics, in other words, does not only involve the acquiring of power and influence but also the pursuit of communal activities. Coordination and administration are important dimensions of politics.

Figure 2.1   Comparison of Scope Among Three Major Approaches to Politics

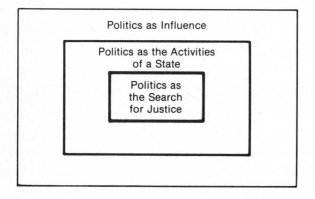

Politics as Influence

Politics as the Activities of a State

Politics as the Search for Justice

Politics as Conflict Management

In this study politics is defined as the process of managing conflict within communities. This definition is similar to the politics-as-influence approach in that it focuses on interpersonal rivalry at all levels of human association. But it differs from that approach in that the unit of analysis is interpersonal or inter-community conflict rather than competition for influence or power. Conflict is the unit of analysis because it is the most fundamental impediment to the development of harmonious and peaceful human communities. Conflict is the cause of the problem of community, and politics is the process by which conflict can be managed or resolved so that people can live in peace and harmony. E. E. Schattschneider, a noted American political scientist, states: "All politics begins with billions of conflicts. There are billions of potential conflicts in any modern society, but only a few become significant. A democratic society is able to survive because it manages conflict, usually at the point of origin; it imposes a kind of birth control on conflict." Carl J. Friedrich, another noted political scientist, observed that the primordial function of politics is the "setting of disputes."[10]

In order for politics to occur, two conditions are required. First, individuals, groups, or nations must espouse *mutually exclusive objectives,* i.e., conflict must exist within or between human associations. Since politics involves the management of tensions, disputes, and conflicts, it can only occur where there is discord and disorder. Conflict is thus a necessary precondition. Where there is no conflict there can be no politics. Obviously, since all human communities experience conflict, politics is found to some extent in all of them; however, the level and intensity of political activity varies in direct proportion to the level of conflict. Small, homogeneous communities like a family, a tribe, or a village tend to have relatively low levels of conflict and therefore require comparatively little effort to manage and resolve tensions and disputes. Nations and the international system, by contrast, tend to have frequent and intense conflicts that require enormous human effort to regulate them.

The second requirement for politics is the need for conflict resolution. What is needed is the development of a common policy that reconciles the competing and mutually exclusive interests of individuals, groups, or states. If parties to a conflict withdraw from a community, or if a party voluntarily adopts the opponent's policies or interest, there will be no political activity. Political activity, in other words, begins only when conflict management is undertaken. The elimination or avoidance of conflict does not result in politics.

Maurice Duverger wrote that there are two types of conflict with which political communities must cope. The first, which he calls horizontal, deals with the conflict of man to man, group to group, class to class, nation to nation. Such conflict includes the competition for influence in a school board, the selection of a party chief, the election of parliament, etc. The second type of conflict takes place on a vertical plane between rulers and ruled, leaders and subjects. Such conflict does not occur between individuals and groups and an abstract power called "government." Rather, the conflict is between those who have recognized positions of leadership and authority and those who do not.[11]

Community conflicts can also be divided into those dealing with the direct allocation of scarce resources or positions and those dealing with the creation or modification of standards for effective conflict management. The first type of conflict deals with specific tensions, such as the resolution of a property dispute, the selection of a president, the appointment of a prime minister, the development of new zoning restrictions, or the allocation of public funds. The second type of conflict is far more significant because it involves development of regulations by which conflict is to be managed and resolved. Such conflict involves development or modification of a constitution or establishment of a basic procedural principle for operating the government. In his presidential address to the American Political Science Association, E. E. Schattschneider called attention to the importance of this type of conflict as follows:

If politics is the management of conflict, it is necessary first to get rid of the simplistic concepts of conflict. Political conflict is not primarily or usually a matter of head-on collisions or tests of strength, for good reason: intelligent people prefer to avoid tests of strength about matters more serious than sports, unless they are sure to win.

Nor is political conflict like an intercollegiate debate in which the opponents agree in advance on a definition of the issues. The definition of alternatives is the supreme instrument of power: the antagonists can rarely agree on what the issues are because power is involved in the definition. He who determines what politics is about runs the country because the definition of the alternatives is the choice of conflicts, and the choice of conflicts allocates power.[12]

Since the most important type of conflict management is that which pertains to the administration of the system itself, Schattschneider suggests that the "heart of politics" is the strategy designed to exploit, use, or suppress conflict. He continues:

Conflict is so powerful an instrument of government that all regimes are of necessity concerned with its management. We are concerned here with the use of conflict to govern, the use of conflict as an instrument of change, growth, and unity. The grand strategy of politics deals with public policy concerning conflict. This is the policy of policies, the sovereign policy—what to do about conflict.[13]

In summary, politics as conflict management is chiefly concerned with the establishment of an acceptable community consensus. Its focus is not on the implementation of abstract rights and ideals but on the achievement of a broad consensus regarding ways to regulate community conflicts and the extent to which tensions and incompatibilities will be tolerated within society. Politics is thus concerned with establishment of rules of conflict management and with the application of those rules within society.

FREEDOM VS. ORDER

Historically, one of the central problems of political philosophy has been the maximization of individual freedom and liberty while still preserving community order. The problem, discussed throughout the history of Western philosophy, is posed succinctly by the French political writer Jean Jacques Rousseau. In the opening sentence of the *Social Contract,* he states, "Man is born free, and everywhere he is in chains." The problem, Rouseau thought, was how persons could be as free within political communities as they were before they had become a part of them. What should be the balance between individual freedom and community order?

The relationship between freedom and order is closely associated with the tension between conflict and consensus. Fundamentally, the tension between freedom and order is a different method of defining the problem of community. Since conflict occurs only where there is freedom to pursue incompatible interests, freedom is a precondition for social and political conflict. Similarly, since some consensus is a prerequisite for a permanent and stable community, consensus is a precondition for an effective social order. Just as conflict needs to be regulated to ensure community order, so, too, individual freedom needs to be partially regulated so that the freedoms of all persons are protected.

As observed earlier, an adequate response to the problem of community requires that conflict be managed, not avoided or eliminated. Only when conflict is tolerated can individuals and groups be free to pursue their individual or group goals, thereby ensuring a dynamic and productive society. Too much conflict (freedom) can lead to destructive results, particularly if the conflict becomes intense or frequent. But too little conflict can inhibit the creative energies of society members. Human communities, to achieve their full creative potential, must provide ample freedom for individuals to pursue their particular interests; simultaneously, they must provide order by which those freedoms can be protected. Before examining further the relationship of freedom to order, both concepts must be more precisely defined.

Freedom

Defining "freedom" is a difficult task. Since the concept is used continually in everyday events, its meaning is generally imprecise and unclear. This is particularly the case in a Western democracy like the United States, where the popular notions of politics and government tend to obscure the tension between freedom and order. Freedom is assumed to be a fundamental human need. The assumption that an increase in human freedom always improves the human condition is not necessarily valid. It is possible to have too much freedom. People need freedom, but they also need order to avoid the destructive results of anarchy. It is often said in the United States that the government that governs the least is the best. If this statement is taken to its extreme, then no government (anarchy) is preferable to some government—a clearly absurd view. What is of course needed is some government to ensure community order, in which the valid interests and concerns of people can be expressed and fulfilled. The notion that any limitation of personal freedom by government is automatically detrimental to individuals and groups cannot be supported.

There are two types of freedom: *absolute freedom* and *authentic freedom*. The first can be defined as thinking, saying, and doing what one pleases. It is freedom without a context or framework. The second type is freedom within the context of a community. Authentic freedom involves the saying and doing of all those things permitted by a society. It involves human choice within boundaries.

Since human beings are social creatures, absolute freedom is not only undesirable and unrealistic but also ultimately impossible if people are to remain fulfilled human beings. When individual freedoms are unrestricted, conflict and chaos result from the clash of unchecked interests among individuals and groups. The ultimate consequence of unregulated conflict is that the absolute freedoms of people become limited and uncertain as the unregulated actions of individuals ultimately limit the ability to act freely and independently. Unlimited freedom leads to a chaotic and anarchic environment.

A more significant inadequacy of absolute freedom is its unrelatedness to human existence. No person has ever lived within a community of complete freedom. From the moment of birth, a person lives in an environment that imposes restrictions on the freedoms of action and speech. Children learn early to comply with expected standards of parents and of such social institutions as schools and churches. As persons reach adulthood they become even more acutely aware of how government, religion, work, marriage, and social associations impinge on their ability to say and do what they please.

Perhaps some of the least noticed but most powerful forces in delimiting human freedom are the customs and natural habits regulating everyday life. All societies from the most primitive to the most modern are held together by common folkways passed along to each new generation. These habits and customs, while differing significantly from culture to culture, help to create and maintain common values and behavioral patterns that ensure the maintenance and preservation of community life. Even a robber gang, an outlaw group, or a faction of political anarchists has its own regulatory code; none would be able to exist without it. Similarly, the picture of the lawless savage running wild in the forest is complete fiction, for he too must cling to his own mores to survive.

Since absolute freedom is both undesirable and impossible, the alternative is an authentic freedom — a freedom that places human and group choice within particular rules and standards. Authentic freedom assumes that personal choice must be restricted. The limitation of choice is necessary because, without social order, human freedoms cannot be secured and protected. If the freedoms of all persons are to be assured, some restrictions need to be placed on individual freedoms. The search for authentic, or social, freedom thus involves a paradox: absolute freedom needs to be restricted to obtain the social freedom of all community members. Since only authentic freedom has meaning in society, subsequent references to freedom will be concerned only with the social or authentic version.

Order

The noted political sociologist R. M. MacIver observed that "without order men are lost, not knowing where they go, not knowing what they do."[14] Simone Weil, the brilliant French writer echoes this theme in her slim volume *The Need For Roots,* written in exile from her occupied homeland at the request of the French provisional government. In that volume Weil argues that the fundamental need within and between people is order. Food and shelter are important, she writes, but the human condition is insufferable unless there is a basic harmony and order within society. "Order is the first need of all."[15]

What is order? It is a condition of stable and dependable relationships. Order results when there is a harmonious arrangement among the individuals and groups within a community. Since a community cannot exist without order, the development of a stable, predictable, and peaceful relationship is the *sine qua non,* of any effective effort to deal with the problem of community.

To be sure, there can be no peace and harmony where individual and group interests are disregarded and where the freedoms of persons are totally curtailed. The expression and fulfillment of the just claims of human beings is itself a precondition for long-term harmony and order. It is not surprising that political theorists like Thomas Hobbes and Edmund Burke have argued that the primal need in society is for order and that order subsequently makes justice possible. Goethe is once claimed to have said, "If I had to choose between justice and disorder, on the one hand, and injustice and order on the other, I would always choose the latter."[16]

It is easy to underestimate the need for order. Since most people have grown up in peaceful, stable communities, they have not experienced the catastrophic effects of prolonged civil war or the breakdown of the social and political institutions within society. But war, disorder, and the disintegration of some of the dominant social structures are possible.

The Second World War brought massive transformations to numerous Western European nations occupied by the Nazis. The takeover of China by the Communists at the end of the 1940s brought radical changes to that nation. During the early 1970s the people of Northern Ireland continued to suffer under a continuous battle between Catholic and Protestant forces. The Communist takeover of the Cambodian government by the Pol Pot regime in 1975 brought an immediate disintegration of the traditional patterns and structures within that society; some commentators have estimated that as many as two million people may have perished during that regime. Perhaps the most vivid recent illustration of the terrible consequences of disorder occurred in 1974 in South Vietnam prior to the fall of that country. As the communist forces began to move south, millions of Vietnamese sought refuge from the war by moving toward Saigon (the capital), leaving behind most of their possessions.

The continuing social, political, and economic disorder within nations should remind us that harmony and peace are not automatic byproducts of community life. Order must be created and preserved. Like the preservation of freedom, the maintenance of peace and order requires constant vigilance.

The creation and maintenance of community order is not the task of politics alone. As will be made clear in the following chapter, the function of government is to refine and preserve community harmony. Government cannot be the sole source of community order. Indeed, the foundation of society's political and governmental institutions and the laws by which they operate presuppose a more basic social order — a harmony that results from a common heritage, a common will, a common culture, and other common traits. This is why countries created by the arbitrary will of political rulers and maintained primarily by the power of the state are often unstable political systems. Although political communities can be maintained by power alone, when there are limited social, cultural, and religious ties in society, the task of forging community order becomes all the more difficult.

The Balancing of Freedom and Order

A stable political community requires both order and freedom. The fundamental task of politics is to establish and maintain a desirable balance between the two. Since both qualities are interdependent, an increase in the level of freedom results in a lower level of order and vice versa. Too much individual freedom leads to disorder and threatens the common cooperative activities of society. Too much social order, on the other hand, results in a rigid, unproductive society.

Although nonpolitical processes and institutions contribute significantly to the building of community order, political authorities are the chief determinants of the level of freedom and order in society. Governments make binding rules and regulations. As a result, they can either expand or limit the level of social controls on society. The greater the level of social control established by government, the higher the level of order and the lower the level of freedom. Conversely, as government decreases the level of social controls by expanding the rights of groups and individuals (e.g., to assemble, to form trade unions, to organize opposition political groups, to a free press, etc.), the level of social order tends to decline.

Figure 2.2 illustrates three hypothetical political communities with alternative levels of freedom and order. Community A represents a high level of disorder because of the excessive level of freedom. The international system is similar to this model. In such a rudimentary political community, there is some order, but the dominant feature of the world system is the freedom of each nation-state within that community. This freedom is expressed in the doctrine of political *sovereignty,* which means that the ultimate responsibility for decision-making lies within each individual nation. Given the high level of national freedom, it is not surprising that the world system is continuously faced with international disputes and wars that threaten its very existence.

Figure 2.2 Comparison of Political Communities in Terms of Freedom and Order

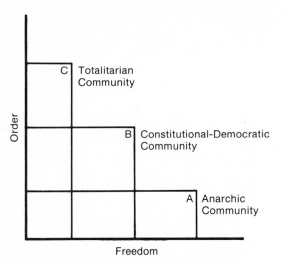

At the opposite extreme are political communities that have a low level of freedom and a high level of order, as represented by point C (Figure 2.2). In such communities, peace and cohesion are the dominant features, while individual and group interests are suppressed or eliminated in favor of more general community concerns. Unlike the world community, where there is much diversity, a communitarian society like China or Cuba tolerates limited levels of freedom. The result is that social and cultural diversity is severely limited. The dominant concern in communist states like these has been to create a society where general interests take precedence over individual or group concerns. Such societies obviously have a high degree of order and stability maintained by continued government surveillance.

Finally, those countries depicted by point B in Figure 2.2 have a general equilibrium between freedom and order. In such countries (represented by the more developed democratic states like Great Britain, The Netherlands, Canada, and New Zealand), freedom and order are both recognized as equally necessary. It is understood that overemphasis on either value can bring undesirable consequences.

Since it is impossible to measure with precision the levels of freedom and order found within society, a classification of countries according to three possible types is at best a heuristic device for understanding different types of political regimes. Moreover, there is no precise, ideal balance between freedom and order. Given the distinctive political, social, cultural, and historical features of each country, states must search for the conflict-management approach that maximizes authentic freedom. Each society must guard against moving to either extreme. Too much liberty leads to unstable, revolutionary conditions and results in an anarchic environment; too much order leads to a repressive totalitarianism with little freedom and liberty. Consequently, each community must deal with its problem of community by managing social and political conflict in order to maintain a healthy balance between freedom and order.

THE SCOPE OF POLITICS

In defining politics as the management of conflict, no clear boundaries have been provided for the study of politics. Since families, churches, schools, neighborhoods, counties, interest groups, corporations, and indeed all inter-personal and intergroup relationships involve conflict and its management to some extent, politics must of necessity be found in all human associations. Communities that are relatively homogeneous and have few members are able to reconcile their incompatibilities and create harmony without much diffi-culty. In such communities politics is hardly noticeable. In larger and more diverse communities like the nation-state or the international community itself, individual and group incompatibilities are far more significant and intense. Here the process of conflict management plays a far more important role. The politics in nation-states thus tends to be far more noticeable than communities like schools and churches.

The lack of clear boundaries for the study of politics is troubling to those who have generally associated politics with activities of the state. The inclusion of political activity beyond the traditional boundaries of the nation-state is based on the assumption that all politics begins with social conflict and that understanding political activity in states can be facilitated by examining con-flict management in communities with which we are most familiar, such as homes, schools, and neighborhoods. The object in approaching politics as an exercise in balancing human freedom with community order is not to define politics so broadly as to make it meaningless but rather to highlight the organic connection between interpersonal and intergroup behavior within small and large communities. The most effective way to understand the conflict-management process within political communities like the United States, the Soviet Union, and the developing nations of Asia, Africa, and Latin America is to understand the sources of conflict and the processes of its management in the common, ordinary activities of life.

One of the most widely accepted definitions of politics is that it is the process of making authoritative decisions for an entire society. According to this definition, the essence of politics is the compulsory quality of decision-making and the society-wide scope of action. Although this definition is almost exclusively associated with the nation-state and its subsidiary organs, the two criteria of politics, compulsoriness and scope, are seldom defined with precision. What, in fact, is an authoritative decision? What are the distinguish-ing characteristics of authoritative and nonauthoritative decision making?

What precisely constitutes a *society-wide* community? Is a church, a school district, or a small village a society-wide community? Although it is generally assumed that it is possible to differentiate between political and nonpolitical communities, the inability to define politics with precision has resulted in much disagreement over the role and scope of politics in different types of human communities.

One way out of this dilemma is to resist defining conflict management in mutually exclusive categories. Rather than define politics as an activity that is either present or not, a more suitable approach is to view politics as an activity found in different degrees. Community conflict managements may then be found along a continuum of much or little conflict. Communities differ therefore in terms of their degree of visible politics, although politics is never totally absent from human social activity.

One way to develop a continuum of political activity is to view human associations along a public sector-private sector continuum based on two criteria—level of authoritativeness and scope of a community decision. The level of authoritativeness (or depth) of conflict management can be determined by the extent to which community decisions are binding and enforceable. The scope (or breadth) can be represented by the number of persons affected by community decisions. The *private sector* can be defined as that portion of society where human associations are largely voluntary and where decisions have limited scope. Most importantly, the "governments" of these associations generally are unable to ensure compliance with their decisions. The *public sector,* by contrast, includes those communities that have conflict-management institutions that can compel obedience from their members. Moreover, not only is membership in such communities less voluntary than in the private sector, the size of these communities is also much larger. Figure 2.3 illustrates differing levels of politics found in some typical human communities.

Figure 2.3 Human Communities Compared In Terms of Levels of Politics

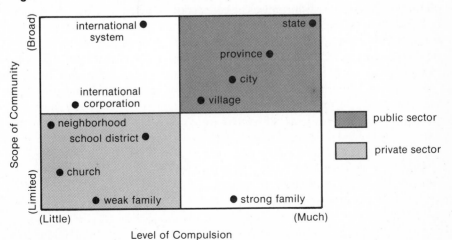

The world, then, is not clearly divided between political and nonpolitical communities. Rather, all forms of human association partake of political activity to some degree. Obviously, those communities like provinces and counties and nation-states have far more politics than do the more limited communities like churches, colleges, and small villages. For this reason political scientists have historically focused on the activities of the state and its agencies.

In this text we shall do the same as we examine the politics and government of some of the major countries of the world and of the international system itself. But our discussion of the politics of the nation-state and of the international system should not obscure the fact that politics is also present in other less noticeable communities. In summary, politics is a continuing activity in all human associations that seeks to reconcile incompatible interests within the context of social order.

METHODS OF CONFLICT RESOLUTION

When mutually exclusive interests arise between individuals, groups, or states, there are essentially two ways that such conflict can be resolved. First, the parties to the conflict may seek to reconcile their differences through compromise; and second, one of the parties may seek to use force to impose its interests and goals on the other.

Compromise vs. Force

Compromise occurs when parties to a conflict decide, either by their own accord or by encouragement of an outside party, to settle the dispute by relinquishing some individual preferences in return for a mutual settlement. This is achieved when parties in conflict decide to seek only a portion of their original interests. In order for compromise to occur, conflicting parties must be willing to seek only relative satisfaction, not full, complete satisfaction that would result without changing their interests and commitments. Since a relative satisfaction of goals involves some dissatisfaction resulting from the change in objectives, all compromise involves both relative satisfaction and relative dissatisfaction of each disputing party. This point has been well stated by Dr. Henry Kissinger, former U.S. Secretary of State, in terms of international conflicts: "An international settlement which is accepted and not imposed will...always appear somewhat unjust to any one of its components. Paradoxically, the generality of this dissatisfaction is a condition of stability, because were any one power totally satisfied, all others would be totally dissatisfied, and a revolutionary situation would ensue. The foundation of a stable order is a relative security—and therefore the relative insecurity—of its members."[16]

It has often been said that the art of politics is the *art of compromise.* One reason for this is that compromise is the most common means of dealing with domestic political conflict. Given the multiplicity of conflicts (many of them of relative insignificance), most parties find it in their interest to reconcile their incompatibilities by adjusting their goals. One of the chief ways to get bills approved in Congress is to make adjustments in the proposed law. These changes are made by amending legislation so that necessary support can be generated for approval.

When conflicts deal with vital issues, as is often the case in international disputes, then compromise becomes far more difficult. This was demonstrated by the second phase of Soviet — American negotiations in the Strategic Arms Limitations Talks (SALT). As with SALT I, the goal of SALT II was the establishment of agreements to reduce further the number of strategic nuclear weapons and vehicles. After the conclusion of SALT I in 1972, the two countries immediately began negotiations on the second phase of SALT. An interim agreement was realized in Vladivostok in November 1974, but the two states were unable to reconcile their incompatible interests until July 1979. The nearly seven years of negotiations to reach an executive agreement about strategic weapons suggests that reconciling incompatible interests on vital issues such as national defense can pose intractable problems.

Another reason why compromise is the dominant form of conflict resolution is that most parties in conflict do not have a clear superiority of force that would permit them to impose their interests on others. Even if a party had a clearly dominant position, the party may consider force as a last resort for only the most important tensions. Thus, for common and relatively unimportant conflicts, parties may prefer to adjust their preferences rather than resort to fighting. Compromise, the dominant form of political activity, is the only effective method of establishing long-term stability and harmony within a community. The role of force is necessary in keeping peace and harmony, but, for reasons discussed below, no association can long remain peaceful if the community's decisions are continually imposed by force.

The second type of conflict resolution involves imposition of a settlement. This type of politics, which can be called *politics of conquest,* is practiced when a party uses superior force to impose its will on a weaker or defeated party. When a conflict is approached in this manner, however, the dispute is not resolved but rather avoided or suppressed. Recall that an effective response to community conflict requires the opportunity to express tensions and incompatible concerns and to seek to resolve these in an open, flexible manner. The suppression of conflict, however, can lead to a temporary peace that could eventually erupt in a storm.

The fundamental weakness of force as an instrument of conflict management is that it cannot ensure long-term peace and stability. When conflicts are resolved through force, individuals and groups continue to prefer their original goals and interests and constantly look for the opportunity to fulfill those

"Mr. President, honored friends, trusted allies, distinguished enemies..."

Drawing by Richter; © 1980 The New Yorker Magazine, Inc.

ambitions. Effective and long-term community harmony not only requires an outward change in behavior but also an inner change. The imposition of order through force is obviously capable of creating external harmony but is unable to establish inward adjustments that can only be created through compromise. The fall of the governments of the Shah of Iran, Anastasio Somoza of Nicaragua, and Idi Amin of Uganda demonstrates the ultimate inadequacy of military force. In each case the leaders had at their disposal superior military forces that were used to buttress and enforce government policies. The unwillingness to listen to popular demands and to adjust public policies to human needs led the masses to violent confrontation with military forces and to eventual collapse of the regime.

Direct vs. Indirect Conflict Resolution

The most common approach to conflict resolution is for the parties themselves to resolve the dispute. The advantage of the direct approach is that it is quick and efficient. Most domestic and international disputes are resolved in this manner, as are virtually all private conflicts. Family tensions, community conflicts, and labor-management negotiations are almost always undertaken and resolved by the parties themselves. Similarly, most tensions and disputes between states are discussed and resolved by diplomats. The tensions in the late 1970s between the United States and Japan over trade restrictions were handled by the two countries alone. Similarly, SALT discussions between the United States and the Soviet Union have been carried out exclusively by representatives from each of the two countries.

If a vital issue is at stake and the parties are unable to resolve the dispute themselves, then an outside agent may assist in settling the conflict. The advantage of the third party is that he is outside the emotional field created by the dispute and can aid in clarifying communication between the disputing parties. In addition, the outside agent may introduce alternative solutions and may even recommend a preferred solution. Whether or not an outside agent is able to assist in a dispute depends on who the outside agent is and the extent to which the parties entrust their interests to him.

The most common third-party processes include conciliation, mediation, and arbitration. In *conciliation* the third party (or conciliator) gathers facts, classifies the issues in dispute, and seeks to bring the parties back to the negotiating table. *Mediation* is a similar process, but the mediator has the added responsibility of recommending a solution. In *arbitration* the parties in conflict accept the arbitrator's authority to issue a final and binding decision. These processes are used in the resolution of private conflicts, such as labor-management disputes, but their most formal and developed expression is in international disputes. The reason for this is that in domestic affairs there are well-established institutions that can assist in the conflict-resolution process. On the other hand, the international system has few institutions that can manage conflict authoritatively. As a result, third-party processes play a much more significant role.

Some third-party interventions in the international system are rather informal, as was the case in Henry Kissinger's Middle East shuttle diplomacy in the mid-1970s. Third-party involvement can also be rather formal, such as when a dispute is turned over to a group of arbitrators affiliated with the International Court of Arbitration in The Hague, The Netherlands, the European Court of Justice, the Court of the European Community, or the International Court of Justice, the world court affiliated with the United Nations.

Government may also be regarded as a third-party agent of conflict resolution. As will become evident in the following chapter, one of the primary functions of government is to maintain peace. This is achieved by developing laws regulating the behavior of individuals in order to manage individual and group conflict. The purpose of a nation's constitution and laws is to create a framework whereby conflict resolution can be carried out efficiently and equitably. When individuals are unable to resolve their disputes, they can appeal to private third-party sources, such as family counselors, labor mediators, and other competent professionals. If a conflict is serious and resolution is impossible, the parties may seek the assistance of their local and national courts. The purpose of the courts is to adjudicate disputes, i.e., to resolve disputes by applying relevant precedents and laws of the state. In some cases, conflicts may arise between institutions of government and the people themselves. The courts are then called upon to issue a final, binding settlement.

SUMMARY

All human communities experience conflict. Since conflict can become destructive and impair social existence, it must be regulated. There are three ways in which communities can respond to conflict: avoidance, elimination, or management. Of these three alternatives, the most effective and desirable approach is the last.

Historically, politics has been approached from three different perspectives — normative, institutional, and interpersonal. Normative politics emphasizes the quest for justice, institutional politics is concerned with state activities; and interpersonal politics emphasizes the continuing struggle for influence in the development of authority structures. Building on the interpersonal approach, politics is defined in this text as the management of conflict.

While political activity occurs in both private and public sectors, the conflict that is most significant and that that has greatest impact on individuals is that which occurs within society. Society-wide conflict must be managed and, in some cases, resolved if the interests of all community members are to be protected.

All human communities need individual freedom to assure a creative and productive society, but they also need a stable order in which the rights of all members are maximized. Too much freedom results in too much conflict; too much order inhibits the development of society's members. The task of politics is to find a desirable balance between freedom and order.

Since all forms of human community experience conflict and its management, politics is found in a rudimentary form in all human interrelationships. The study of politics, however, is primarily concerned with political activity within the public sector, where the decisions of ruling bodies have binding authority over citizens. This text therefore concentrates on conflict management within the nation and its subsidiary communities.

KEY TERMS

normative politics
institutional politics
interpersonal politics
freedom
order
private sector

public sector
compromise
conciliation
mediation
arbitration

NOTES

1. Alexander Hamilton, James Madison, and John Jay, *The Federalist Papers* (New York: New American Library, 1961), p. 78.
2. Martin Luther King, Jr., "A Dream... I Have A Dream," *Newsweek* 62 (September 9, 1963), p. 21.
3. Max Weber, *Politics as a Vocation,* trans. H.H. Gerth and C. Wright Mills (Philadelphia: Fortress Press, 1968), p. 2.
4. David Easton, *The Political System: An Inquiry into the State of Political Science,* 2nd ed. (New York: Alfred A. Knopf, 1971); and *A Framework for Political Analysis* (Englewood Cliffs, N.J.: Prentice-Hall, 1965).
5. Austin Ranney, *The Governing of Men,* 4th ed. (Hinsdale, Ill.: Dryden Press, 1975), p. 35.
6. Karl W. Deutsch, *Politics and Government: How People Decide Their Fate* (Boston: Houghton Mifflin, 1974), p. 3.
7. Harold D. Lasswell, *Politics: Who Gets What, When, How* (New York: The World Publishing Co., 1963), p. 13.
8. Robert A. Dahl, *Modern Political Analysis,* 3rd ed. (Englewood Cliffs, N.J.: Prentice-Hall, 1976), p. 3.
9. Hans J. Morgenthau, *Politics Among Nations: The Struggle for Power and Peace,* 5th ed. rev. (New York: Random House, 1978), p. 30.
10. Carl J. Friedrich, *Man and His Government* (New York: McGraw-Hill, 1963), p. 423.
11. Maurice Duverger, *The Idea of Politics: The Uses of Power in Society,* trans. Robert North and Ruth Murphy (Chicago: Henry Regnery Co., 1966), p. 3.
12. E. E. Schattschneider, "Intensity, Visibility, Direction, and Scope," *The American Political Science Review* 51 (December 1957), pp. 936–7.
13. *Ibid.,* p. 953.
14. Robert M. MacIver, *The Web of Government,* rev. ed. (New York: Free Press, 1965), p. 47.
15. Simone Weil, *The Need for Roots: Prelude to a Declaration of Duties Toward Mankind,* trans. Arthur Wills (Boston: Beacon Press, 1952), p. 11.
16. John G. Stoessinger, *Henry Kissinger: The Anguish of Power* (New York: W. W. Norton, 1976), p. 14.

SUGGESTED READING

ARISTOTLE. *Politics.* Transcribed by Benjamin Jowett. New York: The Modern Library, 1943. Although a difficult work, this volume remains one of the classic statements on government and politics.

CRICK, BERNARD. *In Defense of Politics.* Baltimore: Penguin Books, 1964. An illuminating and thoughtful statement about the nature of politics.

DAHL, ROBERT. *Modern Political Analysis.* 3rd ed. Englewood Cliffs, N.J.: Prentice-Hall, 1976. A short, introductory study on politics from a behavioral perspective by a noted political scientist.

DUVERGER, MAURICE. *The Idea of Politics: The Uses of Power in Society.* Transcribed by Robert North and Ruth Murphy. Chicago: Henry Regnery Co., 1970. A lucid introduction to political sociology focusing on the sources of political conflict and the methods of integration in the modern state.

EASTON, DAVID. *The Political System: An Inquiry into the State of Political Science.* 2nd ed. New York: Alfred A. Knopf, 1971. This is the classic statement on politics from the perspective of systems analysis.

————. *A Systems Analysis of Political Life.* New York: John Wiley & Sons, 1965. This study, based on his earlier work, offers a more refined and elaborate discussion of government and politics from the systems perspective.

LANE, ROBERT E. *Political Life.* New York: The Free Press, 1965. Although dated, this study summarizes some of the major empirical findings about human political behavior.

LASSWELL, HAROLD D. *Politics: Who Gets What, When, How.* New York: The World Publishing Co., 1963. A landmark study on the nature of politics, focusing on the methods of gaining and using influence.

LIPSET, SEYMOUR MARTIN. *Political Man: The Social Basis of Politics.* Garden City, N.Y.: Anchor Books, 1963. This noted political sociologist presents some major generalizations about the sociological foundations of political behavior.

MACHIAVELLI, NICCOLÒ. *The Prince.* Transcribed and edited by Thomas G. Bergin. New York: Appleton-Century-Crofts, Inc., 1947. This short volume, written in the early sixteenth century, is significant because it was the first major study to approach politics descriptively rather than as a quest for normative, moral ends.

MORGENTHAU, HANS J. *Politics Among Nations: The Struggle For Power and Peace.* 5th ed. New York: Random House, 1978. Although an introductory international relations text, the first six chapters present one of the clearest descriptions of the realist perspective of politics.

SCHATTSCHNEIDER, E. E. *The Semisovereign People: A Realist's View of Democracy in America.* Hinsdale, Ill.: The Dryden Press, 1975. Although concerned primarily with American democratic government, this slim volume is an excellent analysis of the nature and scope of politics. This study is written from a conflict-management perspective.

WEBER, MAX. *Politics as a Vocation.* Transcribed by H.H. Gerth and C. Wright Mills. Philadelphia: Fortress Press, 1968. A short, lucid analysis of the nature of politics and government by one of the most influential social thinkers.

3 / GOVERNMENT AND CONFLICT MANAGEMENT

We have noted earlier that all human communities — large and small, simple and complex — experience disharmony and disorder. Although some tension and conflict is necessary to assure the vigor and vitality of community life, too much conflict can be destructive. As a result, instruments need to be found by which order and consensus can be established and maintained within human communities. In this chapter we shall examine the nature, role, and scope of government — the primary institution responsible for building, guiding, and maintaining political community.

THE NATURE AND ORIGIN OF GOVERNMENT

Government Defined

Government can be defined as the individuals and institutions that make and implement rules for society. The term *government* derives from the Greek verb "to govern," which means to steer and direct. Thus, to govern a community means to lead, direct, guide, and manage the affairs of society. The duties of governing are similar to those of a captain of a ship who must make final decisions regarding the speed and direction of a vessel and who has ultimate responsibility for the cargo, passengers, and crew.

As with politics, government may be well developed and institutionalized or may be informal and not easily recognized. Some communities, such as a home, tribe, or college do not have formal institutions or explicit rules and procedures for making and implementing decisions. In cities and states, however, government is generally complex and specialized because of the need

43

for making quick, effective decisions affecting large numbers of people. But whether a community is large or small, simple or complex, there is always a need for some informal or formal process by which decisions can be made, policies established, and conflicts resolved.

In Chapter 2, we observed that politics could be found in both the public and private sectors. Similarly, government can be found in the private sector (e.g. the home, churches, and businesses) and in the public sector (e.g. cities, provinces, states). Government of the public sector, however, is far more significant because of its capacity to command ultimate allegiance and obedience from its members. Since membership in private communities is largely voluntary, there is little or no compulsion to resolve conflict. Government is not authoritative. If participants of a business or school disagree among themselves or with the decisions of those in positions of leadership, they can, if they wish, leave the community. This is not the case in the public sector, where government has the responsibility for making binding rules, formulating and implementing policies, and resolving disputes. The government of society is the final source of decision making because it can use the coercive power of the state to ensure compliance. All other private and public governmental institutions must accept its authority. This study focuses on the government of the state—the government that has final authority within society to manage conflict and build consensus.

The Origin of Government

How did government develop? Why did some individuals become rulers and others subjects? Political thinkers have provided at least three explanations. One theory of the origin of government is that at some point in the course of human civilization a group of individuals, through cunning, force, or deceit, was able to impose their will on others. Government originated, according to this theory, because of the selfish drives of people. As individuals struggled to maximize their power and influence, those who developed superior force were eventually able to impose their will over others. The foundation of government is therefore found in the imbalance of power in society. The powerful rule, and the weak obey. The rulers govern because they have the power to enforce their decisions; the weak obey because they are fearful of the results of their disobedience.

The notion that government has its roots in superior force, however, is not an adequate explanation for the ruler-subject relationship. While force may be an important ingredient in compliance, force is seldom the foundation for all government decision making. As will become clear later on, force alone is not the element that holds communities together. The force that government uses against people must originate with the people. Thus, no government can exist indefinitely when the decisions and actions it takes are against the dominant majority of society and are implemented solely through force.

A second view of the origin of government is the social contract theory. According to this perspective, government was created by people because of the inadequacies of the state of nature—a place where there was no government. Social contract theory suggests that individuals were originally in a state of nature where there was no government and therefore no order or harmony. Because of the shortcomings of this unstable and disorderly environment, people deliberately created, through a contract, a political society in which government would be able to assure peace and harmony and to resolve disputes in an authoritative manner. People, in other words, created government to avoid the disorder and anarchy of the state of nature. Although this utilitarian theory, propounded by such thinkers as Locke and Hobbes, contains some truth (i.e., human beings recognize that they are better off with the order and harmony created by government) it does not provide a satisfactory explanation for the origin of government. From the beginning of mankind, human beings have lived cooperatively with others and their behavior has been "governed," however imperceptibly or informally, by customs, rules, and regulations. To assume that human beings were originally completely free, isolated, and separate individuals without any social order is to build a theory with disregard for historical facts.

A third and preferable explanation for the origin of government is the "organic" theory. According to this approach, government was not established by force or by a deliberate act of individuals but grew out of the social fabric of human association. Government has always existed in a rudimentary form in all human relationships. Its seed was planted when human communities emerged and began to develop hierarchical patterns of authority to ensure survival. People began to establish social order and to obey those in authority because it was in the members' interests to obey. The creation and maintenance of social order has always been an aspect of community life, and wherever this concern has existed there has been some form of government. Robert MacIver has observed that "wherever man lives on earth, at whatever level of existence, there is social order; and always permeating it is government of some sort."[1] Government is an aspect of community life, and wherever people have sought to live in association with others there has been a need for decision making and conflict resolution. According to this theory, then, government is not created or imposed on reluctant subjects by powerful rules. Rather, the seed of government has always existed in all forms of human association.

THE ROLE OF GOVERNMENT

We have already observed that the primary function of government is to lead, direct, coordinate, and regulate the affairs of a political community. From the perspective of conflict management, the task of government is to manage and resolve conflict and establish peace and harmony. In addition, government also helps build community consensus by directing the interests within the state. Government, in other words, builds order not only by prohibiting and punishing unacceptable behavior but also by guiding and leading the development of common goals and ideals.

The immediate outputs of government are its authoritative decisions. These decisions, or *laws,* are the binding rules established by authorized governmental institutions for the entire society. Laws can create programs, establish institutions, define procedures for resolving conflict, establish minimum standards of behavior, prohibit particular practices, and so on. Although not all laws deal directly with social conflict, the bulk of governmental legislation deals fundamentally with the regulation of behavior in order to ensure harmony and to facilitate conflict resolution. Laws, in other words, establish standards for individual and corporate behavior that encourage the development of social order. Traffic laws, for example, delineate acceptable driving practices and help ensure orderly use of highways and roads.

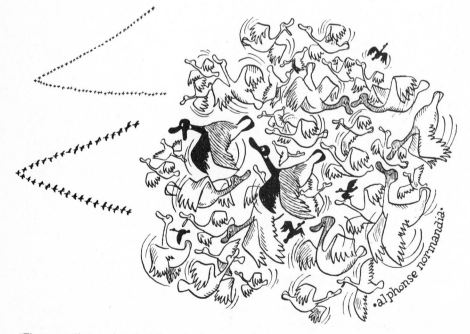

"There are times when I wish we had a somewhat stronger organization."

Reprinted by permission of the artist, Alphonse Normandia. From *Saturday Review,* 1975.

Laws may also be enacted to settle disputes between two or more parties. Since resources are limited within society, individuals and groups are in continual competition for a favorable distribution of a community's scarce resources. These resources may be real, such as economic or social goods, or they may be symbolic, such as the honor and prestige accorded groups with power and influence. When the United States government establishes the national budget, for example, it is in effect voting to resolve the conflicting economic interests of a multitude of American interest groups. Since not every individual and group interest can be fully satisfied, the policies and laws of government benefit some parties more than others. Some groups will be considered winners in the political battlefield, others losers. The decisions of government, in short, are instruments not only for managing community conflict but also for bringing to a temporary halt the competition and conflict among particular groups within society. They are a mechanism for building social order.

Nongovernmental Sources of Order

Although the task of government is to build order in society and to effectively resolve conflicts, government is only one instrument for building domestic harmony. Government does not build order within completely chaotic and anarchic societies; rather, it refines and improves the regulatory processes that already exist in society. The creation of social order is not begun by government but rather completed by it.

There are four important nongovernmental sources of community order. The first of these is the ethical and moral values of people. Individuals generally use ethical values to determine whether actions are good or bad, desirable or undesirable. While such norms may differ among peoples of different societies, there is generally substantial agreement about basic moral assumptions within specific countries. These values tend to justify certain actions and to discourage and inhibit other types of behavior. For example, the value placed on human life tends to inhibit murders and suicides and to discourage abortion. Although laws may help ensure that the behavior of society is in compliance with such an ethical norm, the widespread acceptance of such a value helps to regulate human behavior. Ethical values, in short, play an important regulatory function in developing community consensus.

A second source of community order is the innate, rational competencies of people. Individuals possess reason; they use their minds to protect and maximize their individual interests. Since people are concerned with preservation of their health, improvement of their social welfare, and maximization of their economic gain, there is no need for government to regulate certain types of behavior automatically carried out by the vast majority of the people. For example, since people seek to maximize their economic welfare, they purchase goods at the lowest possible price and sell them at the highest price. No law on frugal living is necessary. Similarly, people do not need to be told to lock their houses and cars, to avoid walking in front of moving vehicles, or to eat a balanced diet. Because people are concerned with their own lives and possessions, it can be assumed that they will use their common sense to protect and maximize their interests. Rational abilities of people can thus help provide a framework in which behavior is consistent and predictable.

Third, the home provides an important nongovernmental source of consensus. Besides serving as a source of customs and values, the home itself is a model political community in which children learn about authority. From an early age, children learn to obey and follow the instructions of their parents and other adults. Family life thus serves as a breeding ground for government in that habits of compliance with authority are first learned in a rudimentary way in the home. Family life thus helps to build consensus among family members and to establish those values essential for the operation of government.

A final and most important nongovernmental source of order is culture, i.e., the common mores and habits of society. People are not always aware of the extent to which culture determines their ideas, values, habits, and patterns of living. But it is clear that from early childhood the habits of dress, work, leisure, rearing of children, work, etc. are deeply conditioned by the folkways of society. These folkways help develop common patterns of communication and action essential to building community harmony. Although most of these values and habits deal with nonpolitical aspects of behavior, they are no less important to the development of order and consensus in political communities. Indeed, the basis of political communities is in the strength of these social, cultural, and religious folkways, which provide the basic harmony and consensus of society. Where people cannot communicate and interact peacefully, there can be no political community.

An important aspect of culture in the development of community consensus is *political culture,* the part of culture that deals exclusively with the political values and ideals of society. Political culture includes the values, traditions, habits, preferences, and emotional attachment toward the political processes and governmental institutions of society. Although the impact of this aspect of culture shall be discussed later, we need to be aware of its major impact on community order.

The government of society is thus based on a well-developed social order emanating from common ethical ideals, standards of rationality, the values and habits of the home, and a common culture, with particular importance given to the political culture. (Figure 3.1) These social and cultural forces help establish common habits of communication and action that facilitate the creation of community order. Government is not the basic source of community consensus but is the means by which society can complete and refine a process established through other nonpolitical means.

We should not conclude from this analysis that the development of culture has always chronologically preceded the development of government. As will be made clear in Chapter 5, the creation of a national identity has generally followed the establishment of the state, not vice versa. The state, in other words, has established the political culture on which its continued existence depends. While the authority of government is based on a community order created by the voluntary habits, customs, and mores of people, the state's institutions have played a major role in creating and maintaining a common culture.

Figure 3.1 Nongovernmental Sources of Order

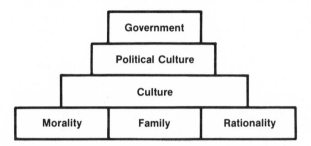

Government and Systems Analysis

A helpful way to understand the role of government within society is to apply systems analysis. Political scientists have found the tools of systems analysis useful because they provide a dynamic method of examining the work of major governmental structures and institutions in society and the relationships between those institutions and the general framework of society. Whereas traditional political science tends to focus primarily on the institutions of government, a large portion of contemporary political science research uses the systems framework to examine the role and function of individuals, groups, and institutions in political communities.

As used in the physical and biological sciences, a system is a set of interdependent parts functionally related in carrying out a particular set of objectives or goals. Thus, the brain, an eye, a tractor, or sewing machine can be identified as systems insofar as they are each comprised of various parts, each contributing toward the completion of a particular goal. In a similar way, political scientists find it useful to describe various governmental institutions and political communities as political systems, i.e., a set of interrelated parts functioning toward particular objectives. The most important type of political system is, of course, the nation-state. But political scientists also use the concept to denote smaller institutions and communities, such as a particular branch of government, a congressional committee, a county board, a school district, a city, or a tribal community.

The value of using the concept of political system is that it highlights the major institutions within the system and their particular functions. In addition, the approach tends to encourage a dynamic analysis of the interaction between various structures of society. There are four major elements among which such interactions occur: inputs, outputs, the conversion system, and feedback. We shall examine how political scientists have adapted these elements to political communities.

In a political system there are two principal inputs — supports and demands. Supports are those resources, abilities, skills, and institutional capabilities that enable a government to carry out its assigned tasks within a political community. Supports include: the wealth of a country, the industrial capacity of a nation, the political organization of a government, the efficiency of a bureaucracy, the homogeneity of a people, the level of literacy, the quality of life, etc. Demands, on the other hand, are the major positive and negative expectations of people with reference to society in general and government in particular. Demands are the expressed wants of people. Since the desires of people are often unlimited, only those demands clearly articulated through organized channels (such as interest groups and political parties) have much impact within the political system. Demands are often conflicting, and there is seldom a clear consensus regarding which interests should be fulfilled and which should be disregarded.

Supports and demands are both channeled into the conversion system, or government. The government, in turn, is responsible for responding to the demands in light of resources and capabilities of the system. Government processes the expectations of society and determines, in light of the system's support capabilities, which actions, programs, and policies should be undertaken. The chief outputs of government are its decisions, actions, regulations, and directives, which are generally in the form of laws. The government's actions may consist of passing new laws (legislative acts), interpreting old laws (judicial decisions), or enforcing existing laws (executive orders).

The enactment and implementation of government decisions has a major impact on society. The response to the government's output is called feedback; it is the means by which the system can adjust, refine, and improve its goal-seeking activities. For example, when the United States' secret bombing of Cambodia became public in 1970, students gave the government a clear and unmistakable message. That feedback put pressure on the United States government to further reduce its involvement in the Vietnam war. Similarly, the continuing escalation of property taxes in the late 1970s resulted in the movement among numerous states to place limits or even reduce the level of property taxes. Feedback, in other words, is the means by which outputs of the political system are translated into new demand inputs. (Figure 3.2 illustrates the interaction among various components of a typical political system.)

Figure 3.2   Major Components of a Political System

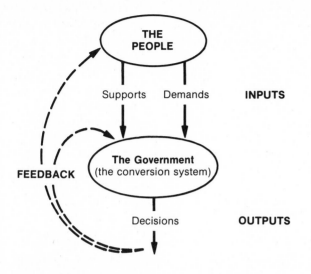

An important element of any political system is a *constitution,* which can be defined as the set of written or unwritten, legal or extralegal principles by which a government operates. Defined as such, the constitution is not a normative set of principles that direct and regulate the behavior of government. Rather, it is a purely descriptive statement of the guidelines that governments follow in carrying out their tasks. Constitutions are the collection of rules and principles by which the political community's conversion system performs. Some of these may be democratic, others dictatorial; some may be well institutionalized from centuries of effective operation, while others may be relatively new. Some may be detailed and specific, and others may be general and philosophic. Thus, while governments differ significantly, all of them are guided by basic constitutional norms. Although we may find some of these norms unacceptable, it is important to recognize that constitutions play an important regulatory function in all political systems.

Constitutions are important instruments of conflict resolution. They are significant because they make explicit the means and instruments by which societal conflict can be regulated and resolved. Duverger has written that there are two basic types of conflict within society—those between people or groups of people and those between government agencies or between government and the people. When conflict arises between or among individuals, groups, or the government, there needs to be an explicit framework for managing it. The function of a constitution is thus to provide rules for the resolution of political conflict.

Since the government has the final authority to resolve conflict, it may or may not seek to protect individual interests when they conflict with the claims of its own agencies. Limited or constitutional regimes assume that the purpose of government is to serve the interests of people—when a conflict arises between individuals and the government, there is no reason why the government should naturally resolve the dispute in its favor. Unlimited or totalitarian regimes, on the other hand, do not seek to preserve and protect individual rights; therefore, constitutional rules would seldom protect individuals from government encroachment. In short, constitutions, whether limited or unlimited, written or unwritten, tend to provide the basic rules of conflict management within a political system. Knowledge of the constitutional framework is thus important if one is to understand the processes and institutions of conflict management and resolution in society.

THE STRENGTH OF GOVERNMENT

The capacity of government to build and maintain order and to make binding decisions for society is dependent on its ability to ensure compliance with its decisions. How can government develop the capacity to enforce its decisions? How can government develop the necessary political strength to ensure that its decisions are binding on society? The capacity of governing a political system is dependent upon two sources: the voluntary compliance of people with the decisions of government; and the political strength and power of the government to enforce its decisions and to use (when necessary) the coercive power of the state to ensure compliance. The ability to govern is therefore partly dependent on the willingness of people to accept voluntarily the decisions of government and partly on the government's capacity to use, or threaten to use, coercive power to enforce decisions. No government can function when its decisions are completely against the wishes of the people. But no government is necessary if all persons voluntarily abide by government decisions without a threat of sanctions.

The Role of Voluntary Compliance

If government is to be effective in building community harmony, most people must support its decisions and actions. When 40 or 50 percent or more of the population of a political community are unwilling to comply with a law, the law becomes virtually unenforceable. The reason for this is that the enforceability of any law is directly related to the willingness of a people to abide by the laws of the government. The greater the compliance with decisions of government, the more effective is the government and the greater the capacity of government to use coercive measures to ensure compliance. Conversely, as voluntary compliance with the law declines, the ability of government to enforce obedience tends to decline. Force alone may be able to ensure sustantial compliance with governmental decisions in the short run, but history suggests that the long-term effectiveness of government can never depend on force alone. When force is the major instrument for implementing laws, force becomes the tool by which government authorities themselves are replaced by those opposing the decisions and policies of government.

The weakness of law to alter habits widespread within society is clearly demonstrated by the American effort at prohibition. Although a constitutional amendment required people to stop making and using alcoholic beverages, the law was unenforceable because a substantial portion of the American people were unwilling to live by that standard. The inability of law to change common habits of people has more recently been demonstrated by the national attempt to lower the U.S. speed limit in order to conserve energy. Although federal and state regulations have set a top speed limit of 55 miles per hour throughout the country, a significant portion of automobiles and trucks on U.S. highways still exceed this limit. The reason is clear: people have not changed their driving habits sufficiently to comply with the new government regulations. The weakness of government force to regulate human behavior is also dramatically illustrated by recent attempts to curb crime in the United States. During the 1970–75 period, expenditures for the maintenance of law and order increased more than threefold, yet the crime rate doubled. Obviously, strengthening the police force does not eliminate crime. What is needed above all is widespread popular support for the government's anti-crime program.

The government's ability to govern is not a function of military and police power but of the willing and automatic compliance of the people. A myth often propounded is that the power of a government and the interests of its people are two distinctly separate and independent phenomena. The above analysis should make it clear that governmental power and the habits of voluntary compliance are two sides of the same coin. A government's ability to govern is directly proportional to the degree that people recognize its authority over them and willingly accept all of its decisions and policies. People obey government not because they are forced to but because they are taught, and expected to do so.

Karl Deutsch suggests that habits of voluntary compliance are the invisible partner of government, yet they do most of the government's work.[2] Indeed, a political community is much like an iceberg, with the visible top one-ninth of it representing the work of government and the submerged, invisible eight-ninths representing customs, habits, and willing compliance with governmental and nongovernmental regulation. If most people refused to pay income tax each year, the collection of income tax would become an impossible task. Similarly, if people refused to stop at red traffic lights, it would be an impossible task to maintain an orderly flow of traffic, even if the police force were doubled or tripled in size. Laws on murder, rape, burglary, or tax evasion are effective because most people do not commit murder, do not rape, do not burglarize homes, and do not evade their income-tax responsibilities. Indeed, the habits of voluntary compliance in these areas are so strong that only a small portion of a government's budget is needed for maintaining compliance with these practices (Figure 3.3).

Figure 3.3   Governmental and Nongovernmental Compliance with Social and Political Norms

Schattschneider suggests that in the United States voluntary compliance with governmental decisions is so strong that the state uses power only marginally to ensure compliance.[3] In 1964, for example, 67 million tax returns were made, reporting 229 billion dollars in taxable income on which 47 billion dollars was voluntarily paid to the federal government.[4] Yet there were only about one thousand tax evasion cases tried that year. Compliance with government is also demonstrated by the relatively low number of persons in prison. In 1974 there were about 218,000 persons in U.S. prisons out of a total population of 212 million persons. For every 1,000 Americans, nearly 999 of them were basically law-abiding citizens.

In Schattschneider's view, coercive power is used by the state but is directed toward other states, not toward its own people. That military and police power is directed chiefly toward other states and not toward the nation's own people is demonstrated by the fact that expenditures for the armed forces is substantially greater than it is for the national police force. In 1974, for example, total federal, state, and local police expenditures in the United States were 8.5 billion dollars, while total armed forces expenditures consumed nearly 30 times that, or 268 billion dollars. Moreover, the total number of federal, state, and local police officers was substantially less than the number serving in the armed forces — 608,000 police officers versus 2,170,000 persons in the armed forces.[5] In short, the coercive power of the state is not the major instrument for enforcing domestic laws. Indeed, compliance is largely voluntary, the bulk of coercive power is used against other states in the international system, not against the state's own citizens.

To believe that people obey their government only because they fear prosecution and punishment is to miss a subtle but important distinction between voluntary and willing support of governmental decisions by most citizens and reluctant and often involuntary compliance by the few. To be sure, some governments generate much of their support from a rather limited group of constituents, but no government can long endure without substantial support from its membership, however that support is developed. Even authoritarian political regimes — systems in which governments make decisions with limited consultation — need to generate support for their policies.

One of the interesting phenomena of comparative politics is the high level of support generated by authoritarian systems. Charismatic, dictatorial leaders, such as Juan Domingo Peron in Argentina, Fidel Castro in Cuba, Mao Tse-tung in the People's Republic of China, and Gamal Abdel Nasser of Egypt, have been exceedingly popular among their peoples. Although such leaders have often granted limited individual freedom and political participation, the level of governmental support and compliance has been surprisingly strong. The reason for this support is that these authoritarian leaders have recognized the important role of the nongovernmental sources of regulation, particularly the common cultural, social, political, and economic values of society. As a result, many of these regimes, and specifically the communist governments, have focused their energies on programs of *socialization,* i.e., programs designed to strengthen the common values of society. Of course, the development of common values is a process that generally goes on in a rather perfunctory manner at home, in schools, at work, and in the common events of life. What many political leaders, however, have recognized is that this process can be deliberately strengthened and guided through systematic programs of indoctrination that can help create a favorable environment for the government's programs. One of the reasons why Mao Tse-tung's government was so effective in transforming China during the 1950s and 1960s was that a vigorous program of political socialization among children and adults was established shortly after the communists gained control late in the 1940s. The high degree of consensus and support for the communist regime was not created by force alone but was a direct result of the systematic development of communist values.

The Role of Enforcement Procedures

If government is to regulate society effectively, it must be able to use its coercive power when people are unwilling to obey its decisions voluntarily. The ability of government to enforce its decisions is determined in great measure by its political strength, i.e., its ability to ensure compliance through coercive and noncoercive means. There are four important elements of political strength: influence, authority, power, and force. We shall examine each of them and the role they play in political systems.

Influence   A person is said to have influence over another person when he can get him to do something he would not do otherwise. Government is said to have influence over its subjects when it can alter the intended behavior of people. Defined as such, personal or institutional influence is not an entity that can be acquired and used but is a type of relationship between individuals, groups, institutions, or political communities in which one party can affect the behavioral outcomes of another. The efforts by government to manage and regulate society are efforts to influence human behavior.

Influence can be brought about either through coercive or noncoercive means. Noncoercive influence involves the altering of human behavior through peaceful, nonthreatening means such as persuasion, manipulation, deceit, propaganda, discussion, argumentation, etc.[6] Although such techniques are important in bringing about compliance with governmental decisions, the ideal form of influence in a political system is the voluntary acceptance of the decisions of government because people accept the authority of government.

Authority   Authority is the capacity of a person or institution to command obedience without coercion.[7] Authority is not based on the superior force of those issuing commands but derives from the popular recognition that some people and institutions have the right to issue commands. Children, for example, obey their parents and teachers because they learn early in life to accept the authority of adults, particularly of their parents and teachers. Compliance with the rules of the home and the classroom does not derive from fear of being punished by some superior, more powerful adult but from automatic acceptance of the validity of the commands of the parent or teacher. Similarly, a government can issue commands and expect obedience from its subjects when its actions are accepted as valid and correct.

Since government authority is based on voluntary acceptance of the right to rule, the degree of authority is directly proportional to the level of *legitimacy,* i.e., the extent to which people are willing to support the government and voluntarily obey commands judged correct and moral. We are not concerned with whether or not people should accord authority to regimes that come to power through nondemocratic means and pursue policies that may be against generally recognized moral values. (The issue of whether or not people should accord legitimacy to regimes and their actions is a separate normative question.) Our concern is with the fact that people do, for whatever reason, accept the authority of government as valid and correct and thereby enable the government to issue binding laws on its people.

Authority is an essential element of all government decision making. It is essential because it is the most efficient way of influencing behavior. When a government possesses legitimacy, all that it needs to influence people's actions is to issue *commands*. Since its authority is accepted, people voluntarily obey.

No coercion, no force, no positive or negative sanctions are required to ensure compliance. People obey voluntarily because they regard the decisions of government as valid.

Max Weber suggests that there are three different sources of legitimate authority.[8] The first type is the *traditional,* found in tribal and other primitive political systems. Authority in such communities is based primarily on the customary patterns of the group. The second type is the *charismatic* authority derived primarily from the character and abilities of the individual leader. Examples of this type of authority are those of Castro in Cuba and Mao Tse-tung in China. The third type is the *legal-rational* authority found in the modern constitutional system. Such authority is not based on the customs of society or the exceptional personal qualities of the ruler but on the legal and constitutional provisions of the government. The authority of prime ministers and presidents in modern democratic systems belongs to this type because the ability to govern is based solely on the constitutional provisions for such authority.

Authority is not static but tends to increase and decrease in response to different types of leadership and in response to popular support accorded the decisions of the government. Leaders such as Franklin D. Roosevelt, Winston Churchill, and Charles de Gaulle, for example, were particularly adept at using their personal abilities to expand the authority of government. The actions, policies, and programs of governments can also affect the level of government authority. When leaders undertake highly unpopular actions the authority of government can be weakened. This was demonstrated during the recent administrations in the United States when the Vietnam war undermined the authority of President Nixon and the continued high inflation undermined confidence in the Carter administration. Moreover, if the authority of government is to be maintained, leaders must gain and maintain office through processes acceptable to the people and must then carry out policies acceptable to most of the society. When political systems enjoy broad popular support, there is little need for coercive action to ensure compliance with governmental decisions. But when popular support declines, the level of authority also decreases and the need for coercive and noncoercive governmental action becomes essential to ensure compliance. Thus, a measure of the extent of authority in any political system is the extent to which government needs to use coercive and noncoercive means to ensure compliance. The greater the need to use instruments of enforcement, the lower the level of authority in the political system.

Power Not all political systems are able to rule through legitimate authority. In some countries, governments gain office by coercive means and are maintained with limited voluntary support. In such systems, power is necessary to ensure compliance with the decisions of government.

Power is the capacity to influence behavior through the threat of coercion. Like influence, power is not an entity that may be acquired but is the successful utilization of tangible and intangible resources in altering human behavior. Unlike influence, power depends upon the use, or threat of use, of negative or positive sanctions. If the threat of sanctions is to be effective, it must be based on resources that can be effectively used to alter human behavior. A physically large person, for example, may appear to have more power than a small person because of his stronger physical features. The town sheriff may similarly possess more power than the ordinary citizen because of his ability to marshal the police capabilities of his other officers against a recalcitrant citizen.

For one party to have power over another it is not necessary that it use direct physical coercion to ensure compliance with the desired goals. All that is required is that one party *perceive* another as being more powerful, i.e., able to alter the behavior of another party by the threat of coercive action. This perception may or may not be based on tangible resources. Sometime ago, for example, a person threatened the life of a bank teller with a water gun hidden in a paper bag and successfully robbed a bank. Although the robbery was carried out with a harmless weapon, the teller perceived the threat as a real one; therefore, the harmless weapon was sufficient to give the robber substantial power over the teller. Conversely, police may be armed and yet powerless if citizens believe that they will not use their weapons to preserve order and protect property. When a major blackout occurred in New York City in 1977, massive looting took place in sections of the city. The violation of property laws occurred not because police were absent but because a substantial number of youth believed that the threat of police action would not be fully carried out.

The importance of perception and credibility in power relationships is most dramatically demonstrated in the irony concerning nuclear weapons. A country possessing a nuclear weapon possesses the most destructive military instrument in the world. Yet, if the weapon is to provide a country with power (i.e., the ability to influence another state), people must believe that such an armament would be used to ensure compliance with a particular desired action. Possession of tangible resources does not automatically ensure power. Power can only be established when one party or state can effectively influence another because of the use, or threat of use, of a particular coercive measure. What is essential, then, in all power relationships is not resources themselves but the perception of the ability to coerce.

Force   Force is the application of coercion. Unlike power, which relies primarily on the image of strength, force involves the application of military and police methods to ensure compliance with government decisions. Just as power is a specific form of influence, so is force a limited aspect of power in which the most extreme sanctions of military violence are used to ensure compliance. The application of force is required when all other less extreme forms of influence have failed. When people refuse to accept the authority of government or to be influenced by the threat of sanctions, the only tool left to government to ensure compliance is force. Force is, in effect, the *ultima ratio* of politics.

THE SCOPE OF GOVERNMENT

All governments seek to regulate and control human behavior. Governments, however, tend to differ significantly among the nations of the world. In some countries, governments play a major role in coordinating and managing social, economic, and political activities; in others, governments play a limited role in social and economic affairs and are chiefly concerned with mediating and resolving conflicts and preserving community order. Whether a government is a prime actor in society or is primarily an empire will depend in great measure upon the values and interests of the members of the political community. The concern is not with whether a government should play a major or minimal role in society. Our interest is simply to observe that governments do in fact play different roles in contemporary political systems.

The scope of government in society can be determined in terms of the *breadth* and *depth* of governmental regulations. The breadth of government refers to the range of activities carried out by the government. It refers to the different types of work that a government undertakes in such areas as the economy, health, welfare, the arts, etc. At one extreme are those societies where governments are primarily concerned with the maintenance of domestic political order and seek to provide maximum national protection from other foreign states. The governments of such communities are chiefly concerned with political order and provide limited social and economic services. This type of government is often called the "minimal state" and functions under the doctrine of *laissez faire,* i.e., the idea that society (and the economy in particular) function best when production and distribution are in the hands of individuals themselves. At the other extreme is the "maximal state," where government is expected not only to maintain community order but also to ensure that all citizens receive certain minimal social and economic standards. In such systems, government may own major industries, produce the primary sources of energy, own and regulate the media, provide education to all citizens, guarantee a minimum income for all families, provide minimal medical care for the aged, provide supplementary payments to the unemployed, etc.

Governments that seek to carry out such a range of activities are generally called *socialistic.* Those that seek to restrict government action and to ensure a strong private sector in social, economic, and other affairs are generally called *capitalistic.* The difference between these two types of governments, however, is not one of kind but of degree. It refers simply to the extent to which governments are involved in the nonpolitical aspects of society. A growing number of governments have sought to play a middle-road position between the two extreme types. These systems, called mixed economies, encourage private initiative while simultaneously ensuring certain minimal conditions in such areas as education, employment, medical care, and retirement protection. The welfare state in the United States is representative of this type of system and differs from the more socialistic systems of Hungary and Sweden and from the more capitalistic systems of Japan and Brazil.

One way of determining the breadth of government is in terms of the total level of government expenditures within society. The public sector, i.e., the breadth of government, may be defined as the proportion of the gross national product (GNP) accounted for by government. Stated otherwise, the public sector represents the percentage of total government expenditures out of the total value of goods and services produced within a country. Countries whose governments account for less than 45 percent of the GNP may be called capitalistic and those that spend more than that may be called socialistic. Although the size of the public sector may vary from as little as 5 percent of the GNP to as much as 90 percent, most contemporary systems allocate between 30 to 50 percent of total national income to public sources.

The depth of governmental regulation refers to the intensity of government's impact on society. The breadth of government gives an indication of the different types of activities carried out by government; the depth of government measures the extent to which individual and corporate behavior is influenced and regulated. Governments that seek to influence all aspects of life and to limit the level of privacy of people are called *totalitarian*. A totalitarian system seeks to penetrate all aspects of a citizen's life and to shape it in accordance with aims of the state. Two political scientists have listed six characteristics of totalitarian regimes:

1. an official ideology dealing with all aspects of human existence which all members of society must accept and promote;
2. a single mass party which leads and directs society in accordance with the official ideology;
3. total control of society through police and military power;
4. virtually total control of the instruments of mass communication;
5. the possession of a monopoly of military power to protect the community from internal or external threats; and
6. central control of the economy.[9]

While totalitarian regimes differ according to the objectives they pursue, they are similar in that they provide no effective protection of individual rights. Government is unlimited. No areas of life are protected from governmental intrusion. Education, the arts, religion, the media, the economy, leisure, are all subject to governmental regulation.

At the opposite extreme are the *constitutional* regimes. Constitutionalism is the doctrine that government responsibilities should be limited so that individual rights can be effectively protected. All political systems have constitutions, i.e., a basic set of rules and principles by which government operates. When these rules effectively limit the duties and powers of government and seek to protect the rights of people from the abuse of governmental power, then the system is said to be constitutional. A constitutional government, thus, has clear boundaries that it or other groups may not violate. (Historically, of course, major violations of human rights have been committed not by individuals or groups but by governments themselves.) The most important requirement for constitutionalism is the effective protection of individual rights from governmental encroachment.

Figure 3.4   Selected Countries Compared in Terms of Scope of Government

POLITICAL INSTITUTIONS

	Constitutional Regimes	Nonconstitutional Regimes
Low Public Sector	Canada Costa Rica New Zealand United States **(Democratic)**	Argentina Saudi Arabia South Korea The Philippines **(Authoritarian)**
High Public Sector	Denmark Norway Sweden United Kingdom **(Democratic-Socialist)**	China Cuba North Korea Soviet Union **(Totalitarian)**

STRUCTURE OF SOCIETY

Figure 3.4 illustrates different levels of governmental responsibility and activity based on a two-dimensional scale. Although it is difficult to precisely determine the scope of government in different societies, we can develop a general assessment based on two dimensions. The first differentiates political systems in terms of the structure of the socioeconomic environment; the other continuum is based on the nature of governmental institutions. The busiest governments are obviously those in totalitarian political systems, where the government has an unlimited role not only in the political sphere but also in the socioeconomic realm. The scope of government is most limited and restricted in those democratic regimes where private enterprise is still dominant and where government plays only a limited role in regulating and distributing economic goods. Governments with an intermediate or moderate scope are found in authoritarian or democratic-socialist systems.

SUMMARY

Government is the primary institution responsible for making final, authoritative decisions in society. Although government is found in all human communities, the institutions that are most significant are those with binding, society-wide authority. As a result, most study of government is concerned primarily with the nation-state.

The central task of government is to make decisions for a political community. These decisions are significant because they bring a temporary closure to the ongoing conflicts and debates within society and thereby create and maintain social harmony.

Government is not the main source of community order, however. The foundation of all political communities is found in the shared values, habits, and customs that help create and maintain a social order on which government authority can rest. Government does not create order out of a totally anarchic environment; rather, government refines and strengthens community consensus.

Government's ability to ensure compliance with its decisions is chiefly dependent on voluntary support. Although government must possess power to ensure compliance, no government can long exist if obedience to its laws can only be realized with threats of coercion. As a result, an effective regime is one that possesses governmental institutions with authority, i.e., with the capacity to elicit voluntary compliance with its decisions.

Governments gain authority when their actions are considered morally correct (legitimate) and when they are in accord with the common practices and mores of society. When a government seeks to gain control without the consent of the people and to carry out actions not in accord with prevailing values and customs, the government must use power, and possibly even force, to gain compliance.

KEY TERMS

government	socialization
law	influence
political culture	authority
inputs and outputs	legitimacy
constitution	power
force	

NOTES

1. R. M. MacIver, *The Web of Government,* rev. ed. (New York: The Free Press, 1965), p. 16.
2. Karl W. Deutsch, *Politics and Government: How People Decide Their Fate,* 2nd ed. (Boston: Houghton Mifflin, 1974), p. 19.
3. E. E. Schattschneider, *Two Hundred Million Americans In Search of a Government* (New York: Holt, Rinehart and Winston, 1969), pp. 17–24.
4. *Ibid.,* p. 21.
5. U. S. Bureau of the Census, *Pocket Data Book, USA 1976* (Washington, D. C.: U. S. Government Printing Office, 1976), pp. 129 and 150.
6. For an excellent overview of the various methods of achieving influence see Robert A. Dahl's *Modern Political Analysis,* 3rd ed. (Englewood Cliffs, N. J.: Prentice-Hall, 1976), pp. 42–53.
7. For an excellent analysis of the meaning of political authority see David V. J. Bell, *Power, Influence and Authority* (New York: Oxford University Press, 1975), pp. 35–69.
8. Max Weber, *The Theory of Social and Economic Organization,* trans. A. M. Henderson and Talcott Parsons (New York: Oxford University Press, 1947), p. 328.
9. Carl J. Friedrich and Zbiegniew Brzezinski, *Totalitarian Dictatorship and Autocracy,* 2nd ed. (Cambridge: Harvard University Press, 1965), pp. 9–10.

SUGGESTED READING

ALMOND, GABRIEL A., and POWELL, G. BINGHAM, JR. *Comparative Politics: System, Process and Policy.* 2nd ed. Boston: Little, Brown and Company, 1978. The authors analyze the major elements of a political system from a structural-functional perspective and present a theory about how political development occurs. A pioneering study that has deeply influenced the field of comparative political research.

BELL, DAVID V. J. *Power, Influence and Authority.* New York: Oxford University Press, 1975. Examines the meaning of these significant political terms.

DAHL, ROBERT A. *Who Governs? Democracy and Power in an American City.* New Haven: Yale University Press, 1961. An empirical investigation of who governs New Haven, Connecticut. Argues that power is distributed among several centers of power.

DEUTSCH, KARL. *The Nerves of Government: Models of Political Communication and Control.* Glencoe, Ill.: The Free Press, 1963. Applies communications theory to political systems in an effort to develop a dynamic understanding of government. Highly theoretical.

FINER, S. E. *Comparative Government.* Harmondsworth, England: Penguin Books, 1970. A comprehensive introductory text to the field of comparative government. Examines the governments of Britain, France, the United States, and the Soviet Union.

FRIEDRICH, CARL J. *Limited Government: A Comparison.* Englewood Cliffs, N.J.: Prentice-Hall, 1974. An analysis of constitutionalism and of the role and function of constitutions in contemporary governments.

MacIver, Robert M. *The Web of Government.* rev. ed. New York: The Free Press, 1965. A brilliant conceptual analysis of the origins, role, and function of government.

Schattschneider, E. E. *Two Hundred Million Americans in Search of a Government.* New York: Holt, Rinehart and Winston, Inc., 1969. A short, lucid account of the role of government in contemporary society. Chapters three and four provide an insightful analysis of democracy.

Truman, David B. *The Governmental Process: Political Interests and Public Opinion.* 2nd ed. New York: Alfred A. Knopf, 1971. A classic reformulation of Arthur Bentley's group approach to politics, with major attention to American interest groups.

4 / THEORIES OF POLITICAL COMMUNITY

Who should govern a political community? How much freedom and order are required in a healthy, stable community? What methods should be used for minimizing and resolving conflict? Who, in other words, should deal with the problem of community, and how should it be dealth with?

Throughout the history of Western civilization, political thinkers have analyzed questions such as these. Although no single superior theory adequately answers all of the fundamental issues of governance and conflict management, numerous theories present alternative perspectives on the nature and resolution of the problem of community that can provide insights about the conflict-management process. In this chapter we shall examine four alternative approaches. The four political thinkers and their distinctive perspectives are:

1. Plato—government by the wise;
2. Thomas Hobbes—government by the powerful;
3. John Locke—government by the majority; and
4. Karl Marx—the abolition of government.

Although our analysis is concerned primarily with each theorist's views on development and maintenance of peace and harmony in human communities, it should be recognized that each thinker is concerned with management of human conflict in a different way. Plato deals only implicitly with the issue of conflict, whereas Hobbes builds a theory based on the need for a stable, peaceful community. Whether or not a theorist deals directly with conflict-management, our analysis focuses on the implicit or explicit ideas regarding the nature of human conflict and the political means available for its management and resolution.

PLATO: GOVERNMENT BY THE WISE

One of the great political treatises of all time is Plato's *Republic* (428–348 B.C.). This study is significant because it presents one of the most profound and eloquent arguments for an elitist government (government by the few). Plato's theory is based on two fundamental assumptions: people are inherently unequal in their capacity to govern; and reason is the effective instrument by which rulers can resolve the problem of community. Although the ostensible purpose for writing the *Republic* was to define the concept of justice, most of the book is concerned with the political issue of who should rule the *polis* (the political community). Plato's answer to this question is singularly clear—the wise philosopher-king should govern. In the words of Plato:

> *Unless either philosophers become kings in their countries or those who are now kings and rulers come to be sufficiently inspired with a genuine desire for wisdom; unless, that is to say, political power and philosophy meet together, while the many natures who now go their several ways in the one or the other direction are forcibly debarred from doing so, there can be no rest from troubles.*[1]

To better understand how Plato comes to this conclusion, we shall examine other aspects of his theory by posing three central questions: Is there a body of knowledge on the nature of a good, ideal political community? If there is such knowledge, can it be attained by people? And if such knowledge is attainable, can people be made to live in accordance with it? Plato's answer to all three questions is in the affirmative.

The Nature of the Ideal Community

According to Plato, the ideal society is one where a natural order results from everyone doing the task he was fitted to do by nature. Since people are born with certain natural interests, abilities, and aptitudes, community order results when people recognize what they are naturally fitted to do and when they do it willingly. When individuals do not carry out the tasks they were designed by nature to fulfill, the result is conflict and disorder.

Plato believes that there are three major tasks in any society and there is a corresponding social class to each task. The most important class is the rulers ("Guardians," as Plato called them), whose task is to ensure that justice is carried out in the political community. The second class is composed of auxiliaries—soldiers and civil servants, who carry out the necessary activities of the state. The most numerous class of persons in a society is composed of artisans, who have responsibility for all production and services within the community (it is the class of professionals, farmers, businessmen, and laborers). At the

Plato

John Locke

T. Hobbes

Karl Marx

All photographs from *The Granger Collection*, New York.

top of the three social classes is the supreme ruler of the community, the philosopher-king, who ensures that all persons have found their proper place in society. Since justice can only occur when people have taken up their natural vocations, the most important task of the ruler is to ensure that everyone is doing what he is naturally fitted to do.

Plato does not provide much specific information about how the philosopher-king is to deal with ongoing problems of government. Rather, he suggests that a properly qualified person who is given the responsibilities of governing a political community will be able to respond adequately to the specific needs and difficulties of a people based on his natural abilities and extensive training. In both the *Republic* and the *Statesman,* Plato suggests that a ruler can develop the competencies to deal with the challenges and problems of a society in much the same way that a doctor develops knowledge and skills to deal with sick patients. Just as a physician has the ability to diagnose human illness and to recommend a remedy, so, too, is a wise ruler able to diagnose the health of political communities and develop policies and programs to ensure a vigorous, healthy, and mature political community. Plato, however, provides little guidance on the specific content of community governance. He argues that a properly chosen and trained ruler will have the skills and the intuitive knowledge to select the actions and policies most beneficial to a community. Although the knowledge of the ideal political community is not spelled out, Plato's theory assumes nonetheless that there is a body of knowledge about the just, ideal society.

The Education of Rulers

How can a ruler acquire the knowledge and wisdom necessary to govern a political community? How can he develop the skills and abilities essential for establishing a just order in society? Since education plays a central role in Plato's theory of government, he devotes a large part of the *Republic* to the selection, development, and training of political leaders.

There are two requirements for becoming a part of the ruling class: first, individuals must have the natural abilities and skills of rulers; and second, they must have undertaken a prolonged and intensive program of theoretical and practical training. Plato assumes that children can be classified at birth into one of the three professional classes. Those with the greatest physical and mental qualities are assigned to the ruling class, while those with the most limited abilities to the artisan class. Although Plato does not indicate how rulers are able to determine into which professional class children should be assigned, he is confident that the differing qualities of children will enable rulers to carry out this difficult task. In addition, Plato thinks the task of placing children into their proper social classes is facilitated because most children will have the same qualities as their parents. Thus, rulers tend to beget prospective rulers;

artisans beget prospective artisans. Plato also allows for the possibility of children from the soldier and working classes to become rulers and children from the Guardian class to become either soldiers or artisans.

The children selected for education, whether male or female, undertake a program of mental and bodily development throughout much of their lives. The program consists of athletics and academics with the purpose of training the mind and developing the will. Plato was well aware that education itself would not guarantee the desired behavior; therefore, one of the essential aspects of his educational program involved the development of character and will. Plato was convinced that a well-developed training program would not only help develop a person's ability to control his passions but would also be able to ensure that those in positions of political authority would pursue the interests of the community, at the expense of, or in disregard for, their individual interests. Education and practical experience would conquer the problem of greed, selfishness, and passion.

Plato's educational program comprises two parts—the academic and the practical. The first part comprises an intellectual development during the first 35 years of life; the second part involves an internship program for approximately 15 years, or until the prospective ruler is about 50 years old. The first dimension of education has two important stages—the elementary, compulsory stage involving the first 20 years of a child's life and the second stage of some 15 years of higher education. During the first period, children are given a regimented and well-planned program of gymnastics (training of the body) and music (training of the mind) to develop the analytical and creative skills of the mind as well as the character and the physical abilities of individuals. Plato was convinced that the minds of youth were so impressionable that great care had to be taken in selection of literature, poetry, art, and music that young people would be exposed to in their educational program. He was convinced that too much soft, lyrical music would lead to the development of weak, emotional character; similarly, poetry had to be carefully screened in order to eliminate any materials that would hinder the development of strong, stable personalities.

Young men and women who distinguish themselves during the early phase of education are selected for a period of further training. During this second phase, the educational program attempts to develop the rational aptitudes of students further. This is done chiefly through the study of mathematics, logic, and other sciences. Those who successfully complete this higher phase of learning are then prepared for the practical stage of the educational program.

The final dimension involves an internship, in which the student can begin to apply his knowledge to the political process. In this phase, candidates are given an opportunity to serve in different but minor posts of the political community. The purpose of the internship is to provide an opportunity for students to begin to apply their knowledge and skills to the problems of society. The objective of this practical experience is to develop judgment in applying knowledge to practical affairs of the state and to ensure that rulers have developed the discipline and maturity necessary for effectively coping with the temptations associated with power. Plato believed that once a student had finished his 15-year internship successfully, he would be ready to undertake a leadership post in a political community.

The Practice of Ruling

The third issue in Plato's political theory asks: how can one ensure that rulers will live in accordance with their knowledge? Plato was aware of the problems involved in giving political power to one person or to one class, but he firmly believed that a properly trained individual could be trusted with unlimited power. Since the misuse of political power was not a byproduct of human nature but of inadequate training and education, there was no need to worry about Lord Acton's famous dictum that "power tends to corrupt, and absolute power tends to corrupt absolutely."

Despite his faith in education, Plato believed that two additional modifications were needed for the ruling class if his elitist theory was to work. The two changes (required for Guardians and soldiers) were abolition of private property and elimination of the family. Plato was convinced that the problems associated with private property and love of family were so pernicious that (rather than attempt to train character to cope with selfishness, avarice, greed, and sex) he abolished property and family life altogether for those involved in positions of political and military authority. Male and female rulers and soldiers would not be allowed to marry and establish families, although they would be allowed to have children in accordance with prescribed regulations. Similarly, rulers and soldiers would not be allowed to possess private property; all the essential needs of housing, clothing, and food would be provided freely by the community. Plato's ideal state would thus be partially communistic. But unlike the contemporary communist ideology, which expouses the abolition of private property for all of society, Plato's communism applies only to rulers and soldiers and would not affect the majority of the community's members.

Given Plato's belief that only wise and properly trained individuals are able to govern, it is not surprising that he is a strong critic of democracy. Unlike democracy, which assumes that no specialization can be developed in the field of government, Plato holds that it is possible to know what is good and desirable in a political community. The task of those in political authority, therefore, is not merely to reconcile competing interests, resolve disputes, or measure public sentiments but to implement the best policies and program regardless of the interests of the common people. The task of governing is not to undertake actions the majority of people may desire; the only authentic task is to do the good.

During the earlier part of his life, Plato was so convinced that education was the proper vehicle for the preparation of good rulers that he completely omitted two themes in the *Republic* that have been central in the role of public opinion and the place of law in society. During his later years, however, Plato's idealism began to wane; he became less optimistic about finding a Guardian class headed by a philosopher-king, which would fulfill the conditions he had stipulated. As a result, in the *Laws* (his last political treatise) Plato was no longer interested primarily in education and the selection of rulers but became more concerned with development of good laws that would create and maintain a good, just society. The foundation of the *Laws,* as it had been for the *Republic,* however, remained the same: good government can result only when reason is applied to the political process.[2]

In summary, Plato is not fundamentally concerned with conflict management but rather with the creation of an ideal, just community. For Plato, the purpose of a human community is to achieve the highest quality of life. This, he believes, can only be realized when wise, knowledgeable people have the authority to rule. When properly trained and able persons are given power, they will be able not only to keep harmony but also to establish the qualities that lead to justice. The problem of centralizing power in the hands of a single, all-powerful philosopher-king is that he may misuse the power, as have so many other political leaders in the past. But Plato was so convinced of the efficacy of reason and training that he continued to believe until his death that the best way of dealing with the problem of community was to give political authority to individuals who have the wisdom and skill to govern. If they did not govern directly, they could at least make laws by which behavior was to be regulated.

THOMAS HOBBES: GOVERNMENT BY THE POWERFUL

Thomas Hobbes (1588-1679) was born in England in an era of great political and religious turmoil. His most important political work, the *Leviathan,* was written in Holland and was inspired in large measure by the English Civil War (1640-1659) which had forced him into exile. The *Leviathan,* a literary masterpiece, is significant because it is one of the most systematic and influential arguments for strong, effective government.

The central problem of the *Leviathan* is the question of fundamental requirements of political society. To answer this question, Hobbes develops a scenario of what the state of nature is like—a place where there is no government, no law, and no order. The state of nature is not necessarily a historical state but a hypothetical condition that precedes the establishment of civil society. It is a place where people are completely free to do what they want and where no common power limits human liberty. The purpose of developing a theory from the primitive conditions of the state of nature is to build a deductive argument patterned after the methodology of geometry, a subject that Hobbes much admired. The object is to set forth basic, essential political axioms and theorems and to draw conclusions deductively from them.

The State of Nature—War

According to Hobbes, the basic quality of the state of nature is conflict. Since there is no government to restrain individual liberty, the state of nature is a place where there is only perpetual war. In the words of Hobbes, life in pre-political society is "solitary, poor, nasty, brutish, and short." Moreover, since life and property are not secure, there is no education, no culture, no civility, no economic growth. Survival from day to day is the chief human concern.

Hobbes's pessimistic assessment of a prepolitical human community is based on two assumptions about human nature. First, Hobbes believes that people are essentially equal in both mind and body so that the strongest and smartest are always susceptible to an attack from the least capable members of society. Second, Hobbes believes that people are essentially selfish and concerned primarily with their individual gain. People may express acts of generosity and kindness, but their fundamental nature is self-interest. Thus, when there is no framework to restrict the ambitions and interests of people, the result is intense, violent conflict. The essential nature of people is not social but competitive. People apart from a political community are like disjointed atoms continuously in tension with others.

Although the human condition in the state of nature is exceedingly bleak, people have the necessary resources to get out of this unfortunate predicament. By establishing a political society (or "commonwealth," as Hobbes called it), their interests would be better realized. The willingness of people to leave the state of nature and move into a civil society is not the result of a desire to help others but rather to promote self-interest. Indeed, the immediate cause for establishing a civil commonwealth is the fear of death and the desire to live in an environment where human life is guaranteed. People have everything to gain by trying to alter the conditions of violence and uncertainty found in the state of nature.

Since people enjoy short-term benefits resulting from unchecked freedom in the state of nature, how can individuals perceive that their long-term interest (their own survival) can only be realized by giving up liberty and freedom? Hobbes argues that all human beings have the rational ability and foresight to perceive the laws of nature by which they are guided out of the state of nature. These laws of nature are not laws as such but rational principles that help people preserve their own lives. Unlike the natural laws of Cicero, Thomas Aquinas, and John Locke, Hobbes's laws are not immutable moral laws that guide the human conscience but simple, rational guidelines for survival. By grasping these rational principles, individuals are able to perceive that their long-term interest lies in an orderly community where there is less absolute freedom but where human survival is no longer the dominant concern.

The major difference between the state of nature and the civil commonwealth is the different levels of freedom and order found in each. In the prepolitical society there is virtually no order, and individual freedoms are without limit. In such a state there is no harmony and no stability. The civil commonwealth, by contrast, is a place where a common authority limits human freedoms and thereby limits the level of conflict. In the state of nature, authority is decentralized; every person is sovereign over his own person. In the commonwealth, authority is centralized and sovereignty rests with a common power. This basic difference is illustrated in Figure 4.1.

Figure 4.1   Comparison of Hobbes's State of Nature and Civil Commonwealth

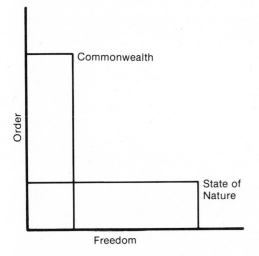

The Formation of Political Society

Hobbes argues that the commonwealth can be established either by acquisition or by institution. When a person naturally acquires superior influence and successfully threatens, or imposes force on, others, a commonwealth is said to be established by acquisition. Communities are created in this manner because of a natural imbalance in the distribution of power, which leads to the dominant individuals' regulating and controlling the behavior of weaker members. Order is thus established by imposition of force. The second (and more significant) method of establishing a community is through consent, i.e., the voluntary creation of a community by joint action. The creation of a commonwealth through this method takes the form of a social contract. In both cases, individuals establish a commonwealth out of fear. The reasons, however, are different: in the creation of community by acquisition, people fear the power of the dominant leader (Sovereign); in the creation of community by institution, people fear each other.

Although the most common historical pattern of creating political communities has been through acquisition, Hobbes's theory of government is chiefly concerned with the creation of commonwealths through consent. The chief characteristic of this approach is the mutual and voluntary character of the contract that establishes the political society. The contract is not an agreement between the people and the Sovereign but rather an agreement among the people themselves. In the contract, individuals agree to give up sovereignty over their own lives to an unknown common power, which Hobbes referred to as the Leviathan, or Sovereign. The purpose of the contract is not to specify rights and duties but to ensure a complete transfer of sovereignty from individuals to the Sovereign. In order for a commonwealth to be created effectively, the contract requires that all individuals unconditionally transfer their rights and liberties to the common power and that all other persons in the community do likewise. The transfer of sovereignty from individuals to the Leviathan must be universal and unqualified.

The Ruler's Responsibilities

Who should be the Leviathan? Anyone, says Hobbes. Since the distinguishing characteristic of the Sovereign is his absolute monopoly of power, any person (or group) who acquires substantial superiority of power automatically becomes the effective Sovereign. While the Leviathan could conceivably benefit by having knowledge and experience about government, the only requirement for the office is to possess a monopoly of force. This ensures peace and order in a community. The ruler is not expected to establish effective social and economic programs, nor is he responsible for caring for the poor or the sick. Moreover, since there are no moral laws and values within the Hobbesian system, there is no need to search for just, equitable policies. The only value to be consistently applied is order and peace, the condition through which life is preserved.

Since government is not part of the social contract creating the commonwealth, the ruler has no duties or responsibilities except to preserve life. The Sovereign's power is absolute and unlimited. Unlike Locke and other modern democratic theorists who have defended the doctrine of inalienable rights (certain inborn rights persons always possess by virtue of their humanity), Hobbes suggests that individuals do not have any rights within the commonwealth except the right to life. Indeed, Hobbes opposed the notion of human rights precisely because he thought it had led to the revolutionary, anarchic conditions of the mid-seventeenth century. His cure for the revolutionary conditions of Britain was to deny the idea of inalienable rights and its corollary—that government was primarily an instrument for maximizing those rights and interests. Rather, Hobbes affirms only one right—the right to life. The task of government is therefore not to ensure justice, the equitable reconciliation of conflicting and competing individual rights, but to ensure peace and political order.

Despite the authoritarianism of Hobbes's theory, there is one limit to the ruler's authority: the Sovereign must protect the lives of his people. If he fails to do this, or if he attempts to kill them, the Sovereign ceases to carry out the function for which he was created. The people then have an obligation to find a new ruler to perform this basic task. Since the chief task of government is to protect life, a ruler may not violate the inalienable right of self-preservation. Hobbes puts it this way: "A covenant not to defend myself from force, is always void." Although there is a condition implicit in the Sovereign's position, it would be incorrect to view Hobbes's theory as a basis for revolution. The thrust throughout the *Leviathan* is not revolutionary politics but authoritarianism, the forceful imposition of order through power.

One of the most distasteful elements of Hobbes's theory is the contention that the Sovereign must have the power to "judge what Opinions and Doctrines are averse, and what conducive to peace." Hobbes was well aware that religious liberty in England had been one of the chief causes of the civil war that had forced him into exile. Not surprisingly, he argues that since the ultimate good is peace and order, any religious and political views and beliefs that get in the way of this objective should not be tolerated. Censorship of ideas is thus one of the important responsibilities of the Leviathan. Some of the ideas Hobbes thinks are averse to a stable community are: (1) military weakness is better than military might; (2) people are good judges of their own actions; (3) actions against the conscience are sin; (4) rulers must abide by the laws they make; (5) property rights should not be violated; and (6) sovereign power may be divided.

Despite Hobbes's concern with the regulation of beliefs, the Sovereign is supposed to regulate only a limited range of activities. Hobbes's theory is authoritarian, not totalitarian. It does not support totalitarianism (the doctrine that government should control all aspects of man) because the vast number of social, economic, and religious activities are to remain in private hands. According to Hobbes, "Private persons are to have the liberty to buy, and sell, and otherwise contract with one another; to choose their own abode, their own diet, their own trade of life, and institute their children as they themselves think fit; and the like." To ensure peace and order, government need not regulate all aspects of human behavior but only those areas that encourage dissention and conflict. Government is therefore only minimally concerned with regulating the economy, the arts, education, and culture, and focuses its attention on developing a strong military and police force to preserve law and order domestically and to protect the state from foreign aggression.

One of the major weaknesses of Hobbes's theory is that it is incapable of differentiating between different types of peace. Thus, some communities may enjoy only short periods of order and stability, while others may enjoy long-term periods of peace and harmony. Communities may also differ in the extent to which peace is achieved through force. In some, arbitrary and repressive policies may create order by intimidation but build up enormous anger against the government. In others, order may result from basic satisfaction achieved through equitable and just policies. Peace, in other words, may be either short-lived or relatively permanent. It may be based on repression or on just, humane policies.

Hobbes's inability to distinguish between various types of order is the direct result of his simple assumptions about human beings. He is so obsessed with the creation of order to ensure the preservation of life that he fails to recognize other values central to human existence. As a result, any political system that keeps order, no matter how repressive, is acceptable. But history suggests that the means used to create community order directly determines the permanence of that order. Political systems that maintain order through humane and equitable policies are more permanent and stable than are those that seek to create order through fear and ruthless, arbitrary police actions.

In summary, Hobbes suggests that the fundamental political issue is the regulation and management of human conflict. Since people apart from government are in a state of continuous war with each other, the basic task of political communities is to manage conflict. This is done, according to Hobbes, by creating a political environment in which power is centralized in the hands of the government. Hobbes's fundamental strategy for managing conflict is to alter the structure of the natural condition of humanity (the state of nature) by creating a central authority to create and maintain order by virtue of its ability to threaten or enforce compliance with its decisions. Since the authority of the Leviathan is so extensive and the freedoms and liberties of individuals so limited, the level of conflict in the political community is limited. Indeed, given the hierarchical structure of the commonwealth, there is little possibility for serious conflict. The frequent, continuous, violent conflict of the state of nature is thus either eliminated or suppressed. The conflict that remains in the political community is regulated by the Leviathan, not by compromise but by force.

Hobbes's theory continues to be relevant to our contemporary world because nations, and particularly the international system, are continuously beset with the conflicts that led him to write the *Leviathan* in the 1650s. While the theory may suffer from inadequate assumptions, his study remains the most consistent argument for a clear and unambiguous sovereign authority in a political community. To be sure, a permanent peace requires more than force. But it is also clear that whenever a community ceases to have sovereign authority backed by power, the community's life is placed in jeopardy both from within and without. An essential requirement for any stable, orderly community is therefore the presence of a sovereign authority possessing a monopoly of force. Peace and power are not two different aspects of the world but rather two different sides of the same coin.

JOHN LOCKE: GOVERNMENT BY THE MAJORITY

Another important theorist who has analyzed the problem of community from the perspective of a social contract is the English writer John Locke (1632–1704.). Locke's most important political work is the *Second Treatise on Civil Government,* a study that has often been regarded as the bible of democracy. This essay is important because it presents one of the most complete and logical arguments for a limited, representative government. The ideas of the *Second Treatise* deeply influenced Thomas Jefferson and other American Founding Fathers and found expression in the state and national institutions and practices of the early American republic. Subsequently, political leaders around the world have continued to find wisdom and inspiration in Locke's theory of conflict management.

The State of Nature

Locke, like Hobbes, begins his analysis of the problem of community by examining the characteristics of the state of nature. In his view, the prepolitical society is a relatively happy, peaceful, harmonious environment where people pursue their own concerns and interests with limited interference. The reason why the conditions in this state are not brutish and warlike (as in Hobbes's theory) is that people are assumed to be kind, generous, and thoughtful. Unlike Hobbes's people, who are only interested in maximizing self-interest, Locke's individuals are assumed to behave in accordance with moral norms, or what Locke calls the laws of nature. These moral laws, which all people can perceive through reason, help guide behavior and restrain the conflict that would otherwise ensue in the state of nature. Although people interpret these laws differently, the principles of nature are sufficiently clear to help establish a significant level of harmony without the assistance of government. People apart from government do not act completely maliciously or totally in disregard for the general community's interests, as Hobbes had argued. Rather, a person apart from government is a relatively social, happy, and peaceful person who gets along rather well with others. The state of nature, in short, is not a state of continuous war but a state of uncertainty in which peace and harmony reign intermittently.

What are the laws of nature? Locke suggests that they are principles that individuals perceive through reason. Some of these laws are: (1) people desire peace; (2) people are naturally free; (3) all individuals have a right to liberty — to do what they want as long as they do not violate the natural rights of others; (4) individuals have a right to own property; (5) people have the right to punish wrongdoing; and (6) people have the right to protect themselves or someone else. Underlying these principles is the most fundamental right of all — the right to life — from which Locke deduces two corollary obligations: the right to preserve one's own life and the right to preserve the lives of others. Locke states the moral obligation to defend human life as follows:

> *Everyone, as he is bound to preserve himself and not to quit his station willfully; so by the like reason, when his own preservation comes not in competition, ought he, as much as he can, to preserve the rest of mankind, and may not, unless it be to do justice on an offender, take away or impair the life, or what tends to the preservation of the life, the liberty, health, limb, or goods of another.*[3]

Although Locke is aware that men use and interpret natural law to suit their own particular interests, he also believes that men act in accordance with them with sufficient regularity to result in a relatively peaceful state of nature. The task of government is thus not to destroy the fundamental rights and freedoms enjoyed in the state of nature but to refine and improve an already amicable state of nature through the establishment of a common source of power.

Inadequacies of the State of Nature

But if conditions are relatively productive and peaceful in the prepolitical society, why do people give up some of their liberty to establish civil society? The reason is that the prepolitical environment has three shortcomings. First, the laws of nature are not sufficiently clear and specific to effectively regulate all human conflict. This weakness is not because of the laws of nature but because of human inability to correctly perceive the laws. Locke writes that "for though the law of nature be plain and intelligible to all rational creatures, yet men being biased by their interest as well as ignorant for want of studying it, are not apt to allow of it as a law binding to them in the application of it to their particular cases." The second imperfection in the state of nature is the lack of a common judge to interpret the laws of nature. Since people tend to perceive and interpret such laws in accordance with their own interests and perceptions, there is a need for a final, authoritative judge. Finally, the state of nature is deficient because there is no effective political authority to implement the laws of nature. There is no sovereign power to ensure that the right and acceptable interpretation of natural law is enforced. In short, while Locke is optimistic that natural law guides human behavior in the state of nature, he is also realistic in recognizing that passion and self-interest hinders the operation of natural law. What results in the state of nature is a relatively stable and peaceful community with periodic confusion, uncertainty, and conflict. In short, Locke assumes that the state of nature is "inconvenient."

Locke suggests two other reasons for establishing civil society: to avoid the state of war and to preserve private property. The state of war, says Locke, is a condition where force is used without right (where power is employed illegitimately). Although war may occur in civil society (such as when a man commits a crime), it is mostly found in the state of nature, where there is no common power to prevent the use of arbitrary power. The second reason for establishing a commonwealth is to help protect property. Property is important not only because it involves the goods a person may rightfully own but also because it is an essential aspect of a person. People acquire property through their own ingenuity and work; property is thus a reflection of one's creativity and diligence. Locke suggests that property and personality are so closely related that to deprive a person of his property is to deprive him of his humanity. Thus, Locke argues that property (which he defines as "life, liberty, and estates") is the chief end of political society.

The Creation of the Commonwealth

The principal characteristic of civil society is it's legitimate authority to resolve conflicts within a community. It is a community where a government has been instituted to make decisions on behalf of all members. Locke distinguishes civil society from the state of nature as follows:

> *Those who are united into one body and have a common law*
> *and judicature to appeal to, with authority to decide*
> *controversies between them and punish offenders, are in civil*
> *society one with another; but those who have no such common*
> *appeal, I mean on earth, are still in the state of nature...*[4]

A fundamental difference between the state of nature and political society lies in the different levels of conflict in each. These in turn are the result of different levels of freedom and order in each of the communities. In the state of nature some order is provided by the laws of nature. But the dominant feature is freedom, and the large amount of freedom is the source of much human conflict. Political society, however, has substantially more order and less absolute freedom — a condition made possible by the creation of government. Although the differences in the levels of freedom and order (and therefore of conflict) are significant (Figure 4.2), they are not nearly as noticeable in Locke's theory as in Hobbes's. The latter theory requires people to shift from a condition of anarchy to a stable authoritarian environment. The distinctions in this model (compare Figure 4.1) are much more drastic than in Locke's.

Figure 4.2   Comparison of Locke's State of Nature and Civil Society

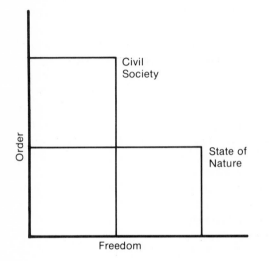

Locke believes that the only acceptable way of establishing political society is through consent. Since the shift from the state of nature to the commonwealth involves a fundamental alteration of the human condition, Locke contends that the only valid method by which this transfer can occur is through the unanimous and voluntary consent of the people, which is expressed in the form of a social contract. The contract, of course, does not involve government but only people who desire to establish the commonwealth.

In accepting the social contract, individuals make two important commitments. First, they agree that the social contract is a perpetual act, i.e., it is for the life of the persons involved and is automatically passed on to other generations. As Locke notes, once a person has consented to the social contract, he is "perpetually and indispensably obliged to be and remain unalterably a subject to it, and can never be again in the liberty of the state of nature."

Second they agree that decisions of government will be made by majority vote and that they will abide by those decisions even if they conflict with personal interests. Locke recognizes that unanimity is desirable in community life, but because of the political paralysis resulting from such a system, he argues that people should operate government under the prudential rule of majority voting.

The Nature of Government

A chief characteristic of Locke's political theory is the limited scope and power of government. One of the primary reasons for this is that government is viewed as an instrument by which people's interests can be realized. The government itself has no rights or privileges, only duties. Rights are always assumed to be with the people.

According to Locke, government is created by a conditional (fiduciary) trust. Although the establishment of government occurs at the same time that civil society comes into being through the social contract, the creation of government is an act independent from the creation of the commonwealth. Thus, while government and society are always closely associated, Locke assumes that they are distinct entities.

One of the most influential aspects of Locke's theory is the idea that people have basic *human rights* that can never be legitimately denied or abrogated. The purpose of government is not to limit these inalienable rights but rather to make them more secure in civil society than they would be in the state of nature. In creating government, Locke suggests that people assume the role of trustors (creators of the trust) and beneficiaries, while government serves as trustee, i.e., the agent to whom the community's interests are entrusted. Since the trust provides that people are always the beneficiaries, government must always protect and maximize the rights and interests of people. When government attempts to limit or deny the inalienable rights it was established to protect, people have the right to establish another government to carry out more effectively the responsibilities of trustee. Locke states the revolutionary character of his theory as follows:

> *For all power given with trust for the attaining of an end being limited by that end; whenever that end is manifestly neglected or opposed, the trust must necessarily be forfeited, and the power devolve to the hands of those that gave it who may place it anew where they shall think best for their safety and security.*[5]

In short, the conditional foundation of government helps ensure that people's rights are protected and that political power remains limited.

There are two other, more specific, ways by which a *limited government* is maintained. First, the legislature is a representative body subject to periodic elections. Since the authority of the legislature derives from consent, legislators must ensure that their decisions and actions are in accord with the interests of the people. Given the conditional nature of government, the work of legislators and the interests of the people would seem to be in continuous tension. This is unlikely, since the people and the legislature do not hold political authority simultaneously. According to Locke, once a legislature has been established, people cease to exercise their power and authority as long as the government faithfully carries out its duties. As long as a government exists, the legislature has final political authority over the community. The authority vested in the legislature is periodically renewed through elections by which political leaders can be either reappointed or replaced. Thus, elections help make government responsive to the interests of the people.

The second method of maintaining a limited government is through *separation of powers.* Locke argues that the responsibilities of making and enforcing laws — the two primary tasks of government — should be carried out independently through separate governmental institutions. The reason for separating the legislative and executive branches is that human nature is unable to cope with the temptations of power when legislative and executive powers are combined. Unlike Montesquieu, who supported a relatively equal or balanced separation of political responsibilities, Locke suggests that the legislature should have supreme power over the executive. The reason for this is that making laws is the most difficult and fundamental task of government. The legislature's supremacy is to be manifested only as it dutifully carries out the interests of the people.

The purpose of the executive branch of government is to enforce the actions and policies of the legislature. In addition, the executive has certain "federative" responsibilities, which do not result from the actions of the legislature but from the existence of the political community itself. (Such responsibilities include the need to keep peace and to protect the community from foreign aggression.) Moreover, since the legislature is not always able to foresee the needs and problems of the future, Locke grants the executive the use of "prerogative" power, discretionary authority to act when there are no laws or when there is insufficient time to enact the law. Some have suggested that an energetic executive branch might lead to an undemocratic system. This is unlikely, since the authority of the executive derives from the legislature in much the same way that acts of the monarch and his cabinet are subject to the Parliament under royal prerogative.

In conclusion, Locke, like Hobbes, suggests that the means of developing harmony and consensus within human communities is to create a commonwealth in which government is given the responsibility of conflict management. Unlike Hobbes, Locke, much more optimistic about the nature of man, believes that individuals are far more enlightened about the process of building harmony. Indeed, the rational and moral principles of natural law enable people to live a relatively comfortable and harmonious existence apart from government. The task of government, therefore, is not to create order out of disorder but to refine and improve the conditions of the state of nature. The task of government is not to create just any type of order but to establish a particular type of peace—a just peace that protects the natural rights of people. Conflict resolution and conflict management are to be carried out according to moral standards based on reason. When governments seek to create order at all costs (as Hobbes had suggested), they undoubtedly violate some human rights in order to preserve life. Locke regards such a solution as unacceptable. The task of government is not only to ensure the right to life but all other basic rights as well.

KARL MARX: THE ABOLITION OF GOVERNMENT

The political thinker who perhaps has had the most profound impact on the twentieth century is Karl Marx (1818–1883), the German theorist and social critic whose ideas have provided the foundation for the communist ideology. Although many of Marx's ideas have been popularized by communist governments, his writings do not lend themselves to easy summation or analysis. This is partly because his publications are so extensive, covering philosophy, history, economics, politics, and sociology; also his interests and theoretical concerns tended to shift over his lifetime from philosophical and humanistic subjects to more political and economic ones. The following analysis is primarily concerned with his two principal works: the *Communist Manifesto,* a tract coauthored in 1848 with his lifetime colleague, Friedrich Engels, and *Capital,* a three-volume work that was not published completely until after his death. *Capital,* Marx's *magnum opus,* is essentially an economic theory of production from which he builds an exhaustive critique of capitalism; the *Manifesto* is a short analysis and guide to political action in the light of shortcomings of the capitalistic system.

The Foundation of Marxism: Materialism

The foundation of Marxism is a materialistic conception of the person and the universe. Unlike Hegel, from whom he borrowed the notion of a dialectical historical development, Marx believed that ultimate reality is not found in the abstract, rational elements of life but in the concrete, material human environment. The main determinants of life are not religious ideas or rational principles, as so many people have thought; ideas and values are themselves the product of the material environment in which people live. In other words, Marx believed that economic aspects of society provide the basic source for other areas of life.

According to Marx, the economic foundation of society is composed of two elements: the productive forces of society and the social relations of production. The *productive forces* represent the material means by which people produce goods to survive and make a living. They include not only machines, tools, and raw materials but also skills, knowledge, and interests people possess and use in making a livelihood. Since people's knowledge and skills have been refined over time, productive capacities have tended to become more proficient. The result has been a continuing improvement in the general productive capacities of society.

The second element, the *social relations of production,* represents the pattern of human relationships resulting from the way people produce and exchange their goods. These social relations, which Marx believed are directly determined by the productive forces, are concerned with such aspects of society as the organization of workers, the relations between management and labor, employment and compensation of workers, and property ownership. Social relations thus give rise to the fundamental structures of society, including its social and economic institutions. They represent, in effect, the institutions of the organization of society.

As productive forces give rise to a particular mode of production and exchange and change over time, so do productive relationships. In Marx's view, there have been four major modes in the historical development of civilization—primitive or communal, slave, feudal, and capitalistic—each of which results from a particular refinement in the productive capacities of human beings. But it is also Marx's contention that history is moving ineluctably toward another, final phase—the communist mode of production.

A fundamental assumption of Marx's theory is that the economic structures of society (i.e., the productive forces and the social relations of production) are the fundamental source of all other elements of society. Marx called these noneconomic areas of society the *superstructure,* which would include the ideas, values, and institutions of such areas as law, politics, culture, religion, and so on. In contrast to Plato, Hobbes, and Locke, who assume the primacy of politics over economics, Marx assumes that economics determines not only politics but also every other aspect of society (Figure 4.3). For example, Locke suggests that there are fundamental moral principles from which individuals derive their knowledge of individual rights; Marx not only denies the existence of such rights but also affirms that natural law and inalienable rights are themselves the result of economic foundations of society. Since the values and institutions of society are a consequence of a particular mode of production, a fundamental change in the social relations of productions leads to a new set of values, ideas, and structures. The shift from a slave society to a feudal society, for example, resulted in significant social, political, and governmental developments, as did the shift from feudalism to capitalism. The basic Marxist assumption of economic determinism has been best articulated by Marx himself in the following famous statement:

> *In the social production of their existence, men inevitably enter into definite relations, which are independent of their will, namely relations of production appropriate to a given stage in the development of their material forces of production. The totality of these relations of production constitutes the economic structure of society, the real foundation, on which arises a legal and political superstructure and to which correspond definite forms of social consciousness. The mode of production of material life conditions the general process of social, political, and intellectual life. It is not the consciousness of men that determines their existence, but their social existence that determines their consciousness.* [6]

Figure 4.3   The Economic Foundations of Society

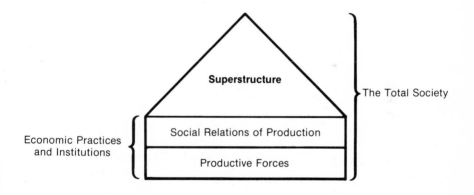

The Problem: Capitalism

The basic cause of community conflict, according to Marx, is capitalism — an economic system that exploits the majority of laborers and alienates them from their work and from other human beings. This exploitation and dehumanization results from the profound division of society into two economic classes: the *bourgeoisie,* who own the means of production and maintain their superior position by controlling all the major institutions of society, including government and politics; and the *proletariat,* the laborers who earn their living by working for the bourgeoisie. According to Marx, the dominant value in capitalist society is the maximization of economic gain. Since greed, avarice, and profit are the primary values, Marx thought that the system tends to degrade people by focusing on possessions rather than on the intrinsic worth of people. Although Marx deplored the squalid living conditions, inadequate working environment, and the spread of disease associated with the industrialization of Europe, he believed that these unfortunate developments were not the result of selfish, evil men but of the system itself.

Although Marx's critique of capitalism was in part inspired by the misery and social cost of the rapid growth of industrialization in continental Europe and particularly in England, his fundamental criticism of capitalism is based not on empirical observations but on a carefully developed economic theory of production. In *Capital,* Marx presents the major elements of this theory and critiques the capitalist mode of production. His critique, however, consists of far more than offering an alternative way of looking at economic reality. Marx is fundamentally concerned with the development of a scientific analysis of historical change, and his theory of production is the method by which he seeks to explain how and why capitalism will inevitably disintegrate and be replaced by another economic system — communism. Although Marx personally detests the capitalist system, in his writings he seeks to grasp the objective truth about the origins and development of this system and to provide a scientific assessment of the future of the world. Despite his concern to be dispassionate and scientific, Marx's writings reflect a tension between the effort to be objective, scientific, and predictive and the concern to motivate and direct personal action to alter the values and institutions of bourgeois society.

The central axiom of Marx's economic theory is the labor theory of value. According to Marx, the value of a good is determined by the quantity of labor required to produce it. The labor theory of value is in direct contrast to capitalist assumptions, which hold that productive value is a function of labor plus three additional factors — land (raw materials), capital, and management. Marx knew that capital (such as machinery and tools) generally played a part in the production of goods. Since capital is nothing more than "stored-up labor" (i.e., labor that had been used in inventing and constructing machines, tools, assembly lines, etc.) the only value capital contributes is determined by the proportion of labor required to eventually replace it. As a result, Marx valued capital less than capitalist thinkers such as Adam Smith and David Ricardo.

Since only human labor contributes to the value of a product, the total value of a commodity is equal to the total wage costs involved in its production. Within a capitalist system, however, the cost of a good always exceeds paid wages. The reason for this is that the employer, by virtue of his superior economic position, is able to obtain the full services of workers without paying them fully for the value of their productivity. Wage costs, in other words, are always less than the value of goods produced. Marx called the difference between the two *surplus value;* it represents the value created by the laborer but appropriated by the employer. Since the ownership of a factory or business firm could not itself contribute to the value of production, any surplus value generated by a business manager represented the illegitimate appropriation of wealth by the bourgeoisie from the proletariat. Surplus value (profit), in other words, is a measure of the exploitation in society.[7]

From his theory of surplus value, Marx developed three important conclusions about the capitalist system. First, capital becomes increasingly concentrated. This occurs as a result of increasing competition among business firms to maximize profits through more efficient operations. As business firms increase in size and wealth through the application of economies of scale (i.e., through the application of mechanized techniques to mass production of goods) they tend to eliminate smaller, less efficient producers. The growing concentration of production in fewer businesses and corporations thus leads to an increasingly unequal distribution of wealth among members of the bourgeoisie.

A second important result associated with capitalism is the increasing misery of the labor class. Since a capitalist's interests of maximizing profits are achieved by minimizing wage costs, an employer attempts to hire the fewest workers at the lowest wage. This is realized, in part, by the introduction of labor-saving technology, which leads to an increase in the proportion of capital to labor required in production. As the demand for labor declines, Marx assumed this would lead to lower wages and eventually to mass unemployment. Rather than making the proletarian class better off, the growth and expansion of business thus has a negative economic impact on laborers.

Third, the growth and development of capitalism eventually leads to the system's destruction. Given the growing concentration of wealth and the increasing misery of workers, Marx believed that these trends lead to a lower rate of profit and that the continuing decline of profitable production eventually causes the capitalist system to suffocate and die. Since wealth becomes increasingly concentrated in the hands of a few, the lack of money in the proletarian class leads to a declining purchasing power among the masses. The rich capitalists are thus unable to sell all of their products; this in turn leads to increasing competition among firms. As firms reduce prices to clear their inventories, the profit margin of businesses tends to decline. In the end, the imbalance between the supply of goods and their demand becomes so serious that capitalism eventually destroys itself. The very engine of capitalism—the profit motive—leads to the poverty first of the proletariat and then of the bourgeoisie. Since the problems of capitalism are inherent in the system, Marx believed that no human innovation could alter the course predicted by the scientific laws of historical change. Capitalism would be replaced by communism.

We have suggested that the Marxist theory places the blame for community conflict on the capitalist system. At a more fundamental level, however, community conflict is the result of class struggle between the bourgeoisie and the proletariat—a class struggle that not only gives rise to labor-management tensions but is also the source of the ideas, values, and institutions that engender community conflict. For example, such notions as private property, profit maximization, and savings have their basis in the bourgeois-dominated capitalist society. Such concepts distort human relationships and encourage social and political conflict. Marx's solution to the problem of societal conflict is not to resolve or manage it. Rather, he assumes that the cause of conflict is systemic and that what is needed is a fundamental alteration of the foundation of contemporary economic society. Seeking to manage conflict through political institutions may delay the eventual destruction of capitalism, but it will not alter the long-term consequences.

The Ideal Community: A Classless Society

Marx believed that the inexorable laws of historical change ultimately leads to the ideal society, which is an association of workers where people contribute according to their capacities and are rewarded according to their need. This voluntary, free, and nonrepressive community is possible, Marx believed, because the economic foundations of society would no longer be based on class distinctions. The ideas, values, and institutions in communist society would be in accordance with the communitarian consciousness growing out of the new, classless, social and economic structures. Greed and profit maximization associated with the capitalist system would no longer be present. Similarly, the institution of private property vanishes as the public assumes full ownership and control of all means of production.

Above all, the state and the institutions of government also vanish in a classless society. According to Marx, a state is the organization by which one class maintains superiority over another. Since the state originates and is maintained by class struggle, a classless society no longer requires the state. Similarly, since political power is nothing more than organized use of power by one class over another, the establishment of a classless society not only makes political power unnecessary but is also contrary to the values of the new community. In the *Manifesto,* Marx and Engels observe: "When in the course of human development, class distinctions have disappeared and all production has been concentrated in the hands of a vast association of the whole nation, public power will lose its political character." Thus, as capitalism is replaced by communism, the institutions of government become increasingly unnecessary. The new society is a place where individual interests and general interests are identical. Disagreements about production and distribution may occur, but the systemic conflict of prior communities no longer exists. Since harmony is a natural byproduct of the classless society, political activity is no longer present, government becomes unnecessary, and the state withers away. All that is needed to maintain the new society is an administrative agency to direct and manage production and distribution.

Marx's ideal community is therefore an apolitical society — a human environment where no conflict-management processes and institutions are at work. Unlike the approaches of Plato, Hobbes, and Locke, which manage conflict through government, Marx assumes that the only adequate and possible solution to human conflict is to eliminate it completely. The communist society does not attempt to resolve conflict but rather to create an environment where human discord is no longer possible. The goal, therefore, is not to refine the work of government but to make government and politics altogether unnecessary.[8]

Establishing the Communist Society

Marx suggests that the transformation of capitalism into communism involves two phases. Following a revolution in which the proletarian forces overcome the organized power of the bourgeoisie, a *dictatorship of the proletariat* is established. In this first phase, the proletariat uses dictatorial power in order to completely eliminate the bourgeoisie's power and to begin the gradual and difficult process of transforming the structure of society. During this transitional phase of socialism (what Marx called the first phase of the classless society), the power of the state is used to eliminate the vestiges of capitalism and to begin to create a culture and institutions that give support to a communitarian consciousness. During this socialistic phase, most private property is abolished and the state becomes the instrument through which the public interest is organized and protected.

After a prolonged period under socialism, society gradually evolves into communism, the higher phase of the classless society. In this ideal environment there is no conflict and therefore no politics and government. The institution of the state is no longer required, for the basic incompatibilities existing in capitalism are no longer present. All that is needed in this classless association of workers is an administrative organ to coordinate the production and distribution of goods. (Such an institution will not have the coercive power of the bourgeois state.) Society is orderly and harmonious, but the source for the stability is not the compulsory power of law and government but the voluntary behavior of people resulting from the new values of the classless society. The distinctive quality of the communist society is that people automatically contribute according to their abilities and are rewarded according to their needs.

How should such dramatic change be brought about? Marx provides two alternatives, one growing out of his scientific orientation and the other from his more voluntaristic emphasis. The first orientation led Marx to the conclusion that the capitalist system would inevitably be destroyed and replaced as a result of the inherent laws of social change. Marx's faith in the inexorable laws of human development gave him the hope of realizing his ideal community apart from planned, organized activity. On the other hand, Marx was concerned with encouraging human action that would lead to communist victory.

The need for organized political activity is most forcefully articulated in the *Manifesto*. The clarion call of that political tract is: "Workingmen of all countries, unite!" The central argument of the *Manifesto* is that the creation of the classless society comes about only through a revolutionary process and requires organized leadership. The leaders, or communists, are distinguished from other members of the proletariat by their ability to understand "the march, the conditions, and the ultimate general results of the proletarian movement." Marx, however, did not explain how these leaders were to be selected or in what manner they would direct the revolutionary transformation from capitalism to communism. This task was to be carried out later by Lenin, the Soviet leader who led the Communists to victory in Russia in 1917.[9]

Lenin's most important contribution is that he believed (unlike Marx) that the automatic laws of social development do not ensure the evolution of capitalism to communism. He saw capitalist values and ideas as being too deeply implanted in the consciousness of workers for them to recognize their own predicament. Lenin believed that the proletariat needed to be led and educated by a group of revolutionary leaders. What he did was to demonstrate through his writings and by his personal example how power was to be taken and used in destroying the capitalist system and in transforming bourgeois society. Because of Lenin's profound influence in applying Marxism to the twentieth-century state, the ideology of communism is generally referred to as Marxism-Leninism.

In conclusion, Marxism is largely an economic theory of human development. The theory seeks to explain the past and to predict the future in terms of the existing mode of production. But Marxism is also a theory of political community — a theory that analyzes the weaknesses of the nineteenth-century capitalist political economy and presents an alternative way of dealing with the conflicts and problems resulting from such a system. Marx suggests that the only possible solution to social and political difficulties is to alter the economic foundations of society. His proposal calls for the establishment of a classless society, a change that will bring about new ideas, values, and institutions to make harmony the automatic byproduct of human interrelationships. Since human conflict disappears, politics and government become unnecessary and the state gradually withers away. Marxism is therefore not a conflict-management theory but an approach that eliminates conflict altogether.

SUMMARY

The major elements of the preceding four theories are summarized in Table 4.1. For Plato, the fundamental political problem is the establishment of a community where individuals work in areas in which they have a natural aptitude. Plato believes that this natural vocational order can only be realized when knowledgeable rulers are in power.

For Hobbes, the basic political problem is the elimination of conflict and the establishment of peace. Hobbes believes that order, not human rights, is the chief need of society, and until harmony is established in society no justice can exist. The task of government is therefore to establish and maintain order.

Locke, by contrast, views the problem of political society in more optimistic terms. For him, the basic problem is the creation of political structures to ensure people's individual rights more effectively. The main function of government is to provide a framework that protects human rights. A government that does not accomplish this is not legitimate and may be replaced.

Finally, Marx assumes that the basic causes of social disorder and economic injustice are the exploitative structures and practices of capitalism. If social conflict is to be managed effectively and eventually eliminated, then the economic foundations giving rise to capitalism must be replaced. Marx believes that the division of society into competing economic classes needs to be replaced by the creation of a one-class society.

One of the important functions of political theories such as those examined above is that they help define alternative approaches for managing political conflict and for solving the basic problems of political society. More significantly, the ideas of political thinkers have been influential in the shaping of political beliefs and values found in contemporary societies. When these ideas become widely accepted in a country, they become part of a nation's political culture or of a government's ideology. (The role of political culture and ideologies in building political consensus is examined in Chapter 7.)

KEY TERMS

philosopher-king
state of nature
laws of nature
civil society (commonwealth)
Leviathan
authoritarian
state of war
consent

human rights
limited government
separation of powers
bourgeoisie
proletariat
surplus value
communism

TABLE 4.1 Comparison of Key Elements in the Political Theories of Plato, Hobbes, Locke, and Marx

	NATURE OF PROBLEM	TYPE OF CONFLICT	METHOD OF CONFLICT MANAGEMENT	WHO SHALL RULE?	PURPOSE OF GOVERNMENT
PLATO	determining justice with the state	social disorder resulting from people not fulfilling their natural abilities	Restructure all society in accordance with knowledge	Philosopher-King	to ensure that people are in their proper classes
HOBBES	anarchy	continuous, violent conflict resulting in possible death	establish a civil society where the Sovereign rules with absolute authority	anyone who has a monopoly of force	to preserve life
LOCKE	state of nature is inconvenient	conflict over property	establish a civil community with a limited, representative government	anyone elected by the people	to preserve the inalienable rights of people
MARX	alienation	economic conflict	establish classless society	During the phase of transition, communists rule; in the "higher" phase, no rulers are needed.	During the phase of transition, the government destroys all values and institutions of bourgeois society; in "higher" phase, government does not function.

NOTES

1. Plato, the *Republic,* trans. Benjamin Jowett (Chicago: Encyclopedia Britannica, Inc., 1952), p. 369.
2. For a useful commentary on the *Statesman* and the *Laws,* see Chapter 4 of George Sabine's *A History of Political Theory,* 3rd ed. (New York: Holt, Rinehart & Winston, 1961).
3. John Locke, *The Second Treatise on Government,* ed. Thomas Peardon (Indianapolis: Bobbs-Merrill, 1952), p. 6.
4. *Ibid.,* p. 49.
5. *Ibid.,* p. 84.
6. Karl Marx, *A Contribution to the Critique of Political Economy* in *The Marx-Engels Reader,* ed. Robert C. Tucker (New York: W.W. Norton, 1972), p. 4.
7. For an analysis of the essentials of Marx's theory of value, see Angus Walker, *Marx: His Theory and Its Context* (London: Longman, 1978). John Gurley, a Marxist, presents a more sympathetic account of Marx's economic theory in *Challengers to Capitalism: Marx, Lenin, and Mao* (San Francisco: San Francisco Book Co., 1976).
8. See Marx's "Critique of the Gotha Program," in which he provides guidelines on the establishment of a communist society and discusses features of the ideal community.
9. Lenin was a prolific writer. His major works include: *What is to be Done?, Imperialism: The Highest Stage of Capitalism,* and *The State and Revolution.* For an excellent compilation of his works, see Robert C. Tucker, ed., *The Lenin Anthology* (New York: W.W. Norton, 1975).

SUGGESTED READING

BLUHM, WILLIAM T. *Theories of the Political System.* 3rd ed. Englewood Cliffs, N.J.: Prentice-Hall, 1978. An introductory political philosophy text combining both traditional and contemporary theories. The text is organized around two themes (freedom and virtue), and each chapter includes an analysis of a traditional and contemporary perspective.

EBENSTEIN, WILLIAM. *Great Political Thinkers: Plato to the Present.* 4th ed. Hinsdale, Ill.: Dryden Press, 1969. This excellent text combines primary source materials and an analysis of the essentials of each political theory.

HALLOWELL, JOHN H. *Main Currents in Modern Political Thought.* New York: Holt, Rinehart & Winston, 1963. Using a Christian perspective, Hallowell examines the major political theorists from Machiavelli through the early twentieth century. The book focuses on three major areas—liberalism, socialism, and nihilism.

HUNT, R.N. CAREW. *The Theory and Practice of Communism.* Baltimore: Penguin Books, 1966. This is a lucid and balanced account of the essentials of Marxism and Leninism and how those theories have been applied within the Soviet Union.

MENDEL, ARTHUR P. *Essential Works of Marxism.* New York: Bantam Books, 1971. An excellent compendium of major writings of Marxists, including Engels, Lenin, Stalin, Djilas, and Mao.

SABINE, GEORGE H. *A History of Political Theory.* 3rd ed. New York: Holt, Rinehart & Winston, 1961. The classic history of political thought.

SIGMUND, PAUL E. *Natural Law in Political Thought.* Cambridge: Winthrop Publishers, 1971. A collection of readings and commentaries on natural law.

THORSON, THOMAS LANDON, ed. *Plato: Totalitarian or Democrat?* Englewood Cliffs, N.J.: Prentice-Hall, 1963. This volume includes essays that present Plato both as defender of democratic principles and proponent of totalitarianism.

TINDER, GLENN. *Political Thinking: The Perennial Question.* 3rd ed. Boston: Little, Brown, and Company, 1979. This succinct and interesting volume is organized around some 31 "perennial" questions of political theory. Tinder skillfully uses the ideas of political philosophers to demonstrate the range of answers that have historically been given to the major issues.

TUCKER, ROBERT C., ed. *The Marx-Engels Reader.* New York: W.W. Norton, 1972. A superior anthology of writings by Karl Marx and Friedrich Engels, preceded by a helpful introduction by the editor.

PART II
PROCESSES OF CONFLICT MANAGEMENT

5 / THE NATION-STATE AND CONFLICT MANAGEMENT

The world is divided into hundreds of thousands of political communities of all types and sizes. These include school districts, villages, cities, counties, provinces, and confederacies. Of the various types of political communities in the contemporary world, the most significant is the nation-state. Often simply referred to as the state, nation, or country, this political organization is significant because it has ultimate responsibility for maintaining peace and order in the present international system. No other political community can claim a higher authority over human beings.

The purpose of this chapter is to examine the nature and role of the nation-state in the contemporary world. Since states have not always existed in their present form, we shall briefly examine the major types of political communities that preceded the rise of the modern state. We shall then analyze the chief features of nations and states, examining how the modern country has come into existence and become the dominant mode of political organization. In the last part of the chapter we shall examine the major ways that governments are organized and the different ways that they manage and resolve conflict.

THE NATION-STATE

Since the nation-state is the dominant form of political community, it is easy to assume that it is the only conceivable method of organizing the contemporary world. A brief examination of political history, however, indicates that there have been numerous other forms of political organization and that the present approach of dividing the world into some 150 to 155 political communities called *nations* is a relatively recent phenomenon dating from about the mid-seventeenth century.

Political Communities in Historical Perspectives

History suggests that there has been a tendency over the course of civilization for mankind to shift political commitments between large powerful states and small, weak communities, between general, universal concerns of an empire and specific interests of localities. Political history, in other words, has not been static but has demonstrated a continuing tension between the forces that bring cohesion and integration and those that bring disunity and disintegration. We can demonstrate this tension by briefly examining some of the major types of political communities that have dominated civilization from, say, the year 3000 B.C. through the present (Figure 5.1).

Figure 5.1 Changes in Patterns of Political Organization Throughout Western Civilization

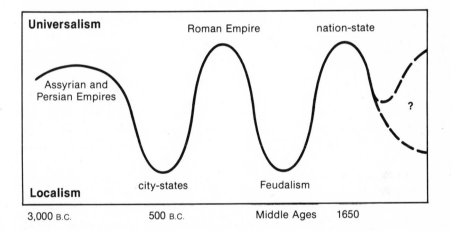

The Early Empires Some of the earliest political settlements developed in Mesopotamia in the valley of the Tigris and Euphrates Rivers as well as in Egypt in the valley of the Nile River. Other political communities also existed in China, India, and Latin America, but the center of civilization appears to have been the Middle East. Little is known about the political institutions and form of government of these early communities, although it is clear that these early civilizations did have governments that performed the rudimentary regulatory functions of the state. Legal codes were used to regulate trade, commerce, and marriage; law enforcement was strict and often cruel. A significant trait of these early regimes was the high level of coercion in building and maintaining political order. Political leadership was achieved largely by military force and those who succeeded in the battlefield were rewarded with positions of political influence. Political power was highly centralized and regimes were dictatorial and quite often despotic.

The City-State   About 500 B.C. the focus of civilization shifted from the Middle East to Greece. One of the most significant political achievements of the Greeks was the development of the *city-state system,* a collection of small, independent, and relatively self-sufficient political communities. The most advanced city-state was Athens, which became a center of learning and culture and served as a model for other states. City-states were generally characterized by a vigorous pursuit of commercial, intellectual, and cultural activities. Since politics was considered an all-encompassing process of developing community excellence, it was the most important concern of its citizens. Much time and energy was devoted to the development of governmental institutions that would protect the city and improve the quality of life. Political processes were much more developed than those in the Assyrian or Persian civilizations; governmental structures were established that could effectively make, enforce, and interpret law. While the city-state had many of the governmental features of the modern state, the city's people were not a nationality and thus failed to meet a condition of the modern nation-state. Their societies were highly stratified, with limited social integration; only about one-fourth to one-third of its people were eligible to participate in political affairs. City-states were states but not nations.

The Roman Empire   The development of the Roman empire grew out of the foreign-policy pursuits of the city-state of Rome. Although the origins of the empire began to be established in the fifth and fourth centuries B.C., the empire does not emerge until the first century following the collapse of the Roman republic. The collapse came partly as a result of the expansion of Roman influence, first throughout Italy and then throughout much of Europe and Northern Africa. As city-states and other territories were conquered, new political institutions were required by which the Roman rulers could maintain control over their new territories and subjects. One of the significant political contributions of the Romans was development of a system of law and administration through which they could effectively govern the empire. Although the legal and bureaucratic institutions were insufficient to prevent the decay and fall of the empire in the middle of the fifth century, the governmental apparatus established by the Romans was an enormously effective instrument for maintaining cohesion for more than four centuries.

Feudalism   With the decay of Roman universalism, a new political order began to emerge that would last for nearly 1,000 years. This new order, perhaps less a political system than a way of life, was called *feudalism.* Feudal communities were based on the manor, a large territory controlled by a lord. Unlike the Roman empire, which was held together by a large impersonal bureaucratic system, the foundation of the feudal order was a private estate. As owner of a territory, the lord granted vassals the privilege of farming his land and offered them protection. Vassals, in turn, agreed to work the land and contribute to the maintenance of the manor. The relationship of vassal to lord was thus personal and mutually contractual. Unlike the impersonal political systems of the Greeks and the Romans, feudalism was limited in scope and highly individualized. In a sense, there was no public sector; community life was nonpoliticized.

The Nation-State   Just as the fragmentation of city-states gave way to the Roman universal order, so too the particularism of the feudal kingdom gradually gave way to the establishment of the modern nation-state. Although the establishment of the modern state dates from 1648 (The Treaty of Westphalia), the emergence of this new order began in the late medieval period when rulers began to consolidate their power into larger, more powerful political communities. By fusing duchies, baronies, large feudal estates, and other small political communities, political rulers began to consolidate their power over significant territories and to claim undisputed political authority. The recognition of this claim by subjects and rulers from other states marks the beginning of the nation-state.

Three developments in particular encouraged the shift from the parochialism and localism of the feudal estate to the modern state. First was the development of an influential commercial class that championed the cause of a larger and more centralized political order; second was the development of a more secular society through the advent of the Renaissance; and third was the loss of influence of the Catholic church. As politics became more secularized, the economic demands for administrative efficiency increased. People came to recognize the inadequacy of the decentralized distribution of power under the feudal system. Support grew for the centralization of sovereign authority so that commercial activity could be more effectively regulated and political and religious conflicts more easily resolved. The rise of the nation-state was in direct response to the needs of the time.

Whither the Nation-State?   Since the emergence of the modern state in the mid-seventeenth century, the number of states has grown from a handful to more than 150 (in 1980). As diagrammed in Figure 5.2, the world was divided into less than 50 states at the beginning of the twentieth century. Following the Second World War, however, the world experienced a distintegration of the European colonial system and the creation of more than 70 new states. In this century, and particularly in the last forty years, the world has witnessed a resurgence of political localism and national parochialism as it has become increasingly threatened by the forces of fragmentation. At the same time, a number of developments have strengthened political integration of states. Among these are the regional economic and military alliances that have strengthened relationships among states. Of the various regional organizations, the one that has most directly sought to qualify the power of the state and to strengthen transnational integration is the European Economic Community. But whether the forces of integration or disintegration, of universalism or particularism will rule is not yet certain.

Figure 5.2 The Growth of Nations, 1775–1975

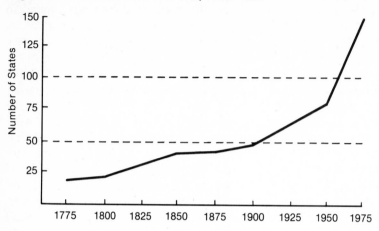

THE NATURE OF THE NATION-STATE

Although the terms *nation* and *state* are commonly used interchangeably, the two concepts have different meanings. The term *state* refers to the political dimension of human organization, while *nation* refers to the social and cultural aspects of human community. The state is almost as old as man himself. The nation, by contrast, is a relatively new development, coming into existence with the modern state about the mid-seventeenth century. The fusion of the state and the nation has of course resulted in the modern nation-state and its propelling force — nationalism.

The State

The central feature of a state[1] is it's final binding authority to manage and resolve social conflicts within particular territories. "The state," writes Frederick Watkins, "is a geographically delimited segment of human society united by common obedience to a single sovereign."[2] From this definition, it is clear that most premodern political communities, such as empires, city-states, and feudal kingdoms, have had some form of government that could ultimately make binding decisions and therefore be considered states. To be sure, many of these premodern communities had governmental institutions and political processes that were rudimentary and informal, yet they did perform the function of making ultimate decisions for subjects. (Not all human communities are of course political. As noted in Chapter 2, some forms of human association do not have individuals or institutions with the authority to issue commands. Such nonpolitical communities are stateless societies, i.e., societies without public government.)

One of the doctrines clearly associated with the rise of the modern state is *sovereignty*. This legal concept was developed by Jean Bodin, the sixteenth century French political historian, to symbolize the ruler's supreme authority over subjects. He defined sovereignty as "the state's supreme authority over citizens and subjects." It was the ruler's power unrestrained by law, except the moral laws the ruler himself perceived by reason.[3]

As the concept has come to be used in the twentieth century, sovereignty has a number of implications both foreign and domestic. From a foreign perspective, a sovereign state must be free and independent from others and therefore has the right to resist any outside interference in its internal affairs. Aggression and invasion by an outside state is a challenge to the independence of the state. In addition, sovereignty implies juridical equality among states. If each state is completely free to determine its own affairs, states can be considered legally equal. Although states are not equal in social, political, and economic resources, the legal fiction of equality is central to the contemporary international system. The United Nations Charter, for example, explicitly states this principle in Article two as follows: "The Organization is based on the principle of equality of all its members." Domestically, sovereignty means that within the state one supreme governmental authority has the power to make binding decisions and to enforce their compliance. Sovereignty represents undivided authority within a specific territory.

Although states have existed throughout history, the modern state differs from the ancient and medieval political communities in a number of ways. Max Weber, the noted German political sociologist, believed that the modern state has three distinctive features. First, the modern state has an efficient and well-organized administrative organization to carry out the decisions of government. This administrative organization or bureacracy is ultimately responsible to the executive and the legislative branches of government. Second, the modern state has a government that is sovereign (i.e., has supreme authority within a particular territory). This characteristic, often called the territorial principle, means that government has the authority to make binding decisions on persons within a state's territory whether or not they are citizens. Finally, the modern state is the only agency that could use force or violence or could sanction its use by others. The state not only possesses a monopoly of force but it also determines when it could be legitimately used within its boundaries.[4]

We have thus far emphasized the importance of political and governmental institutions in the state. From a more practical standpoint, states need two additional requirements: people and land. If government is to exert its sovereign authority over citizens, it needs to exercise that authority over particular countries, i.e., territories with people. Table 5.1 provides some comparative data on the size of territories and populations for selected states.

TABLE 5.1 Large and Small States Compared by Size of Territory and Population, 1981

COUNTRY	SIZE OF AREA (SQUARE MILES)	SIZE OF POPULATION (JAN. 1981 ESTIMATES)
Largest States		
Soviet Union	8,649,538	267,605,000
Canada	3,851,809	24,152,300
China	3,691,514	1,039,270,000
United States	3,615,122	216,816,000
Brazil	3,286,488	123,675,000
Australia	2,967,909	14,691,900
India	1,269,346	672,541,000
Medium States		
Argentina	1,068,296	27,261,500
Saudi Arabia	830,000	8,492,180
Mexico	761,605	73,157,300
Iran	636,296	37,188,100
Peru	496,225	18,025,400
Venezuela	352,145	15,267,700
France	211,208	55,175,000
Italy	116,304	57,410,000
Small States		
Switzerland	15,941	6,273,700
Netherlands	15,770	14,181,000
Israel	8,019	3,895,920
Qatar	4,247	175,452
Mauritius	790	960,179
Bahrain	240	443,597
Barbados	166	255,043
Seychelles	156	65,478

Source: Reader's Digest 1981 Almanac and Yearbook *(New York: W. W. Norton, 1981), pp. 469-471. Copyright © 1981 The Readers Digest Association, Inc. Copyright © The Reader's Digest Association (Canada) Ltd. Copyright © 1981 Reader's Digest Association Far East Ltd. Philippine Copyright 1981 Reader's Digest Association Far East Ltd.*

The Nation

Nations are social and cultural conglomerations of people. When large numbers of persons are joined by common social, cultural, economic, or linguistic ties, they comprise a nation. Whereas a state is primarily a political entity, a nation is a social union based on such factors as a common historical heritage, similar linguistic patterns, an integrated economy, common social and cultural mores, and common ethnic ties. Nations are not formed by governments; they grow and evolve. The foundation of the nation is not the coercive power of the state but the voluntary habits of a people and their common goals and aspirations.

Elements of a Nation   Although numerous forces have helped establish nations, four elements have been particularly salient in the development of modern nations.

1. First, the process of modernization has been of critical importance in bringing cohesion and unity to territories formerly governed by tribal chiefs, feudal lords, or local caudillos. Two aspects of modernization have strengthened national unity and interdependence, one economic and the other social. Economic modernization or development is the process of increasing productivity by transforming the economic values and institutions of society. Although economic growth has depended on numerous conditions (including capital formation, economies of scale, and transformation of attitudes toward work and education), an essential requirement for the modernization of the economy has been the development of an integrated and interdependent market. Economic prosperity has certainly had an enormous impact on the improvement of the quality of life in most communities. But from the standpoint of building nations, the most important contribution of economic development has been the increasing interdependence among the various regions and districts of a nation.

   Another dimension of modernity is social integration. Although closely associated with growth of the national market, development of social cohesion has involved the growing interaction between urban and rural areas and among rural communities themselves. In traditional societies there is limited interdependence among the villages and towns; as a result, there is little awareness about the world beyond immediate territorial boundaries of the local community. The process of modernization, however, challenges the parochialism and isolation of rural villages and encourages the growth of interdependence among various political units of countries. Expanding and strengthening of social integration leads to the development of new political loyalties.

2. The second element of nations is cultural homogeneity. Development of a common culture depends upon the breakdown of regional barriers. Karl Deutsch, a leading student of nationalism, defines a people "as a group with complementary communication habits whose members usually share the same language, and always share a similar culture so that all members of the group attach the same meaning to words."[5] Perhaps one of the most accurate indicators of nationhood is the extent to which people can understand each other. If people are to understand each other, they must be able to communicate through verbal and nonverbal means. Thus, both a common language and a common culture are important in building national cohesion.

Although some social scientists have thought that a single language is essential for building and maintaining nations, history suggests that nations can be maintained even where there is more than one common language. Switzerland, a country of three major languages, is a significant example of a modern nation with a multiplicity of languages. But if nations can exist with more than one tongue, clearly the process of nation-building involves the breakdown of dialects and the consolidation of language in most cases. The development of the Soviet nation involves the increasing dominance of the Russian language throughout the country. In the United States, immigrants have gradually given up their ethnic languages and accepted English both at work and at home. In Latin America most Indians still use their own languages, although official transactions are generally carried out in Spanish.

If establishment of a common language is significant in nations, development of a common culture is perhaps even more significant. Although people may not be able to communicate verbally, it is essential that they be able to understand each other's actions. Trust among human beings is, to a significant extent, the result of predictability of human behavior. No predictability means no trust; no trust means no sense of community. An alien is an outsider precisely because he or she is unable to communicate as well as or to predict as accurately the behavior of other members of a nation. A group of athletes or musicians from different countries easily agrees on the essentials of good soccer or basketball or on techniques of piano playing or on the qualities of a good orchestra. When they begin to discuss manners, food, dress, or other topics closely related to each nation's culture, however, they find much disagreement. Members of a nation may and do disagree significantly on subjects like religion, politics, and economics, but if they are to communicate effectively with each other they need to understand each other's jokes, patterns of behavior, and cultural mores. (The citizens of Peru and Chile, for example, disagree about political and economic issues, but they tend to share common attitudes toward time, work, and leisure. To be a half-hour late to a business appointment in either country is not considered unacceptable behavior. But in American society, characterized by its emphasis on punctuality and efficiency, such action is regarded much less favorably.) Nationals, in short, are at home with each other because they can understand each other's subtle messages and can predict each other's behavior.

3. The third element of a nation is the desire for self-government. When people seek to gain political power and to rule themselves separately, they become a nationality — a clearly differentiated group of people who desire to express their linguistic and cultural distinctions in a political

manner. "A portion of mankind may be said to constitute a Nationality," observed John Stuart Mill in the nineteenth century, "if they are united among themselves by common sympathies, which do not exist between them and any others — which make them cooperate with each other more willingly than with other people, desire to be under the same government, and desire that it should be government by themselves or a portion of themselves, exclusively."[6] As noted above, nations are not political organizations but social and cultural communities. But what distinguishes nations from previous social organizations is that people have a self-conscious awareness of their common heritage and culture and seek to deliberately promote their distinctive characteristics within the world. Nations, in other words, are social organizations that have become partially politicized. This politicization may be successful and lead to the formation of a nation-state, i.e., a nation with independent, sovereign political institutions. But nations may often achieve only some political self-consciousness and exist under the control of a government dominated by another nationality.

4. A final element of modern nations is ethnic homogeneity. Although no nation is completely homogeneous racially, most countries have a dominant ethnic group that provides the unity and cohesion for its people. Walker Connor has examined the nature of contemporary nation states and found that few states are ethnically homogeneous. In fact, of the 132 states that Connor examined he found the following: (a) 12 states had a single nationality; (b) 25 had a dominant nationality accounting for 90 percent of the population; (c) 25 had a dominant nationality accounting for 75 to 89 percent of the people; (d) 31 had a dominant nationality accounting for 50 to 74 percent of the people; and (e) 30 had no nationality representing more than 50 percent of the people.[7]

Most states, in other words, had a dominant nationality of more than 50 percent of the country's population, although many had significant minority groups that continued to preserve their distinctive ethnic and racial characteristics.

Since the number and intensity of common bonds among the peoples of nations vary, the strength of nationhood is also different among nationalities. Some groups are strongly unified by religion, race, language, and traditions, while others tend to be weakly integrated. The Jewish people, for example, are a relatively small nation, yet they have demonstrated enormous cohesion and determination over many centuries of adversity. The Palestinians, too, are a people who (although without a country) have demonstrated a high level of commitment toward their national identity. Numerous African countries, on the other hand, have been beset with tribal and regional rivalries and a weak sense of national pride. In a relatively developed and cohesive country like the United States, the political system has remained strong and vigorous despite internal tensions, some of which arise from the heterogeneous nature of the American nationality.

As a general rule, nations achieve their greatest level of cohesion and development when they are governed by a separate political system. Although the joining of a nation with a state is the basis of the modern state, many nations are not directly associated with a particular state. Indeed, there are many more nations than there are states. In the Soviet Union, for example, there are more than 100 nationalities. The Soviet state is thus a multinational state joining numerous ethnic groups, including Byelorussians, Estonians, Latvians, Lithuanians, and Ukranians. The dominant nationality are the Russians, and it is their political system that provides the basis of cohesion to the Soviet political system. Nationalities in the Soviet system have continued to exist in particular territories and have refused to give up their religious, cultural, and ethnic traits; in the United States, however, immigrants have been absorbed in significant measure into a common "melting-pot" nation. But even in this heterogeneous nation, groups like blacks and Mexicans have maintained many of their individual cultural and racial distinctions, even though they have not sought political self-determination.

Nationalism Since the early nineteenth century, but particularly during the mid-twentieth century, the world has witnessed an increasing politicization of nations. National groups formerly content to live under the political rule of a king, emperor, or dictator, ought to establish a political system based on the specific traits and interests of the nationality. The force or movement leading to the politicization of the nation is nationalism. Hans Kohn, noted student of nationalism, defines this movement as "a state of mind, in which the supreme loyalty of the individual is felt to be due the nation-state."[8] Whereas in ancient and medieval periods citizens gave their attention to local and trival loyalties, nationalism is a force directing people's supreme loyalties toward the nationality.

Nationalism is often associated with patriotism, but this is not correct. *Patriotism* is an expression of loyalty to the state and to the country in which people live. To be patriotic means to support the actions and policies of the country. This support is offered symbolicly by saluting the flag, singing the national anthem, volunteering for military service, etc. Nationalism, by contrast, is the political creed justifying self-determination of a nation. To be sure, it is a form of egotism — of preferring certain people over others. Nationalism also provides the general theoretical justification for the modern nation-state, while patriotism is the quality that sustains states. In comparing patriotism to nationalism, Baradat has observed that "patriotism is a form of secular

worship of the nation-state."[9] It is linked to nationalism in m
as religious worship is tied to theology. Nationalism is the p
modern state; patriotism is the visible manifestation of that be

As noted earlier, nations are based on numerous features, but
sable element in developing and maintaining a nationality is self-det
Kohn writes: "Although objective factors are of great importanc
formation of nationalities, the most essential element is a living an
corporate will. It is this will which we call nationalism, a state of mind i
ing the large majority of a people and claiming to inspire all its member
This corporate will is significant because it channels the interests and vision
the people toward the ideals of the nation-state. Moreover, it provides the
justification for the authority of the government and for the policies that it
carries out. Nationalism is thus the dominant integrative force of the modern
state and, as such, a major force for building cohesion among people.

Nationalism was created in the seventeenth and eighteenth centuries with
the development of the notion of popular sovereignty (the theory of "consent
of the governed"), the growth of secularism, and the modernization of society.
Kohn thinks that the first great expression of nationalism has spread throughout the world and has become the most powerful political movement of the
last half of the twentieth century. The most dramatic explosion of nationalism
began in the late 1950s when former European colonies began to seek political
self-determination. This anticolonial nationalism developed such strength that
in the course of three decades more than 70 nations became politically independent. Although most former colonial territories have now achieved statehood, nationalism is still a dominant force in the contemporary world.

From a standpoint of conflict management, nationalism has played both
an integrative and disintegrative role. When nation-states first began to
emerge in the seventeenth and eighteenth centuries, nationalism proved to be a
powerful integrative force. Former disjointed territories were brought under
the control of a single government. Whereas the fifteenth and sixteenth
centuries in Europe were characterized by continuous religious and political
turmoil among small kingdoms and emerging states, the development of
strong, powerful sovereign rulers brought increasing domestic harmony and
cohesion to territories formerly divided by rivalries. With the explosion of
anticolonialism, however, nationalism encouraged further division of political
communities, resulting in the disintegration of European empires and the further breakup of nation-states. Whereas nationalism had been a potent force
for national consolidation in the eighteenth and nineteenth centuries, in the
twentienth century nationalism became a movement for further disintegration
of the international system. To be sure, the effort to establish self-determination
in the Asian and African states was a logical outgrowth of the previous historical manifestations of nationalism. Moreover, many of the former colonies

...ss of nation-building. But the potency of
...ll and underpopulated territories to seek
...vere not well prepared for nor had the
...ndence.

...expressions of nationalism, three
...first type is the *indigenous* nation-
...ael. The chief feature of this form
...tate and mostly on political and
...ion was largely an indigenous move-
...of the French constitution. British nation-
...ng incremental process in which its people sought
...constitutional system of government. The chief feature
...alism has been its search for a homeland and, since 1948, the
...of Israel.

The second type of nationalism is *social revolution.* Epitomized by the
movements in Cuba, Mexico, and the Soviet Union, revolutionary nationalism
is primarily focused on the restructuring of society to establish a new social
and political order. The central unifying force in contemporary Cuba, for
instance, is the National Revolution led by Fidel Castro. Since 1959, Cuban
nationalism has been concerned with the transformation of Cuban society.
Soviet nationalism also grew out of a social and political revolution led by
communists.

The third type of nationalism has its source in the opposition to the European colonial system. The *anticolonial* nationalism of Asia and Africa is characterized by its single-minded concern with self-determination. Whereas
social-revolutionary nationalism provides some programmatic guidance to
governments, anticolonial nationalism is primarily concerned with political
independence. Once that objective is realized, however, the new nationalism
provides little assistance in establishing new governing institutions.

NATION-BUILDING

Nation-building is the name given to the group of processes involved in the
growth and development of the nation-state. The subject of how nations grow
and develop became of significant concern to political scientists as nationalism
swept through the Third World and led to the political independence of more
than 70 states. What students of politics were particularly interested in discov-
ering were the major stages of establishing political maturity in the new
nations. What were the prerequisites for effective nation-building, and in what
sequence and at what rate should political leaders carry out major changes and
reforms? Since some of the significant theories of political development of

nations is examined in Chapter 13, our analysis of nation-building is limited to major elements of the process. The nature of development of nations and states is briefly discussed, followed by a review of some major stages, or "crises," that tend to occur in the development process.

Building Nations and States

As noted earlier, the development of a nationality is a slow, incremental process. Nations are not created but tend to grow slowly, evolving out of the fabric of social, cultural, and economic forces in society. Since there are many important elements in a nation, establishing one of them — such as a common language, an integrated economic system, a modern communications and transportation network, a dominant ethnic group, a prevailing group of cultural patterns — does not ensure the growth and maturity of a nationality. What is needed is simultaneous social, economic, linguistic, cultural, and religious reforms that strengthen national interdependence. Many of these needed changes result directly from the process of modernization. In addition, nation-building requires the corporate will — the determination to make a nation. The force of nationalism itself requires that other reforms be under way. Nationalism cannot start the process of nation-building but can only function where the social, economic, and cultural preconditions of national development are well established. Nationalism is thus not the beginning but the ending of nation-building.

Closely associated with the development of nations is the building of states. Whereas nation-building concerns the creation of a homogeneous, consensual, and integrated society, the creation of the state involves the establishment of an effective political system to govern the nation. However harmonious and consensual a society might be, nations inevitably need structures to manage and resolve social conflict. Without governmental institutions, no nationality can long survive.

Historically, states have generally been created by the arbitrary will of a few powerful leaders. Although we tend to assume that the creation of the nation-state is a response to grave social injustices, the most common source of states has been the desire for self-rule by political elites. The independence of most Latin American countries, for instance, was achieved largely through efforts of a small group of Creole military and political leaders who sought to secede from the Spanish empire. The movement of independence was not a concern to the Indians or the black slaves but focused on whether leadership should be in the hands of the Spanish king or a group of resident leaders. The objectives of the independence movement were thus not to upgrade the quality of life for the indigenous masses nor to establish democracy; rather, the goal was to perpetuate a feudal and exploitative economic and social system without external accountability. After the military forces of Simón Bolívar, Gen.

Sucre, and José de San Martín had defeated the Royalist forces in South America, sovereign authority passed to resident European oligarchic elites in each of the new states. The lives of the masses, however, were hardly touched by these political events.

The creation of states has also generally involved violence. Since people have generally identified their loyalties with a village, hamlet, city, or district, the consolidation of these distinct territories has often involved force. The consolidation of Germany under Bismarck and Italy under Cavour, for example, was achieved by diplomacy and military violence. Similarly, the creation of states like Belgium, Holland, and Italy involved the expansion of people's political identities from their cities and provinces to those of a nation. In each of these countries, however, the expansion of this new identity occurred partly by force. In their quest for state-building, military and political leaders often used persuasion to gain the allegiance of new subjects; but when peaceful means of consolidating power failed, they did not hesitate to use force to eliminate political resistance and ensure unqualified obedience to the new institutions of government.

In establishing the modern nation-state, the creation of political and governmental institutions generally preceded the development of nations. For most countries, the processes of nation-building generally followed those of state-building. The origin of Latin American states, for example, illustrates this pattern. When the Spanish conquerors arrived in the Western Hemisphere, they defeated the Indians and imposed their colonial system on them. The English colonists in America sought to create a nation without Indians, but the Spanish settlers subjugated the Indians and sought to establish a feudal or dualistic society (a nation with modern and traditional societies existing side by side). Thus, when South American countries became independent early in the nineteenth century, most countries were divided into two nations—a white, European, aristocratic society and an Indian society. The creation of Spanish colonial states in the sixteenth century or of the independent countries in the nineteenth century was based not on an integrated nation but on a deeply divided society. (Indeed, the continued presence of dual societies has been significantly responsible for the political turmoil that most countries in the region have experienced over the past two hundred years.) State-building may precede the development of nations, but if a country is to be stable and orderly, the evolution of an integrated and relatively homogeneous society is essential.

The creation of states has quite often been associated with self-determination in the postwar era. State-building, however, involves more than the initial creation of a politically independent state and the governmental institutions to implement decisions for the state. Indeed, the easiest part of state-building is the creation of an independent state. The more difficult task lies in developing political and governmental institutions by which conflict can be managed and resolved. If achieving statehood is a relatively easy and quick process — witness the explosion of new African states in the 1960s — the establishment of political parties and effective legislatures and executives is far more complex and likely to be realized only through many decades of slow, incremental change.

Crises of Nation-Building

The creation and development of nation-states is an ongoing process. No country can ever hope to establish a completely homogeneous and consensual nation or a perfectly balanced set of governmental institutions to channel and direct the interests of its citizens. Although the pattern of nation-building is partly unique in each country, social scientists have tried to determine some of the common features of the process. One significant comparative study was carried out by the Committee on Comparative Politics of the Social Science Research Council. Based on a number of studies in comparative research, the committee found that every country must overcome five major "crises" in its quest for modern statehood. These crises are: identity, legitimacy, penetration, participation, and distribution. Although the order of these crises varies, many of the modern states, including Britain and the United States, have faced these hurdles in this sequence.[11]

Identity   Identity defines the political and governmental institutions to which individuals give ultimate allegiance. This crisis is significant because it involves the transformation of individual loyalties from villages, cities, and rural districts to the nation. The identity crisis generally involves the expansion of political boundaries and the acceptance of supreme allegiance to these new, larger, and more powerful governmental institutions. No longer do people accept the local caudillo or the tribal chieftain as their boss; rather, the new institutions of the state become the ultimate source of political authority. The problem of developing a common identity can be a continuing challenge to nations. The desire for self-rule by Kurds in Iraq and Iran and by the French Canadians in Québec illustrate the continuing process of building a common national identity.

Legitimacy   This refers to the extent to which citizens accept the institutions and actions of the government. When people accept the governing institutions as legitimate, they enable the government to rule with authority, i.e., without having to carry out decisions by coercion. Legitimacy is a matter of degree. No government is considered legitimate by all its subjects; on the other hand, no political system can long survive if a substantial portion of its members are unwilling to accept the actions and rules made by the government. Quite often governments come to power illigitimately (without much popular support) but can develop substantial approval over time. On the other hand, some rulers are chosen through free competitive elections but after gaining power may lose popular support. Of the five "crises" discussed here, legitimacy is clearly the most elusive and one of the most difficult to overcome.

Penetration   This involves the ability of government to implement its policies, programs, and rules. The degree that a government penetrates a society can be determined by the extent to which citizens comply with the decisions of government officials. The greater the level of compliance, the higher the level of penetration. Conversely, the greater the reluctance of local chiefs and village leaders to comply with edicts, laws, regulations, and decrees of the central government, the lower the level of penetration. In the early phases of nation-building (when countries are not well integrated), it is exceedingly difficult for the national government to enforce its rules uniformly throughout the state. This is why law enforcement in Third World countries becomes weaker the farther one moves from the capital toward the perimeter of the state. But as society becomes more socially and economically interdependent and people identify more deeply with the state, compliance with the decisions of government tends to increase. The problem of penetration is also closely associated with the development of legitimacy. When substantial numbers of people are opposed to the actions of rulers, it is difficult to enforce them, no matter how much force the government applies. As a result, no nation is ever completely penetrated by its government. The level of compliance is always a matter of degree.

Participation   One of the central problems of any state is to determine who will participate in the decision-making process and in what manner. Historically, the government of states was in the hands of relatively few persons. The process of modernization brought a demand for greater involvement in the public affairs of the nation. The most common way of satisfying this demand for participation has been through suffrage, although there are doubts about the extent to which universal suffrage alters the real influence and authority of the masses. In many countries where universal voting is widespread, political power is still tightly controlled by charismatic figures and party leaders. The significance of the participation crisis is that it forces a country to formally recognize the relationship of subjects to rulers. While governments may continue to be controlled by elites, the masses nonetheless have the opportunity to publicly express approval or disapproval for policies and actions taken by a government.

Distribution   This crisis involves the manner and extent to which government becomes involved in distributing and redistributing goods and services. Whereas the first four crises contribute toward establishment and maintenance of social and political order, distribution is chiefly concerned with establishing social justice. Since no community is capable of distributing its goods equitably through private mechanisms alone, governments become involved in transferring resources from some individuals to others. One of the important distributive functions of the modern state is to guarantee a minimal standard of living to its citizens. To do this, governments tax their people and utilize the funds to provide all members of the community with minimal social and economic services. In addition to directly providing material goods and public services, governments also redistribute income through taxation. The progressive income tax structures of modern democratic states is the most common method of carrying out this redistribution. When such taxation is difficult, states may tax consumption of luxury goods, which are generally consumed by the wealthier groups.

THE ORGANIZATION OF THE MODERN STATE

The Role of Constitutions

A constitution is the body of written or unwritten rules by which a state manages and resolves conflict. Since no nation-state is totally harmonious, it needs a set of guidelines for managing political tensions and conflicts. These guidelines and rules are ordinarily set forth in a written document called the *constitution*. The primary function of a constitution is to establish the fundamental principles and procedures by which conflict should be resolved.

Constitutions, which are similar to bylaws or charters of private organizations, generally have at least three major elements: (1) a statement of purposes and goals; (2) identification of the major institutions of the organization or state; and (3) the definition of procedures by which the state or institution makes its decisions. In the U. S. Constitution, for example, the purposes of the country are spelled out in the Preamble, while the division of government and the functions of each branch are defined in the first three articles.

From the standpoint of conflict management, constitutions are the chief instruments defining how social and political conflict is to be managed and resolved. Every community needs a widely accepted system of rules for making decisions and resolving disputes. In football and soccer, for example, there are a set of rules by which these sports are played. The purpose of the umpire is to determine when athletes violate the rules. With constitutions, however, the provisions of conflict management are even more extensive because constitutions need not only to provide rules for decision making but also to define how officials are selected for making and enforcing rules.

The creation of a constitution is generally the result of conflict resolution among competing groups within society. In deciding what the fundamental rules of governing will be, the major groups of society seek to maximize their interests in this process. During the U. S. Constitutional Convention in Phila-delphia, for example, the dominant conflict was between the large and small states, who ultimately agreed to compromise their differences with the creation of a bicameral legislature based on representation of states (Senate) and of people (House of Representatives).

The significance that groups attach to the making of constitutions or other procedural issues is totally justified. The most crucial decision making in assemblies, committee hearings, or plenary sessions involves the determination of how a decision will be made. Thus, although the discussion of substantive issues is often considered the crucial part of the deliberative process, in actual fact the determination of the procedural rules tends to predetermine the outcome of the subsequent substantive debate. This is why one of the most powerful committees of the U.S. House of Representatives is the Rules Committee, which determines the conditions under which a bill is to be debated in the full House.

If a constitution is to be an effective instrument of conflict resolution, it must be widely accepted by the citizens of society. This means that the various sectors of society must accept the fundamental rules, even if their interests are not entirely represented in the document. Constitutions are generally estab-lished by competing groups. Obviously, if there were no conflicts in society there would be no need for a framework for resolving conflict. But once a set of rules has been established there needs to be wide acceptance of the constitu-tion if it is to be an effective instrument of conflict management. Continued conflict over the fundamental rules of government will make conflict resolu-tion impossible.

In making constitutions for the modern state, a number of important qualities help ensure that the instruments are effective. First, constitutions should deal primarily with the fundamentals of governing. This means that the constitution should not be too long or too specific. The major problem with a long, complex document is that the more specific and complex a statement of rules becomes, the more difficult it is to apply the provisions to the governing process. The United States Constitution is a brief six or seven pages, yet it is the oldest written constitution. The next oldest constitutions are those of Sweden (1809), Norway (1814), Holland (1815), Belgium (1831), and Switzerland (1848); each of them is similarly brief in scope. The importance of emphasizing essentials in a constitution was clearly articulated by Chief Justice Marshall in *McCulloch* v. *Maryland,* when he stated that a constitution "requires that only its great outlines should be marked, its important objectives designated, and the minor ingredients which compose those deduced from the nature of the objects themselves."

Second, constitutions should provide a mechanism by which provisions can be interpreted authoritatively. In Great Britain the responsibility for inter-preting its unwritten constitution lies with Parliament's lower house (House of Commons). In the United States, by contrast, the authority for judicial interpretation lies with the Supreme Court. Although the principle of *judicial review* (i.e., determining the legality of federal and state statutes in terms of more fundamental rules of the constitution) is not explicitly stated in the U. S. Constitution, it is an implied power Chief Justice Marshall articulated in *Marbury* v. *Madison* when he stated that it was "the province and duty of the judicial department to say what the law is." While most presidential systems place the authority of interpretation of laws and constitutional rules within the judiciary, the implementation of this principle is difficult to achieve in most states. The reason for this is that the executive tends to dominate the government and to disregard the courts when it is in its interest to do so. (The effective interpreter of rules, decrees, and laws in Third World or communist states is generally the executive.)

A third requirement of constitutions is a formal mechanism by which they may be changed. Since society is continually changing, constitutions need to be modified periodically to ensure that procedures and principles are in accord with prevailing values and practices in society. Where basic constitutional rules are in an unwritten form (as in Britain), there is no need for a formal amendment process. But in all written documents it is essential to define the process by which the constitution can be altered. In unitary states, the power to amend the constitution is generally carried out by popular referendum or by the legislative and executive branches. In federal systems, however, changes in constitutions most often need to be adopted by the states themselves.

Finally, effective constitutions must be suited to the specific needs and values of society. Montesquieu, the eighteenth-century political theorist, argues in *The Spirit of the Laws* that the fundamental rules of society must be related to the social climate of the country: "The government most comfortable to nature, is that which best agrees with the humour and disposition of the people in whose favour it is established."[12] Although this requirement appears self-evident, failure to ensure an organic connection between constitutional rules and society is a source of much tension and turmoil in developing nations. The constitutions adopted by most African countries following independence, for instance, are largely based on principles and practices adopted from the colonial powers. The adoption of foreign constitutional principles that had little relation to the values and practices of society is even more vividly illustrated in Latin America. When South American countries became independent in the early nineteenth century, most states established constitutions patterned after the United States' document. Since the principles of constitutionalism, separation of powers, limited government, and checks and balances were not widely accepted or appreciated, the adoption of constitutional rules that had little relationship to the political realities of the region tended to discredit the new constitutions from the outset. As a result, Latin America has been a region of much constitutional instability. Most countries have had at least 10 constitutions and several (Bolivia, Haiti, and Venezuela) have had more than 20.[13]

Constitutions need to have a normative component. Some idealism is necessary if a political system is to become more developed in the conflict-management process. On the other hand, if the main provisions of the constitution are normative goals that have little relation to procedures and practices widely accepted in society, the constitutions themselves will lack credibility and have little influence on the patterns of government.

The Formal Division of Governmental Authority

Constitutions may be formally classified as confederal, unitary, and federal. Although nearly four-fifths of all governments are unitary in structure, we shall examine the main features of each of these systems since they are the chief methods by which nation-states can be organized.

The Confederal System   A confederal system is one where the subunits of government (generally states or provinces) are powerful but where the central government is relatively weak. Under a confederal system, people grant authority directly to the constituent units but not to the national government. As a result, the central government does not exercise direct control over citizens. It cannot tax people nor can it compel them to serve in the armed forces. The only governing institutions that can do this are the subunits of governments. Since the powers of the central government are derived directly from the states or provinces, the central government can undertake only those tasks requested or approved by the constituting governmental units. Power is thus highly decentralized. (A classic example of a confederacy was the United States immediately following independence.) While there are no longer any states organized confederally, the European Community is perhaps the best example of a confederation in the contemporary world. The European Community can be considered an emerging confederation because, while political authority still resides in each of the nine member states, an increasing supranational role has been played by the governing institutions of the Community.

The major strength of a confederacy is that it allows much diversity within a political community. Its major weakness, and the reason for the demise of confederal systems in the world, is that it leads to weak political and economic integration. The thirteen American states gave up the confederal system precisely because they desired greater economic centralization to encourage greater internal and foreign commerce and greater centralization of military and political authority to strengthen diplomacy and military defense.

The Unitary System   The unitary system is directly opposed to the principles of decentralized political power found in a confederacy. As noted in Figure 5.3., the dominant authority is the central or national government. In unitary systems, people grant authority directly to the central government; it in turn may delegate some responsibility and authority to provincial and local units as

Figure 5.3 Formal Structures of Government

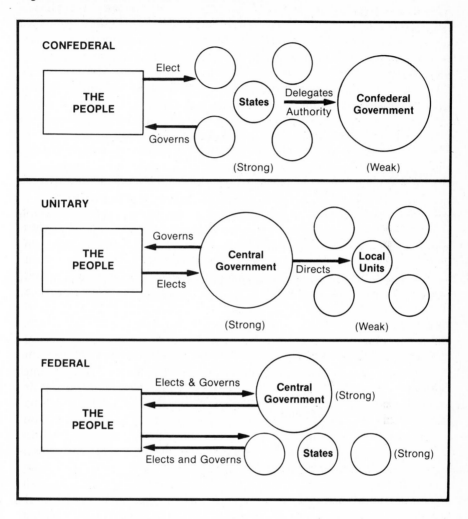

it sees fit. The authority of the subunits of government is thus dependent entirely on the will of the central government. In the contemporary system, virtually all small and medium-size states are unitary in structure.

A major advantage of a centralized system is that it leads to efficiency in decision making, since one central government can make major decisions for all subunits of government. A second advantage is that it can encourage economic integration and thereby promote economic development. The major liability of the unitary system is that it creates uniformities throughout the subunits, which may not be desired.

The Federal System   The federal system is a relatively recent political invention dating from the late eighteenth century. The first country to implement fully a federal constitutional structure was the United States. Since then, some 20 other states have adopted federalism as an organizing principle of government. Federalism has remained a popular form of government for large nations of the world, like Australia, Brazil, Canada, India, Mexico, and the Soviet Union. The reason for this is that it allows for strong central government while also permitting significant regional self-rule. Thus, where significant ethnic, social, and economic diversity exists, the federal formula provides a means to ensure national strength and domestic diversity.

The central feature of federalism is that government operates simultaneously at two levels — the national and the subnational. As diagrammed in Figure 5.3, people grant political authority to two separate and distinct governments; each in turn has the responsibility for carrying out particular governmental functions. The operation of dual government can and does result in a duplication of activities and may even lead to conflict between the central and provincial governments. But such conflict is rare, for most federal constitutions provide for a judicial mechanism for resolving conflicts.

Kenneth Wheare, a leading student of federalism, suggests a number of elements that are essential if a federal union is to succeed. These include:

1. the will to implement federalism;

2. a common fear from an external enemy or a common economic goal;

3. a common race, language, religion, and nationality;

4. similarity of social and political institutions among the units of the federal community; and

5. a competitive political system, for "dictatorship, with its one-party government and its denial of free election, is incompatible with the working of the federal principle."[14]

Of these factors, the most significant are the first and the last. Federalism, above all, requires a corporate will and a political culture to make it succeed. Constitutional provisions themselves do not ensure a federal structure. The experience of the Soviet Union clearly demonstrates this. Although the Soviet political system is theoretically a federal system, in practice the central government in Moscow has supreme authority over the fifteen union republics.

In addition, three constitutional requirements are essential in operating and maintaining federalism. First, federal systems need constitutions to delineate specific powers and responsibilities of the central and constituent units of government. In fact, no federal system exists without a written constitution. Second, the subunits of government need to be treated equally on some legal and political issues if they are not to be absorbed by the central government or by the more powerful states. Since there are generally substantial differences in the size, population, and resources in the subunits, some method of maintaining juridical equality among them needs to be ensured. Such methods may include equal representation in the upper house of Parliament, equal participation in the amending process of the constitution, and equal participation in changing territorial boundaries of the subunits. Finally, federal unions need a method of resolving conflicts between the constituent units and the central government. In the democratic federal states this is generally achieved through the nation's highest national court. In qualified federal states, (such as Argentina and Brazil), conflicts can be resolved politically by the central government's intervention in the affairs of the constituent states. This presidential intervention may involve direct placement of governors in each of the provinces along with a suspension of all political activity at the subnational level. The conflict is thus resolved by the imposition of the central government's will on the provinces.

The primary advantage of the federal system is that it combines centralization of political authority found in unitary systems with decentralization of authority found in confederal systems. Federalism stresses cohesion on essentials (e. g., economic development, national defense, control of the environment) and diversity on the less important issues. It is for this reason that Wheare observes that a federal union requires "some agreement to differ but not to differ too much."[15] Countries likely to enjoy the benefits of decentralization the most are those with numerous different nationalities. Countries like India, the Soviet Union, and Yugoslavia are comprised of numerous distinct ethnic groups, and the federal formula permits constituent territories to maintain some level of self-rule while still preserving national unity.

A second advantage of federalism is that it builds a close bond between provincial governments and their constituents. The establishment of a close relationship between the subunits of government and the people is particularly important in large countries like Australia, Canada, the Soviet Union, and the United States. Given the enormous distances between the capitals of these countries and their outlying territories, the subunits provide another important level of governmental decision making with which citizens can become more readily associated and identified.

One of the important disadvantages of federalism is that it is less efficient in carrying out public actions. Since government operates at two levels, the development and implementation of policies is slower and more cumbersome. A second, closely related shortcoming is that federal union leads to duplication of activities. In the United States, for example, law enforcement, social welfare, and health care are concerns of both the national and state governments; the result is that services and programs are often duplicated due to lack of coordination.

Informal Organizations of Nation-States

Nation-states can also be classified in terms of the informal or actual method of operation. One of the earliest informal classifications of governments was developed by Aristotle, who in his *Politics* suggests that there are six major forms of political organizations. According to him, government may be classified according to the number of people holding ultimate power; these in turn may be distinguished by whether they govern in the interests of the total community or only in their self-interest. Although Aristotle's typology of governments is helpful in identifying possible alternative ways that states can be ruled, it is of limited use because of the difficulty of determining whether governments are ruling in the community's interest or not (Table 5.2).

TABLE 5.2   Typology of Governments in Terms of Number and Concern of Political Rulers

	RULE IN INTEREST OF ALL	RULE IN INTEREST OF SELF
Power held by One	Monarchy	Tyranny
Power held by Few	Aristocracy	Oligarchy
Power held by Many	Polity	Democracy

A more useful method of classifying the governments of states is in terms of scope of operation and level of competitiveness.

Constitutionalism vs. Totalitarianism   Constitutions were previously defined as fundamental rules by which governments manage and resolve social conflict. Since all states have written or unwritten norms, they are all to some extent "constitutional" insofar as they operate in terms of their own prescribed rules. *Constitutionalism,* by contrast, is the practice of keeping government limited. The goal of constitutionalism is to restrict the scope and operations of government so that individual rights can be protected. Constitutionalism is not achieved automatically with a constitution. Indeed, many constitutional regimes (i.e., regimes with constitutions) do not effectively protect the rights and freedoms of individuals. What is needed is effective societal and political conditions to maintain limited government. History suggests that two conditions are essential for all limited regimes. The first is an independent judiciary to help protect individual rights and freedoms from possible government encroachment; the second is a competitive political system in which groups are able to freely compete for political office.

At the opposite extreme are the unlimited or totalitarian systems. Whereas constitutionalism seeks to define areas over which government can exert no control, totalitarianism assumes that there are no spheres the state cannot transgress. Since the chief goal of totalitarian regimes is not the maximization of individual rights but the fulfillment of national community goals, there are no areas of a citizen's life that cannot be regulated by the government. For example, the Nazi totalitarian system sought to regulate not only political life but also social, cultural, religious, and educational aspects of German society.

Quite often the terms *dictatorial* and *totalitarian* are used interchangeably. This is not correct. Whereas dictatorship refers to a government that has seized and used power illegitimately, a totalitarian system is one that (regardless of how power is acquired) attempts to control all aspects of human life. Thus, while a dictatorial regime may often be totalitarian, there is no necessary connection between the way a government gets and maintains power and the extent to which it attempts to regulate the lives of individuals. Theoretically, a dictatorship could be either totalitarian or constitutional, although the latter is highly unlikely in practice. On the other hand, a democratic country could conceivably be constitutional or totalitarian, although the former is far more probable.

Totalitarian political systems are by definition noncompetitive and undemocratic. But what distinguishes a totalitarian regime from one that is constitutional is the degree to which the government seeks to regulate human behavior. Friedrich and Brzezinski observe that totalitarian systems are generally governed by a well-organized political party that seeks to operate in terms of an official ideology. Since the ruling party has the "truth," it not only seeks to eliminate political opposition and to control the media but also assumes that any activity in accordance with the goals and objectives of the ruling officials is legitimate. Thus, the elite-guided party attempts not only to regulate political behavior but also to bring about significant control in other areas of society.[16]

It should be recognized that the extent to which any state is totalitarian is a matter of degree. Totalitarianism and constitutionalism are not mutually exclusive categories but ideal conditions along a continuum. No nation-state is totally totalitarian (totally dominated by the government), and no country is totally constitutional. Most countries are between those two extremes. During the Stalin era, for example, the Soviet Union was far more totalitarian than during the Khrushchev era. Similarly, during the Second World War the United States became less constitutional (government became less limited) as it sought to cope with the challenge of international war.

Competitive vs. Noncompetitive Systems The second important informal distinction among contemporary states is in terms of the level of political competition tolerated within society. Political competition is significant because it is one of the most important ways of ensuring that sovereignty, i.e., ultimate political control, is maintained in the whole of society, not just among a small portion of its members. Since the notion of competition is central to the operation of democracy, we shall first examine the nature of democracy and then show why the freedom to criticize and compete is essential for democratic government.

Democracy may be defined as government by the people. This simple definition, however, does not provide a precise understanding of how democratic communities govern themselves. To say that people govern themselves does not explain how or who makes the decisions within a society. Since all communities experience discord and conflict, decision making seldom, if ever, is unanimous. The problem is therefore to establish a process by which people can maintain ultimate control of the government without being responsible for making all decisions.

In reviewing the literature on democratic theory, we can distinguish two types of democracy; direct and indirect (Figure 5.4). In *direct democracy* all members directly participate in decision making. In such a system there is no elected legislature; the people themselves are the Parliament. This idealistic theory, popularized by such Enlightenment thinkers as Jean Jacques Rousseau, assumes that since sovereignty resides in the people no government can act until it has received instructions directly from the people. Examples of direct democracy include the seventeenth century New England town meetings as well as the government of Swiss cantons. Although applying direct democracy to a large state such as Canada and the United States poses enormous difficulties even with sophisticated computers, the shortcomings of direct democracy are not technological but substantive. As Schumpeter points out, direct democracy falsely assumes that people hold opinions about major public issues and that they are willing to articulate these to the government.[17] Moreover, even if people had opinions about major issues and communicated those in the decision-making process, the multiplicity of opinions would lead to government paralysis.

The second type of democracy is indirect or representative. In *indirect democracy,* people hold sovereign authority but delegate the responsibility for making and enforcing community rules to a government. Unlike the classical model of direct democracy (where people themselves make laws), in representative democracy people elect officials who can carry out this task for specified terms. There are three major advantages in delegating the ongoing decision-making authority to a group of elected government officials: (1) the number of persons directly involved in making public decisions is limited to a manageable number; (2) elected officials are given responsibility for policy initiation and political leadership; and (3) elected officials are held accountable for their actions in periodic competitive elections.

Democratic governments do not become more democratic by increasing popular participation. Increasing the number of elections, for example, does not necessarily lead to more responsible government. Indeed, too many elections leads to "electoral fatigue." What is important is not frequency of

Figure 5.4   Direct and Indirect Democracy

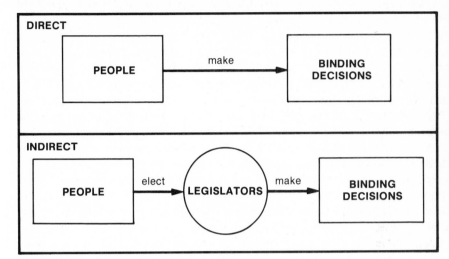

participation but continued possession of ultimate control over the fate of governments. Popular sovereignty does not mean that people should always participate directly in public decision making but that they should hold ultimate authority for making and abolishing governments. As long as people maintain this authority, they can significantly control their political fate. Schattschneider observes:

> *The ultimate power of the people to pass judgment on the government is not perfect power but it is enough. The people cannot judge every detail of the work of government. They can make only a general, overall judgment about the broad tendency of the government and the general results of public policy. They cannot vote every day. What this amounts to is a few large decisions on questions of general policy confirmed or reversed when they throw the party in power out or continue it in power. But it is enough.*[18]

People may not have the capacity to evaluate laws and complex policies and programs. But they do have the capacity to judge the general effect of governmental decisions. Just as people judge the quality of food prepared by a chef ("The proof of the pudding is in the eating"), so, too, do they pass judgment on the overall impact of governmental actions.

The essential requirement of all representative or indirect democracies is that people be completely free in passing periodic judgment on the work of government. It is not enough to have elections. What is significant is that elections be totally free. People must be able to criticize the government and to develop political parties to oppose the governing party. Thus, although there are numerous aspects to democracy (protection of minority rights, majority rule, political equality, etc.), the essential requirement is political freedom and periodicity of elections. Without periodic competitive elections, people have no method of holding government accountable and are therefore unable to control their political fate. In the last analysis, the distinguishing feature of democratic governments is not whether governments rule in the interests of the people or even if the people themselves rule by regular participation. The essential requirement for democracy is a competitive political system.

Nation-states that are politically noncompetitive are generally ruled by dictatorial or authoritarian governments. A *dictatorship* is a government in which political authority is held by one person (the dictator) or a small group of political officials (the elite). The term *dictator* originated with the ancient Roman practice of appointing a leader with absolute power to save the city when threatened by foreign invasion or domestic violence. Gradually, the term came to denote any individual who seized and held power without the support of the Roman senate. Dictatorships thus came to signify regimes that held power illegitimately. In contemporary usage, a dictatorial regime is one that, in contrast to representative democracy, has gained and maintains power without the consent of the people. Dictatorships, in other words, are noncompetitive regimes. Rulers do not gain office through competitive elections, nor are their programs and actions evaluated periodically in free electoral contests. In fact, most dictatorial regimes seek to consolidate power by abolishing elections, suppressing the media, and significantly curtailing human rights.

Like constitutionalism and totalitarianism, political systems vary according to their level of political competitiveness. No state is purely competitive or noncompetitive. Countries tend to vary along a continuum. By avoiding the fallacy of dichotomous thinking, i.e., believing that reality is divided into mutually contradictory categories, we can avoid the erroneous view that governments are either democratic or dictatorial. Table 5.3 lists selected countries on a continuum based on level of political competition.

TABLE 5.3   Selected Countries Classified According to Level of Political Competitiveness, 1980

POLITICALLY COMPETITIVE			POLITICALLY NONCOMPETITIVE	
Democracies	*Partial Democracies*	*Mixed Systems*	*Partial Dictatorships*	*Dictatorships*
Belgium	Brazil	Algeria	Haiti	China
Colombia	Egypt	Argentina	Iraq	Cuba
Norway	Mexico	Jordan	Pakistan	Saudi Arabia
United States	South Africa	Paraguay	Tanzania	Soviet Union

SUMMARY

The dominant type of political community in the contemporary international system is the nation-state. Dating from the mid-seventeenth century, this form of political community represents a fusion of a dominant nationality with sovereign governmental institutions.

Governments of nation-states can be differentiated both formally and informally. Formally, state constitutions provide for either centralized administration (unitary organization) or partly decentralized administration (federal organization). The highly decentralized model of confederacy is no longer a viable option for organizing a state.

Informally, states can be distinguished either by scope of government or level of political competitiveness. Countries that effectively limit the scope of government are constitutional regimes; those that do not become totalitarian. Regimes also differ in terms of level of political competition. Countries that tolerate complete freedom of expression and opposition tend to be democratic, i.e., to preserve the ultimate authority of government in the hands of the members of society. Rulers that come to power illegally and remain in power without consent are dictatorial. Dictatorships are, by definition, noncompetitive regimes.

KEY TERMS

city-state	constitution
feudalism	confederal
state	federal
sovereignty	unitary
nation	constitutionalism
nationalism	totalitarianism
patriotism	dictatorship
nation-building	competitive system
legitimacy	democracy

NOTES

1. The term *state* is of relatively recent origin, dating from about the sixteenth century. Machiavelli was one of the first writers to popularize the term. Originally, the term was used interchangeably with "status" and "estate" and was used to denote the privileges and responsibilities of the owner of an estate. Gradually, as feudal estates were consolidated into kingdoms, the concept came to signify the king's final authority over his subjects.
2. Frederick Watkins, "State: The Concept" in *International Encyclopedia of the Social Sciences,* vol. 15 (New York: The Macmillan Co. & The Free Press, 1968), p. 150.

3. Jean Bodin, *Six Books on the State* in *Great Political Thinkers: Plato to the Present,* 4th ed. William Ebenstein (Hinsdale, Ill.: Dryden Press, 1969), pp. 354–355.

4. Max Weber, *Economy and Society,* eds. G. Roth and C. Wittich (Totowa, N.J.: Bedminster Press, 1968), p. 56.

5. Karl W. Deutsch, *Political and Government: How People Decide Their Fate* (Boston: Houghton Mifflin, 1974), p. 130.

6. John Stuart Mill, *Representative Government* in *Great Books of the Western World,* vol. 43, ed. Robert Maynard Hutchins (Chicago: Encyclopedia Britannica, 1952), p. 424.

7. Walker Connor, "Nation-Building or Nation-Destroying," *World Politics* 24 (April 1972), p. 320.

8. Hans Kohn, *Nationalism: Its Meaning and History,* rev. ed. (New York: D. Van Nostrand, 1965), p. 9.

9. Leon Baradat, *Political Ideologies: Their Origins and Impact* (Englewood Cliffs, N.J.: Prentice-Hall, 1979), p. 45.

10. Kohn, *Nationalism: Its Meaning and History,* p. 10.

11. Leonard Binder et al., *Crises and Sequences in Political Development* (Princeton: Princeton University Press, 1971), pp. 52–67.

12. Montesquieu, *The Spirit of the Laws* in *Great Political Thinkers: Plato to the Present,* 4th ed. William Ebenstein (Hinsdale, Ill.: Dryden Press, 1969), p. 429.

13. Jacques Lambert, *Latin America: Social Structures and Political Institutions* (Berkeley: University of California Press, 1967), pp. 258–259.

14. K.C. Wheare, *Federal Government,* 4th ed. (New York: Oxford University Press, 1964), pp. 44–48.

15. *Ibid.,* p. 48.

16. Carl J. Friedrich and Zbigniew K. Brzezinski, *Totalitarian Dictatorship and Autocracy,* 2nd ed. (Cambridge: Harvard University Press, 1965), pp. 9–10.

17. Joseph A. Schumpeter, *Capitalism, Socialism and Democracy,* 3rd ed. (New York: Harper and Row, 1950), pp. 269–273.

18. E.E. Schattschneider, *Two Hundred Million Americans in Search of a Government* (New York: Holt, Rinehart & Winston, 1969), p. 76.

SUGGESTED READING

BINDER, LEONARD et al. *Crises and Sequences in Political Development.* Princeton: Princeton University Press, 1973. This volume, the seventh in a series on political development, summarizes some of the major conclusions of a ten-year project on nation-building by the Committee on Comparative Politics of the Social Science Research Council.

DAHL, ROBERT, ed. *Political Oppositions in Western Democracies.* New Haven: Yale University Press, 1966. A collection of essays on political conflict and opposition in selected democratic countries. Chapters 11 and 12, by Professor Dahl, summarize some of the dominant patterns of opposition and offer some explanations for the findings.

————· *Regimes and Oppositions.* New Haven: Yale University Press, 1973. A com-
to *Political Oppositions in Western Democracies,* this volume explores the nature
of political opposition in the more restrictive political systems, including the
Soviet Union, Czechoslovakia, Spain, and the one-party states of tropical Africa.
DEUTSCH, KARL W. *Nationalism and Its Alternatives.* New York: Alfred A. Knopf,
1969. A general, nontechnical introduction to the theory and practice of nationalism. This study, which summarizes some of Deutsch's research on nation-
building, focuses on nationalism in Western and Eastern Europe and in the
developing nations.
FRIEDRICH, CARL J. *Limited Government: A Comparison.* Englewood Cliffs, N.J.:
Prentice-Hall, 1974. A short introduction to the doctrine of constitutionalism and
how it is applied in contemporary democratic systems.
KOHN, HANS. *Nationalism: Its Meaning and History.* rev. ed. New York: D. Van
Nostrand Co., 1965. The first part of this primer analyzes the nature and histor-
ical development of nationalism; the second part includes short readings illustrat-
ing the different expressions of nationalism from the sixteenth through the twentieth century.
SCHATTSCHNEIDER, E.E. *Two Hundred Million Americans in Search of a Government.*
New York: Holt, Rinehart & Winston, 1969. Chapters 3 and 4 of this slim volume
give an insightful defense of indirect democracy.
SCHUMPETER, JOSEPH A. *Capitalism, Socialism and Democracy.* 3rd ed. New York:
Harper & Row, 1962. A penetrating study of the economic systems of capitalism
and socialism and of their relationship to democracy. Schumpeter criticizes the
simplistic notion of classical democracy and suggests that the only way of establishing responsible government is through representative government.
WHEARE, K.C. *Federal Government.* 4th ed. New York: Oxford University Press, 1964.
A well-written primer on the nature and practice of federalism by a noted British
scholar.
————· *Modern Constitutions.* New York: Oxford University Press, 1951. A lucid and
succinct comparison of some of the central features of modern constitutions. A
useful introduction to the role of constitutions.

6 / INSTITUTIONS OF CONFLICT MANAGEMENT

Four types of institutions participate in the making of authoritative decisions in modern political systems. These institutions are the legislature, the political executive, the court, and the bureaucracy. The first three organizations make, implement, and interpret the laws of the state, while the last assists in making and enforcing laws.

Traditionally, political scientists have defined the major responsibilities of government in terms of legislative, executive, and judicial functions. More recently, however, political scientists have increasingly used Almond's terminology of rule making, rule application, and rule adjudication to describe the major functions of government.[1] Two advantages of this terminology are that it emphasizes all types of government decisions whether or not they are laws, and it avoids the possible Anglo-Saxon bias of preferring duly passed laws and of neglecting rules passed by government institutions without the support of representative legislatures. Thus, while we are chiefly concerned with the law-making and law-enforcement functions of modern government, we need to recognize that all political systems — traditional or modern, simple or complex — make binding decisions about community conflict.

The purpose of this chapter is to examine the role of legislatures, executives, courts, and bureaucracies in the modern state. Our concern is to analyze the nature and function of these organizations in developed political systems. One of the difficulties in assessing the effective role of legislatures, executives, and courts is to determine to what extent formal institutional rules are applied in the decision-making process. In many cases, political systems have elaborate constitutions delineating functions for various governmental institutions, yet the constitutional norms may have little bearing on the actual operations of government. In Latin America, for example, numerous countries have patterned their institutions after those of the United States, yet legislatures have been far weaker in the Southern Hemisphere than in the United States. Similarly, the Soviet Union has an elaborate parliamentary constitutional structure (much like that of Western European parliamentary systems), yet the actual operation of the Soviet government is significantly different from those in Holland or Norway. Recognizing, then, the gap between constitutional norms and practice, we shall focus our attention in this chapter primarily on countries where formal rules and constitutional institutions effectively regulate community conflict. Although many authoritarian regimes have symbolic legislatures and courts, our primary focus is on those systems in which these institutions play a significant rule-making and rule-adjudicating function.

THE ORGANIZATION OF GOVERNMENT

One of the significant differences of competitive political systems is between presidential and parliamentary regimes. *Parliamentary systems* are characterized by a fusion of law-making and law-enforcing responsibilities, while *presidential systems* are characterized by a separation of governmental powers. Thus, a central difference between these constitutional structures is the extent to which governmental power is centralized in one political body. Before examining in greater detail the primary differences between presidential and parliamentary systems, we need to review the principle of separation of powers, the doctrine by which the two constitutional structures can be differentiated.

Separation of Powers

Although separation of powers is associated with Montesquieu, the origins of the doctrine can be traced to antiquity.[2] Throughout the history of Western political thought, philosophers have debated the question of centralization of political authority. Political thinkers have recognized that a strong government is necessary for governing society, yet they have also realized that an overly powerful government can result in tyranny. Thus, throughout the history of political philosophy, thinkers have tried to find the correct balance between an effective, yet responsible government—a strong but self-regulating regime. Perhaps the first traces of the notion of separation of powers are found in the writings of Aristotle and Polybius; both emphasize the need for partitioned authority through a balanced constitution—a government based on a proper mix of social classes and of the appropriate monarchical, aristocratic, and democratic elements representing each class. The notion of a clear separation of governmental functions, however, is a modern doctrine that emerges in the seventeenth and eighteenth centuries with the writings of John Locke, the Baron de Montesquieu, Jean Jacques Rousseau, Thomas Jefferson, James Madison, and others. As the doctrine emerged, it was partly a description about how political systems operated and partly a prescriptive formula for how governments should operate if they were not to become tyrannical. Let us briefly examine the essential elements of the doctrine.

According to the notion of separation of powers, three major responsibilities need to be performed by government: the making of laws (the legislative function), the enforcement of laws (the executive function), and the interpretation of laws (the judicial function). The chief insight of seventeenth- and eighteenth-century thinkers, however, was to associate the division of governmental responsibilities with the creation of a responsible, nontyrannical government. As articulated by Montesquieu, (the most influential exponent of this doctrine) the creation of a limited government requires that governmental functions be divided and that the responsibilities of each branch be carried out by different people. The security against tyranny is achieved by ensuring that no individual or group of individuals may perform all three governmental functions. The classic expression of this doctrine is found in the constitution of the state of Massachusetts:

> *In the government of this commonwealth, the legislative*
> *department shall never exercise the executive and judicial powers,*
> *or either of them; the executive shall never exercise the legislative*
> *and judicial powers, or either of them; the judicial shall never*
> *exercise the legislative and executive powers, or either of them:*
> *to the end that it may be a government of laws and not of men.*

One of the important corollaries of separation of powers is *checks and balances,* the notion that the divided powers review and check the work of each other. Although Montesquieu appreciated the relationship between separation and balance among the branches of government, nothing is gained if dividing authority results in a feeble government. What was needed was an energetic and responsible government. The statesman who was perhaps most responsible for integrating separation of powers with checks and balances was James Madison, the father of the American Constitution. Madison believed that if partitioned authority is to result in an effective yet nontyrannical system, the two principles need to be integrated. In *The Federalist* No. 51 he observes:

> *But the great security against a gradual concentration of the*
> *several powers in the same department, consists in giving to*
> *those who administer each department the necessary*
> *constitutional means and personal motives to resist*
> *encroachments of the others. The provisions for defense must in*
> *this, as in all other cases, be made commensurate to the danger*
> *of attack. Ambition must be made to counteract ambition.*[3]

Madison thus believed that government must be framed so that it is forced to control itself. The only way to accomplish this was by modifying the doctrine of separation of powers so that the branches of government overlap each other. Power must be partitioned, but it must be separated so that the activities of any branch can be reviewed and checked by the other two.

Presidential and Parliamentary Democracies

Presidential Democracies   The origins of the presidential form of government are associated with the United States constitutional system established in 1789. Although the Founding Fathers did not deliberately seek to create a completely new alternative to the English parliamentary system, they did establish new institutions and practices that would eventually result in a radical new method of organizing the tasks of government. The term *presidential* was not originally used to denote the American governmental system but came into existence shortly before the Civil War. In *The English Constitution,* Walter Bagehot used the term to describe the American constitutional system to differentiate it from the British "cabinet" system. Subsequently, Woodrow Wilson criticized Bagehot's description of American government in his *Congressional Government,* and argued that the essential feature of American politics is the Congress, not the Presidency. Time, however, has vindicated Bagehot's analysis and not Wilson's.

The central feature of a presidential system is that it is based on the doctrine of separation of powers. As developed in the United States and copied by most Latin American countries, the three functions of government are carried out by different branches, each of which has its own specific duties and each of which is staffed by different officials. No person may serve in more than one branch at a particular time. Although legislative, executive, and judicial responsibilities are carried out by separate governmental institutions, some overlapping authority among the three areas of government is encouraged to facilitate the practice of checks and balances. In our review of the American political system in Chapter 10 we examine some of the ways by which this principle is applied in the United States. The most significant implementation of this principle is *judicial review,* the practice of a court declaring a law inconsistent with the constitution and therefore void.

Ordinarily, presidents and legislators are directly elected by the people, while justices are generally appointed and confirmed by the other two branches. Since both the chief executive and the legislators are elected directly by the people, their mandates and terms of office are independent of each other. In the United States, the President is elected for a four-year term, while members of the House of Representatives and the Senate are elected for two and four years, respectively. In Mexico, on the other hand, the president serves a six-year term, as do legislators of the upper house (Chamber of Senators). Legislators of Mexico's lower house (Chamber of Deputies) serve a three-year term. One of the interesting consequences of the dual basis of elections is that the executive and legislative branches may represent different political parties. Where legislatures are bicameral—i.e., where legislative responsibilities are shared by two different chambers—it is possible for three parties to share power, one controlling the executive and two others controlling each of the two legislative bodies.

Another significant feature of presidential systems is that the functions of chief of state and head of government are both performed by the president. The *chief-of-state* function is mostly symbolic and ceremonial; in parliamentary systems it is carried out by a figurehead monarch or elected president. The *head-of-government* function is concerned with the leadership of government, and in parliamentary systems this function is carried out by a premier or prime minister. In presidential systems, however, both of these functions are combined in one. The president wears two hats—one as ceremonial leader and the other as head of government. A president both rules and reigns.

When compared with the parliamentary system, presidential regimes have a number of strengths. One of these is their stability. Since the terms of the president and legislators are fixed, presidential systems tend to be more stable than parliamentary systems. In only the most extreme cases—such as impeachment—can legislators and presidents be forced out of office before their terms expire. A second strength is a close bond between the chief executive and the people. Since the president is elected directly by the people, the president acquires a direct mandate to lead and direct the nation. Moreover, once the president has been elected, he is better able to utilize the media to achieve his goals and objectives than is a prime minister. Third, the presidential system has the advantage of dual representation. Since the executive and the legislature are elected independently, both the president and the parliament provide independent representation of the popular will.

Presidential systems have two important weaknesses. First, since the executive and legislative branches can be controlled by different parties, the inability to reconcile goals and objectives can lead to governmental paralysis. Even if one party controls both branches, the fact that the president and the legislators have an independent mandate may result in irreconcilable differences. During the term of President Carter, for example, the Democratic party controlled both Congress and the Presidency, yet the inability to resolve differences between the two branches resulted in numerous deadlocks on major legislation. A second major weakness of the presidential regime is that the chief executive is unable to effectively lead and direct the work of the legislature. Since the president and the legislature have entirely separate functions, leadership of parliament must arise from the legislature itself. Unlike the parliamentary system, where the prime minister serves as leader of the parliament, the president has few opportunities to work with legislators in directing the enactment of legislation.

Parliamentary Democracies   Unlike the presidential system, which is largely an invention of the American Founding Fathers, parliamentary government was not created or invented but rather evolved out of a long, complex political history in England. The rise of the parliamentary system is associated with the gradual decline of the power of the monarch and the growth of influence of the parliament. Originally, English kings possessed virtually absolute power. But as wealthy lords and businessmen came to share increasing economic and social power, the influence of the monarch declined and was eventually eclipsed by the parliament. Since the Glorious Revolution of 1688, it has claimed supreme authority within Great Britain. The establishment of constitutional government was not achieved through a constitutional convention as in the United States but through an extended period of incremental evolution.

A central feature of parliamentary government is the supremacy of the parliament. Unlike presidential systems, which provide distinct governmental responsibilities to each of the three branches of government, parliamentary systems do not function in terms of separation of powers. Rather, legislative and executive responsibilities are fused together, with ultimate authority residing in the elected legislature. Executive authority, which ordinarily is in the hands of a cabinet headed by a premier or prime minister, derives from the parliament. After a new parliament has been assembled, the lower house of the legislature (e.g., the House of Commons in Britain, the Bundestag in West Germany, the Knesset in Israel) constitutes the government, i.e., selects the prime minister and the cabinet. Ordinarily, the prime minister and the cabinet are leaders of the majority party of Parliament and hold their executive posts as long as they can retain the confidence of the members of Parliament. Executive authority is therefore dependent upon continuing support from the lower House of Parliament. As a result, executive-legislative responsibilities are "fused," not separated as in presidential systems.

Classic parliamentary theory dictates that executive authority be in the hands of a cabinet, which shares decision-making power collegially. In the early phases of parliamentary development, the prime minister was not considered chief executive but chairman of a committee—the first among equals. Since executive authority was assumed to reside in the cabinet, decision making required complete public agreement among senior cabinet ministers. The need for public consensus among cabinet members is indicated by the doctrine of *collective responsibility,* which means that if cabinet members are unable to support publicly the decision of government they had to resign. Increasingly, however, modern cabinets have become less collegial. Since the prime minister establishes the agenda for cabinet meetings, leads and directs the work of government ministries, and decides when Parliament should be dissolved and new elections held, the prime minister clearly plays a dominant political role. Although cabinets play a far more significant role than do their presidential counterparts, their collegial nature has undoubtedly declined in modern parliamentary systems as the chief executive has come to play a more dominant role in countries like Britain, Sweden, and West Germany.

The term of a prime minister and his cabinet (commonly called "the government" in Britain) is dependent on the parliament. The prime minister gets his position by virtue of being leader of the majority party and is able to retain that position as long as he maintains the "confidence" of a majority of members of the legislature. When the prime minister's party can no longer command majority support, the chief executive must resign. Thus, unlike the president who serves a fixed term of office, a prime minister can lose his job in one of two ways: first, if the lower House of Parliament passes a vote of "no confidence" in the leadership of the executive, the prime minister must dissolve Parliament and resign; and second, a prime minister can be forced to resign if a major legislative program is defeated. The reason why a major legislative defeat can lead to the collapse of the executive is that failure to obtain legislative support is an indication that the government no longer has the necessary "strength" to govern.

When a parliament is dissolved, it is customary for the prime minister and cabinet to continue as an interim or caretaker government. After the parliamentary election, the party with the largest number of legislative seats is asked to form a government. If a single party commands majority control of the parliament (as has been the case in Britain), then it alone can select the prime minister and cabinet. On the other hand, if no party receives a majority of legislative seats (as is generally the case in multiparty systems such as Holland, Italy, and Israel), then two or more parties must form a *coalition,* or temporary political union, to provide the necessary parliamentary strength to govern. Since coalition governments require continued support from two or more parties, they tend to be more difficult to create and maintain than those where one party controls the parliament. The difficulty of creating coalition governments has been dramatically illustrated in the Netherlands, where in the early 1970s political parties bargained for more than six months in establishing an effective coalition. On the other hand, no country better illustrates the difficulties of establishing political stability through party coalitions than does Italy, a country whose governments during the postwar era averaged less than a year in duration.

The second important characteriestic of parliamentary government is that the leadership of the state and the leadership of the government are carried out by different officials. The *chief of state* may be a hereditary monarch, as in Belgium, Denmark, Holland, Norway, and Sweden, or may be an elected official, as in Israel, Italy, and West Germany. But whether the position is hereditary or elective, the function of the chief of state is essentially the same — to carry out symbolic and ceremonial functions representing the state and to ensure that there is a government that can rule society. As chief of state, the monarch or elected president appoints the prime miniter and cabinet, approves laws, receives ambassadors, officially calls for elections, opens Parliament, and ultimately has responsibility for protection and welfare of the nation. While the chief of state has no political authority, the figurehead executive function is not unimportant. One of the significant tasks of the chief of state is to encourage domestic consensus during periods of domestic turmoil and instability. During the Nazi occupation of the Netherlands, for example, Queen Wilhelmina played an important role in encouraging Dutch resistance. Although the Dutch government fell to occupying German forces, the Dutch monarch had escaped to England and continued to provide hope and leadership to her people through regular radio broadcasts.

The functions of *head of government* are carried out by a prime minister or premier (in the case of West Germany, a chancellor). As leader of the government, the prime minister has the responsibility for leading, guiding, and directing the nation. Whereas the chief of state is primarily concerned with the integrity of the nation-state, the head of the government is chiefly concerned with politics—with the making and implementing of decisions. As chief political executive, the prime minister must prepare legislation, develop new policy initiatives, direct the making and implementing of foreign policy, and help reconcile conflicting and competing interests. Since the ability to govern depends directly upon continued parliamentary support, one of the primary responsibilities of the prime minister is to ensure continued party support for the policies and programs of the executive.

One of the strengths of the parliamentary system is that it encourages a close union between the executive and the legislative branches. Unlike the presidential system, where prolonged conflict is tolerated, the life of a parliamentary government depends upon continuing legislative support. A positive result of this fusion of executive and legislative tasks is that the prime minister's programs are either supported by the legislature or the government is forced to resign. The prolonged executive-legislative tensions in the United States over Watergate would never have occurred in a parliamentary system. Once the irregularities had been discovered, the legislature would have investivated the alleged improprieties and made a quick determination on whether or not the chief executive could retain the confidence of the legislators. In 1974 the West German government experienced a comparable crisis when it was discovered that a close aid of Willy Brandt, the chancellor, had been a spy for the Communist government of the German Democratic Republic. Chancellor Brandt resigned immediately (unlike Mr. Nixon), and a new head of government was elected with ten days.

Another advantage of legislative-executive fusion is that it facilitates enactment of legislation. Legislative paralysis is far more difficult in parliamentary systems than in presidential regimes. For example, although the

United States needed a comprehensive energy program in the late 1970s, President Carter and Congress were unable to agree on a general energy conservation program. Under a parliamentary system, the inability of the executive to obtain legislative support for such a program would have resulted in the resignation of the cabinet and in new elections.

A second strength of the parliamentary system is that the chief-of-state and head-of-government functions are separated. Fusion of roles makes it impossible to criticize the head of government and his policies and programs without also criticizing the chief of state. In constitutional monarchies, it is customary to evaluate and critique the head of government but never the hereditary chief of state, who is assumed to be above politics. In presidential systems, however, the president's dual role of chief of state and head of the government makes it difficult to separate the two functions; the result is that challenges and criticisms made against the president not only call into question his political leadership but also his symbolic role as chief of state as well.

The chief weakness of the parliamentary system is the lack of stability of the government. Since the prime minister and cabinet can only function with ongoing support of the parliament, the close fusion of the executive and the legislature can lead to political instability when there is no clear parliamentary consensus. Unlike a presidential system, where the president and legislators serve for fixed terms, cabinets and members of parliaments serve for variable terms, depending in great measure on the capacity to establish harmonious executive-legislative ties.

More than two-thirds of the countries of the world have organized their governmental institutions according to the parliamentary model (Table 6.1). The popularity of parliamentarianism derives largely from the colonial tutelage of European states in Asia and Africa. Most developing countries have established constitutional structures that they received from the European parliamentary systems. The Western Hemisphere, by contrast, is dominated by presidential structures. Most Latin American countries became independent in the early nineteenth century and were deeply influenced by principles of government adopted previously by the United States.

The French System   The French political system is of interest because it is a hybrid of parliamentary and presidential structures. Under the Third and Fourth Republics, France had functioned as a parliamentary system but had experienced much governmental instability because of the inability to develop political consensus. The French people were deeply divided over fundamental issues, and the deep cleavages among political parties made it difficult to achieve compromise and conciliation within the legislature. The result was governmental paralysis. In 1958 under the leadership of Charles de Gaulle, the French adopted a new constitution, bringing an end to the instability of the Fourth Republic. The major changes in the new constitution of the Fifth

TABLE 6.1 Formal Organization of Government of Selected Nations

COUNTRY	HEAD OF STATE	HEAD OF GOVERNMENT
Presidential Systems		
Argentina	President	President
Colombia	President	President
Ecuador	President	President
Kenya	President	President
Ivory Coast	President	President
Mexico	President	President
Nicaragua	President	President
United States	President	President
Venezuela	President	President
Parliamentary Systems		
Bahamas	Governor-General*	Prime Minister
Belgium	Monarch	Prime Minister
Canada	Governor-General*	Prime Minister
Federal Rep. of Germany	President	Chancellor
Finland	President	Prime Minister
Jamaica	Governor-General*	Prime Minister
Japan	Emperor	Prime Minister
Israel	President	Prime Minister
Netherlands	Monarch	Prime Minister
Norway	Monarch	Prime Minister
Sweden	Monarch	Prime Minister
Turkey	President	Prime Minister

*Acts as a representative of the British Crown.

Republic provide the president with increased authority and greater limitations are placed on the power of the National Assembly (lower house). The French system retains a significant fusion of executive and legislative functions but shifts authority from the National Assembly to the president.

When compared with presidential and parliamentary systems, the French governmental system maintains partial fusion of executive and legislative branches found in parliamentary systems and fusion of symbolic and governmental functions of the presidential executive. The fusion of executive and legislative functions is maintained in part by making the premier and his ministers accountable to the National Assembly, the 490-member national legislative chamber. According to the Constitution, the Assembly has the right to censure the premier and can thus force his resignation, requiring the president to replace him or call for new elections. To counterbalance the parliament's authority to challenge the premier, the president has the power to dissolve the Assembly and call for new elections. The president can only dissolve the Assembly once within a 12-month period.

Despite the partial resemblance of the French system to other parliamentary systems, the French structure of government is similar to presidential systems in its fusion of head-of-government and chief-of-state functions in one office. Unlike parliamentary systems, the president of Franch is both chief of state and head of government and as such, has many of the same responsibilities and tasks of the presidential chief executive. Unlike a presidential executive, he chooses the premier and cabinet ministers to carry out his governmental programs and policies. When the premier is unwilling or unable to serve the president, as was the case with Premier Jacques Chirac in President Giscard d'Estaing's administration, then he must resign and allow the president to appoint a political leader who can more effectively carry out his goals and objectives. The French premier is therefore not the head of government as in the parliamentary systems of Britain and Holland but a figurehead political leader through whom the president can carry out his policies. The real prime minister is the president.

The significant position of the president in the French political system derives from two sources. First, the president is elected in a national election for a seven-year term. Like the American president, the French chief executive is elected in a popular election and thus receives a direct mandate from the people—a mandate that allows him to challenge and act independently of the national legislature. Second, the French Constitution provides the president with broad powers, some of which are not even granted to chief executives in presidential systems. Two of the most significant powers are the right to refer government legislation directly to the people and thus bypass a hostile legislature and the right to declare a state of emergency. The intent of the first constitutional provision is to give the chief executive the privilege to amend the Constitution through a national referendum. Charles de Gaulle used this procedure twice: to change the selection of the president from indirect to direct election, and to increase the power of regional governments and thereby alter the role of the French Senate. When this last constitutional amendment was defeated in 1969, de Gaulle interpreted the referendum as a defeat of his own leadership and resigned. The second presidential power is based on Article 16, which provides that in case of a threat to the integrity of the French state, the president may assume emergency powers. This was done in 1961 in the face of an imminent military coup by army officials in Algeria.

Although no other country has fashioned its governmental institutions after the political system of the French Fifth Republic, the "hybrid" system is significant because it seeks to combine the strength and independence of the presidential executive with the partial fusion of powers of parliamentary systems. Some of the major elements of the French system are compared diagrammatically with those of presidential and parliamentary systems in Figure 6.1

Figure 6.1 Comparison of Presidential, Parliamentary, and Hybrid Government Structures

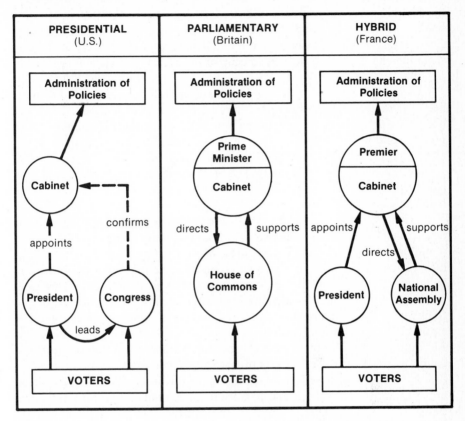

LEGISLATURES

Most political systems have parliaments, congresses, or other similar assemblies that participate in the management and resolution of national conflict. In 1970, Blondel estimated that 108 nations had national legislatures.[4] Although each of these collective bodies differs in terms of its role and function in its respective political system, in most countries legislatures play a significant role in making rules and in giving legitimacy (and therefore authority) to governmental decision-making process.

Structural Features

Legislatures can be either one-chamber (unicameral) or two-chamber (bicameral) assemblies. Of the 108 national legislatures in 1970, more than one-half (56) were unicameral. As a general rule, such legislatures are found in small states; bicameral assemblies are found in large nations, where dual representation can strengthen the relationship of the central government to the subnational units of government.

Although the development of bicameral legislatures is associated with the need for representing aristocratic interests, only a small number of "upper" houses are designed to represent such interests. Where upper chambers seek to preserve and protect the values of the aristocratic elite, membership is generally based on heredity or executive appointment (as is the case in Canada, Jordan, Barbados, and Trinidad). The most significant example of an aristocratic upper chamber is the British House of Lords, a body of some 1,150 hereditary and life peers.

The two major justifications for having dual legislative chambers is the desire to ensure constitutional democracy and the requirement for dual representation imposed by federal structures. Most developed competitive democracies have bicameral legislatures to strengthen the principle of checks and balances. Notable parliamentary democracies without dual chambers are Denmark, Finland, Iceland, Sweden, and Norway. The primary argument for two chambers is that it can strengthen representation of popular interests and can ensure that actions of the legislature are not the result of a capricious majority. Although the establishment of the American bicameral legislature grew of a compromise between the interests of large and small states, a common justification for a two-chamber legislature during the ratification debates was that an upper chamber could check and balance the irrational and tyrannical tendencies of the lower chamber. Moreover, some of the Founding Fathers thought that the most powerful branch of government would be the legislature and that an internal regulatory system (such as bicameral checks and balances) could ensure that legislative power would not become excessive. Defenders of democratic government point out that, while bicameralism may strengthen the tradition of limited, constitutional government, single-chamber legislatures tend to be more democratic insofar as they do not have an upper chamber whose representatives are selected indirectly by subunits of governments or appointed by the chief executive.

The second major justification for bicameral legislatures is federalism. As one might expect, virtually all federal systems have bicameral legislatures. The lower chamber directly represents popular interests, and the upper chamber represents subnational territories. As a general rule, the selection of legislators to the upper chamber is carried out by provinces and states of a country. Some federal systems, such as those of Argentina, Brazil, Switzerland, and the

United States, provide that each of the subunits (cantons, provinces, and states) have equal representation. Other federal systems, such as those of the Soviet Union and West Germany, provide for variable representation based on the size of the republic (USSR) or state (West Germany). In the Soviet system, each Union Republic is allowed thirty-two delegates, Autonomous Republics eleven, and Autonomous Regions five. West German states may have from three to five representatives in the *Bundesrat*.

Legislatures vary significantly in size. One of the smallest is the Diet of Liechtenstein (15 members). Without a doubt the largest assembly is the National People's Congress of the People's Republic of China, which at its Fifth Congress in 1978 had 3,500 delegates. Technically, however the Chinese Congress cannot be called a legislative assembly because it is not an institutionalized, ongoing assembly. The largest, established lower legislative chambers include the Soviet of Unions of the USSR with 767 members, the Italian Chamber of Deputies with 630, the British House of Commons with 630, and the West German *Bundestag* with 518.

Table 6.2 provides the average size of legislative constituencies for lower houses. In most countries there is substantial variation among the size of the legislative districts. In some cases this variation is planned, but in others it results from demographic changes. In the United States, congressional districts may vary by as much as 50,000 people, even though redistricting according to the "one man, one vote" principle occurs every ten years. Ideally, legislators should have to represent relatively small constituencies, such as those found in the principality of Liechtenstein, Iceland, or even in some of the Western parliamentary systems (average constituency is less than 100,000). When a legislator is responsible for constituencies of more than 250,000, representation of all interests becomes difficult. This is the case in India, where a typical legislator of the lower house has responsibility for more than one million persons.

Functions of Legislatures

Making Laws　　The most significant task performed by parliaments is making laws. Legislatures share this function with the executive, but the extent to which the latter is involved in enacting legislation depends upon the formal structure of government and the effective influence of the officials in each of the two branches of government. In parliamentary systems, legislatures play a *law-assenting,* rather than a law-making, role. Since prime ministers and cabinets are expected to lead and direct the work of parliaments, most bills are prepared, introduced, and guided through the maze of legislative deliberations by a government minister. In Britain and West Germany, for example, virtually all significant legislation is initiated and directed by the cabinet. The task of

TABLE 6.2   Legislatures of Selected States

COUNTRY	UPPER HOUSE	LOWER HOUSE	AVERAGE SIZE OF CONSTITUENCY[a]
Australia	Senate (64)	House of Representatives (124)	113,700
Belgium	Senate (106)	House of Representatives (212)	47,170
Brazil	Senate (67)	Chamber of Deputies (420)	278,700
Canada	Senate (104)	House of Commons (264)	90,150
Costa Rica	———	Legislative Assembly (57)	37,800
Denmark	———	Folketing (179)	28,575
German, Fed. Rep.[b]	Bundesrat (45)	Bundestag (518)	117,160
Iceland	———	Althing (60)	3,783
India	Council of States (243)	House of People (525)	1,233,980
Italy	Senate (315)	Chamber of Deputies (630)	91,100
Japan	House of Councillors (252)	House of Representatives (511)	225,650
Jordan[c]	Council of Notables (30)	House of Deputies (60)	———
Liechtenstein	———	Diet (15)	1,466
Netherlands	1st Chamber of States-General (75)	2nd Chamber of States-General (150)	94,130
Sweden	———	Riksdag (349)	23,815
Switzerland	Council of States (44)	National Council (200)	31,910
U.S.S.R.	Soviet of Nationalities (750)	Soviet of Unions (767)	335,075
United States	Senate (100)	House of Representatives 435	496,550

Source: Arthur S. Banks, Political Handbook of the World: 1979 *(New York: McGraw-Hill, 1979), passim.*

[a]The size of constituencies was determined by dividing the number of seats in the lower chamber by the total estimated population for 1979.

[b]Of the 518 seats in the Bundestag, 22 are from West Berlin, and those legislators can participate in procedural issues only.

[c]Jordan's lower house was dissolved in 1974.

the popular assembly (more particularly, of the majority party) is to support the initiatives of the government. In short, law making is primarily a cabinet function in parliamentary systems. On the other hand, failure to support legislative initiatives of the cabinet can result in dissolution of the parliament. Thus, effective authority for making laws and rules resides in the legislature, from which the cabinet derives its legitimacy.

Legislatures play a more significant role in enacting laws in presidential systems. Since the authority of the congresses is derived independently from that of the executive, the legislature has a central role in preparing laws for a nation. To be sure, in virtually all competitive presidential systems the assent of the chief executive is required before a bill can become a law. Moreover, presidential executives generally initiate most major legislation. But once introduced, the role of the legislature is far more significant in refining, amending, and reformulating bills.

Nowhere is this legislative *law-making* role illustrated more dramatically than in the United States, where both the Senate and the House of Representatives play the dominant role in enacting laws. Not only do legislators modify and substantially alter bills prepared by the presidential executive, but legislators themselves initiate (on behalf of their own constituencies) bills of a more limited scope. These private bills, which generally far outnumber public bills introduced by the government, are more common in presidential systems than in parliamentary systems. In the United States an average of more than 10,000 bills are initiated per year, of which all but 250 are private bills. (In the United Kingdom, on the other hand, more than three-fourths of all bills are initiated by the government.[5])

The importance of legislatures in making laws derives from their representative character. Making rules, decrees, and laws is not difficult; what is difficult is to make rules that, when enacted, will be widely obeyed. A dictator can rule by decree, but if people are to comply with such decrees he must use coercion to ensure compliance. On the other hand, if representative assemblies enact laws, the vast majority of people accept and obey such regulations because they accept the decision-making process as legitimate. Thus, because of their representativeness, legislatures are acceptable conflict-management institutions and possess the authority to make laws that are recognized as binding on the people.

In most bicameral legislatures, enactment of laws requires the consent of both chambers. If membership in the upper house is not carried out by direct election, the legislative authority of this chamber is often reduced. This is commonly the case in parliamentary systems where the upper house serves more aristocratic interests. In Britain, India, Ireland, and South Africa, for example, the upper house has the authority to delay significant legislation (i.e., money bills) but not to veto them. Similarly, when the French Senate and National Assembly cannot resolve an incompatibility on a bill, the National Assembly can make the final decision. In presidential systems, both upper and lower houses generally have the same law-making authority; when different bills are passed by each chamber, a compromise needs to be established. Failure to do so results in the defeat of a bill.

Representation   A second major function of legislatures is the representation of popular interests in government. Since legislatures are elected collective assemblies, they are better representative institutions than is the executive. Given the pluralistic nature of society, legislatures are better equipped to represent the many competing and conflicting concerns of people. From a democratic perspective, legislatures represent different interests in society and then seek to generate harmony from those competing and conflicting concerns.

In order for a legislature to develop a policy or approve a bill, it needs at least the support of a majority of its members. Ordinarily, however, this consensus needs to be generated through a process of compromise and bargaining. When compromise and bargaining become unacceptable, the process of conflict resolution becomes difficult, if not impossible. Legislatures, in short, provide a chamber for developing harmony out of competing interests in society. Every bill approved by the legislature can thus be viewed as a successful effort in conflict management.

To facilitate the conflict-resolution process, parliaments are organized structurally in terms of committees and politically in terms of party affiliation. Most legislatures have specialized committees and subcommittees to carry out preliminary investigations before proposals are brought to the full assembly. In the United States, for example, most scrutiny of legislation is carried out by specialized committees. Failure of a committee to act favorably on a bill automatically results in its defeat. Committees thus facilitate the conflict-management process by dealing with problems in small, specialized organizations.

The second method by which parliaments are organized is in terms of party affiliation or political orientation. In Britain, for example, the House of Commons is divided into the government party (Her Majesty's Loyal Government) and the opposition party (Her Majesty's Loyal Opposition). In France, on the other hand, members of the National Assembly are grouped into parties organized from the political left to the political right. The role that political parties play in managing and resolving conflict within legislatures is determined in great measure by their number and strength. Legislatures controlled by two parties (as in Great Britain or the United States) are able to manage conflict much easier than are multiparty systems like Holland and Italy. In addition, the cohesion and organizational strength of parties is also important in facilitating conflict resolution. As a general rule, the development of party discipline tends to encourage bloc voting among party legislators. This cohesion in turn tends to facilitate bargaining and ultimately compromise among the dominant party interests within the legislature.

In some countries, legislatures play a relatively insignificant role in the management and resolution of conflict. This situation most likely occurs in political systems dominated by one political party, as in China, Cuba, and the Soviet Union. In such countries, there is no competition between parties, and conflict within the party is seldom discussed openly. Legislatures in communist systems therefore do not effectively represent interests; rather, they serve to support and approve the work of the executive. Conflict management by legislatures is also limited in states where political parties are weak or nonexistent. In developing countries, legislatures play a relatively insignificant role because of dominance of the executive and also because legislatures are themselves not well organized. Thus, political systems with one or no political parties seldom have legislatures that manage conflict effectively. The most common result in such institutions is avoidance of politics altogether in the search for a quick consensus.

There are two ancillary issues relating to political representation that need to be briefly examined. The first deals with the role of a legislator and the second, the impact of electoral systems.

A. Legislative Roles. One of the age-old questions of democratic theory is how a legislator should perform his duties once elected. One school of thought assumes that a legislator should serve as a trustee, i.e., as an independent agent seeking to maximize the welfare of the nation irrespective of the particular interests of the legislator's constituency. When a legislator acts as a trustee, he does not seek to represent the preferences of his constituency but rather to act in their behalf in the best possible manner. To do this, the legislator depends on his own ideals, concerns, and conscience. The most eloquent defense of this position is given by the famous British statesman Edmund Burke. In 1774 he wrote a letter to the voters of Bristol, the district he represented in the House of Commons, and said:

> *Parliament is not a congress of ambassadors from different and hostile interests; which interests each must maintain, as an agent, and advocate against other agents and advocates; but Parliament is a deliberate assembly of one nation, with one interest, that of the whole; where, not local purposes, not local prejudices, ought to guide, but the general good, resulting from the general reason of the whole. You choose a member indeed: but when you have chosen him, he is not a member of Bristol, but he is a member of Parliament. If the local constituent should have an interest, or should form a hasty opinion, evidently opposite to the real good of the rest of the community, the member for that place ought to be as far as any other from any endeavor to give it effect.*[6]

There are a number of difficulties with the trustee perspective, not the least of which is that legislators need to act responsibly if they are to be reelected. A legislator may wish to disregard the sentiments of his own people; if he does so regularly, the chances that he will be supported in the next election are substantially diminished.

At the opposite extreme is the view that legislators should be "ambassadors" from their districts. According to this perspective, legislators should act as messengers, voting in accordance with the interests of the district's constituents. They should not seek to apply their own values and principles or to direct public opinion toward their own goals; rather, the legislator should reflect the views and interests of the constituency. The problem with this approach is that it assumes that the people are informed about major issues on which a legislator must vote, that they are sufficiently interested in public policy issues to communicate their views to him, and that the people are in sufficient agreement regarding the proper course of action. Generally, the average adult is not well informed about public affairs and seldom communicates with his legislator. When people are interested and informed, the result is often a pluralistic distribution of public opinion. Seldom do all constituents agree on what the government should do. As a result, even if a legislator wanted to carry out his representative function as an ambassador, he would find the task impossible.

In practice, most legislators are partly trustees and partly messengers. On the one hand, they seek to bring their own values and interests to bear on their legislative work; on the other hand, they seek to determine the particular concerns of their district and to represent those concerns in the legislature.

B. Electoral Systems. The two most common methods for selecting legislators are through territorial and proportional systems of representation. The most common type of *territorial representation* is the *single-member district (SMD)*, which involves the selection of one legislator per legislative district on the basis of an election plurality. Used in Britain and the United States, the SMD electoral system has the advantage of being simple and easy to use. One major limitation is that it does not ensure that the proportion of the popular vote will result in a comparable proportion of the legislature's seats. For example, in 1945 the British Labor Party received 48 percent of the vote but received more than 61 percent of the seats. As a general rule, the selection of legislatures on the basis of plurality voting in SMD results in an average imbalance between votes and seats of at least four or five percent. A second major disadvantage of the SMD system is that it discriminates against third parties. Since the only parties likely to be successful are large and well organized, political parties that enjoy less than 20 percent support have difficulty obtaining representation in the legislature, unless all its supporters are concentrated in a few districts. In the 1979 parliamentary elections, for example, the British Liberal Party received close to 14 percent of the national vote but less than 2 percent of the seats in the House of Commons.

To rectify the problems with territorial systems, some countries have adopted *proportional representation*. The main idea of proportional systems is to ensure that the number of legislative seats and the party's popular vote are approximately the same proportion. The two most common forms of proportional representation are the party-list system and the single-transferable vote system. The first is designed for political systems where the role of individual legislators is relatively insignificant but where the party organization is of critical importance. The second is designed to give voters greater control over the selection of legislators while also ensuring proportional representation for the party. Of the two systems, the party list is the most common and is used in such parliamentary systems as Belgium, Finland, Holland, Israel, Norway, and Sweden. Although proportional representation may be considered more democratic insofar as people's party preferences are more accurately represented in the legislature, the system has the disadvantage of weakening ties between legislators and the people. Since legislators do not represent districts but party concerns, there is no representation of special territorial concerns. A further liability of proportional systems is that they are complex and difficult to comprehend.

Forming, Maintaining, and Supervising the Executive   The last major function of parliaments concerns executive-legislative relationships. In parliamentary systems, the lower house has the responsibility for making and maintaining the government. Since the prime minister and cabinet hold office by virtue of majority control, legislatures play an enormously significant role in providing political support required for the government to rule. In presidential systems, the authority of the executive does not derive from the legislature but from the people themselves. As a result, legislatures in presidential systems can oppose and defeat policy proposals but they cannot defeat the executive. As Wheare observes of presidential legislatures, "they can defeat the government without destroying it."[7]

One function that both parliamentary and presidential assemblies share is their supervision of the executive and its bureaucratic agencies. Oversight of the executive can be carried out in one of two ways: by directly questioning and investigating the work of each of the government ministries within a full plenary legislative session or by delegating the oversight function to specialized committees. The first method is generally used in parliamentary systems and the second in presidential systems. Oversight of cabinet ministries is perhaps best institutionalized in Great Britain, where three to four times a week a question period is set aside in the House of Commons to allow its members to ask questions concerning operations of the ministries. Through this device the legislature continually checks on the executive and ensures that there is continuing confidence in each of the ministries. It is estimated that between 75,000 to 100,000 written and oral questions are put to the British government every year.

In presidential systems the investigatory and supervisory functions are carried out by specialized committees. Such committees are perhaps most developed in the United States. Since Congress appropriates all funds, each of the cabinet members and their respective assistants are continually defending, explaining, and justifying their programs. In addition, committees frequently investigate alleged improprieties within the bureaucracy or the executive itself. The Watergate hearings, for example, were carried out by the Senate Judiciary Committee and ultimately led to the resignation of President Nixon.

EXECUTIVES

With the exception of some competitive parliamentary systems, the executive branch of government clearly dominates the legislative branch in most countries. Indeed, many states do not even have a legislature because the executive has suspended its function. In others, legislatures may exist, as in some communist states or Latin American presidential systems, but may have a limited impact on the decisions taken by the government.

Nature of the Executive

Governmental executives differ significantly among the nations of the world. Three major differences may be observed:

1. Executives can be distinguished in terms of their effective political role in the state. In some states, the legal chief executive is a figurehead leader through whom another person rules. In other words, the executive power of a state does not reside with the formally elected or appointed chief executive but with another leader. This condition has occurred frequently in Latin America where strong, charismatic *caudillos* have placed puppet presidents in power to give the illusion of democratic politics. Omar Torrijos, head of the Panamanian national guard forces, decided to give up (formally) his title as head of the Panamanian government in 1978; nonetheless, he continued to hold ultimate political authority even after the nation had elected a new president. This situation was also evident in Iran following the fall of the dictatorial regime of the Shah in 1979. Although a president was elected and numerous prime ministers were appointed, effective political power remained in the hands of one religious leader—the Ayatollah Khomeini.

    In most countries where figurehead and political executives are two different individuals, the distinction between the real and the symbolic authority of the state is formally explicit. In parliamentary systems, for example, the figurehead chief of state performs only symbolic and ceremonial functions and has no political power to carry out executive policies and programs. In such systems, the figurehead duties are ordinarily performed by an elected president or a hereditary monarch. The presidents of parliamentary systems such as in Cuba, India, Israel, and Italy, have relatively limited influence on the decisions of the state. Effective executive authority lies in the prime minister or premier who carries out the leadership of the government.

2. Executives can be distinguished in terms of their levels of competitiveness. A competitive or limited executive is one who: (a) is elected directly or indirectly by the people through free and competitive elections; (b) serves for a limited tenure; (c) abides by constitutional limitations imposed on his office; and (d) preserves fundamental constitutional rules without seeking to change them to his advantage. A noncompetitive or authoritarian executive, by contrast, has the opposite characteristics: (a) the executive comes to power without free, competitive elections; (b) the government restricts the freedom to oppose the executive and uses coercion to impose its decisions on the people; and (c) the executive does not hesitate to alter fundamental constitutional rules either to expand its own influence or to control individuals. In most cases the differences between competitive and noncompetitive executives are not found in constitutional provisions of the state but in the manner in which executives rule.

3. Finally, executives can be distinguished in terms of their size. By far the most common type is the single executive, i.e., a government where one individual holds ultimate executive authority. In presidential systems this person is the president; in parliamentary systems this official is the premier or prime minister; and in authoritarian systems, the chief executive is the dictator, military ruler, or party chief.

The other, less common type of leadership is the collective executive. To the extent that executive authority is shared collectively by all members of the senior cabinet in constitutional parliamentary systems, countries such as Britain and Holland may be considered as having collective executives. Another type of government that can be considered a collective executive is the military *junta* (a group of military officers sharing executive authority). The most recent military coups in Latin America have been carried out by the combined efforts of the armed forces. After civilian officials have been removed from office, the leaders of each of the different branches of the military form a collective executive. In most cases, however, one military ruler eventually becomes chief of the group and tends to dominate the decision-making process.

The collegial executive is a type of leadership that is most developed in Switzerland. In the Swiss political system, executive authority resides in a seven-member Federal Council elected jointly by the bicameral legislature for a four-year term. The Council elects a president and a vice-president, who replaces the president after he has completed one year as chairman of the Council. The president serves as symbolic head of state and has responsibility for chairing the work of the Council. Uruguay copied the Swiss collegial system in 1951 but reverted to the single executive in 1967.

Functions of the Executive

Political executives perform at least five major tasks: First, they are the primary institutions responsible for the symbolic and ceremonial functions of state. All nations are held together by a common heritage, a national identity (nationalism), and common goals and aspirations that make people prefer their own nation to others. These predispositions to live with one's own people are commonly expressed through symbols such as a flag, national anthem, and the pledge of allegiance to the state. Virtually all states have one official who serves as the ultimate symbol of the state. In presidential systems the chief of state is the president, who also serves as head of government; in parliamentary systems that task is carried out by a hereditary monarch or elected official whose sole function is to be symbolic leader of a country.

Second, political executives are responsible for leadership of the country. Like the chief executive of a business corporation, the political executive is responsible for setting goals and priorities for the nation and for determining the role of the government in achieving those goals. Since the government plays a dominant role in the lives of most people, the chief executive must decide how and to what extent the government should be involved in the various aspects of society. In the United States, for example, the president annually prepares the budget, which is then turned over to Congress for it to modify, alter, and eventually approve. The initiation of the goal-setting process is in the hands of the executive, although in democratic systems approval by the legislature is required before funds may be allocated and programs implemented.

Third, executives are responsible for managing the bureaucracy. The bureaucracy, or civil service, is the group of career employees within the government who support the implementation of programs established by the executive and the legislature. Unlike political executives, who are concerned with the highly conflictual process of policy making, the task of the bureaucracy is to apply rules and to implement policies and programs. (Bureaucrats are considered to be apolitical in that they are not formally involved in making public decisions.) Since the executive is responsible for carrying out the laws of the state, presidents, prime ministers, and their supporting cabinets must coordinate the work of many ministries, agencies, bureaus, and commissions of government and maintain political control over their staffs. Only through continued control and supervision can the political executive ensure that its bureaucratic apparatus is responsive to the political will of government.

Fourth, executives are responsible for managing conflict. Since no political system is completely harmonious, the executive must preserve order within the nation. Political executives perform two major conflict-management tasks. First, they help ensure a stable and orderly society through effective enforcement of laws. Every state holds a monopoly of force by which it can effectively punish those who seek to threaten the laws and institutions of government. The second and more important method by which executives manage conflict is by developing consensus. Since force is a relatively inefficient method of ensuring order, executives tend to establish domestic harmony by seeking to build a consensual public opinion. Some of the ways by which chief executives do this are: (1) by seeking to regulate the media and influence the political education of children and adults; (2) by directing the attention of the public away from domestic problems and conflicts toward international concerns over which there is substantial agreement; and (3) by tending to develop policies and programs that satisfy significant elite groups within society.

Finally, political executives are responsible for carrying out the foreign policies of the state and for protecting the nation from possible foreign aggression. The chief executive is thus the chief diplomat and the commander-in-chief of the nation. Although these responsibilities are partly shared with legislatures in democratic systems, the initiation and implementation of foreign policy is largely in the hands of the president or prime minister. Similarly, the decision of whether or not to go to war is ordinarily in the hands of the legislature in competitive states. But the chief executive is responsible for ensuring that the nation is adequately prepared to defend itself from external aggression or internal subversion. Once a major conflict develops, the chief executive serves as ultimate decision maker in directing the use of military force.

THE JUDICIARY

The major purpose of courts is to resolve social and political conflicts publicly. Every day thousands of tensions, incompatibilities, and conflicts occur in society. Most of these are not serious and therefore have no impact on the level of stability and social harmony within a community. Of the potentially serious conflicts, many of these are resolved by the parties themselves or by an intermediary. One common way to resolve labor-management disputes is to use a mediator or arbiter who can facilitate compromise between the two parties. Resorting to third parties to settle private disputes is an entirely voluntary process.

Courts and Conflict Resolution

To facilitate the resolution of conflict, most political systems have established public courts by which government can render a binding decision on both public and private disputes. The major differences between private mediation and public action of courts are: court officials (judges) are government appointed and resolve disputes by applying laws passed by the government; and one or both parties in conflict can be forced to settle disputes through the court. Conflict resolution by judges thus differs from private mediation in that government action is not voluntary and the method for resolving disputes depends not only upon reconciliation of the private interests of the parties but also upon application of the interests of society as expressed in its laws.

From the standpoint of conflict management, *laws* are general rules passed by legislatures to develop consensus and social harmony. Laws direct human behavior by prohibiting or commanding certain types of actions. The function of the judge is to impartially interpret and apply appropriate laws to resolve a dispute between private parties or one involving the government itself. Since judges have substantial discretionary authority, democratic countries try to develop elaborate procedures to ensure that judges are competent to apply and interpret laws and that they remain immune from political pressures. Maintaining an independent judiciary is particularly difficult, since judges are often appointed by the executive and can be pressured or disregarded by the more powerful and influential executive.

In many developing and noncompetitive systems, courts are either nonexistent or serve as instruments of the executive. Only in developed democratic countries do courts have the political strength and independence to challenge the legality and constitutionality of actions of government officials and to ensure that law-enforcement officials do not abuse the legitimate rights of the people.

Although it is recognized that courts function most effectively if they are entirely independent from political executives, it is equally recognized that the application and enforcement of the law is the responsibility of the executive branch. As a result, most executives have elaborate bureaucracies for apprehending and prosecuting persons who violate the law. In the United States, the Attorney General is responsible for prosecuting those who violate federal laws, while each state has its own attorney general to ensure compliance with state statutes. When persons violate national or state laws, they are sought and apprehended by law-enforcement agents; if evidence is sufficient, they are charged (indicted) with a criminal act and brought to court to determine their guilt or innocence. Unlike civil proceedings, where the plaintiff is normally a private party, in criminal cases the accusing party is always the government. A government prosecutor presents evidence in an impartial court to obtain the conviction and punishment of a criminal.

Court procedures and organization vary significantly among countries. Two of the dominant judicial systems are the Anglo-American approach of common law and the European approach of civil law. The Anglo-American approach views the court as an impartial battleground where the judge's primary task is to maintain order and direct the deliberations of the court. His chief responsibility is to ensure "due process." The decision of whether crimes have been committed or not is in the hands of an impartial jury—a group of men and women who listen to the court proceedings and then issue a verdict on the case. The continental approach differs from the Anglo-American in that the judge plays a far more significant role in the court's decision. Instead of using a jury to convict a criminal, the judge himself hears the evidence and then determines the guilt or innocence of a party based upon his understanding of the law.

The different roles that judges play in Europe and in the United States and Great Britain derive in great measure from differences in legal systems. The system of law in Britain, the United States, and most English-speaking countries is called common law. Common law is essentially judge-made law, i.e., the interpretation and application of law is based on previous decisions of judges.[8] For example, when a judge hears a case, he determines the relevancy of previous cases and then applies the judicial precedents he believes have a bearing on the specific dispute at hand. Common law is flexible and adapts to changing conditions; it provides the judge with much discretionary authority in the manner in which he applies it in his judgments.

Civil law, by contrast, is based on Roman law and is generally far more explicit and rigid. Unlike common law, civil law is codified, and the task of the judge is to apply the written law to cases. Little discretionary authority is allowed to judges in applying the law. When civil codes must be interpreted and explained, the task is left more to teachers than to judges. The responsibility of the judge is not to make or even find the law. His task is to apply the statutes with legal precision and with little or no concern for precedents or general principles of equity.

Functions of Courts

1. The primary task of courts is to *settle disputes*. Unlike compromise, which is essentially a political process, courts resolve conflicts by applying the law. Whether the conflict is between two private parties or between the government and an individual or group, the task of the judge is to apply and interpret society's laws to resolve the conflict.

   Two major types of conflicts are brought to courts: civil disputes and criminal disputes. The first type normally involves a private dispute in which the general interests of society are not at stake. For example, such conflicts may include a property settlement between two neighbors, the settling of a divorce case, or the determination of guilt or innocence of a physician in a malpractice suit. Criminal cases, by contrast, involve crimes against the entire society—i.e., they involve violations of national laws designed to protect the general interests of society as distinct from the private interests of individuals. Examples of such crimes include gambling, printing counterfeit money, arson, homicides, kidnapping, etc. Since every society has laws designed to protect its people from crimes such as these, when such laws are violated a conflict develops between the government, the agent for society, and the individuals committing the crime. Whereas private parties generally bring civil disputes to court, criminal cases are always brought to court by the state.

2. Another major function of courts is to *interpret the law*. This responsibility falls most heavily on judges in common law countries, although no state has a legal system so clear and precise that it does not require some interpretation periodically. Even in civil law countries, judges must ascertain the meaning of the codes and then apply them to the cases. Ideally, laws should be written as clearly as possible, but no group of lawmakers can write rules that are always relevant to the changing circumstances of life. Inevitably, questions arise about the meaning and purpose of laws, and the task of the judge is to apply the partly imperfect or imprecise rules to the changing needs of society. This interpretive function, called *adjudication,* is significant not only because the law is applied to changing conditions in society but also because judicial interpretations themselves have a binding effect on common-law societies.

3. Another closely related function of the judiciary is to *determine the law*. Courts do not make law; that is the function of legislatures. But since they interpret the law, they can establish what the law is. The task of determining the law is primarily found in common law countries. In civil law countries the task of the judge is to apply the written codes rigidly, regardless of how changing circumstances affect the original goals and purposes of the legislation. Perhaps the most extreme expression of judicial authority in "finding" the law is in those countries that practice judicial review. Judicial review is the action of a court in declaring a law unconstitutional when it is inconsistent with the fundamental constitutional rules of a country. Such a practice can only occur in countries with separation of powers, for only in those states do courts have the authority to contravene the combined action of the legislature and the executive.

THE BUREAUCRACY

Prior to the twentieth century, political theorists generally thought that there were three major branches of government — the legislative, the executive, and the judiciary. The growth and expansion of the government in the modern, industrial state, however, engendered another area of government that exerts an enormous, independent influence on the course of public policy. This new branch of government is the bureaucracy, or what has traditionally been called the "administration," or civil service.

Nature of the Bureaucracy

The bureaucracy may be defined as those institutions and personnel responsible for implementation of policies and programs established by the government. As defined by the German sociologist Max Weber in the nineteenth century, bureaucracy refers to modern, efficient, and well-organized public institutions that carry out the goals and objectives of the government.

Weber considered a modern civil service (or administration) so important that it was impossible to conceive of a modern state without a bureaucracy. Indeed, the chief characteristic of the modern state (as distinguished from a feudal or patrimonial state) is that it has institutions that rationally allocate human resources and direct human energies toward defined objectives.[9]

If bureaucracy is chiefly a creation of the modern state, the role of civil servants is associated with the history of the state. The ancient Assyrian, Babylonian, and Egyptian empires each had organizations to carry out the king's wishes and commands, whether it was organizing for war, collecting taxes, developing irrigation systems, or carrying out trade with other political groups. The Roman Empire had an enormously well-organized administration by which the emperor could maintain control over his subjects and direct the actions of his people. When the Spanish conquerors arrived in America at the beginning of the sixteenth century, they found that the Incas had a well-organized administration by which the rulers in Cuzco (Peru) could effectively govern vast Andean territories to the north and south.

Administration is found in all types of organizations and communities. For example, private colleges have administrations to carry out policies of the board of trustees. Professional associations, such as the American Bar Association and the American Institute of CPAs, have professional staffs to serve the interests of their members. At the public level, school boards, city councils, and county governments hire professionals to carry out programs and policies established by elected officials. Thus, whether private or public, associations and communities generally have administrative staffs to support their organizations and help achieve their goals.

It is important to distinguish the functions of political executives and their bureaucracies. The task of elected executives is to determine policies, programs, rules, and decrees. Fundamentally, political executives set the goals for a nation. The role of the bureaucracy, by contrast, is to support the executive in making its decisions and, most importantly, in carrying them out. The differing roles of the politician and the bureaucrat are clearly illustrated in parliamentary systems. After a minister is appointed, he becomes chief executive officer of his ministry. As part of the government, the minister is responsible not only for directing and coordinating the work of his ministry but also for ensuring implementation of specific goals and objectives established by the cabinet. As chief political official, the minister gives instructions to senior civil servants, who must carry out his directives. Ordinarily, senior civil servants in countries like France, Great Britain, and Holland are professional career employees who have worked in a ministry for many years. While civil servants may have much more knowledge about the personnel, organization, and history of an organization, senior bureaucrats are still under the political authority of the executive.

What are the major characteristics of a modern bureaucracy? Peter Blau, building on Max Weber's important analysis of bureaucracy, suggests six important features:

1. Bureaucracy is organized on the basis of specialization of tasks. In the modern organization, tasks become specialized and only people with proper education and training fill administrative positions. The concept of division of labor is what distinguishes the factory system from previous productive efforts, and a bureaucracy is simply the application of the notion of division of labor to the public sector.

2. Bureaucracy has a clear administrative hierarchy. This means that heads at lower levels are supervised and controlled by heads at the next higher level. Thus, a policy decision passed by a minister to a chief civil servant is quickly passed along through various chains of command within an organization.

3. Operations are governed by a consistent system of rules. Unlike public administration in undeveloped political systems, bureaucracies in the modern state establish standards of operation to ensure consistency and regularity in performance. As a result, bureaucratic organizations place much importance on routine procedures and rules—an importance symbolized by the common expression "standard operating procedures."

4. To ensure optimum effectiveness, bureaucracies are expected to be formalistic and impersonal. Civil servants must be impartial and maintain a detached attitude toward their work so that their own personal interests and prejudices do not influence their official decisions.

5. The bureaucracy is a well-developed employment organization that offers long-term careers to its people. The civil service is characterized by a system of promotions according to seniority or achievement, or both. Personnel policies are explicit and well developed.

6. Bureaucracy is the most efficient method of implementing goals. This efficiency derives from specialization and employment of personnel on the basis of technical qualifications.[10]

Functions of the Bureaucracy

We have observed that the primary task of a bureaucracy is to implement policies and programs of the government. Since most of the goals and objectives established by the executive and approved by the legislature are in the form of laws, the administrative bureaus of government are responsible for executing and enforcing laws. Before the rise of the modern state, the task of implementing laws was in the hands of the executive; with the development of modern society, the now complex task of governing and providing public services and implementing programs has been transferred to a civil service. Although the executive branch is ultimately responsible for the execution and implementation of national goals and objectives, the actual responsibility has been placed in the hands of civil servants.

A second task of the bureaucracy is rule making. Although bureaucracies do not have constitutional authority to make laws, they nonetheless make decisions that have the binding authority of laws. The rule-making authority entrusted to bureaucracies has largely resulted from unwillingness or inability of legislatures to pass laws that are comprehensive in delineating both the goals and the means to realize goals. Given the complexity of problems within modern societies, legislatures tend to pass laws that state purposes and objectives but leave implementation of goals in the hands of the bureaucracy. Legislatures thus delegate responsibility for working out the details of program and policy implementation; civil servants are thus given authority to issue rules and regulations that have the binding authority of laws. In the United States, the "underlegislation" by Congress has resulted in a mushrooming set of federal guidelines, rules, and provisions (known as the *Federal Register*) which have the same effect as laws, even though they were never approved by a legislative assembly.

A third task of the bureaucracy is to gather information on the impact and effect of government legislation. The bureaucracy, in other words, serves as a feedback mechanism for both the executive and legislative branches of government. Sometimes the bureaucracy can adjust the programs of government to ensure that the purposes of laws are realized; in other cases programs must be dismantled and redesigned. Since bureaucrats have the greatest amount of information on the actual impact of the government on the lives of people, they provide essential data for the maintenance and alteration of policies and programs. Because the bureaucracy is such a rich repository of data, it is playing an increasingly important role in designing legislation for the executive, which in turn introduces it into the legislature.

Fourth, bureaucracies are the primary institutions for providing essential public services. Every province, city, local district, and village has essential public needs. These needs include education, fire protection, law enforcement, and health care and are provided directly or indirectly by civil servants. At the national level some government ministries and departments provide direct economic, social, and medical services to citizens, while others seek to regulate selected areas of society to ensure economic protection and consumer welfare. In the United States, for example, governmental institutions such as the Weather Bureau, the Veterans Administration, the Social Security Administration, and the National Institute of Mental Health directly serve the needs of people, while the Securities and Exchange Commission, the Food and Drug Administration, and the Environmental Protection Agency regulate individual and corporate behavior for the benefit of all members of society.

Because of the proliferation of public services in contemporary nation-states, the bureaucracy plays an increasingly important role. The dominant impact of the bureaucracy on modern society was recognized long ago by Weber, who believed that the actual ruler in the modern state would be the bureaucracy.[11] Although Weber's assessment may still be an exaggeration, there is little doubt that the role civil servants play in contemporary political systems is growing. One of the indicators of this growing influence is the size of the bureaucracy. In most modern states, government expenditures account on the average for more than 40 percent of the gross national product. In addition, the number of government employees has been steadily increasing during the postwar years. In the United States, for example, the number of civilian government employees at the national, state, and local levels in 1950 was 6.4 million. By 1974, however, the total number of civilian government employees had climbed to 14.7 million, or slightly more than 16 percent of the total labor force.[12]

Many people seem to regard the growth and expansion of the bureaucracy with apprehension. They correctly recognize that the bureaucracy tends to result in slow, inefficient, and impersonal decision making in the public sector. Moreover, the growing complexity of the government leads to duplication of work and in some cases to the establishment of programs that are counterproductive to the general welfare of the community. On the other hand, the development of the bureaucracy ensures society of many services and benefits it would otherwise not enjoy. In addition, the presence of an effective bureaucracy serves as a check on the power of the executive and helps ensure the practice of limited government in presidential and parliamentary systems. There can be little doubt that, despite problems associated with the growth of bureaucracy, modern states are better off with their large impersonal administrative staffs than were the feudal kingdoms and patrimonial societies with their smaller group of loyal servants.

SUMMARY

The two major types of competitive political systems are presidential and parliamentary regimes. A primary feature of presidential systems is that they are based on the principle of separation of powers. Parliamentary systems, by contrast, maintain a fusion of executive and legislative powers. Another important distinction between these two types of systems is that presidential executives have one person who carries out symbolic chief-of-state functions and head-of-government responsibilities, while parliamentary systems entrust those two duties to two different leaders.

Most political systems have institutions that make, enforce, and interpret the rules or laws of a country. Although the nature and organization of legislatures, executives, courts, and bureaucracies vary among countries, in most nations they perform many common tasks. The following functions are common to most of these four institutions:

Legislatures:	Make laws
	Represent popular interests
	Form, maintain, and supervise the executive
Executives:	Perform chief-of-state duties
	Carry out political leadership
	Manage bureaucracy
	Manage national conflict
Courts:	Settle disputes
	Interpret laws
	Determine laws
Bureaucracy:	Implement policies established by government
	Make rules to enforce laws
	Examine effects of policies
	Provide social services

KEY TERMS

parliamentary
presidential
separation of powers
checks and balances
judicial review
chief of state
head of government
collective responsibility
prime minister
cabinet

bicameral legislature
unicameral legislature
territorial representation
proportional representation
collegial executive
law
common law
civil law
adjudication
bureaucracy

NOTES

1. Gabriel A. Almond and G. Bingham Powell, Jr., *Comparative Politics: A Developmental Approach* (Boston: Little, Brown & Co., 1966), Chap. 1.

2. For an excellent study of the history of the doctrine of separation of powers, see Paul K. Conkin, *Self-Evident Truths* (Bloomington: Indiana University Press, 1974), Chaps. 7 and 8.

3. Alexander Hamilton, James Madison, and John Jay, *The Federalist Papers* (New York: New American Library, 1961), pp. 321–322.

4. Jean Blondel, *Comparative Legislatures* (Englewood Cliffs, N. J.: Prentice-Hall, 1973).

5. Valentine Herman, *Parliaments of the World* (New York: De Gruyter, 1976), p. 636.

6. Quoted in Leo Strauss and Joseph Cropsey, eds., *History of Political Philosophy* (Chicago: Rand McNally & Co., 1972), p. 672.

7. K. C. Wheare, *Legislatures* (New York: Oxford University Press, 1963), p. 122.

8. The legal practice of following previous court precedents unless there is a compelling reason to break with past practices is known as *stare decisis.*

9. Max Weber, *Economy and Society,* eds. Guenther Roth and Claus Wittich (New York: Bedminster Press, 1968), vol. I, pp. 54–56.

10. Peter M. Blau, *Bureaucracy in Modern Society* (New York: Random House, 1967), pp. 53–57.

11. Weber, *Economy and Society*, vol. III, p. 1393.

12. U. S. Bureau of the Census, *Pocket Data Book: USA 1976* (Washington, D. C.: U. S. Government Printing Office, 1976), p. 111.

SUGGESTED READING

ABRAHAM, HENRY, J. *The Judicial Process.* 3rd ed. New York: Oxford University Press, 1973. A valuable introduction to judicial institutions and processes in modern democratic states, with emphasis on France, Great Britain, and the United States.

BLAU, PETER M. *Bureaucracy in Modern Society.* New York: Random House, 1967. A lucid and succinct account of the role and functions of bureaucracy in the modern state. An excellent introduction to the subject.

BLONDEL, JEAN. *Comparative Legislatures.* Englewood Cliffs, N.J.: Prentice-Hall, 1973. An informative study of the structure and function of modern legislatures. Blondel's analysis is based on comparative data from 108 countries.

HERMAN, VALENTINE. *Parliaments of the World.* New York: Walter De Gruyter, 1973. Prepared for the Inter-Parliamentary Union, this comprehensive volume includes data on the composition, organization, functions, and powers of the legislaturs of 56 countries. An excellent reference volume.

KING, ANTHONY, ed. *The British Prime Minister.* New York: St. Martin's Press, 1969. An invaluable collection of essays on the contemporary role of the prime minister in the British political system.

LA PALOMBARA, JOSEPH, and RIGGS, FRED, eds. *Bureaucracy and Political Development.* Princeton: Princeton University Press, 1963. A collection of essays on the nature and role of bureaucracy in the developing nations.

NEUSTADT, RICHARD E. *Presidential Power: The Politics of Leadership from FDR to Carter.* 2nd ed. New York: John Wiley and Sons, 1980. An insightful analysis of how the American president exerts influence in the decision-making process. Argues that the major source of executive power is the capacity to persuade.

PITKIN, HANNA F. *The Concept of Representation.* Berkeley, Calif.: University of California Press, 1966. A superb analysis of the most important theories of representation.

RAE, DOUGLAS W. *The Political Consequences of Electoral Laws.* rev. ed. New Haven: Yale University Press, 1971. An illuminating study of how various electoral systems affect the number and strength of political parties.

ROSSITER, CLINTON L. The *American Presidency.* New York: Harcourt, Brace, Jovanovich, 1960. A general introductory study on the role of the president in the American political system. Interesting and well written.

SIMON, HERBERT A. *Administrative Behavior.* 2nd ed. New York: Crowell-Collier and Macmillan, 1957. An influential study of the role and functions of public administration, written from a behavior perspective. Simon won the Nobel Prize in economics for his studies on organizational behavior.

WHEARE, K.C. *Legislatures.* New York: Oxford University Press, 1963. A lucid summary of the composition, organization, and functions of legislatures in contemporary democratic countries. An excellent introductory volume.

WILDAVSKY, AARON. *The Politics of the Budgetary Process.* 2nd ed. Boston: Little & Co., 1974. An informative case study of how governmental and administrative staff participate in making the U.S. federal budget.

7 / THE DEVELOPMENT OF CONSENSUS: POLITICAL CULTURE AND SOCIALIZATION

In Chapter 3, we suggested that the peace, harmony, and order found in political communities is largely the product of shared values and habits. Government is not the prime initiator of community order; rather, it helps refine and improve a relatively harmonious and consensual environment.

Children are not born with a knowledge of culture. Their minds at birth are a political *tabula rasa* — i.e., devoid of political knowledge and feelings. As a result, if culture is to help build community consensus, children need to learn the generally accepted norms, beliefs, and patterns of behavior of the community of which they are a part.

The purpose of this chapter is to examine the nature and role of culture in supporting the political practices and governmental institutions of the state. In addition, we shall examine the more specific sets of political beliefs and ideals found in most political communities, which serve to guide and direct the political behavior of people. These belief systems, called *ideologies,* play an important role in directing the motivations and actions of a state. Finally, and most significantly, we shall analyze the nature of *political socialization,* the process by which people learn about the political values, ideals, and orientations of the community in which they live.

POLITICAL CULTURE

Culture refers to the widely shared values, beliefs, and customs of a society. As portrayed in Figure 7.1, one of the important components of culture is the *political culture* — the norms, values, and fundamental orientations toward the political system. Although all cultural dimensions help build community unity, we are primarily concerned with the dimensions of culture that deal with the political processes and governmental institutions of the state.

162

Figure 7.1 Components of Culture

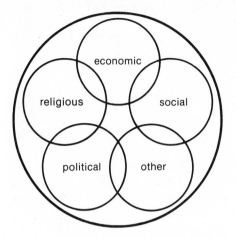

According to Almond and Powell, a political culture has three major components: empirical beliefs, affective responses, and value preferences.[1] Empirical beliefs include people's knowledge and awareness about the political institutions and dynamics within a state. For example, in the United States, empirical beliefs include knowledge about domestic and foreign policies, actions of the president, Senate, and House of Representatives, recent decisions of the Supreme Court, party activity, and so on. What is significant within a society is not the accuracy and validity of the beliefs of people but the determination of prevailing views about the political system.

The second component of political culture is the affective responses to political objects. Such responses include: favorable and unfavorable feelings toward the people and institutions of government, and level of pride and commitment toward political processes and governmental institutions. For example, a cross-national survey indicated that 85 percent of Americans polled felt pride in their governmental and political institutions. (This compares with 46 percent for the British, 30 percent for the Mexicans, 7 percent for the Germans, and 3 percent for the Italians.)[2] Another study measuring the affective political responses of Americans suggests that the level of trust and confidence in their institutions declined in the 1960s. In 1964, for example, 14 percent of those surveyed indicated that they always trusted the national institutions of government, while 63 percent indicated that they did so most of the time. By 1970, however, those who said they always trusted the government in Washington had declined to 6.4 percent and those who said they trusted the government most of the time had declined to 47.1 percent.[3]

Finally, political culture includes ideals and preferences about how the political system should operate. These value preferences may include general principles of government, such as political equality or separation of powers, or

more specific policy goals, such as changes in government budgetary alloca-
tions, restructuring of government programs, and changes in foreign-policy
interests. In addition, these preferences may include political values that individuals believe should be maximized within the political community. These
individual predispositions may include preferences such as stricter enforcement of the law, greater economic and social justice, or preservation of
individualism.

Every political culture is to some degree unique. Every society has its own
norms and beliefs and these in turn help to support the processes and institutions of the political system. Political cultures, however, can be compared in
terms of consensus and participation.

A *consensual political culture* is one in which there is a high level of
agreement about common empirical beliefs and value preferences and where
people tend to have a positive predisposition toward political and governmental institutions of the state. We are not concerned about how such a political
culture is established and maintained. Our interest is to recognize that, however achieved, some nations enjoy a high level of agreement about fundamental
principles, norms, values, and beliefs regarding political conflict management.

A *polarized political culture* is one in which substantial numbers of
people within a community are divided over political norms, ideals, and
beliefs. When a political culture is polarized, people are unable to agree on the
methods and rules of conflict management and on what policies, programs,
and actions should be undertaken by the agencies of government. As a result,
people become increasingly disillusioned with the political system. This is what
happened during the American Civil War—the American people became
deeply divided over the issues of slavery and states' rights. Similarly, the revolutions in Iran and Nicaragua in 1979 also resulted from extreme polarization
over political values and governmental institutions. Other areas over which
societies can become divided include religion, ethnicity, language, distribution
of wealth, and political ideals. (Figure 7.2 portrays political cultures in terms
of ideological orientation.)

The importance of widespread agreement about general political norms
and positive feelings toward the institutions of government cannot be emphasized enough. The bedrock of a political system is a consensual political culture. No nature can hope to survive without substantial agreement about basic
rules, preferences, and goals. Of course, no political system enjoys complete
consensus among the elements of a political culture. But when a substantial
portion of the people espouse conflicting interests and values, the differences
may result in increasing polarization and distrust among the people and
between the people and the government. The institutions of government then
lose authority and are unable to direct and lead the society. As a result, the
only means by which the nation can be preserved is through the establishment
of a military government to rule temporarily until greater harmony can be
achieved.

Figure 7.2   Polarized and Consensual Political Cultures

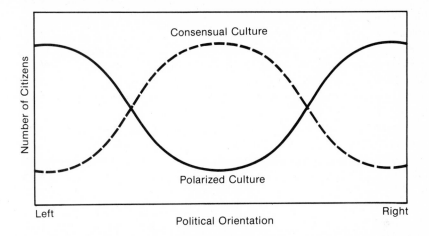

Another way of distinguishing among political cultures is in terms of level of participation. The three types of cultures are most common: participant, passive, and traditional.[4] A *participant political culture* is one where there is a high level of awareness and knowledge about the institutions of government and where a substantial portion of the people are active in the decision-making processes of the state. This type of culture is primarily found in modern democratic states. A *passive political culture,* by contrast, occurs when people have a relatively high level of knowledge and awareness about the politics and government of the state but are either unable or unwilling to become involved in voting or some other type of participation in politics. In such cultures the institutions of government may be relatively modern but individual, group, or party involvement in the decision-making process is limited. This type of culture is represented in some of the authoritarian military regimes of Latin America, such as in Brazil and Argentina. Finally, a *traditional political culture* is one where people have little knowledge and awareness about political and governmental institutions and play a passive role in public affairs. Such a culture is essentially apolitical and is found in developing nations with substantial illiteracy and limited socioeconomic modernity. Countries like Bolivia, Chad, Ethiopia, and Haiti are characterized by such political cultures.

IDEOLOGIES

An important part of political culture is *ideology.* Ideologies represent simplified political belief systems that provide direction, motivation, and emotional support to governments. Whereas political culture is general and diffuse in orientation, an ideology is a systematic set of concrete political ideals and values. Political culture is the political framework in which political institutions and processes function; an ideology, by contrast, is the belief system that directs and supports the actions of those in power or of those seeking to gain political office.

There has been much disagreement among political scientists as to the precise definition of an ideology and the role that it should play within society. Originally, the term was used by the French scholar Destutt de Tracy (1754–1836) to describe the ideas of the Enlightenment, which he believed could lead to the improvement of society. As first used by him, ideology is a "science of ideas" that can direct the modernization and development of society. Subsequently, Marx and Engels defined ideology as the belief system created by the bourgeoisie to perpetrate their control over the masses. Thus, whereas Tracy thought that an ideology is an instrument for directing a political community to social and economic improvements, Marx and Engels consider ideology a tool of oppression, an illusory aspect of the superstructure of the capitalist system.

The more contemporary approach to ideology is to use a value-free approach that neither supports nor rejects ideologies. Rather than view ideologies as beneficial or detrimental tools, most contemporary scholars use the concept to describe belief systems widely accepted within nations that help guide and direct the actions of a political community. Whether ideologies are narrow or broad in scope, complex or simple in structure, or rational or irrational in content is not considered important to the student of politics. What is significant is that people accept (consciously or unconsciously) certain belief systems that direct their actions and develop their values. Ideologies may or not may lead to the improvement of society. But as a simplification of the values and ideals of a community, they help build domestic consensus and facilitate the justification of government actions.

Most ideologies have at least three major dimensions. An ideology provides a philosophical perspective about the world. As a world view, an ideology provides justification for the values, preferences, and actions of people and a method of criticizing those ideals and events that are not in accord with the world view. Since most ideologies tend to be relatively simple sets of systematic assumptions and principles, they provide an effective means by which information can be filtered. Ideas not in accord with the world view are automatically dismissed. For example, an American who believes in the concepts of inalienable rights or political equality automatically dismisses totalitarian government practices.

An ideology provides values and goals about the future of a political community, i.e., it informs people about what ought to be. Although ideologies differ as to the specificity with which they describe the ultimate purposes and goals of society, all provide some vision of what the good life entails. For socialists, for example, the good life is a highly egalitarian economic society; for the communist, the *summum bonum* involves the creation of a community without private property and where people can contribute according to their ability and be rewarded according to their needs; and for the liberal democrat, the ideal society involves the preservation and maximization of individual freedoms within society.

Finally, ideologies give some guidance about ways to realize desired goals and objectives. While ideologies differ in the extent to which they cover methods and tactics, all ideologies implicitly include values and norms for realizing ideals of an ideology. In the case of democracy, for example, the principles of majority rule and minority rights give direction to democratic regimes about the realization of particular goals. In communism and fascism, on the other hand, the realization of national objectives is considered more important than protecting individual rights. In short, ideologies serve as a simplified cognitive map. As a world view, they tell people what to believe; as a prescriptive formula, they tell people what purposes and goals to realize as a nation; and as a methodological guide, they describe acceptable means to realize ultimate purposes.

Ideologies are significant tools of conflict management. Since ideologies facilitate the creation and maintenance of common beliefs and values, they are highly efficient means of creating community consensus. Moreover, ideologies themselves are tools for justifying particular processes and institutions of conflict management. Under Hitler, the Nazi ideology was used to justify totalitarian rule and the elimination of all political opposition. In competitive systems, on the other hand, democracy is used to justify the rights and freedoms of all persons, even when the ideas and practices of people are not entirely in accord with those of the government.

One of the important political developments of the twentieth century is the use of ideologies by certain totalitarian parties to establish greater control over subjects. What Communist regimes in Cuba, China, and the Soviet Union demonstrate is that the popularization of ideology can be an important tool for solidifying political control and developing domestic unity. Although totalitarian regimes use substantial terror and force in maintaining government control, the stability and order of these regimes derives less from continued application of coercion than from political indoctrination. Communists understand that the most economical way of building domestic unity is not through force but through programs of political socialization based on a simple ideology.

In competitive political systems there is no single acceptable world view. As a result, democratic systems generally have more than one ideology, or at least substantially different ideological perspectives. In the United States, there is general agreement about the principles of democracy yet substantial difference between conservatives and liberals over the role of government in the economy.

Conservatives believe that government should play a limited role in regulating the economy, while liberals believe that government should be instrumental in the production and distribution of goods in order to guarantee minimum social and economic conditions.

POLITICAL SOCIALIZATION

Socialization is the process by which people acquire the habits, knowledge, and orientations that enable them to function effectively within society. *Political socialization,* an aspect of the total socialization process, is concerned with the acquisition of knowledge, skills, and predispositions about politics and government. It is the means by which members of society (particularly children and immigrants) learn to accept and support the basic political norms and aspirations of the country in which they live. It is, in effect, the means by which each generation transmits its political culture, and more particularly its ideology(ies), to a new generation. Since political socialization is chiefly concerned with the perpetuation of the values and practices of a nation, the process is essentially conservative. It attempts to preserve and maintain the norms and institutions that manage and resolve social and political conflict.

Methods of Political Socialization

The process of political socialization is carried out by two methods. First, individuals are directly socialized by formal institutions of government. Although all public institutions contribute to the socialization of political values and predispositions, nations differ in the extent to which institutions of the political system become agents of planned and directed socialization. In the United States, the local, state, and national institutions of government participate in political socialization, but there is no systematic program for directing political education processes. In countries like China and the Soviet Union, by contrast, the Communist party tries to direct and control the socialization of children and the resocialization of adults in order to ensure a deep commitment to the goals and aspirations of the Communist regime. The political socialization program of the Nazi Party also involved the establishment of a new political culture in Germany. Since the goals of the Nazi regime were substantially different from those of earlier governments, Hitler believed that it was essential to bring about a planned alteration in the political values and commitments of the German people. He accomplished this through well-organized programs of political instruction for both children and adults.

The second method by which political socialization occurs in through informal institutions of society, such as the home, schools, churches, neighborhoods, and so on. Children learn about the need to obey authority figures within their home and school; this learning tends to facilitate their acceptance of political authority. Similarly, young adults learn about the norms and ideals of the political system from their peers, while family relationships and professional ties may influence the socialization process of adults. Unlike the more direct approach of political socialization through governmental institutions, this method of transmitting political knowledge and values is much more discrete.

One of the major differences between pluralistic and totalitarian regimes is the different role that government plays in the transmission of political values. In pluralistic systems there is no official political culture or ideology. As a result, numerous different agents of socialization help transmit a number of different sets of values and political beliefs to the younger generation. In totalitarian systems, by contrast, government is committed to a single ideology; the task of the regime, if it is to survive, is to inculcate among all members of society a deep commitment to the goals and aspirations of the state. This involuntary process of transmitting political knowledge and commitments is called *indoctrination.* It is the most common means by which totalitarian regimes develop popular support for their goals and aims.

The Nature of Political Socialization

The nature of the socialization process differs throughout various stages of life. There are four stages that can be differentiated in the socialization of political attitudes and values: childhood, adolescence, adulthood, and old age. We shall focus our attention on the nature of the process in childhood and adulthood.

The Socialization of Children Until recently, social scientists had little knowledge about how children develop political attitudes and learn to accept the norms and orientations of the political system in which they live. During the past two decades, however, a number of major studies on the political education of American children have provided useful data on the socialization process. While the subsequent discussion is based largely on these studies, the findings clearly have implications for other countries as well.

Research shows that children become aware of politically relevant information early in life. By age four or five they have a vague, rudimentary awareness of government. These impressionistic feelings and ideas are strengthened greatly when children begin to attend school and to recognize the importance of such symbols as the flag, the national anthem, and the Statue of Liberty. The practice of pledging allegiance to the flag is a particularly important activity in the early political socialization of children. During the first three grades, children develop strong positive feelings about the government and its leaders. They tend to see government as an institution that helps people, protects them, and cares for their needs, even though their knowledge of government is limited. The development of supportive feelings is thus significant because it tends to precede the acquisition of information on the political system. Just as children develop strong, positive feelings of affection toward their parents and learn to depend upon them for their needs, they also develop strong, positive perceptions about the government. Government, like parents, is assumed to be a beneficial source of authority. To a large degree, then, early socialization is a process of building loyalties.

Studies of American children indicate that political knowledge that is first acquired is vague, general, and idealistic. Children first begin to associate the functions of government with key figures like the president and the policeman, not because they are aware of their specific functions but because they are recognized as central authorities within society. In a major study of the development of political attitudes of children, Robert Hess and Judith Torney found that most students surveyed in second and third grade identify government almost exclusively with the president. More than three-fourths indicated that he was the chief source of the laws, and more than four-fifths indicated that he "ran" the country. Not only do they assign a major role in government to the president but they also have strong positive feelings toward him. They think that he is a helpful and supportive person.[5] In addition, the researchers found that second-grade students tend to view the president and the policeman in only slightly less positive terms than they view their own father.[6] As a general rule, early political socialization is highly personalized and idealistic.

As noted earlier, politics involves management and resolution of conflict. During early childhood, however, children tend to view conflict and disagreement as undesirable and are anxious to minimize interpersonal and intergroup tensions. For them security is found in orderly, stable institutions characterized by peace and cooperation. To the extent that tensions do arise, the purpose of authority figures like a father, policeman, or president is to help resolve tensions and conflicts as quickly as possible. Since children desire to minimize conflict, it is not surprising that an awareness of politics as a conflict-management process does not emerge until much later in life (in late adolescence or even adulthood).

As children mature, they begin to acquire specific information about the role of political leadership and to develop an awareness of the function of governmental and political institutions. As political knowledge becomes more specific and less personalized, children become more aware of the complexities of government and of the interaction of the various branches of government. Figure 7.3, based on a survey of attitudes of children in the United States, indicates some of these changing perspectives. As children become better informed about politics and government they tend to become less idealistic and supportive of leaders and institutions of government and begin to question and evaluate institutions of political authority.

Adolescence and Early Adulthood   Whereas early childhood encourages the development of vague, idealistic, and supportive values toward the political system, socialization in adolescence and early adulthood involves an increasing awareness about the role of political institutions in managing society. No longer is politics idealized; rather, young people begin to understand that politics involves tension and conflict and that the function of governmental institutions is to help manage such conflict. With increasing knowledge of the political system comes a decreasing affective commitment toward institutions

Figure 7.3   Changes by Grade in Perceptions of Source of Law and Who Runs the Country

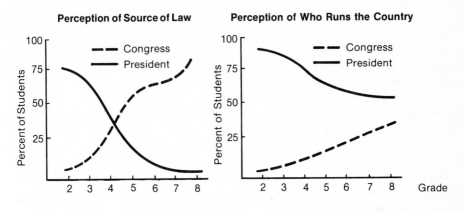

Source: Data adapted from Robert D. Hess and Judith V. Torney, The Development of Political Attitudes in Children *(Garden City, N. Y.: 1967), p. 43.*

of political authority. Feelings, beliefs, and loyalties developed in early childhood are questioned and evaluated, and the level of positive feelings toward the political system tends to decline significantly until early adulthood, when people begin to increase their stakes in society.

One of the reasons for the weakening of affective responses toward the political system among young people is that they are searching for their own values and questioning established authority patterns within society. As a result, students tend to be critical of traditional institutions and to be relatively uninvolved politically (except for opposition movements to ruling authorities). For example, the lowest portion of turnout among eligible voters in the United States is the college-age-group (persons 18 to 22 years of age). Similarly, opposition to political authority has been most strongly associated with young adults, particularly those who are relatively educated. In the developing nations, university students have historically been a source of opposition to government. The overthrow of Anastasio Somoza's regime in Nicaragua in 1979, for example, was accomplished chiefly by teenagers and young adults. In China, the Cultural Revolution of the 1960s and the demands of the late 1970s for liberation were carried out largely by young adults. In the United States, the typical rioter during the civil disturbances of 1967 was a teenager or young adult. Clearly, positive commitments toward the political system developed in early childhood are substantially weakened during adolescence and young adulthood. "It is clear," write Easton and Dennis, "that teenagers and young adults appear to be the bearers of political discontent, the harbingers of possible instability in many countries."[7]

Fortunately, weakened commitment to the political system does not persist. As people increase their social and economic stakes in society—i.e., as they increase their ties to neighborhoods, churches, schools, businesses, etc. — positive feelings toward the political system increase. Similarly, the level of involvement with public affairs becomes more significant. Adulthood is thus a period when commitment toward the people and institutions of political authority is strong and awareness about and involvement in the decision-making process of the state is considered important.

Figure 7.4 portrays the changing levels of commitment toward a political system. To the extent that changes in affective responses occur in political systems as suggested in the diagram, two implications must be emphasized. First, if the major emotional ties to a nation's political institutions are developed in early childhood, countries that hope to achieve a modicum of stability need to ensure that the political socialization of children in society is effective. (This is the view of Plato, who in his *Republic* suggests that the establishment of a healthy, stable society can be accomplished only when rulers have some control over the education process.) If communist regimes achieve a high level of order and stability, it is in great measure a result of establishing and maintaining effective socialization programs for children. When deep commitments are not established in the early years, the increasing disillusionment with authority found among adolescents and young adults puts undue strain on the political system.

Figure 7.4   Changing Levels of Commitment Toward Political Institutions During Major Stages of Life

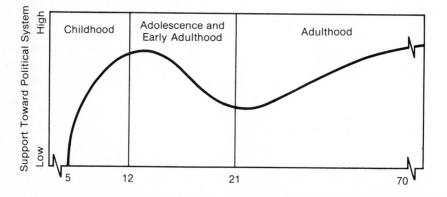

A second important implication is that a stable country needs to have a relatively large population of adults who can provide the necessary support for the institutions of government. When more than 50 percent of the population

is under the age of 20, a society has an unusually large percentage of teenagers and young adults who may place undue political demands on the institutions of government. This is the condition in many developing nations of Asia and Latin America, where population growth rates have been two to two and a half times those of industrial states. We shall explore the impact of the population explosion in Chapter 13.

AGENTS OF SOCIALIZATION

The Family

There are two ways by which a family transmits political values and orientations to children. First, it can help develop an awareness about and appreciation for society's institutions of authority and encourage compliance with established norms and rules. Since the home is a rudimentary political system with its patterns of authority and expected behavioral norms, the family environment provides children with their first encounter with hierarchical relationships. From their earliest years, they are taught to obey their parents and other adults and to comply with behavioral norms expected within the home, the classroom, the church, or other institutions with which they are associated. Since their emotional security is tied to the home, they develop positive feelings toward persons in authority, and such feelings help children subsequently to understand and accept patterns of authority within the political system of society. When patterns of authority are weak within the home, children have less positive views toward authority figures and are less likely to automatically comply with expected norms and rules. Moreover, where the father is not perceived as strong within the home, the children have greater difficulty in understanding and appreciating the political and governmental institutions of government. A study of Jamaican and American children shows that children in families with no father tend to have less interest in politics than in families where the father is present.[8]

A second way that a family influences the process of socialization is by modeling certain political values and beliefs. Parents not only transmit affective responses to their children but they also teach them specific values, orientations, and beliefs that they themselves hold. It is well documented that children acquire the party attachments of their parents and that they do so well before they understand the nature of politics or the functions of political parties. Obviously, when parents have different party affiliations, the process of transmitting party orientations is significantly impaired. In such circumstances, the most important political learning that is transferred is the common political values and aspirations shared by the parents.

One of the important determinants of the level of political socialization by parents is the extent to which they discuss politics within the home. A comparative study of French and American family patterns showed that French fathers are much less likely to discuss their political concerns with their children than are American fathers. As a result, while nearly 86 percent of the Americans surveyed could describe their fathers' party preferences, only 26 percent of the French had any knowledge about their fathers' political preferences.[9] The implication of this study is clear: parents that discuss political issues with their children have a greater influence on their children's political socialization.

Schools

Whereas the family provides the environment in which children first learn about affective political orientations, the school is the institution through which children first begin to acquire specific political knowledge. Hess and Torney, based on their extensive survey of political attitudes of children, go so far as to suggest that the school is the single most important influence in the political socialization of children. According to them, the school is "the central, salient, and dominant force in political socialization of the young child."[10]

What do children learn at school? In the early grades children acquire a rudimentary awareness of symbols of public authority and the importance of compliance with decisions of government leaders. In the early primary grades the school tends to reinforce the values of loyalty to the state and patriotism to the nation. As children grow older, however, they become more aware of the complexities of government through civics courses and through groups with whom they associate.

It is well known that democratic and nondemocratic systems regularly include civics courses, which help develop an awareness of institutions and processes of government. The impact of such courses, however, varies significantly among political systems. A study of American high-school students, for example, indicates that civics courses have been overrated in the United States. They have demonstrated little impact on the students' interest in politics, on their loyalty to the country, or on their feelings of political competence. "There is a lack of evidence," write Kenneth P. Langton and M. Kent Jennings, "that a civics curriculum has a significant effect on the political orientations of the great majority of American high-school students."[11]

Another agent of socialization, perhaps even more important than curriculum, is the social and cultural patterns within schools. Schools generally reflect the values of society and thus tend to reinforce the fundamental norms and orientations of the political system. In his study of American and Russian schools, Urie Bronfenbrenner found that American schools tend to emphasize individual performance, while Soviet schools tend to emphasize group achievement. According to Bronfenbrenner, the emphasis in American schools on individual success leads to a competitive environment where organized and structured activities are considered less significant than personal achievement. In the Soviet Union, on the other hand, the emphasis on group activities leads to a more structured, orderly, and communitarian learning environment.[12] These different styles of teaching not only reflect different cultural patterns but they also help reinforce different dimensions of political culture found in the two nations.

The level of education of the nation's people is also an important determinant of the political awareness. Studies have shown that within democratic systems the higher the level of education of the people the more aware and politically involved they are likely to be. In their survey of British, German, Italian, Mexican, and American political attitudes, Almond and Verba found that educated persons are more likely to be informed about political issues and more willing to discuss political subjects with others. In addition, they found that educated persons are more likely to have broader political perspectives, feel more capable of influencing their governments, and be an active member of some organization.[13] These findings are clearly in accord with many studies of American voting behavior, which show that college-educated persons tend to be more interested and better informed about political issues than are those who do not have a college education.

The national level of education also has a significant impact on political participation. A study of six developing nations shows that the level of formal education is the most powerful influence in the development of an active citizenry.[14] It is not surprising that regimes trying to consolidate their national power seek to strengthen primary and secondary education. Nonpluralistic countries seek to directly use schools to direct the formation of new political values and orientations.

When Fidel Castro assumed dictatorial power of Cuba in 1959, one of the ways by which he sought to solidify control of the nation was by directing the political socialization process of children and the resocialization process of adults. As Richard Fagan demonstrates in *The Transformation of Political Culture in Cuba,* Castro and his advisors tried to transform the political values and orientations of the Cuban people so that a new society could be established. This change was undertaken by directly controlling the educational institutions and by directing and guiding the political learning of adults. In 1961 shortly after Castro nationalized all private schools, a massive literacy campaign began as part of the creation of the new Cuban — an individual with new values and orientations who was active in supporting the ongoing struggle *(la lucha)* to establish a socialistic society. The goal of political socialization was not only to alter the political beliefs of people but also to mobilize the masses to follow the goals of the Cuban revolution. Castro's success is amply demonstrated by the degree to which traditional values and institutions have been replaced by noncompetitive socialist practices. Clearly, education can be used not only to increase political knowledge but also to mobilize people toward particular goals.

Other Agents

In addition to the family and the school, there are a number of other dominant forces in the political socialization process. Two significant sources of influence are peer groups and the mass media.

Peer Groups   These are composed of individuals who share similar values, orientations, or social status. Such groups play a significant role in either reinforcing or undermining the political learning that has occurred during the child's early years at home or at school. As a child matures, he begins to place greater importance on peer relationships and to develop ideas and views independent of those learned from parents or teachers. As adolescents begin to question persons in authority, they place increasing trust on their friends. These new ties can either help support or undermine the orientations and affective feelings developed earlier in life. The impact of social relationships on young adults is demonstrated by a study of Jamaican high-school students. According to the survey, students of working-class homes who attend schools with children of upper-class homes tend to develop political values and attitudes more characteristic of the upper classes (such as development of positive attitudes toward voting, minority rights, political involvement) and are less supportive of the regime.[15] Working-class students who associate only with peers from their own social class tend to develop values and orientations associated with their own social class.

The Mass Media   Ever since the invention of printing made communication possible with a large segment of society, the mass media has played an increasingly important role in politics and the political socialization process itself. As literacy increased and the availability of newsprint expanded in the eighteenth and nineteenth centuries in Europe and North America, written communication became a more significant medium of politics. With the development of radio and television in the twentieth century, instant communication has become possible not only within nations but also throughout the world. To be sure, the mass media plays a more profound role in the political socialization of children and resocialization of adults in the more modern nations. Yet no state, however backward, is immune from the influence of transistor radios or printed materials.

Within developed societies the most influential agent of the mass media is television. It has been estimated that children in the United States watch television an average of three hours a day. (Adults watch only slightly less than this.) Thus, by the time a young person completes high school, he has spent almost as much time watching television as he has in school. What is significant about television as an agent of socialization is not that it is an efficient means of transmitting and dramatizing political events. The importance of television is, according to Marshall McLuhan, that the medium is itself the message. Television not only is a medium of communication but also tends to have a profound impact on the nature of society and of the social and political interrelationships. In short, while modernization of the mass media increases the impact of the press, radio, and television on the political system, those instruments themselves help to shape a different type of society.

POLITICAL SOCIALIZATION AND CONFLICT MANAGEMENT

A basic assumption of this text is that a fundamental task of politics is to regulate human conflict in order to ensure order and stability within political communities. The most visible and extreme way by which states can manage conflict is through force. But force is not an economical method of ensuring stability and consensus. If they are to be effective in governing society, governments need to have the voluntary support of a substantial portion of the nation's population. Since the voluntary support can only emerge from common political values, orientations, and behavioral patterns, the strengthening of society's political culture is the most effective way by which order and consensus can be generated in the long run.

From a conflict-management perspective, political socialization performs two important functions: first, it helps create and maintain common political ideals, aspirations, and patterns of behavior that preserve and strengthen the nation. While much of the political socialization process proceeds imperceptibly, the development of common cultural norms is essential to a political community. It is the most effective way of establishing a framework in which the process of conflict management can be carried out. Second, political socialization helps establish goals and objectives for a political community. Without the creation of common wants, people would automatically pursue interests that are competitive and conflictual. The socialization process is significant because it limits the level of diversity and develops areas of consensus on which governments can act.

Developing a consensual political culture, however, does not provide the agreement required to pursue specific policies. The political culture is too general and too diffuse to support specific goals and objectives of a state. What is needed is the strengthening of ideology. Unlike political culture, ideology is a systematic belief system that provides specific policy direction to the government. When children and adults are socialized in terms of an ideology, the political consensus resulting within society is much more concrete and permanent.

Political socialization and ideologies play an important role in building national consensus. But the goal in states is not just establishment of political cohesion but also creation of social harmony on which government authority can rest. If governments are to make binding decisions for its members, a substantial number of people must support the policies and actions of government. Political culture and ideologies, however, are too general for building the necessary political support for government. As a result, additional political institutions must participate in the development of a more permanent foundation for the state.

Figure 7.5 illustrates the major institutions involved in building national consensus. As will become apparent in the following chapters, the roles of these institutions in building national cohesion vary among different types of political systems. In totalitarian countries, for example, ideology and the ruling political party play a dominant role, while public opinion and interest groups are carefully regulated by the government. In competitive systems, by contrast, public opinion, interest groups, and political parties play a vigorous role in competing for influence.

Figure 7.5 Relationship of Socialization and Political Culture to Government Decision Making

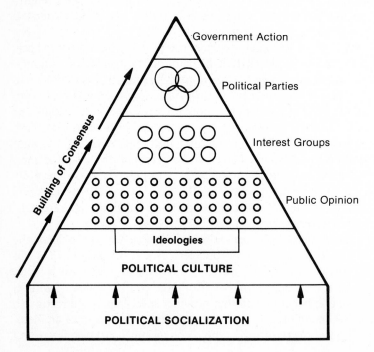

In Chapters 8 and 9, we shall examine the roles of public opinion, political participation, interest groups, and political parties in generating a more specific and developed political consensus. It is sufficient at this point to recognize that public opinion is public views that individuals hold about policies and actions of government. Although such opinions are related to a person's ideological views, public opinions are specific ideas of individuals about public issues. Interest groups and political parties are those institutions that organize public opinion and participate in the policy-making process. They are the institutions that channel the opinions of individuals into the arenas where public policy is made. Interest groups are chiefly concerned with influencing the actions of government, while political parties are primarily interested in gaining control of political power.

SUMMARY

An important aspect of a nation's political system is its political culture, i.e., the values, norms, and customs relating to political and governmental activities of the state. Two dimensions by which political cultures may be classified are levels of consensus and political participation. Some cultures are strongly consensual, and others are highly conflictual; on the other hand, some cultures may emphasize participation, while others may be nonparticipatory.

Ideologies, which are a part of political cultures, represent systematic and cohesive political belief systems. Whereas political cultures are a broad and diffuse set of political norms and orientations, ideologies are far more concrete and specific and can thereby provide direction and motivation for the actions and policies of government. Political cultures establish the framework in which politics is carried out within the nation; ideologies, by contrast, establish the political goals and aspirations of people.

Since no child is born with a knowledge of political culture or ideologies, the common values and orientations of the state must be taught to all new members of society. This process, known as political socialization, is of particular importance to children and immigrants. Since societies are continually changing, the values and orientations that are transferred in the socialization process change with time. As a result, political socialization must be a continuous process for all members of society.

The main agent of socialization is the government. In addition, families, schools, peer groups, and the mass media play a significant role in socializing young persons and adults.

KEY TERMS

political culture	political socialization
ideology	indoctrination

NOTES

1. Gabriel A. Almond and G. Bingham Powell, *Comparative Politics: A Developmental Approach* (Boston: Little, Brown & Co. 1966), p. 50.
2. Gabriel A. Almond and Sidney Verba, *The Civic Culture* (Princeton: Princeton University Press, 1963), p. 64.
3. Arthur H. Miller, "Political Issues and Trust in Government: 1964–1970," *American Political Science Review* 68 (September 1974), p. 953.
4. Gabriel A. Almond, ed., *Comparative Politics Today: A World View* (Boston: Little, Brown & Co. 1974), pp. 51–54.
5. Robert D. Hess and Judith V. Torney, *The Development of Political Attitudes in Children* (Garden City, N. Y.: Doubleday, 1967), p. 64.
6. *Ibid.,* p. 51.
7. David Easton and Jack Dennis, *Children in the Political System* (New York: McGraw-Hill, 1969), p. 306.
8. Kenneth P. Langton and David A. Karns, "The Relative Influence of the Family, Peer Group, and School in the Development of Political Efficacy," *Western Political Quarterly* 22 (1969), pp. 813–826.
9. Philip E. Converse and Georges Dupeux, "Politicization of the Electorate in France and the United States," in Angus Campbell et al., *Elections and the Political Order* (New York: John Wiley & Sons, 1966), pp. 279–281.
10. Hess and Torney, *Development of Political Attitudes in Children,* p. 250.
11. Kenneth P. Langton and M. Kent Jennings, "Political Socialization and the High-School Civics Curriculum in the United States, *American Political Science Review* 62 (September 1968), p. 866.
12. Urie Bronfenbrenner, *Two Worlds of Childhood: U. S. and USSR* (New York: Russell Sage, 1970), Chapters 2–4.
13. Almond and Verba, *The Civic Culture,* pp. 317–318.
14. Alex Inkeles, "Participant Citizenship in Six Developing Countries," *American Political Science Review* 63 (December 1969), p. 1132.
15. Kenneth P. Langton, *Political Socialization* (New York: Oxford University Press, 1969), Chapter 5.

SUGGESTED READING

ALMOND, GABRIEL A., and VERBA, SIDNEY. *The Civic Culture.* Princeton: Princeton University Press, 1963. One of the most significant comparative studies of political culture based on a survey of political attitudes in the United States, Great Britain, West Germany, Italy, and Mexico.

DAWSON, RICHARD E., and PREWITT, KENNETH. *Political Socialization.* Boston: Little, Brown & Co. 1969. A general survey of political culture and socialization.

EASTON, DAVID, and DENNIS, JACK. *Children in the Political System.* New York: McGraw-Hill, Inc., 1969. An analysis of the agents and process of political socialization in children. The study is based on a large survey of political values and attitudes in American children in primary and secondary education.

FAGAN, RICHARD R. *The Transformation of Political Culture in Cuba.* Stanford: Stanford University Press, 1972. A case study of how the Castro regime transformed the values and attitudes of the people of Cuba during the 1960s.

GREENBERG, EDWARD, ed. *Political Socialization.* New York: Atherton Press, 1970. A short but excellent collection of eight significant studies on political socialization in the United States, covering areas that are both consensual and conflictual.

GREENSTEIN, FRED I. *Children and Politics.* rev. ed. New Haven, Conn.: Yale University Press, 1969. A study of political socialization of 700 children of New Haven.

HESS, ROBERT D., and TORNEY, JUDITH V. *The Development of Political Attitudes in Children.* Garden City, N. Y.: Anchor Books, 1968. This study, based on a survey of 17,000 students in elementary schools in the United States, examines the process of political socialization in early childhood. As one of the most significant studies on the subject, this book is an excellent introduction to political socialization.

JAROS, DEAN. *Socialization to Politics.* New York: Praeger Publishers, 1973. A useful introduction to the agents and process of political socialization. Because it is short and well written, this is a helpful volume to the beginning student.

LANGTON, KENNETH P. *Political Socialization.* New York: Oxford University Press, 1969. This is a cross-cultural analysis of the agents of political socialization.

PYE, LUCIAN, and VERBA, SIDNEY, eds. *Political Culture and Political Development.* Princeton: Princeton University Press, 1965. A collection of ten studies on the role of changing political values and attitudes in the development process of the emerging Third World States.

SARGENT, LYMAN TOWER. *Contemporary Political Ideologies: A Comparative Analysis.* 3rd ed. Homewood, Ill.: Dorsey Press, 1975. One of the many studies of different ideologies, this is one of the best short introductory volumes. It examines nationalism, democracy, communism, fascism, anarchism, and socialism.

SOLOMON, RICHARD H. *Mao's Revolution and the Chinese Political Culture.* Berkeley: University of California Press, 1971. A study of the development of the Marxist-Leninist political culture in China. The author examines the traditional values of Confucian culture and shows how Communist leaders have tried to modify these through political socialization.

8 / THE REPRESENTATION OF INTERESTS: PUBLIC OPINION AND POLITICAL PARTICIPATION

In the previous chapter we examined the process by which people learn the basic values, orientations, and patterns of behavior of the political system. Although political socialization is essential in establishing and maintaining a political community, the authority of government does not and cannot rest solely on the general conflict-management framework sustained by socialization. A political culture is too general, too diffuse, and too amorphous to provide the necessary support for government decision making. Government action rests on something far more specific—public opinion.

Americans have become accustomed to the view that democracy is founded on public opinion but that Communist regimes are based only on the interests of party leaders. In reality, all governments depend in some way upon popular support, however it may be generated. When a substantial majority of a nation's people is opposed to a regime, the authority of government is undermined and its ability to rule becomes impaired. A noted American political scientist observes:

> *Governments must concern themselves with the opinions of their citizens, if only to provide a basis for repressing of disaffection. The persistent curiosity, and anxiety, of rulers about what their subjects say of them and of their actions are chronicled in the histories of secret police... Although a government be erected on tyranny, to endure it needs the ungrudging support of substantial numbers of its people. If that support does not arise spontaneously, measures will be taken to stimulate it by tactical concessions to public opinion, by management of opinion, or by both.*[1]

Whether democratic or authoritarian, whether constitutional or totalitarian, all governments need popular expression of support for actions and policies that are undertaken. They may not have continuing majority approval, but they do need the support of significant portions of the populace if they are to remain in authority.

In this chapter we shall examine the nature of public opinion and its role in competitive and noncompetitive political systems. We shall then review some of the major ways by which people participate in order to express their opinions and interests in the political system. While there are many types of participation, we are concerned primarily with voting — its role and significance as well as factors that influence voting behavior.

PUBLIC OPINION

Definition

What is public opinion? According to V. O. Key, Jr., it consists of "those opinions held by private persons which governments find it prudent to heed."[2] To further understand this concept, it is useful to highlight three essential qualities of public opinion.

First, public opinion is concerned with the expression of a view or perspective on a particular issue. Public opinion is not a feeling or attitude, nor is it a philosophic orientation toward the political system. Rather, public opinion is a specific position or preference toward a particular political object. It is a specific, concrete view about a political issue or problem.

Public opinion is also concerned only with those opinions expressed publicly. Until a person articulates his views and ideas, they cannot be considered political opinions. Inward feelings are, of course, significant in that they give rise to public expression of opinions. But until a person expresses his views, opinions do not enter the realm of public discussion and debate. Only articulated opinions comprise public opinion.

Finally, public opinion deals only with those issues that have a society-wide impact. People hold views and opinions on thousands of different issues, but most of these are concerned with essentially private issues of the home, the church, vacations, work, etc. The issues of significance in a political system are those that have general import to a large segment of society; they include such concerns as taxes, foreign economic assistance, legalization of drugs, funding of public education, and so on. If an issue is to have a society-wide impact, it must also have the support of a large number of people or be sufficiently visible as to gain broad public support. The goal of public opinion is to influence the course of public policy, and only well-organized expressions of public opinion have much impact on the decision-making processes of government.

Public opinion is not automatically harmonious and consensual. Indeed, the very essense of community life is continuous tension and conflict among members of society, and nowhere is this conflict felt more continuously (at least in democratic societies) than in the arena of opinions and ideas. The natural state of public opinion is discord and conflict. If consensus is to be achieved among the opinions and interests of people, it has to be created by deliberate, planned efforts. (The two primary institutions for organizing people's opinions and interests are interest groups and political parties.) It is sufficient at this point to recognize that the natural condition of public opinion is conflictual, although the extent of consensus differs among states. In some countries, such as more politically mature democracies and authoritarian Communist regimes, there is a high level of consensus on the general rules and values of the political system, as well as the major goals and objectives of the government. In the transitional societies of Africa, Asia, and Latin America, however, political institutions are much less developed; the result is a much less consensual public opinion.

The Distribution of Public Opinion

If public opinion is to have an impact on the decisions of government it needs to be organized. When public opinion is unorganized and many different competing and conflicting views are expressed to the officials of government, it is difficult for any particular group to influence the course of public policy. Political influence results when there is a large, well-organized expression of public opinion.

The distribution of public opinion depends upon two dimensions: direction and intensity. Direction of public opinion indicates whether people are for or against some issue; intensity indicates the degree to which people support or oppose an issue. The impact of public opinion depends both upon the extent of support — i.e., the number of people supporting or opposing an issue — and the intensity with which they hold that view. As Figure 8.1 illustrates, when a large segment of the population supports a specific issue intensively, the impact of public opinion is significant. As the level and intensity of support decline, the predicted impact of public opinion similarly tends to decline.

Public opinion can be either harmonious or conflictual. A *consensual public opinion* is one where there is substantial agreement about an issue. This agreement is manifested on issues where a substantial majority of the people support or oppose a particular issue. In Figure 8.2, diagrams A, B, and C are consensual distributions of public opinion because in each one of them a clearly dominant view is expressed. In diagram A the people obviously agree that the United States should defend Europe from an invasion by the Warsaw Pact countries, while in diagram B the people are generally opposed to mandatory busing to achieve integration. In each of these two cases, there is a clear preference on which government can act if it so wishes. Diagram C may

Figure 8.1 Predicted Impact of Public Opinion on Government Decisions Based on Level and Intensity of Popular Support

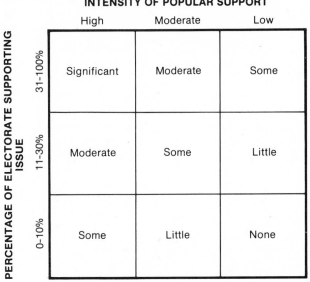

INTENSITY OF POPULAR SUPPORT

	High	Moderate	Low
31-100%	Significant	Moderate	Some
11-30%	Moderate	Some	Little
0-10%	Some	Little	None

PERCENTAGE OF ELECTORATE SUPPORTING ISSUE

also be considered a consensual expression of public opinion, but it provides no clear mandate to government. In this distribution, the American people are largely indifferent to changes in the level of economic assistance to the Third World. The late V. O. Key, Jr., called this distribution a "permissive consensus" because it provides no clear mandate to government and allows it much freedom to act.[3]

A *conflictual public opinion* is one where people are polarized around two or more perspectives on a particular issue. One type of polarization is the one depicted in diagram D, where people are deeply divided into two separate groups. In such a distribution, the members of a community are divided into two mutually exclusive groups and hold their opposing opinions with much intensity. This was the situation during the U.S. Civil War, when Southern and Northern states disagreed over the nature of slavery. More recently, this polarized public opinion has been evident in countries like Iran, Nicaragua, Rhodesia, and Northern Ireland. No nation can long exist when an intense conflict divides a society. Either war or revolution brings victory to one of the factions, or the community eventually divides into separate political entities.

A conflictual public opinion can also exist when groups are deeply divided along more than two lines. In such a situation, people are not divided along two clearly delineated positions; rather, the public is grouped around

Figure 8.2   Patterns of Public Opinion Based on Level and Intensity of Popular Support of Selected Issues

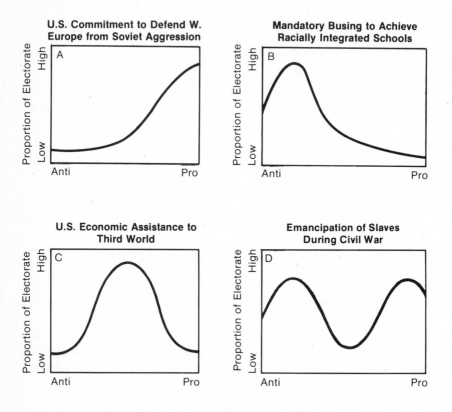

four or five different positions, each of them held intensively by ten to 30 percent of the population. In 1973 George Gallup, Jr. polled the American people to determine their views on the most effective ways to achieve racial integration in public schools. The results were: 22 percent favored creation of housing for low-income people; 27 percent favored changing of school boundaries; 5 percent favored busing; 22 favored something other than the first three; 18 percent indicated they opposed racial integration; and 17 percent indicated they had no opinion.[4] Although we do not know the extent to which the individuals surveyed supported their expressed views, the heterogeneity of public opinion on the issue of integration obviously made it difficult for government to develop an effective racial integration policy. When such a conflictual distribution exists, not only do the actions of government enjoy limited popular support but also, depending upon the intensity of the opinions, the actions themselves may be determined by significant opposition. An unorganized, conflictual public opinion is thus a weak foundation for any public action.

Public Opinion in Different Political Systems

The role of public opinion is also determined by the nature of the political system. In pluralistic, democratic states, public opinion has an existence independent from government. In such countries, people are free to organize and express their interests with few or no restrictions. The task of government is not to control public opinion but to serve it. In noncompetitive systems, however, the task of government is to create, mold, and direct the public interests of people. In such systems, public opinion does not have an independent existence and people are not free to express, assemble, and mobilize public interests as they desire. In both competitive and noncompetitive systems, public opinion is significant in giving authority to government and in supporting policies of the state. Whereas the development of public opinion in competitive countries is carried out largely apart from the government, in noncompetitive, authoritarian, or totalitarian regimes, government is the major agent for creating and maintaining a supportive and consensual public opinion.

Public Opinion in Competitive Systems   According to classic doctrines of democracy as expressed in the writings of John Locke, the function of government is to be an agent for the interests of the majority. The government should do what 51 percent of the people desire. This simplistic notion assumes, however, that people have an ongoing interest in affairs of the state and that those interests are largely consensual — or at least capable of developing majority agreement. While both assumptions may be realistic for direct democracy (found in seventeenth century New England towns and in contemporary Swiss cantons and villages of Switzerland), they are not realistic for the public affairs of a large, complex country like the United States or Canada.

In dealing with the many vexing issues confronting contemporary democratic societies, it is virtually impossible to expect citizens to be informed about all major issues and to be prepared to cooperate with others in developing broad agreement on ways to cope with problems and challenges. Contemporary issues within modern societies are too numerous and complex for citizens to become sufficiently informed so that they contribute to the formulation of public policy. Even if they could regularly offer their views to government officials, it is doubtful that people would want to do so. As Walter Lippmann observed earlier in the century, the average person has little time for the affairs of state. After people work at their jobs to sustain a reasonable standard of living, they have little time left for the weighty matters facing government. Even if they are interested in participating in the decision-making process, the information available to the common man, Lippmann thought, is limited and inadequate.[5]

If public opinion does not and cannot lead and direct the actions of competitive political system, what role does it play? Public opinion influences the actions of government in two significant ways. First, periodic elections in democratic systems allow people the opportunity to vote for candidates whose political views and orientations best represent their interests. Although elections cannot ensure that public opinion will be translated into public policy, it provides a periodic mechanism by which people's popular concerns can be identified with political leaders who will most likely carry out the interests of their supporters. Once political leaders are elected, the relationship of political action to constituency support becomes far more complex. Sometimes the politician may not know how all of his constituents feel about an issue; at other times he may feel that they are not sufficiently informed; and in still other instances there may be little time to consult public opinion within his district.

When leaders take the initiative and act without demonstrable public support, they may continue to receive constituency support but only if the actions and decisions they have made are fundamentally in accord with the interests of constituents. Within democratic systems there is a clear provision for taking bold, decisive action. But if candidates hope to be reelected, they need to ensure that actions and policies receive substantial public support after they have been made. The role of decisive action without public support was clearly demonstrated by then-President Nixon when he first announced the strengthening of political and economic ties between the United States and the People's Republic of China after more than 20 years of total separation. Nixon allowed his aide Henry Kissinger to make a number of secret visits to China and then announced publicly that he, too, would visit the country. Had these preliminary steps been made public, it is doubtful that the president would have won public support. But by acting secretly he was able to put in motion a process that itself altered public opinion and eventually led to the establishment of full diplomatic relations between the two countries in January 1979. Clearly, Nixon's original actions on China were taken without the knowledge and support of public opinion, but the administration's actions themselves eventually altered public opinion.

At times, however, governments may act but never gain the support of the people. This was the case when President Ford pardoned Mr. Nixon from all wrongdoing in the Watergate affair. While most scholars agree that President Ford had the constitutional right to pardon the former president, his action was strongly opposed by a large segment of Americans and may have been a decisive cause of his failure to win reelection in 1976. In short, elected officials may not always have public support for actions and decisions that they make, but periodicity of elections provides the means by which people can continue the support for the incumbent or some other candidate.

A second way by which public opinion influences the course of public action is through interest-group lobbying. Although the influence of interest groups varies among countries, in most western democracies pressure groups provide a means by which public opinion can be brought to bear on actions of government. The ratification of the Panama Canal Treaty in the U. S. Senate, for example, elicited significant lobbying by various interest groups concerned with national security issues. Similarly, the continuing debate in the 1970s over the place of women in society focused on the ratification by states of the Equal Rights Amendment. Persons who felt that women should receive further legal protection for their social, political, and economic rights generally identified with interest groups that supported ERA; those who held more traditional values tended to support interest groups opposing such a measure. Thus, in expressing opinions on major national issues, interest groups are a convenient and effective method by which to generate and channel influence toward government. Because of the importance of interest groups in democratic society, we shall examine their role and function more carefully in the following chapter.

The real significance of public opinion in competitive systems is not that it informs the decision-making process either indirectly through elections or directly through interest groups. The distinctive feature of competitive systems is that public opinion is not regulated by the government. Unlike totalitarian regimes, competitive systems are based on the assumption that the organization of public opinion should be carried out with complete freedom of the press and assembly. Only public opinion created through vigorous, open debate can be considered legitimate. To ensure free expression of popular opinions and interests, elections in competitive systems generally involve numerous parties, each of which is free to select its own candidates and to maximize its popular support. Losing parties continue to participate in the political system by challenging and opposing the actions of government.

The role of interest groups is also different in competitive systems. Whereas in noncompetitive systems they may be controlled and influenced by the ruling authority, in democratic systems the role of interest groups is not necessarily to support the government but to try to challenge, direct, and influence actions of government. Interest groups, in other words, are independent organizations. They are created and maintained by the free and voluntary action of citizens.

John Stuart Mill (in his essay *On Liberty*) observes that the value of democratic society ultimately depends upon the quality of its people, and the quality of people ultimately depends upon freedom and liberty within the society. Mill states:

> *The worth of a State...is the worth of the individuals*
> *composing it; and a State which postpones the interests of their*
> *mental expansion and elevation, to a little more of administrative*
> *skill, or of that semblance of it which practice gives, in the*
> *details of business; a State which dwarfs its men, in order that*

they may be more docile instruments in the hands even for beneficial purposes — will find that with small men no great thing can really be accomplished; and that the perfection of machinery to which it has sacrificed everything, will in the end avail it nothing, for want of the vital power which, in order that the machine might work smoothly, it has preferred to banish.[6]

Mill lists three reasons for the presence of absolute freedom of thought and opinion. First, an opinion that is silenced may be true; in silencing it we assume our own infallibility. Second, even though the silenced opinion is false, it may contain some truth. This is so because most truth is found not within a single source but by "the collision of adverse opinions." Third, even if the prevailing opinion were the complete truth, freedom of thought and discussion is essential if the truth is not to become dogma. "If all mankind minus one, were of one opinion, and only one person were of the contrary opinion," wrote Mill, "mankind would be no more justified in silencing that one person, than he, if he had the power would be justified in silencing mankind."

For Mill, as for so many other liberal-democratic thinkers, freedom of opinion is a prerequisite for a competitive, pluralistic political system. While the existence of such freedom of thought and opinion may make the development of a consensual public opinion more difficult, the creation of a harmonious public opinion through any other process except the free competitive exchange of ideas leads to a weak, artificial, and contrived society. Competitive political systems are thus deeply committed to political freedom, with the hope that political institutions can organize the multitudinous interests of people and develop a stable, domestic political consensus.

Public Opinion in Noncompetitive Political Systems   To understand the role of public opinion in noncompetitive political systems, we need to differentiate between authoritarian and totalitarian regimes. In authoritarian systems, the authority of government is based on the force of military institutions. Such regimes gain and maintain power because they have the support of the military. Since authoritarian systems are not supported by a political party but by a group of military leaders or a single dictator, the major objective is not to develop support for a new political ideology but rather to avoid politics altogether. Authoritarian regimes are concerned above all with one objective — staying in office. As a result, their primary concern is to eliminate all forms of political opposition or practices that might threaten its power. Thus, such regimes curtail freedom of speech and assembly, limit and control freedom of the press, control all radio and television, and seek to regulate all organizations that might threaten its political power.

Unlike totalitarian regimes, authoritarian military systems such as those in Argentina, Brazil, and Chile generally do not attempt to develop a new political culture or a new set of political ideals and orientations. Rather, their objective is to control political power by eliminating all sources of political dissent. Although reliance on military force provides authoritarian regimes with many coercive instruments, such systems are ultimately unstable because they fail to cultivate public support.

Totalitarian systems are similar to authoritarian regimes in that they seek to eliminate all forms of political opposition, but they differ in that they attempt to build a supportive political culture through programs of socialization and indoctrination. Realizing that long-term stability ultimately rests on public opinion, totalitarian systems attempt to alter common political values and orientations until prevailing views and ideals within society are in accordance with those of the governing regime. Rather than use force as the basis of the government's authority, totalitarian systems try to develop public support for the goals and ideals of the ruling political party.

The practice of molding public opinion in totalitarian systems is illustrated in communist regimes. The goal of communism is to create political communities in accordance with the principles of Marxism-Leninism. One of the central tenets of Marxism is that the average members of the working class are unable on their own to grasp and understand the goals and ideals of communism. It is for this reason that Marx and Engels suggest (in the *Manifesto*) that an elite group of proletarian workers—the Communists—is necessary to lead and guide the proletariat in developing the ideals, orientations, and habits to help bring about communism. In the words of Marx and Engels, the Communists are those persons who clearly understand "the line of march, the conditions, and the ultimate general results of the proletarian movement."[7] Public opinion cannot be allowed to develop through debate, discussion, and open conflict. Rather, the Communist party itself must assume responsibility for creating a political culture supportive of communist ideals.

The creation of a communist political culture has generally been achieved by maintaining a framework where there is only one acceptable ideology and by creating vigorous socialization programs among children and adults. Like authoritarian regimes, Communist systems generally control the media. All radio, television, and newspapers are regulated directly or indirectly by the ruling party. The liberal-democratic notion of freedom—i.e., the idea of allowing freedom of expression and competition for political influence—has no place in Communist systems. Fidel Castro, Communist dictator of Cuba, has made plain his distaste for the western, or "bourgeois," view of political freedom. The purpose of the press, he once noted, is not to criticize the actions and policies of government but to support them. "As long as the revolution develops, as long as there is counterrevolution supported by the United States, and as long as this struggle exists," he observes, "we will not allow any paper that goes against the revolution."[8] Thus, freedom is not found in opposing the creation of communism but in identifying with the revolutionary goals articulated by the government.

Besides controlling the media, Communist regimes seek to eliminate all political organizations that are not supportive of the goals of communism. The only political organization permitted is the Communist party. Similarly, the role of interest groups is severely restricted, since it is assumed that there is but one group interest—that of the proletariat, as defined and articulated by the party organization. Still, no community or political organization is totally homogeneous, some factions will always exist. Sooner or later, group interests seek to express their particular interests and concerns within the framework of the Communist party.

One of the ironies of Communist ideology is that it seeks to develop a strongly supportive political culture but encourages freedom of expression within the party organization. One of the central tenets of communism is the notion of self-criticism—the idea that party members should constantly seek to purify the beliefs and practices of its members through open criticism. According to the Statutes of the Soviet Communist Party, members have the responsibility to "boldly disclose shortcomings and strive for their removal" and "rebuff firmly any attempts to suppress criticism." Persons guilty of suppressing ciriticism or persecuting anyone for criticism "must be held to strict Party responsibility, up to and including expulsion from the ranks of the Party."[9] Criticism and dissent is therefore tolerated within the framework of the party but cannot be used to oppose or criticize the aims, policies, and actions of the government. The goal of self-criticism is to strengthen party organization, not to contribute to the decision-making process of government.

The second and most significant way by which Communist regimes seek to develop a common political culture is through programs of political socialization. Unlike authoritarian military regimes, which are primarily concerned with elimination of all political opposition, the fundamental aim of Communist governments is to establish a new society based on Marxist-Leninist principles. While Communist regimes differ over the nature and role of these principles, they agree that the creation of a communist society requires a new political culture—a new set of values, beliefs, and orientations. As a result, a major task of Communist parties in countries like China, Cuba, and the Soviet Union is to resocialize adults and establish programs of indoctrination for children. Since the creation of a new political culture is the responsibility of the Communist party, its success has, to a large extent, depended upon the ideological commitment of party members themselves. The precondition for any effective socialization program is therefore a well-informed and deeply committed party cadre.

The alteration of traditional political culture is dramatically illustrated by the enormous changes in political values and orientations in China following the establishment of a Communist government in 1949.[10] Traditionally, Chinese culture emphasized strong kinship ties. Authority patterns were clearly defined and were based on such considerations as age, generation, kinship, wealth, sex, and education. The goal of the traditional order was to maintain peace and harmony in social relationships through these well-defined authority patterns. While the Chinese Communist party has continued some elitist patterns, the fundamental goal of the Party is to challenge traditional values and commitments toward the family, clan, and social class and to replace these particularistic commitments with one toward the people as a whole. As Mao Tse-tung often observed, the goal of his Party is to make individuals desirous of "serving the people." To develop this new commitment, it was necessary to eradicate habits and structures supporting individual and group selfishness. Some of the changes made in China to strengthen the new communitarian ethic include: redefinition of marriage and family ties, a more influential role for women in society, increasing esteem for manual labor, and development of a work ethic without material incentives.

Since Marxists believe that political and social reality is ultimately based on the economic foundations of society, Maoists have tried to establish the new society by directly altering the nature of economic production within society. Besides placing production in the hands of the state, the Chinese have tried to alter economic relationships in more subtle but fundamental ways— breaking down specialization, dismantling bureaucracies, and eliminating practices that give rise to technicians, experts, bureaucrats, and other authorities. The goal of Chinese economic development is not to increase production in order to strengthen consumer satisfaction. Rather, the aim is to alter the process of economic development to create a new person who is supportive of communist goals.[11]

Besides the emphasis on altering economic relationships, Chinese Communists are deeply committed to programs of political education to reinforce structural economic changes. Such programs have been created at all levels of education, at work, and throughout various institutions of society. Since the eradication of "bourgeois selfishness" is regarded as a continuing challenge, Chinese Communists believe that the ongoing indoctrination of children and adults is essential for realizing the goals of the proletarian revolution. Indeed, the process of establishing a Marxist-Leninist society may require a periodic renewal and purification of ideological commitments, such as was undertaken during the Cultural Revolution of 1966-1967.

The creation of a Communist political culture in the Soviet Union has involved structural and attitudinal changes similar to those in China, although the level of ideological change has not been as extreme. Whereas China is committed primarily to establishing new values and orientations, the Soviet Union has sought to establish economic development at all costs. Thus, whereas Chinese productive relations help to instruct and to reinforce development of a Communist ideology, the creation of a new political culture in the Soviet Union is primarily achieved through programs of political socialization. Such programs are found in schools, universities, youth associations, government bureaucracies, work associations, professional associations, and so on. (As noted in Chapter 12, programs of socialization seek to develop a level of awareness about the political economy of communism and to instill a high level of commitment toward the aims and goals of the Communist party. The development of knowledge is chiefly the concern of Party "propaganda"; the development of support toward the actions, policies, and general aims of the Party is chiefly carried out by "agitation.") Thus, through continuing pro-grams of political instruction for children and adults, the Soviet Communist party seeks to develop a political culture that is supportive of its aims.

In summary, public opinion is significant in Communist regimes. Since the authority of government ultimately rests on the voluntary support of people, Communist parties have used force, but primarily as a means of devel-oping a consensual public opinion supportive of the aims and goals of the government. The fact that both the Soviet Union and China have achieved political unity and stability attests to the effectiveness with which the masses have learned and accepted the values, orientations, and beliefs of communism.

The Measurement of Public Opinion

Measuring public opinion is important in modern democratic systems. Since the theory of democracy assumes that government must be a vehicle for transforming popular interests into public policies, it is believed that govern-ment officials should know what the sentiments and interests of people are. In practice, however, the primary interest in public opinion polls in Western democracies has not been to determine popular sentiments in order to establish effective public policies. Rather, the aim has been to predict elections. With increasingly sophisticated methods of polling, interest in measuring public opinion has been growing. Yet (as of the present) no government has devel-oped a system whereby it continually surveys public opinion in order to strengthen its policy-making processes.

Methods of Measurement   The first major attempts to measure public opin-ion were carried out through "straw" polls. Newspapers and weeklies mailed out questionnaires to their subscribers, and election outcomes would be pre-dicted on the basis of the responses. The most important early straw poll in the United States was distributed by the popular magazine *Literary Digest*. From 1916 through 1932, the *Digest* correctly predicted the winner of each presiden-tial election. The theory of the straw poll is that the larger the number of responses from readers, the greater the accuracy of the poll's predictability. For this reason, the *Digest* increased the number of mailed sample ballots so that by the early 1930s nearly 20 million questionnaires were mailed out, and an astonishing five million responses were received. But in 1936 the *Digest* made a major error in its prediction, which eventually led to the demise of the magazine. It predicted that Governor Alfred Landon, the Republican candi-date, would win the presidential election with 59 percent of the popular vote. In actuality the Democratic candidate, Franklin D. Roosevelt, won a landslide victory with more than 60 percent of the vote and all but eight of the electoral votes.

Ever since then, scientific sampling has become the only acceptable method of surveying public opinion. The basic premise of scientific sampling is to measure the public opinions of a relatively small, but carefully developed sample to ensure accuracy in representing the total population. Unlike earlier straw polls, which emphasized size in the sample, contemporary approaches in polling are concerned with representativeness. The two most common methods of achieving this are through probability and stratification techniques. In *probability sampling,* the goal is to create a sample of individuals selected on the basis of randomness alone—i.e., each member of a population has as good a chance of being chosen as any other. The second and more popular approach is *stratified quota sampling.* This approach seeks to duplicate the major characteristics of a population within a small sample. Thus, features such as age, sex, location, party preference, income, etc., are duplicated in the sample in approximately the same proportion as is found in the general population. The assumption of this approach is that these pre-selected traits play a role in the way people behave politically. As a general rule, however, most polling seeks to combine elements of probability and stratification. One way by which these two methods are combined involves the selection of areas, such as towns, cities, or particular county districts, through stratification procedures. Within each preselected territory, people are then chosen through random procedures. The selection of the sample to be polled is thus realized through two techniques.

The Reliability of Polls How accurate are polls? The margin of error in polling, which can be determined by comparing predicted results with electoral outcomes, is generally less than 6 percent among major American polling firms. That is, pollsters' predictions are likely to have a maximum error of 3 percent over or 3 percent under the actual results. This is indeed a notable achievement, particularly when such polls seek to describe the opinions and anticipated voting behavior of 60 to 100 million people based on a sample of less than 3,000 persons. In six U. S. presidential and congressional elections from 1950 through 1960, the Gallup polling organization made an average prediction error of less than one percent. In 1964, its prediction that Lyndon Johnson, the Democratic Party candidate, would receive 64 percent of the vote was off by 2.6 percent; in the 1968 election, its prediction that the Republican presidential candidate, Richard Nixon, would receive 43 percent of the vote was off by 0.4 percent; and in the 1972 election, its prediction that Nixon would receive 62 percent of the vote was off by an infinitesimal 0.2 percent.[12]

Of course, polls can and do make significant errors, as was the case in the May 1970 parliamentary elections in Great Britain. The Labour Party had been elected to office in 1966, but through the following years popular sentiment ran in favor of the opposition Conservative Party. Early in 1970, however, a number of polling firms indicated that popular sentiment had shifted back in favor of the Labour Party. Based on these encouraging results, Harold Wilson, the Prime Minister, decided to call for early elections. From early May (when elections were first announced) until election day on June 18, most polling experts predicted an easy victory for the Labour government. On the day before the election *The London Times,* the most prestigious British daily, carried an article giving the Labour Party a victory by 8.7 percent. The results, however, were far different from what was anticipated. The Conservatives, in a stunning electoral upset, received 46.6 percent of the vote to Labour's 43.4 percent. When these percentages were translated into parliamentary seats in the House of Commons, it meant that the Conservative Party had increased its number from 253 to 330, while the number of Labour seats had declined from 364 to 287.

While polls occasionally fail to predict significant election results, as a general rule they are quite accurate. As a result, most democratic countries depend heavily on polls to provide preelection information on when and how to run for office. Indeed, the decision of parliamentary governments on whether or not to call national elections is often based on the predicted results of polling organizations. In addition, a large part of the interest and excitement of legislative and presidential elections derives from the anticipated results predicted by opinion polls and the actual outcomes. In the 1978 Illinois campaign for the U. S. Senate, for example, a large part of the interest in this contest derived from the growing strength of the Democratic challenger Alex Seith over Republican incumbent Charles Percy. When the contest began, Senator Percy had an enormous lead; just prior to the election, however, the polls gave Mr. Seith a slight advantage.

One common use of opinion polls is to evaluate governmental performance. In the United States it is a matter of routine to evaluate the performance of the president. Pollsters regularly survey American perceptions about how they think the president is carrying out his responsibilities in domestic and foreign affairs (Figure 8.3). While recent presidents have indicated that these "popularity" surveys are not significant, declining popular esteem led President Johnson to decide not to seek another term of office and ultimately forced Richard Nixon to resign. When President Jimmy Carter's popularity sank to levels below those of President Nixon, he hired a media specialist, Gerald Rafshoon, to help improve his image.

Information provided by polls is based on specific perceptions at a particular moment in history. Circumstances can help alter views and attitudes dramatically. In August 1979, for example, Democrats and Independents were polled on the Democratic nominee they would prefer; the results were 58 percent in favor of Ted Kennedy and 25 percent in favor of President Carter. Subsequently, Iranian students took some 50 American embassy staff as hostages, and a major international dispute ensued between the two states that helped strengthen Mr. Carter's image. By December 1979 public opinion had shifted dramatically away from Senator Kennedy back to President Carter. Mr. Kennedy received only 33 percent preference for the presidential nomination, while President Carter received an astounding 53 percent.[13]

Figure 8.3   President Nixon's Popularity, 1972–1973 (Percent Approval)

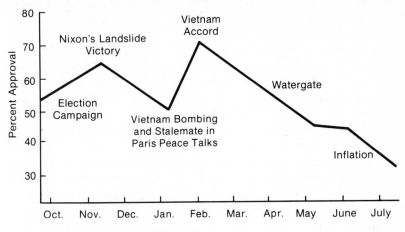

Source: Based on data from the Gallup poll.

In summary, public opinion polls are relatively accurate instruments for measuring public sentiment at a particular time. Although they may provide valuable information to candidates and help satisfy human curiosity, they do little to strengthen the democratic decision-making process. As stated earlier, ideal democracy requires that public opinion be measured continually so that such information can be made available to government officials. While numerous firms regularly survey public opinion in the United States and other democratic countries, there is no established method by which representative institutions of government regularly act on the basis of public opinion surveys. Until this is done, the main function of polling will relate primarily to election campaigns and the measurement of support for individuals and actions of government leaders.

POLITICAL PARTICIPATION

Like many other basic terms in political science, the term *political participation* is used in different ways in the professional literature. Some political scientists use it to cover all individual and collective responses toward a political system. Since individuals vote, pay taxes, abide by laws, and voluntarily live and work in specific countries, their actions automatically underwrite the entire political system. The danger of using political participation as an all-inclusive term, however, is that it loses its analytical usefulness; it becomes difficult to differentiate among various types of individual and collective political activity. At the other extreme, some political scientists use the term in a highly restrictive way to include only those specific voluntary acts that support a political system. Such actions include individual participation in elections as well as collective behavior of parties and interest groups but do not include mass participation in authoritarian regimes or unconventional action such as demonstrations and riots.

In this study we shall use the term *participation* to include those individual and collective responses between the all-inclusive and the restrictive approaches. More particularly, participation will be defined as any type of political action, individual or collective, successful or unsuccessful, organized or unorganized, that seeks to influence the actions of government, the choice of political leaders, or the general conduct of public affairs.[14] Participation will be used to represent the expression of feelings and opinions, whether carried out in a legitimate or illegitimate manner or whether carried out in a democratic or undemocratic regime. Participation, in other words, involves the outward manifestation of the ideas and beliefs of people—the means by which public opinion is turned into political action.

The Rise of Political Participation

Historically, governments have been managed by a relatively small group of political leaders. Throughout most periods of ancient, medieval, and even modern history, most political systems were in the hands of a relatively small, wealthy, and powerful ruling elite. Even during the period of Athenian democracy, the vast majority of the population did not participate in the decision-making process—the right to participate was limited to male citizens. The growth of significant political participation did not begin until the sixteenth century, when the authority of the state became increasingly secularized as a result of the Rennaissance and the Reformation. But even during the seventeenth and eighteenth centuries, the right to participate in the decision-making process of the state was generally restricted to white male property owners—a condition that did not change in industrial European states until the nineteenth century. The most important expansion of political participation in the Western democratic states occurred in the nineteenth and twentieth centuries as new groups demanded and received the right to vote. In most cases, suffrage was first given to males of the middle class, then to males of the lower classes, and then to blacks and women.

While the growth of participation has been different to some degree in each country, a number of common factors have influenced the expansion of the number of participants involved in the decision-making processes of the state. One political scientist has examined political participation and suggests five major factors affecting its growth.[15]

1. Participation results from the modernization of society. As countries become more industrialized, urbanized, and literate, there has been pressure from the more informed populace to become more involved in political and governmental affairs.

2. As new social groups grow and develop (such as the middle class or urban labor), they seek to make their political gains commensurate with their economic achievements. Social and economic changes among new classes thus encourage political changes.

3. Participation has been encouraged by the intellectual leaders of society, who help formulate ideals and goals and arouse the masses to political action. Quite often the intelligentsia of society (i.e., writers, professors, and political thinkers of a nation) encouraged participation in countries where the processes of modernization have not fully taken hold. Since the intellectual leaders of the Third World have been a catalyst for building and guiding political awareness and generating political interest in their nations, they have generally played a key role in establishing nationalist movements and in spreading the notion of equality.

4. Domestic conflict among competing elite groups stimulates political participation. When groups such as the military, landowners, the middle class, and the church compete for political influence, they can increase their influence by getting the support of individuals who did not previously participate in the political system. The expansion of participation in Latin America in the twentieth century has been greatly stimulated in this manner as elites have encouraged the political involvement of urban labor and peasants.

5. The growth of government itself encourages political participation. As government becomes a more pervasive influence in society, people not only become more aware of the impact of politics on their lives but also seek to maximize their benefits from the political system by making demands on those holding public office. While the growth of government results in great measure from the expansion of political participation, government itself is a prime stimulus for mass concern with the affairs of state.

Types of Political Participation

There are numerous forms and degrees of political participation. One distinction in participation is between the behavior of individuals and that of collective groups. Although both individual and group action is significant, we shall be concerned only with individual participation. (The role of interest groups and parties—the most common forms of group participation—are examined in Chapter 9. Sidney Verba and Norman Nie have examined political participation in the United States and conclude that there are six dominant forms of participation among Americans (Figure 8.4).

A similar typology of political participation has been developed by Milbrath and Goel. According to them, three major levels of political participation are found in typical contemporary nation-states—the active, the passive supportive, and the apathetic. Apathetic participants are those who do not become involved at all in political affairs. Passive supporters are those who are

Figure 8.4   Types of Political Participation

Source: Data from pp. 79–80 in PARTICIPATION IN AMERICA by Sidney Verba and Norman H. Nie. Copyright © 1972 by Sidney Verba and Norman H. Nie. Reprinted by permission of the publisher.

regularly but minimally involved in the affairs of state. They tend to show their concern for politics by such activities as voting, attending parades, paying taxes, and flying the flag. Milbrath and Goel distinguish five types of active participants:

1. *protestors*—those who protest laws, participate in riots, refuse to obey unjust laws, or other comparable acts;
2. *community activists*—those who participate in voluntary community activities to strengthen and improve the local welfare;
3. *party and campaign workers*—those who actively work for a political party by attending meetings, giving financial support, or persuading others to support party candidates;
4. *communicators*—those who engage in political discussion and constructive criticism of government affairs; and
5. *contact specialists*—those who contact government officials when their personal needs are at stake.[16]

Political participation can also be differentiated in terms of methods used to influence government. Some forms of political activity are routine or normal, while others may be considered unconventional. Of the five types of active participants listed above, all except the protestors represent conventional methods of political activity. When individuals and groups become disillusioned with a government and are unable to alter its policies, they may seek to oust it through illegal, violent, or even revolutionary methods. An assassination plot, for example, is considered unconventional participation. Other types include demonstrations, riots, guerilla warfare, and revolution. When groups carry out illegal, violent, or revolutionary actions to influence the political system, it means that they have not been successful in using conventional channels of participation to communicate their needs and concerns to the government. Thus, when there is substantial alienation, dissatisfaction, and disillusionment, individuals and groups may resort to extreme forms of violent action to dramatize their demands and seek to alter the outcomes of the government.

Voting Behavior

The most common and widely accepted form of active political participation is voting. It is found in almost all modern political systems, whether democratic or authoritarian. While elections have different implications in different types of systems, voting can be used in all countries as a means of legitimizing authority of government — as a means of giving public support for the leaders of government and the public policies they are seeking to carry out in society. It is for this reason that most governments, regardless of their ideological orientation, find it advantageous to periodically give people the opportunity to express their support for the governing regime.

Levels of Voting   Table 8.1 compares the size of the electorate and the proportion of voters in selected countries. While the number of countries in each type of political system is limited and the electoral information is dated, two generalizations can be drawn that are valid for most contemporary political systems. First, the highest levels of registered voters are found in Communist systems; the lowest levels are found in developing countries. Although registration requirements vary among countries, virtually all states allow persons from 18 to 21 years of age to register to vote. The major reason for the different levels of eligible voters is not found in the registration laws of states but in the values, orientations, and expectations of citizens, i.e., in the political culture. Where adults are expected to register and vote (as in the case in Communist regimes), young adults are more likely to become part of the electorate than in countries where registration is not considered a central responsibility (as is the case in many developing nations). Indeed, in many of the Third World states, ethnic groups may be unaware of the role of government

TABLE 8.1 Size and Proportion of Voting Electorate in Selected Countries, by Type of Political System

COUNTRY	VOTERS AS PERCENT OF POPULATION OVER 20	DATE	VOTERS AS PERCENT OF ELECTORATE	DATE
I. Communist Systems				
Albania	100	1966	100	1962
Bulgaria	100	1966	99.7	1962
East Germany	92.1	1967	99.2	1963
Hungary	100	1967	97.2	1963
Romania	99.6	1965	99.8	1965
Soviet Union	97.7	1966	99.9	1966
II. Developed Democracies				
Austria	88.9	1966	93.8	1966
Belgium	79.4	1965	91.6	1965
Denmark	86.8	1966	85.6	1963
Italy	89.2	1963	92.9	1963
United Kingdom	72.4	1966	77.1	1964
United States	56.8	1964	58.7	1964
West Germany	77.6	1965	86.8	1965
III. Developing Democracies				
Chile	54.1	1965	77.8	1965
Dominican Republic	82.8	1966	69.9	1962
El Salvador	34.3	1967	33.4	1966
Guatemala	25.9	1966	47.8	1966
Ghana	———	———	47.7	1956
Honduras	67.3	1965	———	———
India	55.8	1967	53.1	1962
Mexico	49.8	1967	54.1	1964
Uganda	———	———	66.0	1963

SOURCE: Charles S. Taylor and Michael C. Hudson, World Handbook of Political and Social Indicators, *2nd ed. (New Haven: Yale University Press, 1972), pp. 54ff.*

in their own lives; many do not understand and appreciate the role of political participation. Thus, the need to become a part of the voting population is not considered significant.

A second major generalization from Table 8.1 is that the proportion of voters is highest in Communist states and lowest in developing countries. Although the voting data in Table 8.1 may exaggerate actual results, it is a generally accepted fact that Communist regimes have the highest level of adults who go through the ritual of voting. One reason for this is that elections are not competitive and free but exercises in gaining and maintaining popular support for the governing authorities. Since there is but one official slate of candidates, to avoid voting can be interpreted as a form of opposition to the Communist party. Elections become instruments for singling out disenchanted persons.

Another reason for the high voter turnout in Communist regimes is due to public pressure to participate in elections. During the period preceding elections in the Soviet Union, for example, the media and party institutions seek to stimulate popular interest in the goals and aims of the Party, and more particularly, in candidates running for office. Parades, meetings, discussions, and media publicity are all used to encourage interest in the election campaign. The goal is not to ensure the selection of Communist party candidates; this is ensured by the lack of political competition. Rather, the goal is to stimulate and agitate the people to express their support for the Party through voting.

Elections are thus significant in Communist systems not because they provide a means of selecting officials to rule but because they provide a means of mobilizing public support for the ruling authorities. Election campaigns are not competitions between parties; rather, they are exercises in generating support for ongoing activities of the government. Voting is significant because it provides public demonstration of popular support for the ruling party.

The lower level of voting in democratic systems can be partly explained by the different purposes of elections from those of Communist regimes. In democratic systems, the chief goal is not to mobilize public support but to select individuals who can serve in government. Elections are the mechanism by which citizens can *control* the government, not merely approve it. As a result, the most significant factor in democratic elections is not the proportion of the electorate who votes (10 to 20 percent lower on the average than in Communist systems) but the extent of freedom and competition in the election process. According to democratic theory, only where there is complete freedom of expression and assembly can the people maintain control over government.

Voting turnout in democratic systems varies significantly. In some European parliamentary systems, the proportion of the electorate who votes is close to 90 percent, while the average American turnout for presidential elections during postwar years is about 60 percent. In order to encourage participation in elections, a number of countries have passed compulsory voting laws to fine or penalize persons who do not vote. Such laws have been passed in Australia, Austria, Belgium, Brazil, Liechtenstein, Switzerland (in a number of its cantons), and Zaire, although they do not appear to have had a significant impact on electoral results.

Despite concern for the relatively low election turnout in some democracies, a low level of voting may not be an indication of the failure of democracy (as has been argued by some) but may be a means of expressing the people's wishes. This may be the case when a large portion of the people are relatively satisfied with the actions and policies of government and believe that their voting participation will not alter the directions of a political system. Lipset suggests that high or low voting levels are not in themselves significant in democratic countries. What is important is a sudden increase in electoral participation, for such a shift may represent a serious problem or tension among a large portion of the electorate.[17]

The lowest level of voting is in Third World states. There are a number of reasons for this. First, many Third World nations are relatively new and are still in the process of institutionalizing elections. Second, since political parties are not well developed, they are unable to direct and mobilize political participation. Third, lack of a well-informed, literate citizenry contributes to a low level of participation.

Determinants of Voting   Why do people vote? What are some of the factors that affect voting behavior? Because of the importance of voting in democratic societies, political scientists have carried out extensive research on voting behavior. In the section below we shall list some conditions that affect the overall level of voting within a state *(macroconditions)* and then review some factors that affect individual voting behavior *(microconditions)*.

Almond has suggested four factors that influence the overall level of voter participation in democratic systems.[18] One factor is the level of popular interest in elections. In the United States, for example, voter turnout is significantly higher in presidential elections than in "off-year" congressional elections (Figure 8.5). One reason for this is that voters tend to perceive the election of the president as a more significant event than the selection of members of the Senate and House of Representatives. Elections, too, tend to generate more interest during periods of crises (such as the French elections of 1958) than in periods of calm and stability. A second factor influencing voter turnout is the frequency of elections. Constant elections may tend to overwhelm citizens and lead to lack of interest in voting. This may be the case particularly when voters are unable to decide on which elections are the most

Figure 8.5 Turnout of Eligible Voters in Presidential and Congressional Elections, 1940–1972 (in percentages)

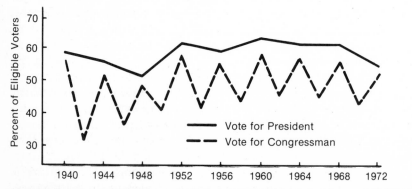

SOURCE: *U. S. Bureau of the Census,* Statistical Abstract of the United States, 1974 *(Washington, D. C.), p. 437.*

important and on the ones in which they can exert the most influence. A third factor affecting the level of voting is the extent of party competition. Partisan competition appears to stimulate interest in political issues and encourage participation. This appears to be the case in many Western European countries, where party competition is frequent and intense. Finally, political culture can also affect voter turnout. In countries where prevailing values and orientations encourage political participation, levels of voting and of other organized political action tends to be higher. In countries where there is limited expectation of popular participation (often in developing countries), the voting turnout tends to be lower. Thus, the relatively high voter turnout in countries like The Netherlands and West Germany may not be an indication of popular concern with issues and problems of society but rather a deep commitment to the civic values of the state.

With regard to specific factors associated with individual voting behavior, a number of indicators have been demonstrated to have a key impact on electoral participation in democratic regimes. Some of the key factors are: personal income and education, age, area of residence, sex, and organizational involvement. Of these, the most significant factor appears to be the first.

1. *Social Class.* Cross-national studies continually demonstrate that well-educated people tend to vote more than do less well-educated persons and that high-income people tend to vote more than do those with low income. Similarly, occupational studies tend to show that manual and clerical workers have a lower level of voter turnout than that of professional or managerial classes. White-collar workers, in other words, have a higher rate of participation than blue-collar workers. Because of the important role of social class, it is not surprising that, where race is directly associated with income and educational levels, different racial groups also demonstrate different levels of participation. In the United States, blacks, who have lower incomes and lower levels of education than whites, tend to vote less than whites. The U. S. Census Bureau estimates that in the 1968 election 58 percent of blacks voted compared with 69 percent of whites; in the 1972 election 52 percent of blacks voted compared with 65 percent for whites. Although much research continues on the impact of social class on voting, it is relatively safe to say that one of the key factors determining voter participation is social status. A recent five-nation study of political culture shows that political participation increases as one's social status improves. Citizens of the same social status in their respective countries (United States, United Kingdom, West Germany, Italy, and Mexico) tend to participate at about the same absolute levels.[19]

Another interesting finding about the relationship of social class to voting is that voters' political preferences tend to be associated with social status. Well-educated and highly paid individuals tend to associate with parties of the right; less well-educated and lower-paid workers tend to associate with parties of the left. Although the relationship between political orientation and social class has been demonstrated to exist in most western democracies, in no country do all members of a social class identify with the left or right. Some workers always identify with the political right, and some members of the upper classes identify with the political left. But as a general rule, ideological orientation and social class tend to be associated. In the United States, the professional, managerial, and business groups tend to support the Republican party, while the less advantageous economic groups (such as blacks, manual workers, clerical staff, etc.) tend to support the Democratic party.

2. *Age.* A second factor associated with voting is age. Since young adults are often involved in opposing governments in dramatic ways—marches, rallies, protests, and even riots—it is commonly assumed that young people are active political participants. But studies show that among various age-groups in democratic societies, the lowest levels of voting come from young people who have recently attained the voting privilege. In most Western democracies, the proportion of voters is highest among middle-aged people 35 to 55 years and older adults over 55. In general, the proportion of the electorate who votes increases with age up until the late 50s and early 60s and then declines after that. It is not surprising that, while a large number of people expected the newly enfranchised American youth (18 to 20) to play a key role in the 1972 presidential elections, less than 50 percent of them bothered to vote.

   It is often assumed that people are liberal and radical politically when they are young but that as they get older they tend to become more conservative. While political orientation appears to be statistically correlated with age, one political scientist suggests that it is not age itself that affects political orientations but the common experiences of a particular age group. The Great Depression, for example, would have tended to develop a set of political attitudes and values different from those created during the American turmoil of the 1960s. What is significant, then, is not age per se but types of generational experiences conditioning attitudes and values.[20]

3. *Area of Residence.* Although there are some exceptions (such as France), urban citizens tend to vote more than those living in rural areas. One reason for this is that voting is much more accessible to city dwellers than to individuals living on farms. It may also be due to the greater level of politicization found in cities than in rural communities. This is particularly the case in developing nations, where rural peasants are generally unaware of political issues and tend to be far more concerned about pragmatic issues of survival and increased agricultural production than with the more general questions of public policy.

4. *Sex.* Traditionally, women tend to vote less than men. Although modernization appears to be altering some of the traditional roles of the various sexes, as a general rule voter turnout in democratic countries tends to be higher among men than among women. One reason for this is that political activity throughout most historical periods was limited to men. Indeed, women's suffrage was not granted in most developed states until the twentieth century, and in some cases (such as Switzerland) only as recently as the 1960s. Another factor that may account for the lower voter turnout of women is that in most societies women still bear greater family burdens than men. The greater demands of children and the home not only restrict the freedom to participate but can also curtail the pressures to vote often found in society at large. Interestingly, sexual differences in participation tend to be highest among the poor and uneducated and gradually decline for the middle and upper classes. Thus, while the difference in voting between upper-status men and women appears to be small, the gap in turnout among the poor and unemployed is much greater. Similarly, women tend to have higher levels of political participation in the rich, developed nations than in the poor, less developed nations of the Third World.

Political preferences also appear to correlate with sex. Although there is some controversy about the role of sexual differences on political values and attitudes, as a general rule women tend to be more conservative than men. For example, the postwar voting patterns of Britain, West Germany, and Italy clearly indicate that women are more likely to be associated with conservative parties. In Germany, women cast a proportionately higher vote for the Christian Democrats than for the Socialists, whereas men do the opposite. In Italy, women tend to support the Christian Democrats, while men tend to affiliate with the socialist or Communist parties. In Britain, a larger percentage of men is associated with the Labor Party, while a larger portion of women supports the Conservative Party. While there are many reasons for the general predisposition of women to be more politically conservative, one significant consideration is that women are often more concerned with maintenance of the economic status quo. For them, economic and political stability is far more important than for men. Religion, too, can influence how women perceive political issues. In Italy, for example, women tend to be stronger supporters of the Catholic church; this no doubt encourages them to support the Christian Democratic movement. Since women as a general rule are more religious than men, their tendency to support conservative movements may be partly strengthened by the stronger commitment of conservative parties to religious values and institutions.

5. *Parties and Other Organizations.* Another significant determinant of voting is organizational affiliation. People who are associated with

various types of organizations (such as professional groups, interest groups, political parties, etc.) tend to vote more often than do those with no such ties. Interestingly, the level of organizational involvement is itself associated with social class. Members of the high income and well-educated class tend to have far more organizational ties than those who are relatively poor and uneducated. But recent research suggests that while social class and organizational affiliation are related, organization membership itself has a strong independent impact on how people vote. One student of politics has examined the determinants of voting and concludes that "the two most important factors that seem to determine whether one participates at all are social class and organizational affiliation."[21] The importance of organizations, like interest groups and parties is obvious. Organizations tend to encourage individuals to be informed about public policy issues, to participate politically, and to encourage others to do likewise. Above all, organizational affiliation tends to encourage and direct political participation in areas where it can have the greatest impact on society.

Not only does organizational affiliation encourage participation; it also directs people how to vote. Studies show that one important predictor of voting behavior is party identification. When individuals are members of a group or party or perceive themselves as affiliated with a group, that relationship or affiliation tends to influence how a voter acts. Partisanship, in other words, helps direct the political awareness and orientation of people and encourages support for the party.

To be sure, issues also play an important role in voting, but studies on American voting behavior indicate that individuals most concerned with and informed about issues are those who have strong party ties. In *The American Voter,* a classic study on American voting behavior, Campbell, Converse, Miller, and Stokes suggest that three conditions are necessary for an issue to play a significant role in voter behavior. First, the issue must be sufficiently recognized by the public; second, it must arouse a high degree of concern so that people consider it in the voting process; and third, people must be able to associate a particular party or candidate with their own position on an issue and to recognize other candidates or parties as opposing the issue. Only when it fulfills these three conditions for a significant number of persons can issues play an important role.[22] But individuals for whom these three conditions are most likely to be fulfilled are those with strongest party ties. Such individuals are most likely to derive their perspectives and orientations from the political party with which they are affiliated.

In conclusion, voting behavior is influenced by numerous factors. In seeking to explain the importance of some of these issues, Lipset suggests four social factors that affect the rate of voting and help account for the varying rates of participation discussed above. According to him, a group is most likely to vote if: (1) its interests are strongly affected by government actions; (2) it has access to information about the relevance of government policies to its particular concerns; (3) it is exposed to social pressures demanding political participation; and (4) it is not faced with opposing or contradictory pressures.[23] Thus, one of the reasons why men may vote more often than women is that they have greater information and spend more time in an environment that encourages them to vote. On the other hand, when individuals are faced with cross-pressures — i.e., when they confront social pressures demanding different political actions — people tend to withdraw from the political arena. Perhaps one reason for the lower voter participation of young adults is that they face a relatively greater number of competing and contradictory pressures than do adults.

SUMMARY

The foundation of a regime's authority and of the actions it undertakes is public opinion. Whether political systems are competitive or noncompetitive, no government can long endure if it does not have continuing support of a substantial portion of its population. The problem with public opinion is that its natural condition is anarchic. Thus, if government action is to have popular support, a unified and supportive public opinion needs to be created. In competitive systems this unity is generated by free and unregulated competition among interest groups and political parties. In noncompetitive systems a cohesive and supportive public opinion is established by the governing authorities, which restrict political opposition and establish programs of political socialization.

Since public opinion plays a significant role in determining who will govern and what policies will be carried out in democratic countries, the measurement of public opinion is generally considered a significant political activity in those societies. By using modern sampling techniques, opinion polls on political issues and candidates can provide reliable information about a population's preferences and the popularity of political leaders.

Political participation, which may be expressed individually or collectively, spontaneously or deliberately, is a means by which public opinion is transformed into political action. When individuals seek to translate their political interests into public policy, they participate in the political system. The most common type of participation is voting.

An examination of voting behavior in contemporary political systems shows many common patterns. The following are some of the most noticeable:

1. Voting rates are higher in Communist countries than in democratic states;
2. Economically developed nations tend to have higher voting rates than developing nations;

3. Voting rates tend to be higher among those who are well-educated, wealthy, older in age, urban residents, male, and affiliated with parties and other political organizations;

4. Voting rates tend to be lower among those who are less-educated, poor, young, rural residents, female, and not affiliated with political organizations;

5. In general, poorer, less well-educated social groups tend to be more radical than those of the upper social status. Similarly, young people and men tend to be more radical than older adults and women; and

6. A key determinant of voting behavior is party affiliation.

KEY TERMS

public opinion
opinion poll
probability sampling

stratified quota sampling
political participation

NOTES

1. V. O. Key, Jr., *Public Opinion and American Democracy* (New York: Alfred A. Knopf, 1961), p. 3.

2. *Ibid.,* p. 14.

3. *Ibid.,* p. 29.

4. *Gallup Opinion Index,* report no. 100 (October 1973), p. 18.

5. Walter Lippmann, *Public Opinion* (New York: Macmillan Co., 1938), Chapters 16–17.

6. John Stuart Mill, "On Liberty" in *Great Books of the Western World,* ed. Robert Maynard Hutchins (Chicago: Encyclopedia Britannica, Inc., 1952), p. 323.

7. Karl Marx and Friedrich Engels, "Manifesto of the Communist Party," in *Great Books of the Western World,* ed. Robert Maynard Hutchins (Chicago: Encyclopedia Britannica, Inc., 1952), p. 425.

8. Barbara Walters, "An Interview with Fidel Castro," *Foreign Policy,* no. 28 (Fall 1977), p. 36.

9. "The Statutes of the Communist Party of the Soviet Union" in *Man, State, and Society in the Soviet Union,* ed. Joseph L. Nogee (New York: Praeger Publishers, 1972), p. 94.

10. For a discussion of the establishment of a communist political culture in China, see Richard H. Solomon, *Mao's Revolution and the Chinese Political Culture* (Berkeley: University of California Press, 1971) and Harold C. Hinton, *An Introduction to Chinese Politics,* 3rd ed. (New York: Praeger Publishers, 1973).

11. John Gurley, "Maoist Economic Development: The New Man in the New China," *The Center Magazine* 3 (May 1970), pp. 27–30.

12. Bernard C. Hennessy, *Public Opinion,* 2nd ed. (Belmont, Calif.: Wadsworth Publishing Co., 1970), pp. 103–104.

13. *Time,* December 31, 1979, p. 12.

14. For a concise analysis of political participation see Herbert McKlosky, "Political Participation," in *International Encyclopedia of the Social Sciences,* vol. 12 (New York: Macmillan Co. and The Free Press, 1968), pp. 252–264.

15. Myron Weiner, "Political Participation: Crisis of the Political Process," in Leonard Binder, et al., *Crises and Sequences in Political Development* (Princeton: Princeton University Press, 1971), pp. 166–175.

16. Lester W. Milbrath and M. L. Goel, *Political Participation,* 2nd ed. (Chicago: Rand McNally, 1977), pp. 12–20.

17. Seymour M. Lipset, *Political Man: The Social Bases of Politics* (Garden City, N. Y.: Doubleday, 1960), p. 229.

18. Gabriel A. Almond, ed., *Comparative Politics Today: A World View* (Boston Little, Brown & Co. 1974), pp. 61–62.

19. Norman H. Nie, G. Bingham Powell, Jr., and Kenneth Prewitt, "Social Structure and Political Participation: Developmental Relationships — II," *American Political Science Review* 63 (September 1969), pp. 808–832.

20. Joseph LaPalombara, *Politics Within Nations* (Englewood Cliffs, N. J.: Prentice-Hall, 1974), p. 447.

21. *Ibid.,* p. 459.

22. Angus Campbell, P. E. Converse, W. E. Miller, and D. E. Stokes, *The American Voter* (New York: John Wiley & Sons, 1960), pp. 169–171.

23. Lipset, *Political Man: The Social Bases of Politics,* pp. 191–226.

SUGGESTED READING

BUTLER, DAVID, and STOKES, DONALD. *Political Change in Britain.* 2nd ed. New York: St. Martin's Press, 1976. The leading study on the British electorate.

CAMPBELL, ANGUS, et al. *The American Voter.* New York: John Wiley & Sons, 1960. This landmark study of American political behavior is based on the 1952 and 1956 presidential elections. Regarded as the leading work in the field, it provides many generalizations on how and why Americans vote. An abridged edition is available.

FLANIGAN, WILLIAM H. *Political Behavior of the American Electorate.* 4th ed. Boston: Allyn and Bacon, 1978. A short, informative summary of the main empirical findings about how and why Americans participate in politics.

HENNESSY, BERNARD C. *Public Opinion.* 3rd ed. Belmont, Calif.: Wadsworth Publishing Co., 1975. An excellent introduction to public opinion, including review of the theoretical and empirical literature in the field.

KEY, V. O., JR. *Public Opinion and American Democracy.* New York: Alfred A. Knopf, 1961. Although the study is concerned primarily with the United States, the insights on the nature and role of public opinion are valid for all competitive political systems.

LANE, ROBERT. *Political Life.* New York: The Free Press, 1959. A comprehensive survey of American voting behavior, focusing on those factors that encourage and discourage political participation.

LANE, ROBERT and SEARS, DAVID O. *Public Opinion.* Englewood Cliffs, N.J.: Prentice-Hall, 1964. A well-written introduction to the nature and role of public opinion in contemporary political systems. The volume also examines the role of political socialization in developing public opinion.

LAZARSFELD, PAUL, BERELSON, BERNARD, and GAUDET, HAZEL. *The People's Choice: How the Voter Makes Up His Mind in a Presidential Campaign.* New York: Columbia University Press, 1968. Originally published in 1944, this significant study stresses the impact of socioeconomic variables on voting behavior. The findings were based on interviews conducted in Erie County, Ohio, prior to the 1940 presidential election.

LIPPMANN, WALTER. *Public Opinion.* New York: The Free Press, 1953. The noted American columnist tries to dispel some common misconceptions about the role of public opinion in Western democracies. This pioneering study was first published in 1922.

LIPSET, SEYMOUR MARTIN. *Political Man: The Social Bases of Politics.* Garden City, N.Y.: Anchor Books, 1963. A collection of essays on the sociology of politics. Chapters 6 through 8 analyze social factors affecting voting.

MILBRATH, LESTER, and GOEL, M. L. *Political Participation—How and Why People Get Involved in Politics.* Chicago: Rand McNally, 1977. A comprehensive account of who participates in politics and why, and the different forms of participation commonly found in modern Western states.

VERBA, SIDNEY, and NIE, NORMAN H. *Participation in America: Political Democracy and Social Equality.* New York: Harper & Row, 1972. This award-winning study presents new insights and empirical generalizations about the nature, causes, and consequences of political participation in the United States. The findings are based on a large-scale survey of the American public conducted in 1967.

9 / THE DEVELOPMENT OF CONSENSUS: INTEREST GROUPS AND POLITICAL PARTIES

Political systems differ in the level of conflict that is openly tolerated in society. Some countries, such as Cuba, Iraq, and the Soviet Union, tend to restrict freedom of speech and of assembly; therefore, they experience a low level of visible conflict. Western democratic countries, by contrast, tend to tolerate a high level of freedom, resulting in higher levels of social and political conflict. Although nations experience differing levels of disharmony and disorder, no community is automatically capable of maintaining peace and consensus without the assistance of political institutions that can organize the competing and conflicting interests of people.

The two primary political institutions that organize the interests and concerns of people are interest groups and political parties. Both institutions play an important role in building harmony among diverse and competing interests within society. While the role of such institutions differs among political systems of the world, every country has some institutions, however rudimentary in form, that carry out this consensus-building function. In this chapter we shall examine the nature and role of interest groups and parties, focusing in particular on their function in building consensus and managing political conflict. We shall also explore briefly the role of these institutions in different types of political systems.

THE NATURE OF INTEREST GROUPS

All people have concerns, desires, and expectations about what the government should or should not do. Depending upon the problem and the type of political system, an individual may occasionally be effective in expressing his personal concerns to government decision makers and influence the actions to be taken. Most often, however, the action of an individual has limited impact on government. The reason for this is clear: the number, scope, and intensity of people's interests and concerns from government are too great and complex for any one individual to successfully influence government policy. As a result, the only effective way for people to express their concerns to government and to alter public policy is to express their interests through groups. Individual interests thus need to be transformed into group interests before they can have much influence on the actions and policies of government.

People become involved in interest groups because government decisions are made partly in response to concerns expressed by groups. Since every decision of government—i.e., laws, decrees, regulations, rules, and policies— either pleases or displeases, helps or hurts individuals, people find it advantageous to become associated with groups whose interests they share.

Definition of Interest Group

Although there is disagreement as to what constitutes an interest group, one of the most widely used definitions is the one formulated by David B. Truman. According to him, an interest group is "any group that, on the basis of one or more shared attitudes, makes certain claims upon other groups in society for the establishment, maintenance, or enhancement of forms of behavior that are implied by the shared attitudes."[1] According to this definition, the distinguishing feature of an interest group is the promotion of common or shared interests within a political system. Unlike a political party, whose goal is to get people into public office, the goal of an interest group is to influence public policy. Interest groups do not seek to win elections or control government; that is the function of political parties. The objectives of interest groups are limited and specific—to influence actions and policies of government without bearing the responsibility for governing.

Not all interest groups become directly involved in political action. Some groups are chiefly concerned with professional and economic concerns and become involved in politics only when their interests are directly challenged by the government or other organizations. Such groups are essentially concerned with private interests; therefore, their focus is chiefly nonpolitical. Other groups, however, are primarily political in orientation because of their continuing concern with the course of public policy. Such groups, known also as *pressure groups,* seek to inform and mobilize the general public on issues of broad, public interest.

Common Cause, established by former HEW Secretary John Gardner, is perhaps the best-known American political interest group. With a membership of over 325,000, Common Cause was created ostensibly to give a voice to the common man. Stated in one of its direct-mail appeals, the purpose is as follows: "Common Cause is a dynamic citizens' movement, a nonpartisan people's lobby. We are Democrats, Republicans, and Independents who have joined forces in our fight for the rights we share. We are a common cause. We came together in Common Cause because we found that everybody was organized except the people!" To express common public concerns, Common Cause has a central office of seasoned lawyers and lobbyists to inform and communicate and, where necessary, pressure government leaders to vote in accordance with the interests of "the general public."

Types of Interest Groups

Interest groups may be differentiated in terms of their scope of concern, their level of organization, and their type and style of operation.

Scope Groups may either represent general or specific interests. Although the distinction between broad and narrow concerns is ultimately subjective, it is useful to distinguish between the general and the private concerns of groups. General interests are most often espoused by mass groups, i.e., groups held together not by specific goals but by broad religious, racial, ethnic, economic, or other similar bonds. Such groups do not seek to protect their members' specific interests but rather their general concerns. Thus, blacks and workers may find it useful to be associated with groups such as the NAACP and the AFL-CIO, which promote the interests of blacks and laborers. Specific interests, by contrast, are represented by organizations that limit membership to individuals who share a common profession, a public concern, or an avocational interest. Unlike mass groups, which are often weakly organized and seldom restrict membership, special-interest groups are generally small and led by a highly professional staff. The American Institute of CPAs, the National Association of Manufacturers, and the American Bar Association are examples of such groups.

It is also possible to distinguish groups in terms of their public or private scope. Some groups exist chiefly to maximize the private interests of their members. Others, such as Common Cause, the Sierra Club, and the Foreign Policy Association, seek to defend goals that are essentially public in character. The goal of the Sierra Club, for example, is to protect the American environment, whereas the goal of the American Medical Association is to protect and maximize the interests of its member physicians.

Level of Organization Groups may be differentiated in terms of their organization. Some groups, like the American Rifle Association and the American Medical Association, are cohesive, well organized, and directed by a competent professional staff. Other groups have an unstable membership, have weak organization and leadership, and are unable to mobilize members toward common action. Cohesion and organization are significant, since the ability to influence government action is directly related to a group's ability to express its interests clearly and forcefully. Groups unable to keep their members apprised of issues and unable to mobilize them to common action are not effective in influencing public action.

Type and Style of Operation   A useful typology of interest groups has been developed by Gabriel Almond and G. Bingham Powell. According to them, groups articulate demands and interests in four fundamental ways, each of which is represented by a particular type of group. The four types of operation are: anomic, nonassociational, associational, and institutional.[2]

1. *Anomic groups* are the spontaneous, unorganized expression of concerns by alienated and dissatisfied persons. Since such groups come into existence largely out of an immediate political difficulty or impediment, the tactics often used are spontaneous violence, including demonstrations, riots, assassinations, etc. The extreme tactic is revolution. Although such groups may emerge in well-developed political systems (this was the case in the United States in the race riots of the 1960s), such groups are most often found in developing or transitional societies where political institutions and the media are not yet well developed.

2. *Nonassociational interest groups* are categoric groups, i.e., groups based upon one or more shared concerns without any formal organization to promote the common interest. Such groups are often based on racial, regional, class, or economic considerations. Since such groups do not have an organization by which group demands can be expressed, the articulation of interests is intermittent and often carried out by individuals and cliques. Nonassociational groups are found primarily in developing nations.

3. *Institutional interest groups* are groups that come into existence with the growth of particular institutions, such as the church, the military, the bureaucracy, or the university. These formal organizations do not develop in order to act as a pressure group—i.e., to articulate group demands—but to maintain a formal organization for the group's membership. Institutional groups do, of course, articulate their members' specific interests, but they also represent the more general interests and perspectives of society. Institutional groups such as the military and the church play a major role in the developing countries, since they are often the most organized political forces.

4. *Associational interest groups* are voluntary organizations or associations that individuals join to promote shared interests. Unlike a nonassociational group, associational interest groups have a formal organization by which they do this. Such groups generally have a well-organized professional staff to direct the activities and concerns of the group. Associational groups are the dominant method by which interests are expressed in the Western democratic states. They are considered the most developed form of interest groups and the most effective in influencing policy.

THE ROLE OF INTEREST GROUPS

The primary function of interest groups is to protect and maximize the shared interests of members. Most group concerns are private and nonpolitical and can be fulfilled by the group itself. But when group interests are challenged by the government or other groups, people seek to protect their shared interests by influencing the political process.

Methods of Influencing Public Policy

There are two ways by which interest groups seek to maximize their influence in the political system. First, they can publicize their demands and try to mobilize public opinion in their favor. Second, they can make demands directly on elected officials. The first approach is chiefly educational; the second is primarily political. The purpose of the first approach is to inform the public about the goals and interests of the group and to show how such interests are also those of the general public. The goal is to persuade the public that the particular interests of the group are identical with the common welfare of society. The second approach, by contrast, assumes that the pursuit of interest group objectives requires a direct appeal to legislators. Such appeals may involve providing information about the issues under government consideration or putting direct pressure on the legislators by group leaders.

Influencing the Public   Because of the significant role of public opinion in democratic societies, one way to influence public policy is to persuade people to support particular policies by informing elected officials of their support or opposition. This is often accomplished by programs of institutional advertising in which groups and institutions provide their perspectives on public policy issues. The goal of such public relations campaigns is to challenge specific beliefs and to seek to develop sympathy for alternative perspectives on issues. A more effective means of mobilizing public opinion is by direct mailings, although such a procedure is costly.

Influencing the Government   Three ways by which interst groups seek to influence government policy directly are: lobbying, party politics, and protest campaigns.

1. *Lobbying* is often called pressure politics because it involves the direct attempt to communicate concerns to legislators. The term *lobbying* arose out of the practice of trying to buttonhole legislators in public assemblies and lobbies. Today, lobbying refers to the efforts of interest groups and other political groups to introduce, modify, pass, or kill legislation.

Perhaps the most widely practiced form of lobbying is the dissemination of information. Since interest groups can often provide the most detailed and current information on issues relating to their trade, profession, or cause, legislators often depend heavily on lobbyists for data. But interests groups can also seek to pressure legislators to support the aims of interest groups. The ability of a lobbyist to gain support for his group's interests depends upon such things as size, cohesion, organization, and wealth. Groups that are large, cohesive, and whose members are wealthy and politically active are more likely to pressure legislators than are small, relatively unorganized groups.

While lobbying is found in different degrees in all political systems, it is obviously most prevalent in democratic societies, where there is open competition and conflict in the creation of public policies. Within competitive systems, lobbying is most common in countries with weak party discipline (where legislative voting behavior seldom follows the wishes of the party's leadership). When party leaders can control the voting behavior of their members, as is the case in a number of Western parliamentary systems, the impact of lobbies is limited. In the United States, party whips have limited influence to ensure organized, bloc voting. As a result, American legislators are much more susceptible to pressure from interest groups than are legislators in parliamentary systems.

2. The second way to present demands to a government is through the structure of a *political party*. The primary difference between a political party and an interest group is that the former is concerned with gaining direct control of the government, while the latter is chiefly concerned with influencing government action. Nevertheless, parties and groups are closely interrelated. In many political systems the support of political parties is channeled through interest groups.

Political parties need the organized support of interest groups; interest groups, on the other hand, need parties in control of government through which their claims and interests can lead to favorable government action. In most political systems, parties and groups are mutually dependent: parties seek to gain the support of interest groups so that they can successfully compete for government office; and interest groups attempt to establish ties with parties so that they can be more effective in making claims on the government. Because interest groups are small, they find it advantageous to become associated with political parties. They must ensure, however, that their ties are with a political party that has some chance of gaining control of government offices. Furthermore, interest groups cannot depend upon political parties for total support. Since many different interest groups become affiliated with political parties, the party may be unable or unwilling to support group interests when they are in conflict with other significant party goals.

Despite the weak and often unpredictable relationship between political parties and interest groups, groups continue to depend upon parties for achieving their goals. In Britain, for example, trade unions continue to have their interests represented in Parliament through the Labour party, while the concerns of professionals and businessmen are channeled primarily through the Conservative party. In the United States, labor groups such as the AFL-CIO and the United Mineworkers are associated with the Democratic party, while farmers and business groups such as the American Bankers Association and the American Farm Bureau Federation tend to ally with the Republican party.

3. The third method of presenting demands to the government is by *protest campaigns*. This may involve organizing a peaceful demonstration, campaign, or strike to dramatize the interests and concerns of a group. For example, when American farmers became disenchanted (in 1977 and 1978) with low prices for grains and other produce and with the absence of government support, they carried out numerous demonstrations on tractors in various state capitals and ultimately in Washington, D.C. When nonviolent methods of protest are ineffective in changing government policies, groups may become so frustrated that they resort to organized violence. In Latin America, the military has often intervened in politics to bring a halt to social and economic change or to encourage a government to undertake a series of actions or programs that the government in office has been unwilling or unable to carry out. On the other hand, groups may sometimes become dissatisfied with authoritarian regimes and use violence to oust military leaders. In 1979 the regimes of Anastasio Somoza in Nicaragua and Shah Pahlavi in Iran were both forcibly overthrown as a result of popular disenchantment with those repressive and autocratic leaders. Groups may sometimes become so disillusioned and frustrated that their opposition to government is expressed in spontaneous, unplanned violent action. This was the case in 1968 when race riots erupted across the United States following the death of Martin Luther King, Jr. The spontaneous violence that erupted in inner cities was not planned or organized but resulted largely from a long history of deprivation among blacks.

Effectiveness of Interest Groups

The ability of an interest group to influence government action depends upon numerous factors. One obvious prerequisite involves the techniques and methods used by groups to publicize demands and pressure governments to accede to their special interests. Other factors that affect a group's influence are size, unity, organization, and wealth.

The size of a group's membership is significant because it represents the proportion of people within a political community associated with a particular interest. Large groups, all things being equal, are more successful in pressing their demands than small groups. But since most large groups tend to have a weak organization and a limited commitment from their members, large categoric associations like religious, racial, or ethnic groups tend to have less impact on public policy making than do smaller but more-organized interest groups.

Group cohesion is a second important determinant of influence. Groups that are divided in their aims or that seek to accomplish many different goals often exert less influence than those with limited, specific objectives. The reason for this is that special-interest groups tend to have a higher degree of unity and a stronger sense of mission than large general-interest groups. In the United States, for example, groups like the veterans, farmers, union laborers, and business managers play an important role in American politics but may be less effective in influencing the making of public policies than the more limited and specific groups such as the Sierra Club, the American Medical Association, or the United Mineworkers.

Closely associated with group cohesion is organization. Schattschneider observes that organization is the major determinant of politics, as it is the key to success in business, war, and athletics.[3] If a group is to be successful in making claims on society and the government, it must have effective leadership and good organization in order to present its demands effectively. Organization is required because the ability of a group to influence public policy is dependent (in competitive political systems) upon the ability of leaders to get members to support their actions. This support can be demonstrated by public expression of concerns to legislators or by voting for those who support the aims of the group and by opposing those who do not. In some cases, leaders themselves can have a major influence even when organization is weak or membership is small. Ralph Nader and his consumer group, for example, have deeply influenced American legislation in great measure because of the force and persistence of Mr. Nader's personal leadership. Similarly, John Gardner and George Meany (former leaders of Common Cause and the AFL-CIO, respectively) enjoyed unusual influence because of the character of their leadership.

A final source of group influence is wealth. To the extent that money can generate influence, wealthy interest groups have an advantage in competing for society's scarce resources over relatively poor groups. To be sure, money cannot legally buy votes or influence in democratic states, but the status and privileged positions of certain professional groups can contribute toward a group's influence in society. In the United States, groups such as the American Medical Association and the American Bar Association are unusually effective in pressing their claims, even though their memberships are substantially smaller than are groups such as the AFL-CIO, a group representing nearly fifteen million workers.

Interest Groups and the Public Good

One of the philosophical issues concerning interest groups is the extent to which they can be instruments of the common welfare. Since an interest group is, by definition, a tool of a particular interest in society, such a group attempts to maximize its goals in the political system, even if it must disregard or overcome the concerns of other interest groups. The central issue is this: is the public interest found independently of the groups in society, or is it found through the accommodation and reconciliation of competing groups' demands? Is the general welfare, in other words, the product of interest group demands, or is it independent of those demands?

Historically, most ancient, medieval, and modern political theorists support the traditional or normative view of the public good. According to such thinkers as Plato, Thomas Aquinas, John Locke, and Walter Lippmann, the public good is not a relative, changing concept found by accommodation of different conflicting and competing interests in society.[4] Rather, traditional theorists assume that there are standards for achieving the public good. The function of politics is to allow enlightened, moral leaders to describe the nature of the public good and to help a political community realize those objectives. Those who assume that the public good can be known and found independently of the competing demands of political groups also generally support the notion of *natural law*—the concept that there are universal moral norms human beings can know by reason and can apply to the political process. Natural law thus provides the standard for evaluating the legitimacy of group interests within society.

One articulate defender of the traditional approach of finding the common good was James Madison, architect of the Unites States Constitution. Madison, in his famous essay, *The Federalist, No. 10,* argues that the fundamental problem in a political community is the conflict produced by groups or factions. Since factions are not concerned with the public good but only with the private concerns of the group, Madison believed that if the public good is to be realized the negative effects of interest groups ("mischiefs") must be controlled. This may be done by establishing a republic, as opposed to a direct democracy. There are two ways by which a republic can control the effects of interest groups: first, it can refine and filter the interests of groups through the representative institutions of government; and second, it can facilitate the selection of legislators able to discern the public good better than the people themselves. For Madison, then, interest groups need to be minimized in society. If the public good is to triumph, then the private concerns of groups have to be regulated in such a way that their effects have minimal impact on society. The public good can be found and applied only when interest group politics play a limited role in a political community.

The modern, democratic approach to the public good assumes that there is no cohesive, monolithic "public good." Rather, the common good is found and applied by the reconciliation and accommodation of conflicting interests in society. Even if universal moral standards of a "public philosophy" did exist, the defenders of this approach argue that its content and applicability can only be established by reconciliation and compromise among the different interpretations of the common good.

Theodore Lowi suggests that the modern view of the public good has three characteristics: first, it assumes that no special or general interest is adverse to the public interest unless it violates the law; second, all interests must be treated equally; and third, government must discover the real interests in society and then accommodate those interests through careful development of public policy. Thus, the common good is not some universal, unchanging set of moral standards but a series of perceptions as to what types of public policies and programs can benefit the most people.[5]

In short, whereas the traditional approach assumes that interest groups are barriers to finding and applying the public interest, the modern approach assumes that interest group politics is the means to maximizing the common good. Private group interests are not inimical to the general interest; they are the foundation for it.

THE NATURE AND FUNCTION OF POLITICAL PARTIES

Definition

A political party is an independent political organization that seeks to mobilize public support in order to gain control of the government. Like an interest group, a political party is a consensus-building institution in that it organizes, coordinates, restricts, and reconciles different interests. But unlike an interest group, a political party is chiefly concerned with personnel and governmental institutions, not with influencing public policy. Interest groups aim to *influence* government action; parties, on the other hand, aim to *control* government.

The concept of a political party first came into usage in the nineteenth century in competitive political systems. The term was used to denote political groups that competed for power in open elections. Political parties, according to this traditional definition, could only exist in competitive political systems. Thus, a noted political scientist observes that since parties require competition, a one-party political system is a contradiction in itself.[6]

More recently, the term *party* has been used in a less restrictive way to denote any political organization that links the people to the government, the society to the state. No longer are party politics and democracy assumed to be synonymous. The distinctive trait of a party is now assumed to be its capacity for organizing human activity toward a particular end—the placement of party representatives in political power. Thus, if the major feature of a party is its capacity to connect people with government, parties cannot be restricted to democratic regimes alone. Institutions like the Communist and Nazi parties can also be legitimately regarded as political parties.

Building on this less restrictive perspective, we shall assume that a political party can exist in any political system provided it meets the following conditions: (1) the life of the party is continuous, i.e., the party is not a temporary institution but a permanent organization whose life continues after an election or other major challenge; (2) the party aims at getting public support for its general and specific aims; (3) the party selects candidates for office and seeks to get them elected; and (4) the party aims to work within the generally accepted political rules of society.

Functions of Political Parties

The primary objective of a political party is to gain control of governmental office. In competitive systems this generally involves nominating candidates and supporting them in elections. In noncompetitive systems, parties generally gain office with the assistance of the military or mass popular support. In either case, the goal is the same—to maximize direct control over the government. In the process of gaining and maintaining political power, political parties perform three significant functions: developing consensus, directing political action, and serving as a personnel bureau.

Developing Consensus   Political parties are a country's principal consensus-building institution. The method by which domestic unity is developed is, however, different in competitive and noncompetitive systems. In the latter, political parties seek to build domestic unity primarily by programs of political education. In communist systems, for example, the Communist party places major emphasis on the development of common political values and attitudes among its members so that they in turn can transfer these values and attitudes to the general public. To be sure, political socialization is carried out in all political systems, although totalitarian systems are conspicuous in their deep commitment to indoctrination of party ideals.

In democratic systems, by contrast, political parties seek to build consensus by reconciling the competing interests and demands of individuals. This is done by organizing and limiting the range of interests within a political organization. A helpful way to understand this consensus-building function is to consider a political party as a funnel. As diagrammed in Figure 9.1, the function of a party is to process the multitude of diverse and conflicting interests of groups and individuals and build them into a homogeneous, cohesive set of demands. The process by which the conflicting claims are delimited in democratic parties is through internal party struggles, which result in victories, defeats, and compromises among various groups within the party structure. Quite often, of course, groups themselves are unable to reconcile their interests; party leaders must themselves lead and direct in the formation and development of goals and objectives. Although party leaders and followers may not at times be in accord, the continued effectiveness of a party depends upon the ability of its members and leaders to speak with one voice. Party effectiveness requires that the actions of leaders be supported by the rank and file.

Figure 9.1   The Development of Party Consensus in Democracies

Heterogeneous, Conflicting Interests → **Party Organization** → Goals, Policies, and Programs Articulated by Party Leaders

Although building consensus is a major concern, the ultimate purpose for building social harmony is to enable the political party to articulate with authority general goals and objectives. But to be effective in its expression of policies and programs, the political organization must have support within the party and from society at large. Thus, *interest aggregation* — i.e., the transforming of individual demands into public interests — and *interest articulation* are two essential tasks of political parties.[7]

Directing Political Action   If parties are to gain office and develop support for programs, they must be able to elicit popular support. This involves mobilizing people (getting them involved in the political process) and directing their behavior toward particular party goals.

Aristotle was of the opinion that man is by nature a political animal, i.e., that he had a natural propensity for becoming involved in the affairs of the state. If this assumption were completely valid, people would automatically participate in political and governmental affairs. Electoral data tends to suggest that many developed democratic countries tend to have a relatively high rate of nonparticipation in elections. This is particularly the case in the United States, where about 60 percent of the electorate vote in national elections. Moreover, if political participation is defined in terms of other types of political activities, such as involvement in community affairs, participation in civic groups, or supporting election campaign efforts, the level of political apathy in most democratic countries is even more significant.

As noted in Chapter 8, Verba and Nie developed a sixfold classification of political participation. Beginning with the least active, the six types of political participants are: the inactives, the voting specialists, the parochial participants, the communal activists, the campaign activists, and the complete activists. According to Verba and Nie, 22 percent of the American adult population is totally inactive, while 11 percent are complete activists.[8] While we do not know the proportion of adults who are inactives and complete activists in the other developed and developing nations, it is clear that all states have varying levels of participation among their people. Whether the society is deeply politicized or largely apathetic, one important function of political parties is to mobilize individuals who are uninvolved politically. This is done by making them more informed about political issues and by eliciting their personal involvement in the affairs of state.

In addition, political parties attempt to guide and direct political behavior both internally and externally. This is accomplished by organizing and supporting the activities of members. Parties select persons to represent them in government and develop goals and priorities. Parties, in effect, structure the vote by limiting the possible alternatives to be considered and supported. A large part of the vote-structuring process is carried out by caucus organizations, which establish informal rules by which parties make decisions and select candidates. The caucus is thus an important institution because it develops the framework by which the party organization is established, maintained, and operated. A member of the British Labour party or of the Dutch Socialist party, for example, is restricted in his choices to those selected by his party's leaders. By delimiting alternatives to party members and supporters, the political party plays an important role in guiding and directing political behavior.

The number and type of political parties within a country—i.e., the type of party system—also affect the way people behave politically. Countries with numerous political parties provide a greater number of alternatives than those with one or two parties. Since multiparty systems present numerous alternatives, vote structuring is more difficult in such systems than in those where selection of candidates, policies, and programs are limited to the choices of two parties. In such systems people can support either the continuation of policies and programs of the party in power or the alternative policies and programs proposed by the opposition party.

Personnel Agency The third major party function is the selection of candidates for political office and the appointment of officials to government following successful elections. If a political party is to gain power, it must nominate candidates who are loyal and who have the skill to elicit popular support. The extent to which candidates must have party loyalty and popular appeal depends upon the type of political system. In Britain, for example, where the selection and appointment of candidates is carried out by the party organization, the most important requirement for candidacy is party loyalty. Once candidates are selected to run for office, the campaign is largely based on the policies and programs of the party, not on the individual qualities of the candidate. In the United States, on the other hand, party organization is weak and election to Congress or the presidency is largely based on the leadership and charismatic qualities of the candidate. The length and quality of commitment to a political party is of comparatively little significance.

Once the election is completed and the political leaders for the executive and legislative branches are selected, the winning party (or parties, if a coalition government is required) has the responsibility for appointing public officials to run the various agencies of government. In practice this means that in parliamentary systems the leader of the majority party becomes the prime minister; he in turn selects a cabinet with whom he will jointly govern. The prime minister and cabinet share the responsibility of filling numerous government positions. In a presidential system, the newly elected president has the primary task of appointing a cabinet (with the concurrence of the Senate) and of selecting many loyal party supporters to direct and manage agencies, commissions, and departments of the bureaucracy.

POLITICAL PARTIES IN ALTERNATIVE POLITICAL SYSTEMS

The role of political parties in contemporary countries depends in great measure upon the type of political system in which they operate. Although parties carry out certain organizational activities in all political systems, the specific role that they play depends upon the nature of political competition and the level of organization within society. There are three major types of party systems: competitive, noncompetitive, and developing. Within the competitive systems, we shall differentiate between presidential and parliamentary structures.

Competitive Party Systems

A democratic country is one in which groups and parties are free to challenge the political views and policies of the governing party. Theoretically, a political system may be competitive when there is only one political party, provided the government does not attempt to limit the political involvement of other groups and does not restrict the freedom of action to opposition groups and parties. Thus, one-party systems—i.e., countries where only one political party successfully controls government—may be considered competitive when they do not restrict freedom of speech and assembly but allow opposition forces to organize and compete for control of government. Mexico, for example, is a competitive one-party system. Since the 1930s, the *Partido Revolu-*

cionario Institutional (PRI) has dominated Mexican politics, but it has done so without restricting the freedom to oppose the government. Similarly, the Congress Party dominated the politics of India from the late 1940s until the mid 1970s, yet opposition parties were allowed to challenge government policies and programs. In some developing countries, single parties dominate society in such a way as to effectively restrict some freedoms and liberties ordinarily associated with competitive systems, yet not sufficiently to regard them as noncompetitive. The developing nation variety of a one-party system often seeks to create unity by a single, mass party. For example, the objective of Tanzania's TANU party (Tanzania African National Union) is to limit the influence of regional factions and to promote the concept of unity within the nation. Unlike totalitarian one-party systems, which seek to establish a complete monopoly of political control, mass parties in developing states are much less restrictive.

Within developed, industrial states, there are two major types of competitive party systems: parliamentary systems and presidential systems.

Parliamentary Democratic Systems A central feature of parliamentary governments is their continuing dependence on the parliament. Whether the executive is supported by one or several parties, the capacity to govern depends on the ability to maintain the continuing support of the legislature. When a prime minister and his cabinet lose the confidence of a parliament — i.e., when they fail to maintain majority support for his programs — then the government must resign. Although the need for continuing support from the legislature can lead to weak and unstable government (as has been the case in postwar Italy), in practice most Western European systems have been stable. The reason for this lies in the strength of their political parties, which derives largely from two sources: parliamentary parties generally have strong central leadership and effective organization; and they exert major influence on the development and implementation of government policies and programs.

One feature of parliamentary parties is their high level of cohesion. Party unity is maintained within Parliament by the principle of *party discipline,* which means that elected legislators must support their party leaders when called to do so if they expect the support of the party in future elections. Within Parliament each party has its own caucus or committee headed by senior party officials. The party head is supported by a "whip," whose function it is to keep his members in line and ensure that they vote in accordance with party platform.[9] The extent of party control is directly proportional to the ability to control a candidate's career. Where legislators depend upon the party organization for their nomination and campaign support, they must either follow the directions of the party whip or face the possibility of not being allowed to run on the party ticket in a future election.

Outside the parliament the party is headed by a bureaucratic office, which exerts varying degrees of influence on Parliament's members. Its most important task, however, is to take care of such matters as party organization, finances, and campaigns. The central office must ensure that there is effective coordination of the various local, regional, and national party concerns so that the party can compete effectively in elections. Since the party organization carefully screens individuals whom it judges will most effectively represent its interests, the party organization has enormous influence on the selection of candidates for the parliament.

The second feature of parliamentary parties is their capacity to control government policy. In presidential systems a victory by a particular party does not ensure that its interests and goals will be implemented. In a parliamentary system, however, the government not only has the ability but also the responsibility to carry out its proposed objectives. To begin with, the leaders of the majority party generally hold the key positions of government, including the offices of prime minister, cabinet, and other key branches of government. These positions are held by virtue of the continuing ability of the government to maintain majority support in the parliament. Thus, party leaders are able to implement their programs because they can depend on parliamentary approval. Indeed, the inability of a party to dictate government policy is considered a vote of no confidence, requiring the government to resign and call for new elections.

Presidential Democratic Systems   Presidential systems are based on the practice of separation of powers. This means that the executive and legislative branches have separate but overlapping functions and that a large part of their decision making is carried out through continuous conflict and tension between the two branches. This conflict between the president and the legislature is heightened when two parties share power. Since the president and the legislature are elected through separate elections, different parties may control the two branches of government. Indeed, in countries where the legislature is divided into two distinct chambers (such as in the United States), the legislature itself may be controlled by different parties. Obviously, when power is shared among different branches of government and different parties control the major representative institutions, developing coherent policies may be more difficult than if only one party controls government. But even when one party controls the executive and legislative branches (as in the United States during the Carter Administration), executive-legislative tensions can be significant when there is little party unity. In short, political parties in presidential systems need to overcome structural impediments created by separation of powers before they can exert major influence on government decision making.

One of the major impediments to party influence in the United States is that the Democratic and Republican parties are highly decentralized. This is partly due to the federal structure of government, which requires that parties function at the national, state, and local levels. Although the Republican and Democratic parties each have a national headquarters to direct and coordinate their work, party leaders seldom have the control that their counterparts in

European parliamentary systems have. Whereas European political parties are generally tightly knit and highly centralized political organizations, North American parties are essentially decentralized organizations, with major power residing in the hands of state and local party officials. The only time American political parties become truly national is during presidential elections every four years.

Noncompetitive Party Systems

Noncompetitive systems are those in which opposition to the ruling political party is restricted or not permitted at all. The governing party maintains its leadership position by restricting freedom of expression and by controlling the level of political activity within the state. In noncompetitive systems there is no "loyal opposition." All opposition, private or public, is viewed as a threat and a challenge to the political authority of the government.

Political systems differ in the extent to which they tolerate competitive political practices. The level of noncompetitiveness in a country is determined to a significant degree by the extent to which it allows three basic freedoms: the freedom of speech, the freedom of assembly, and the freedom to replace political officials through free, competitive elections. The first freedom involves the level of expressing ideas and views in private and in public without fear, penalty, or government interference. The second freedom involves the extent to which people can organize political activity to express views and concerns different from those supported by the government. The third freedom involves the opportunity to replace government officials through free, public elections. If government actions are to be responsive to popular wishes, the most effective way to do this is to ensure that the political party with the largest popular support is permitted to govern.

Countries obviously differ in the levels and types of freedom that they tolerate. The most restrictive systems, like the Communist states of China, Cuba, and the Soviet Union, do not protect any of these freedoms in any significant way. Other countries, such as the African and Latin American military regimes, may restrict the freedom of speech. In still others, the governing party may permit a large amount of freedom of speech and assembly but not elections that might threaten loss of political authority or even the control of government.

The major function of a political party in a noncompetitive system is to lead, guide, and direct the nation. Since there is only one accepted political perspective—that of the governing party—there is no need for the general public to examine and discuss alternatives. The function of the people is to support the ideals and programs of the government. In competitive systems, political parties generally present different perspectives and alternatives to the problems of society. In noncompetitive systems, by contrast, the governing party does not seek to build its policies and programs out of conflicting and competing interests within society; rather, it seeks to build support for its actions and ideals by curtailing the amount of opposition tolerated within the state. In the Soviet Union, for example, the Communist party is the only political institution through which the people can legitimately express their interests. In countries where power is less institutionalized, political influence may be associated with a charismatic leader rather than with an organization. This was the case in Germany, when Hitler ruled with the support of the Nazi party; it has also been the case in Cuba, where Fidel Castro has used the Communist party to foster his goals for the state.

In short, political parties in noncompetitive systems are generally effective instruments for building external consensus and unity. Rather than managing social and political conflict, noncompetitive parties seek to build unity by restricting freedom and imposing order. Little or no attempt is made to manage conflict and reconcile conflicting and competing popular interests. The goal is not to manage but to suppress and eliminate conflict. Although such an approach may lead to an outward peace, the elimination of opposing ideas and proposals deprives a community of valuable input for making governmental policy and, more significantly, for ensuring a healthy, vigorous political climate.

Parties in Developing Countries

In many developing countries of Africa, Asia, and Latin America, political parties are either not well developed or do not exist at all. In 1969 Jean Blondel estimated that there were thirty-one developing countries without political parties and that in countries where parties existed the most common form was the single, mass party.[10] Part of the reason for the lack of effective political institutions in Third World states is that many have been independent only a few decades. As a result, their political parties are not well developed and need more time and experience to mature. Another reason for the absence of effective political parties in these countries is that many of them are still in the process of building national unity. Developing national cohesion is particularly difficult in some of the new states, where tribal and regional interests pose major barriers to the creation of broad, national concerns. When diversity and parochialism dominate politics, the challenge of creating and maintaining effective national parties is exceedingly difficult. When parties are established under such political conditions, the process of nation-building is one of the major challenges to party institutions.

In a widely read study on the politics of the developing countries, Samuel Huntington argues that the political instability of the Third World is largely the result of ineffective political and governmental institutions.[11] In traditional societies political stability is not difficult to maintain, but as nations become more modern and challenge traditional values of society there is a need for political institutions to channel and direct the growing and diverse interests of people. In the absence of effective political parties, public opinion is unorganized and stability is difficult to maintain. Thus, the importance of political parties in modernizing societies is that they are the major vehicles for organizing and directing the political behavior of people.

Huntington suggests that the level of stability is likely to be highest where there is only one party.[12] Multiparty and no-party systems are likely to be unstable. The explanation for this phenomenon, according to him, does not lie in the number of parties itself but rather in the strength and maturity of those institutions. The key determinant of whether or not a country will have a coup d'etat is not the type of party system but the organizational strength of its political parties. Countries with well-organized parties are far more effective in building domestic consensus than countries without them.

The weakness and instability of countries with ineffective or no political parties was dramatically illustrated by the domestic turmoil in Iran in 1978 and 1979 when the Iranian Moslems revolted against their autocratic leader, Shah Reza Pahlavi. Although the Shah brought much social and economic development to his country, the Iranian regime was not supported by any political party. The absence of political institutions to provide channels of communication between the government and the people ultimately led to extreme frustration and alienation from those in power. When the dissatisfaction could no longer be contained, the Iranian people revolted and brought down the Shah's government.

INTEREST GROUPS, PARTIES, AND CONFLICT MANAGEMENT

One of the central arguments of this text is that all human communities experience some conflict and that if they are to be effective and healthy they need to manage and direct the interests of people. Continuing, unregulated conflict impairs decision making and may lead to paralysis. The significance of interest groups and political parties is that they are the primary institutions within political systems by which consensus can be created and maintained. The pattern by which consensus is developed and conflict is controlled depends upon the type of politics practiced by the government.

Authoritarian Conflict Management

In authoritarian systems the government seeks to limit the role of group conflict by restricting the freedom with which people and groups can act in a state. Since the goal of noncompetitive political systems is to suppress and eliminate conflict—i.e., opposition to the interests and programs of the governing party—the presence of interest groups may itself be considered a challenge to the ruling party. Since the goal of interest groups is to provide a means by which a group's specific interests may influence public policy, the existence of interest groups suggests that the governing party's interests are not completely homogeneous. Early postwar studies of the Soviet Union tend to suggest that the Soviet Union was governed by a monolithic Communist party. More recently, however, studies suggest that the Soviet Communist party is itself comprised of numerous "group" interests from which the Party's policies and programs are created.[13] Groups such as bureaucrats, economists, planners, writers, and the military all play an important role in making public policy. Although the extent to which groups can espouse their distinct interests is limited in authoritarian and totalitarian regimes like China, Cuba, and the Soviet Union, interest groups play a limited role in facilitating the development of government policies. No political system is so totally homogeneous that all party interests can be directly processed by the party organization.

Unlike interest groups, which play at best a modest role in conflict management in noncompetitive systems, political parties are essential instruments by which many authoritarian and totalitarian regimes gain and maintain power. Indeed, the most conspicuous twentieth century totalitarian regimes — the Fascist regimes in Italy and Germany and the Communist regimes in China and the Soviet Union — were built by a single political party. The role of political parties in noncompetitive systems, however, is not of managing political conflict but of seeking to suppress it through force.

To begin with, since only one political party is permitted in the state, the governing party not only develops goals but also determines all outcomes. The function of political parties is not to present alternatives but to buttress government. The ruling party is free to eliminate opposing factions and ensure that its goals and objectives are implemented. Moreover, the function of totalitarian parties such as those in Nazi Germany and Communist China has not been to aggregate public interests and develop general goals and policies by carrying out compromises, bargains, and adjustments among the various party interests. Rather, totalitarian parties try to articulate goals and interests formulated by party leaders and then gain support from party members and ultimately from the masses themselves. Totalitarian party organizations, in other words, are not instruments of reconciling conflict; rather, they are instruments by which order and consensus are imposed within the party and within society itself.

Figure 9.2 illustrates the role of political culture, public opinion, interest groups, and political parties in building consensus in noncompetitive political systems. Since the ruling party or military government maintains its authority by eliminating all sources of political opposition, authoritarian regimes attempt to regulate public opinion and interest groups and permit no other political parties to criticize their decisions or challenge their authority. The extent to which interest groups influence public policy depends largely upon the level of competitiveness of the country. Moreover, the political culture and prevailing ideology play a dominant role in establishing common goals and ideals that the government seeks to achieve.

Figure 9.2 The Development of Consensus in Noncompetitive Systems

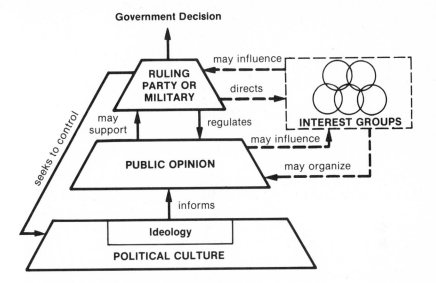

Pluralistic Conflict Management

One of the central tenets of democracy is the assumption that no individual or group has an automatic or continuous claim to government rule. The right of governing a political community, according to democratic theory, rests on one source alone—the consent of the people. The problem in competitive political systems, however, is how to develop a majority consensus among the numerous conflicting factions in society.

Unlike noncompetitive systems, pluralistic, competitive states seek to regulate political conflict by providing structures that organize group interests and then by maintaining a framework in which conflict may be resolved through elections or other related mechanisms. In pluralistic systems each of the groups comprising society has a legitimate right to express its views and try to influence public policy. Group interests are therefore essential factors in organizing individual interests and in articulating demands to officials in government. Since competitive systems place no restrictions on the political activities of groups, the resolution of group conflict is largely determined by the effectiveness with which groups make their claims. The success or failure of interest groups is thus determined by the ability to articulate demands in a highly competitive political environment where other groups are seeking similar scarce resources.

Political parties in pluralistic systems also play a critical role in managing social and political conflict. The function of the party is not to determine policy outcomes but to organize public opinion. Conflict is not resolved by political parties — that is done by the people when they elect leaders to public office. What parties do is structure political competition so that people can select officials representing different perspectives on society's issues and problems. Depending on the number of parties competing for elective office, political conflict is narrowed to the various alternatives represented by party organizations. Although competitive pluralistic systems have an infinite number of group and individual conflicts, the role of parties is to direct social and political conflict into the periodic electoral competititons. Social conflict is thus managed by converting incompatibilities and disagreements into competition for political office. When a party wins office and gains the right to carry out the decision-making process for a specified number of years, then the cycle of conflict is terminated temporarily.

The function of interest groups and political parties is thus to channel popular conflicting interests into a framework in which a temporary resolution can be achieved. The periodic resolution of political conflict requires that the losing party or parties allow the successful party to govern for the term specified by the constitution. When a party is unwilling to accept defeat (as has occurred periodically in some developing countries), then the resolution of conflict through democratic processes becomes impossible. In such an environment, political factions may continue to compete until one of them is defeated by force. The development of consensus in democratic regimes is therefore ultimately dependent upon the willingness of parties and groups to compete for political power and accept the results of political competition.

Although continuing conflict among interest groups and political parties can be beneficial, an excessive amount of conflict can weaken and even paralyze a political system if there is no satisfactory resolution of incompatible interests within society. If democracy is to effectively serve as a mechanism of conflict resolution, then debates, disagreements, and incompatible interests of society must lead to satisfactory conclusions. In democratic systems the end of discussion and debate comes primarily with the announcement of election results and the peaceful transfer of power to those who win office. It also comes through the many laws, decrees, and policies established by government agencies. The result of electoral victory or of government decisions is a temporary suspension of social and political conflict.

Figure 9.3 illustrates the major steps involved in building consensus within pluralistic countries. The development of public policies is based on a nation's political culture, which informs and structures public opinion. Ideologies also help build and maintain the values and orientations supporting the decisions of government, although their role is much less significant than in noncompetitive regimes. Political values lead to the creation of individual interests; these in turn are channeled into group interests and eventually into political parties. In pluralistic systems, the principal political competition is between political parties that compete for the right to make policies for the

Figure 9.3 The Development of Consensus in Competitive Systems

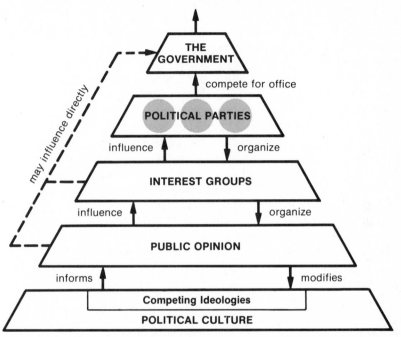

entire society. While parties are the major organizations for making public decisions in competitive systems, individuals and interest groups can (and do) directly influence the decisions of government.

SUMMARY

The two principal political institutions that organize public opinion are interest groups and political parties. Although interest groups vary in terms of their composition, organization, and function, they all perform a common task — the development of group consensus. This task is carried out either by molding and informing public opinion or by directly influencing policy making through lobbying, party organization, or protest campaigns.

Political parties differ from interest groups in that they are primarily concerned with gaining control of government. The chief aim of parties is not to influence the making of public policies but to establish direct control of the decision-making agencies of government. In achieving this aim, parties perform three significant tasks: they build regional and national consensus; they direct political action, and more particularly, structure the manner in which people vote; and they select personnel who can serve in government once the party wins an election.

Political parties perform different roles in competitive and noncompetitive systems. In noncompetitive countries, only one political party is tolerated, and the main task of that organization is to lead, direct, and mobilize public opinion. In competitive countries, by contrast, the chief aim of political parties is to compete for power and to gain office in free elections. When a political party wins an election, it gains the right to govern. When it loses, it continues to function by challenging and criticizing the policies of government and holding those in authority accountable for their actions.

Unlike the active role of parties in competitive and noncompetitive developed countries, political parties in the Third World are often absent or undeveloped. As a result, no political institutions can effectively organize and mobilize public opinion and thereby provide support for the ongoing decisions of government. If developing nations have had a high level of political instability in the past two decades, a major reason for this lies in the absence of institutions to organize public opinion.

KEY TERMS

interest group

protest campaign

natural law

political party

lobbying

interest aggregation

interest articulation

party discipline

NOTES

1. David Truman, *The Governmental Process: Political Interests and Public Opinion,* 2nd ed. (New York: Alfred A. Knopf, 1979), p. 33.
2. Gabriel Almond and G. Bingham Powell, *Comparative Politics: A Developmental Approach* (Boston: Little, Brown & Co., 1966), pp. 75–79.
3. E.E. Schattschneider, *Political Parties and Democracy* (New York: Holt, Rinehart, & Winston, 1964), p. 6.
4. For a short, general overview of natural law, see Paul E. Sigmund, *Natural Law in Political Thought* (Cambridge: Winthrop Publishers, 1971). See also Walter Lippmann's *The Public Philosophy* (New York: Mentor Books, 1955) in which the need for a public standard is set forth in order to limit the private interests of society.
5. Theodore J. Lowi, *American Government: Incomplete Conquest* (Hinsdale, Ill.: Dryden Press, 1976), p. 212.
6. Sigmund Neumann, "Toward a Comparative Study of Political Parties" in *Modern Political Parties,* ed. S. Neumann (Chicago: University of Chicago Press, 1956), p. 395.

7. For a general discussion of the role of interest aggregation and interest articulation in political systems see Chapters 4 & 5 of Almond and Powell's *Comparative Politics: A Developmental Approach.*

8. Sidney Verba and Norman H. Nie, *Participation in America: Political Democracy and Social Equality* (New York: Harper & Row, 1972), pp. 77–79.

9. The term "whip" was originally used in British politics and was derived from the "whippers-in," who kept the hounds from straying from the scent in fox hunting.

10. Jean Blondel, *An Introduction to Comparative Government* (New York: Praeger Publishers, 1969), p. 140.

11. See Chapter 1 of Samuel Huntington, *Political Order In Changing Societies* (New Haven: Yale University Press, 1968).

12. *Ibid.,* pp. 422–426.

13. The most explicit study of Soviet politics from a pluralistic perspective is H. Gordon Skilling and Franklyn Griffiths, eds., *Interest Groups in Soviet Politics* (Princeton: Princeton University Press, 1971).

SUGGESTED READING

DUVERGER, MAURICE. *Party Politics and Pressure Groups.* Translated by David Wagoner. New York: Thomas Y. Crowell, 1972. A general introduction to parties and interest groups based on a comparative analysis of European political systems.

———. *Political Parties: Their Organization and Activity in the Modern State.* 2nd ed. Translated by Barbara and Robert North. New York: John Wiley & Sons, 1967. A highly conceptual study of political parties, with a view of outlining a general theory of their rule and function in contemporary democratic states.

EHRMANN, HENRY W., ed. *Interest Groups on Four Continents.* Pittsburgh: University of Pittsburgh Press, 1958. A collection of studies on the role of interest groups in selected nations.

EPSTEIN, LEON D. *Political Parties in Western Democracies.* New York: Fredrick A. Praeger, 1979. A comparative study of political parties in Western democratic states. Less theoretical than Duverger's study.

FINER, S.E. *Anonymous Empire—A Study of the Lobby in Great Britain.* 2nd ed. New York: Humanities Press, 1966. Although dated, this remains the standard work on British interest groups.

HUNTINGTON, SAMUEL P., and MOORE, CLEMENT H., eds. *Authoritarian Politics in Modern Society.* New York: Basic Books, 1970. A collection of essays on the nature of politics in various one-party countries. The introductory and concluding chapters provide a valuable discussion about the issues and problems of single-party politics.

KEY, V.O., JR. *Politics, Parties, and Pressure Groups.* 5th ed. New York: Thomas Y. Crowell, 1964. The most influential introductory text of American parties. A classic.

LAPALOMBARA, JOSEPH, and WEINER, MYRON, eds. *Political Parties and Political Development.* Princeton: Princeton University Press, 1966. A comparative study of the role of political parties in selected emerging nations.

MICHELS, ROBERT. *Political Parties.* Translated by Eden and Cedar Paul. New York: Collier Books, 1962. Originally published in 1915, this influential study sets forth the "iron law of oligarchy," which predicts that the inevitable result of organized politics is elite rule.

MILBRATH, LESTER. *The Washington Lobbyists*. Skokie, Ill.: Rand McNally & Co., 1963. A detailed study of the role and methods of American interest groups.

NEUMANN, SIGMUND, ed. *Modern Political Parties*. Chicago: University of Chicago Press, 1956. A useful, but dated collection of essays on the nature of party politics in various states throughout the world. Newmann's introductory essay provides a clear description of the role and function of political parties.

SCHATTSCHNEIDER, E.E. *Party Government*. New York: Holt, Rinehart & Winston, Inc., 1942. An influential analysis and critique of American political parties. See also Schattschneider's *The Semisovereign People* (Hinsdale, Ill.: Dryden Press, 1975), which offers a more recent presentation of the author's perspective on parties and competitive politics.

SKILLING, H. GORDON, and GRIFFITHS, FRANKLYN. *Interest Groups in Soviet Politics*. Princeton: Princeton University Press, 1971. A study of selected political groups that influence the governmental decision-making process in the Soviet Union. Especially valuable is the concluding chapter analzying group politics in the Soviet system.

TRUMAN, DAVID. *The Governmental Process: Political Interests and Public Opinion*. 2nd ed. New York: Alfred A. Knopf, 1971. The standard introductory text on politics from the group perspective. This influential volume updates Arthur Bentley's *The Process of Government,* published in 1908.

ZEIGLER, L. HARMON, and G. WAYNE PEAKE. *Interest Groups in American Society*. 2nd ed. Englewood Cliffs, N.J.: Prentice-Hall, 1972. A widely used introductory study of American interest groups. Chapter 1 provides a useful conceptual overview of the role and organization of interest groups.

PART III
THE PRACTICE OF CONFLICT MANAGEMENT

10 / CONFLICT MANAGEMENT IN THE UNITED STATES

The American political system is significant because it is the oldest presidential regime and one of the oldest existing democracies. Unlike many other presidential systems, the United States has been able to establish and maintain constitutionalism, separation of powers, and periodic competitive elections to ensure continued representative government. In this chapter we shall examine some of the social and political factors that have helped to facilitate democratic conflict management within American society. We shall first examine some of the major impediments to social order and then review some key factors that have facilitated the development of social and political consensus. Our primary concern, however, is to analyze the fundamental norms, procedures, and institutions by which consensus is maintained and conflict is managed and resolved.

THE NATURE OF THE STATE

It is easy to forget that the United States was a part of the British Empire for almost as long as it has been an independent country. Although the United States became a separate nation in 1776, its origins date from the early seventeenth century when British colonists arrived along the northeastern coast of America to establish communities that would be free from the political and religious restrictions of the British state. The early settlers were able to find the religious and economic freedoms they had sought, but their aspirations for complete political independence were not fulfilled until some 150 years later. During the colonial period the British Crown maintained direct rule over each of the colonies. In local affairs, however, colonial communities were nearly completely independent from the British imperial government and were able to develop skills and traditions of self-government.

Local government practices were significantly influenced by British political conventions and practices. Among the values and practices the English immigrants brought to America are such notions as limited government, trial by jury, due process of law, common law principles, and political legitimacy based on representation. These ideas, along with the participatory pattern of congregational church government, helped sow the seeds of democracy early in the development of colonial local government. While many aspects of intolerance existed in the early New England colonies, the notion of political legitimacy based on direct participation became deeply imbedded in American political culture with the continuing practice of democratic town meetings. Indeed, the practice of local participatory democracy ultimately paved the way for the creation of a separate, independent republic.

During its formative years, North America was divided into thirteen colonies. As a result, when the American colonists formally proclaimed their independence on July 4, 1776, the new American country did not become one sovereign state but thirteen distinct political units. The first formal alliance among the thirteen states was created some five years later with the establishment of the Articles of Confederation, which provided for a weak central government to assist in developing and coordinating domestic and foreign policies of states. Since ultimate political authority was in the hands of each state, the *confederal* association was unable to develop effective common programs and policies in such difficult areas as banking, interstate commerce, foreign trade, military defense, and foreign policy.

In 1787 political leaders from the various states met in Philadelphia to review some common domestic and foreign problems facing the states and to propose changes that would result in "a more perfect union." The report from the Philadelphia Convention was the U.S. Constitution, a document that proposed the establishment of a *federal presidential system,* in which the central government would have more authority than that under the confederal system but less authority than under a unitary system (such as the British government). Since its ratification in 1789, the U.S. Constitution has functioned continuously as the fundamental norm for conflict resolution in the American political system.

Although the basic structures of the American political system remain largely the same since they were first established in 1789, many significant changes in the country have altered the processes of building consensus and managing conflict. Politically, American governmental institutions have become far more specialized and developed, while the scope of political activity has increased dramatically. In the late eighteenth century the public sector of the United States was probably less than 5 percent of the GNP, but by 1975 it had climbed to nearly 40 percent. In addition, there have been twenty-six major additions (amendments) to the Constitution; they have not altered the fundamental structures of government but have made the document more relevant to the changing socioeconomic climate of the country.

Territorially, the state has expanded dramatically—from thirteen states to fifty states. With nearly 3.6 million square miles, the United States is now the fourth largest country in the world. Its population, too, has grown significantly—from about 2 million in 1790 to about 216 million in 1980, making it the fourth largest nation. The social makeup of the people has changed from a relatively homogeneous white Anglo-Saxon culture to a highly heterogeneous, melting pot of nationalities. Economically, the United States has grown from a largely agrarian structure to a country with the most advanced technology in the world (average annual personal income was nearly $8,000 in 1979). Despite these political, social, and economic changes, the basic governmental norms of the American political system remain largely the same as when they were first established in the late eighteenth century by the Founding Fathers.

CONFLICT AND CONSENSUS

Government plays a central role in managing social conflict in America. Because of its monopoly of force, the state is able to make authoritative decisions about conflict management and ensure that its decisions are enforced. But by far the most significant source of conflict regulation is the American society itself. Because of its diversity and cultural heterogeneity, the American society is able to automatically manage conflict through the balancing and counterbalancing of competing group interests in society.

The notion of a self-regulating society is clearly set forth by James Madison, architect of the U.S. Constitution, in *The Federalist No. 10,* one of the newspaper articles written in support of the Constitution during its ratification campaign in New York. In that essay, Madison argues that one of the important advantages of a large republic, like the proposed thirteen-state nation, is that its large size inhibits the development of a dominant and continuing majority that can threaten the legitimate rights of minorities. Diversity of interests, he argues, tends to encourage political competition which in turn inhibits the development of a permanent group of rulers with unlimited power.

To a large extent, Madison's views have proven correct. Despite the significant pluralism in America, there has been a relatively firm political consensus in the United States. This consensus has not been created by the government's imposition of order on the people but has resulted from the automatic interplay of divergent interest groups. Indeed, the existence of a basic political and social harmony enables governmental institutions to carry out their regulatory functions. Of course, the American community has not always been a harmonious and consensual society. There have been periods, such as the Civil War and more recently during the 1960s and early 1970s, when the fundamental consensus of society appeared deeply threatened. In examining American political processes it is important to recognize some factors that have been barriers to widespread social and political consensus and those that have facilitated the development of social harmony.

Impediments to Consensus

A number of factors have inhibited the development and maintenance of consensus in American society. The first of these is the cultural heterogeneity of the people. Unlike some European countries, which are dominated by a single nationality, the United States is composed of numerous immigrant groups. From 1820 to 1965 some 43 million immigrants settled in the United States, of whom 35 million came from Europe—mostly from Italy, Austria, Hungary, Poland, Ireland, Russia, England, Sweden, and Canada. Of the 8 million non-European immigrants, the largest ethnic group is from Mexico. (Another significant ethnic group are blacks, who number about 22 million, or roughly 11 percent of the total population. Blacks, of course, did not immigrate but were brought in bondage to America to work in plantation farming in the South.) The United States is thus based on a conglomeration of numerous different ethnic groups, which are largely integrated into a common melting-pot culture. Nonetheless, American ethnic heterogeneity continues to provide a challenge to the development of a stable, consensual society.

A second impediment to consensus is the large size of the country. With nearly 3.6 million square miles, the United States is almost thirty-six times the size of the United Kingdom. The distance from the East Coast to the West Coast is nearly 3,000 miles, or more than twice the distance from London to Moscow. While the absence of natural barriers permits the development of a highly integrated transportation and communications network, the country's vast territory continues to permit significant diversity among the people. Some of the most noticeable cultural differences are between the North and the South, although there are significant differences among other regions as well. While political conflict is not directly based on regional differences, the vast territory makes it difficult to develop a highly homogeneous and integrated culture.

A third factor affecting the development of consensus is the cultural heterogeneity of the rural population. Although the rural population is only about one-fourth of the total number of Americans, the broad geographical dispersion of these people impedes the development of homogeneous cultural and social patterns. In 1970 it was estimated that nearly 53 million people lived in rural areas, of which 10.5 million lived in some 13,700 towns of less than twenty-five hundred persons. The remaining 41 million Americans lived in other rural areas.[1] Given the vast expanse of the country, small rural communities tend to develop their own distinct, parochial folkways. Despite modern communications and transportation systems, the geographical isolation of towns and rural communities tends to preserve "small-town" mores. Thus, despite a relatively high level of urbanization, large distances between cities, towns, and rural communities impedes the development of a homogeneous culture and a tightly integrated nation.

Sources of Consensus

One might expect that because of its size and diversity the United States is a highly disorderly and conflictual society. But this is not the case. Three factors help maintain the American consensus: first, wide acceptance of certain basic values; second, impact of economic development on the society's integration and urbanization; and third, broad acceptance of American political institutions.

Shared Values Two widely shared values facilitate the maintenance of national harmony—the notions of *political equality* and *individualism.* From the earliest times, Americans have believed in the political ideals of an egalitarian society. Indeed, the formal declaration of American independence written by Thomas Jefferson affirms that the legitimacy of political authority must rest on the consent of politically equal human beings. Thus, from the beginning of the republic, Americans have assumed that one of the foundational principles of a free and democratic country is the notion of equality. To be sure, the meaning of this ideal has been given different concrete expressions during various states of American political development. But however inconsistent the practices may have appeared with the ideals of equality (the historic discrimination against blacks is the most visible of these), Americans generally agree about the validity of the notion of equality. The duplicity between theory and practice did not result because of a renunciation of one of the fundamental norms of the American community but because of differing interpretations about the meaning of this ideal.

One of the reasons for the broad acceptance of the notion of equality is that from its early development the American community was characterized by a pervasive social, political, and economic equality. Unlike the more aristocratic countries of the European continent, eighteenth- and nineteenth-century America was characterized by egalitarian patterns and values. In the early nineteenth century, Alexis de Tocqueville, a young Frenchman, travelled to the United States and wrote one of the most insightful commentaries on American society and its government. In the following passage, he describes the most distinctive quality of American society as the pervasiveness of social, economic, and political equality:

> *Among the novel objects that attracted my attention during my stay in the United States, nothing struck me more forcibly than the general equality of condition among the people. I readily discovered the prodigious influence that this primary fact exercises on the whole course of society; it gives a peculiar*

> *direction to public opinion and a peculiar tenor to the laws; it imparts new maxims to the governing authority and peculiar habits to the governed. I soon perceived that the influence of this fact extends far beyond the political character and the laws of the country, and that it has no less effect on civil society than on government; it creates opinions, gives birth to new sentiments, founds novel customs, and modifies whatever it does not produce. The more I advanced in the study of American society, the more I perceived that this equality of condition is the fundamental fact from which all others seem to be derived and the central point at which all my observations constantly terminated.*[2]

While the United States has changed much since Tocqueville made these observations in 1832, the country continues to be characterized by a pervasive political and social equality. This egalitarianism has been strengthened in great part by the fluidity and mobility of American society. Although there are significant differences in wealth among people, these differences are based, in great part, on the ingenuity and skill of individuals and not on social class differences. Indeed, one of the characteristics of American society is the absence of firm class distinctions. Whereas social class is the basis of political parties for a number of European countries, American politics is not significantly related to levels of economic prosperity or types of vocation. As a result, national cleavage is rarely based on social or economic distinctions alone.

The other widely shared value in American society is competitive individualism. From the time of early colonization, Americans have assumed that economic prosperity is a direct result of individual effort and initiative and that the limit to realizing the American dream is in the hands of each person. American optimism about the future and the deep commitment to self-help are partly the result of the country's vast territory and the unlimited natural resources that were available to the early settlers.

As Americans were rewarded economically for their hard work, and as economic prosperity was shared by farmers, industrialists, and businessmen alike, competitive indivivdualism developed as the dominant economic ethos of the country. From the inception of the United States, governmental regulation was viewed as an unimportant or even unnecessary activity. Europeans, by contrast, have ascribed a far more favorable role to the state, largely because the economic development of many of their countries was influenced directly by the policies and programs of their governments. To be sure, the competitive individualistic ethos of the early Americans has lost some of its popularity as government has assumed a more significant role in directing the economic affairs of the country. But even with the increasing size of the public sector, individualism remains a widely shared belief among the American people.

Economic and Social Integration   Another source of American unity is the high level of economic development. Community consensus has not been encouraged directly by the rise in the standard of living but rather through the processes associated with economic growth. The most important of these are economic integration and urbanization. As noted earlier, the territory of the United States is vast and has the potential for creating major regional cleavages. With the exception of a few cases, however, geographical distinctions have not been a major source of conflict in American politics. One of the reasons for this is that, as the United States has become more economically developed, it has also become more integrated through modern transportation and communications systems. Since economic interdependence is essential for increased production and distribution, one of the important byproducts of greater industrialization is more and better highways, railroads, airlines, and communications systems to facilitate mobility.

Societal consensus is also encouraged by the rise in urbanization, which has historically accompanied economic growth. In 1850, when the U.S. was just beginning its dramatic growth in productivity, the proportion of the urban sector was only 15 percent. Yet fifty years later it had climbed to 40 percent and by 1970 it had reached 74 percent. By challenging the diversity of rural folkways and encouraging the development of more universal, cosmopolitan values, urbanization facilitates the development of a more homogeneous culture. Moreover, the shift from rural to urban communities makes people far more flexible and mobile. It has been estimated that one-fifth of the American people (almost all of them from the urban sector) move annually. The continuing movement of the American population thus weakens any firm regional cleavages and makes people far more adaptable and flexible.

Acceptance of Institutions   A third source of American unity is the broad acceptance of governmental structures and political processes. In the early 1960s two political scientists surveyed the political views of people in the United States, the United Kingdom, France, Germany, Italy, and Mexico. They found that the British and American people were far more likely to support their governmental institutions than were the citizens of Germany, Italy, or Mexico. When Americans were asked what aspects of society they were most proud of, 85 percent mentioned their political institutions. This was nearly twice the level found in Britain and much higher than that found in the other three countries. Furthermore, more than two-thirds of the Americans said that they found satisfaction in voting, while only about one-third of the respondents from the other four countries said they did. In addition, when asked if they felt they could do something to change an unjust law at the national or local level, more than three-fourths of the Americans indicated they did. This was about the same level for Britain but was higher than for the other three countries. Finally, one-half of the Americans said they would expect serious consideration from government officials or from police, and nearly 90 percent indicated they thought they would get equal treatment from government officials or the police.[3]

These cross-cultural findings are further reinforced by other opinion surveys. Robert Dahl summarizes the findings of some of these studies as follows:

1. It was nearly impossible to find an American who said that he was opposed to democracy or favored some alternative—at least for the United States. Quite the contrary—nearly everyone professed to believe that democracy is the best form of government;

2. Although substantial numbers of citizens approved of proposals for specific constitutional changes, the broad elements of the system were widely endorsed;

3. There was substantial agreement that if defects existed in the laws and the Constitution, they should be cured by traditional legal and political processes of change;

4. Most people continued to believe in the virtues of compromise; and

5. Most Americans claimed that life in the United States was the best they could attain anywhere in the world; few wanted to emigrate. They expected their own material conditions would improve, and that for their children life would be much better provided there is no war.[4]

In short, while Americans may disagree on political issues, they tend to concur on the fundamental rules and procedures of conflict management and conflict resolution. Like the British, Americans agree widely on the scope and methods of regulating social conflict.

The Nature of American Conflict

Despite the wide acceptance of governmental institutions and the conditions facilitating social and cultural consensus, the United States has experienced significant cleavages from time to time. By far the most important domestic conflict was the Civil War of the mid-nineteenth century when the North and the South fought over the legitimacy of slavery. While there has been no significant national conflict since then, during the 1960s and early 1970s American peace and harmony became increasingly threatened by economic and social tensions among urban blacks and university youth and by the rising level of crime and violence in the central cities.

This high level of conflict is well documented by a number of studies that show that the United States has ranked comparatively high in terms of overall levels of tensions and disorder. In one cross-cultural study of civil strife, Ted Gurr found that the United States ranked forty-first out of the 114 nations in terms of level of strife during the 1961–1965 period. When compared with the other developed democracies of the world, however, the United States ranked fifth; a higher level of conflict was found only in Belgium, France, Greece, and Italy.[5] In another comparable study of political violence during the 1948–1965 period, the United States ranked fourteenth out of 84 nations and had the highest level of violence of any Western democracy.[6] *The World Handbook of Political and Social Indicators* indicates that during the 1948–1967 period the United States had far more riots and protest demonstrations than did any other nation.[7]

Part of the explanation for the high level of conflict and tension in American society may be that democracy itself encourages open expression of disagreement and tends to tolerate greater conflict than do the less competitive political systems. Social and political conflict in the 1960s was clearly more frequent and more intense in the United States than in other competitive political systems. As a result, it was commonly assumed that the social and political tensions of the 1960s had their roots in fundamental cleavages within society.

A major source of the social tensions of the 1960s was related to the plight of the urban black communities. Inner-city blacks, discouraged and alienated by a long history of discrimination and economic deprivation, began to express their frustrations through acts of violence that ultimately resulted in riots in numerous American cities. The first major racial confrontation occurred in Harlem and Rochester in 1964, but riots quickly spread to other cities, including Watts and Chicago in 1965, Cleveland, Jacksonville, and New York City in 1966, Newark and Detroit in 1967, and Washington, Chicago, and Baltimore in 1968. By one count, from 1962 until 1969 there were more than twenty-four hundred civil disorders involving blacks.[8]

Another source of the conflict was disenchantment of university students with the political system, and more particularly with the Vietnam War. Beginning in 1964 with the Free Speech Movement at the Berkeley campus of the University of California, student groups began to demand a greater role in governing university affairs and a more significant part in the American political process. While campus radicals tended to support the demands of blacks, the issue that brought about the most militant student participation was the Vietnam War. Throughout 1969 and 1970 thousands of student groups expressed their opposition to American foreign policy through massive demonstrations, and in some cases acts of violence, in Washington, D.C., and in university campuses throughout the country. The most dramatic moment in the student opposition movement occurred at Kent State University in May 1970 when four students were shot by the National Guard.

Along with the rise in group conflict is a significant rise in the rate of individual crime and violence. As shown in Figure 10.1, serious crime rose dramatically during the 1960s. For example, from 1960 to 1974 the rate of crimes of violence (murder, forcible rape, robberies, and aggravated assaults) and the rate of property crimes (burglaries, larceny, and auto theft) increased more than threefold. By 1975 it was estimated that the total number of serious

Figure 10.1   Increase in Serious Crime in the United States, 1960–1974

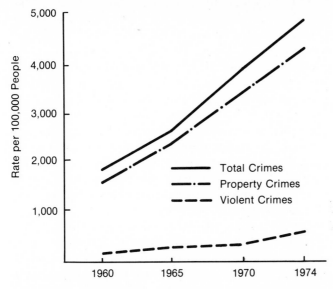

Source: U.S. Bureau of the Census, Pocket Data Book: USA 1976 (Washington D.C.: U.S. Government Printing Office, 1976), p. 142.

crimes exceeded eleven million per year. The dramatic increases in American crime not only placed growing stress on law-enforcement agencies but also called into question the effectiveness of the fundamental norms of conflict resolution in the state.

The inability of government to ensure political order and stability and to respond to the demands of people led to an increasing dissatisfaction with the political process and, in some cases, to an increasing alienation from government. A 1964 survey of American public opinion showed that 76 percent of the respondents felt that they could trust government to do the right thing almost always or most of the time. Only 54 percent of the respondents in that survey felt similarly toward government in 1970. On the other hand, the proportion of those surveyed who thought they could trust the government only some of the time increased from 22 percent to 44 percent during the 1964–1970 period.[9]

THE NATURE OF AMERICAN GOVERNMENT

Philosophical Foundations

The structures and functions of American government are based in great measure on two fundamental documents — the Declaration of Independence and the U.S. Constitution. The Declaration provides the lofty aspirations and ideals to be pursued by the American republic. The Constitution, on the other hand, sets forth the realistic guidelines necessary for generating and using political power in pursuit of the Declaration's ideals. Philosophically, American government is based on the interdependence of the idealism of the Declaration of Independence and the realism of the Constitution.

The Idealism of the Declaration   While the Declaration delineates reasons for creating an independent United States, the real significance of the document lies in its articulation of the fundamental assumptions of legitimate government. According to the Declaration, authored by Thomas Jefferson, a child of the Enlightenment and political thinker deeply influenced by the ideas of John Locke, there are three basic assumptions for establishing and maintaining legitimate political authority; first, government must protect the inherent rights of individuals, among which are life, liberty, and the pursuit of happiness; second, government must be based on the notion of human equality; and third, government power and decision making must be based on the consent of the governed. According to Jefferson, the only reason for establishing government is to preserve the inalienable rights of people; when a government fails to do this, it is the right and duty of the people to establish a new government. The legitimacy of government thus derives solely from the doctrine of *popular sovereignty*.

Although the Declaration expresses the dreams and moral sentiments of a republican government, it provides little guidance on how to establish and maintain such a political system. The Declaration affirms ideals and assumptions, but it does not articulate how the principles of popular sovereignty, political equality, and inalienable rights are to be realized in the political arena. What specifically are the concrete individual rights of people? What is the meaning of political equality, and how is it to be realized? If government power is to be derived from consent, how much conset is required before a government can implement a policy? Furthermore, should consent be continuous or periodic? The Declaration does not answer these questions but simply affirms the aspirations of democratic government. The development of implementation procedures for the Declaration's ideals was left to the Constitutional Convention delegates, a group of well-seasoned politicians concerned with the practical affairs of politics.

The Realism of the U.S. Constitution   Unlike the Declaration's idealistic Lockeian sentiments about man, the underlying assumptions of human nature in the U.S. Constitution are far more grim and restrained. The Declaration, infused with the eighteenth-century optimistic spirit of the Enlightenment, tended to assume that man was kind, rational, generous, and altruistic; the Constitution, developed by political leaders who were deeply influenced by Calvinist theology and the practical, pragmatic concerns of human political behavior, was based on assumptions of man as passionate, wicked, and selfish. Writing in the late nineteenth century, Lord Bryce observes that a "hearty

Puritanism" pervades the U.S. Constitution, a document which, in his view, was developed by "men who believed in original sin, and who were resolved to leave open for transgressors no door which they could possibly shut."[10] More recently Richard Hofstadter, the noted American historian, writes that the men who wrote the Constitution "had a vivid sense of human evil and contentiousness... They did not believe in man, but they did believe in the power of a good political constitution to control him."[11]

The Founding Fathers' major difficulty in creating effective governmental institutions was in ensuring that government be strong enough to govern the people but not so powerful that it would not be able to control itself. Given the human tendencies toward ambition, pride, and selfishness, peace and justice are not expected to result automatically from human association, but can only be established through careful management of political power. The fundamental task of the Founding Fathers was the development of a governmental framework that was strong enough to bring about peace and justice but also weak enough to avoid misuse of political power. What was needed, and to a large extent created, was a *limited* yet *powerful* government.

The task of creating a more powerful national government than had existed under the Articles of Confederation was a relatively easy task. All that had to be done was to shift political authority from the states to the central government. The more difficult problem was to create a limited or constitutional government—a government regulated by laws and not by the arbitrary wishes of men. This was done in two ways: first, specific constitutional provisions explicitly prohibit governmental and nongovernmental encroachment of individual rights; and second, governmental power is divided among several institutions and branches so that the power of one institution is checked by others.

Numerous constitutional provisions restrict and prohibit government. The most important listing of individual freedoms is the first ten amendments to the Constitution, or what is commonly called the "American Bill of Rights." These guarantee, among other things, freedom of religion, freedom of speech, freedom of press, freedom of assembly, right to trial by jury, and protection from unlawful search and seizure. The Tenth Amendment, in particular, reinforces the doctrine of limited government; it states that "the powers not delegated to the United States by the Constitution, nor prohibited by it to the States, are reserved to the states respectively, or to the people." The Fourteenth Amendment also places specific restrictions on the political authority of states by denying them the power "to deprive any person of life, liberty, or property, without due process of law."

Although explicit prohibitions against the government are important in maintaining a *limited government,* history suggests that they are not a sufficient safeguard. Many countries have bills of rights that offer little protection for human rights. This suggests the importance of internal structuring of political authority so that government power is self-limiting. In the American system this is achieved by partitioning government authority and providing that separate centers of power check and balance each other. The Founding Fathers held a pessimistic view of human nature; they believed that government would provide a means by which the selfish tendencies of people led to corruption and injustice if proper checks were not placed on government leaders. Government, they believed, can not alter human nature; it simply reflects it.

The Founding Fathers sought to develop a system that could lead to limited but effective government (given the nature of people). This was to be accomplished by the *principle of counterpoise,* i.e., the maintenance of balance of power between distinct and separate centers of power. In the words of James Madison, officials in the separate branches of government check and balance each other's interests by making "ambition counteract ambition."[12]

The principle of counterpoise is applied to the structure of American government in three ways: *separation of power, federalism,* and *bicameralism.* The first provides that the powers of government be divided among three branches. The second provides that governmental authority be partitioned between the states and the national government. The third requires the creation of a dual or bicameral legislature in which the law-making authority of the state is shared by two legislative bodies. Since separation of powers and federalism are the main doctrines for ensuring a limited government, we shall examine how these principles are applied in the structure of American government.

Separation of Powers

The system of government outlined in the U.S. Constitution is a *presidential system*—a framework in which executive, legislative, and judicial functions are separate and carried out by different officials. The first three articles of the Constitution, which comprise the bulk of the document, set forth the structure, responsibilities, and source of authority for each of the three governmental branches. The power of the Congress and of the president is to be derived directly from the people. The justices of the Supreme Court are to be appointed by the president and confirmed by the Senate. Although it was originally envisioned that the legislative branch would be the most powerful of the three governmental bodies, in practice the presidency tends to dominate the legislature.

The division of the central government's responsibilities into three distinct branches does not lead to a forceful, effective government. Dividing authority only weakens a government. What enables the American system to work is that the authority of each of the three branches overlaps (Figure 10.2). This practice, known as *checks and balances,* enables the three branches to coordinate their work and strengthen the authority of the central government. At the same time, the overlapping authority allows a branch of government to review and examine the work of another branch and to check its authority when it believes that it is contrary to the best interests of the state. Some of the ways by which the practice of checks and balances is implemented in the U. S. government are:

1. Federal laws need the consent of both the Congress and the president (Congress may override a presidential veto with a two-thirds vote in each chamber of the legislature);
2. The House of Representatives may impeach the president and Supreme Court justices; the Senate tries them;
3. The president signs treaties; the Senate ratifies them;
4. The president nominates ambassadors, federal judges, and cabinet officers; the Senate confirms such appointments; and
5. The Supreme Court may declare a law passed by Congress and signed by the president invalid if it is not in accord with the Constitution.

Figure 10.2   The Overlapping Authority of the Separate Branches of Government

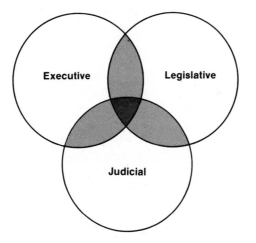

The Federal Framework

The United States was the first federal system of government. After the nation became independent in 1776, the thirteen states established a confederal relationship to encourage cooperation and unity. The confederacy, however, proved to be an inadequate instrument to coordinate the policies and actions of the separate units of government. As a result, delegates to the 1787 Constitutional Convention met in Philadelphia to deal with the structural weaknesses of the confederacy. They proposed a novel experiment — federalism. The new system combined elements of the existing confederal system and of the unitary system of Britain. The power of the central government would be increased substantially, yet the governments of each of the thirteen states would continue to play a significant role. Government would operate simultaneously at the national and state levels.

Although the U.S. Constitution does not use the term *federal,* the principles of that document clearly provide for dual government since it sets forth the duties and responsibilities of each level. Some of these duties are given to either the national or the state government. Others, such as the power to tax, borrow, or spend for the general welfare, are shared or concurrent responsibilities. Moreover, the Constitution also delineates specific prohibitions on both national and state governments. For example, the central government may not give preferential treatment to states in commercial matters, nor can it admit states on a basis of inequality with existing states. States, on the other hand, are prohibited from such things as taxing imports or exports, passing laws that impair contractual obligations, or coining money. To be sure, specific Constitutional provisions do not eliminate all tensions between national and subnational units of government. When tensions arise over competing regulatory claims, the central government has final authority. The Constitution provides that laws of the federal government are to be considered the supreme law of the land.

Given the federal structure of government, conflict management in the American nation occurs basically at national and state levels. All residents in the United States are subject to the rules and regulations of the national government, regardless in which state or locality they live. Additionally, persons are subject to the laws of the state in which they reside. Each of the fifty states has its own legislative, executive, and judicial institutions for making, enforcing, and enterpreting laws; it is the responsibility of all persons to live in accordance with the state statutes to which they are subject. Americans are thus continuously responsible to two levels of governmental authority. No matter where they reside or visit, they are always subject to national and state laws.

INSTITUTIONS OF CONFLICT MANAGEMENT

Government is a pervasive force in American society. Whether at the village, city, county, state, or national level, governmental institutions are always present to maintain community order, settle disputes, protect the rights of citizens, and provide needed social services. In a city such as Chicago or New York, hundreds of governmental institutions make authoritative policies for citizens. One political scientist has estimated that there are nearly eighty thousand government units in the United States that help regulate the behavior of citizens.

Of the many formal institutions of conflict management, the most important are those of the national government. They are the most significant institutions because they have final responsibility for decision making within the state. We shall therefore examine the nature and role of each of the three major institutions of government—the presidency, Congress, and the courts.

The Presidency

The American political system is called a presidential government because the president has a dominant position in the state. As head of the government he rules; as chief of state he reigns. The president is the central figure for ensuring community consensus and for managing societal conflict. The president's power in the government is derived in great measure by his numerous functions and by the popular support generated in his election to office. Although the final selection of a president is in the hands of an electoral college,[13] ordinarily the presidential candidate who receives the most popular votes also becomes president. Unlike a prime minister, whose term is dependent on the continuing support of the parliament, the president is elected to serve for a term of four years. If he is impeached, tried, and convicted of a crime, or if he resigns (as President Nixon did in 1974), the vice-president takes over as chief executive. A president may be reelected only once.

The president has five central constitutional duties. First, he is the chief of state. This means that he performs the major symbolic and ceremonial functions of a state, tasks undertaken by a king or queen in a parliamentary system. As head of state, the president must ensure that peace and order prevail in the country and that consensus is encouraged through the symbols of executive authority.

Second, the president, as head of the government, is responsible for administering all government programs and policies and for managing a federal bureaucracy of more than 6 million civilian and military employees. The president's ability to control federal institutions comes largely from his ability to appoint close to fifteen hundred administrators, including twelve cabinet officers to head the major executive departments. The president also has his own White House administrative staff of some five hundred persons who assist him in coordinating the various departments and agencies of the government.

Third, the president is commander-in-chief of the armed forces. Although Congress must declare war and appropriate funds for defense, the responsibility for developing, training, supervising, and deploying military forces is the president's. It is he who must ensure that the nation is prepared to defend itself from foreign aggression; it is he who, as leader of the armed forces, must ultimately direct military operations during time of war.

Fourth, the president is chief diplomat. As head of the foreign-policy-making establishment, he has the responsibility for coordinating foreign relations and for ensuring that U.S. national interests are maximized within the international system. While the secretary of state ordinarily has ongoing responsibility for developing foreign policy, the final responsibility for American foreign relations is in the hands of the president. He must ultimately decide how the nation's national interests can best be achieved within the competitive world system.

Finally, the president is chief initiator and implementor of legislation. Although each year more than ten thousand bills are introduced into Congress, the most significant bills are those prepared by the White House. The executive develops the major legislative programs and prepares the proposed annual budget of the government. With few exceptions, the initiative for all major bills comes from the executive branch. In addition, the president also must ensure that bills once enacted into law are "faithfully executed." This means that the president must carefully implement the policies, programs, and regulations established by federal law and, where necessary, use federal law-enforcement agencies to ensure compliance.

The Congress

The United States Congress is a bicameral legislature of 535 elected members — 100 senators and 435 representatives. Although the division of the legislature into two separate chambers provides a mechanism by which the work of legislators can be internally checked, the original reason for establishing a bicameral legislature was expediency, not the application of the principle of checks and balances to ensure a limited government. The most difficult problem for the authors of the U.S. Constitution was the issue of legislative representation. Small states wanted equal representation; large states wanted representation based on population. In the end a compromise reconciled the two conflicting perspectives: the interests of small states would be protected in the Senate, where each state has two representatives; the interests of large states would be protected in the House of Representatives, where representation is determined on the basis of population.

Originally, the difference in population between large and small states was not that large. In 1790, for example, the non–slave population of Virginia was about eight times that of Delaware. Today, however, the population differentials between large and small states are many times greater. In 1970, for example, the population of California was nearly 20 million, while the population of Alaska was only about three hundred thousand. The result of the fixed representational character of the Senate is that underpopulated states have a significant representational advantage. Thus, there is one senator for every 150,000 persons in Alaska but only one senator for every ten million Californians.

Apportionment of seats in the House of Representatives is much more difficult than in the Senate. Since 1911, the number of members in the House has been fixed by law at 435, but the distribution of seats has continuously shifted among states. Since representation in the lower chamber must be based on relative size of population, increase or decrease in population relative to other states changes the number of representatives. Thus, between 1950 and 1970, the number of California representatives increased by thirteen, while the number of representatives for New York and Pennsylvania declined by four and five, respectively.[14]

Besides representational differences, the House and Senate differ in other important ways. First, the Senate tends to be more informal and slower in its deliberations. This is partly due, perhaps, to the smaller size of the Senate, which permits a more relaxed and intimate relationship among its members. In addition, the longer term of the senators (six years as opposed to two for the House) results in a greater freedom to focus on substantive work. Second, senators tend to be concerned with broader, more general concerns than are representatives. Since senators are elected by the entire population of a state, they must represent the general interests of the state. Members of the House, by contrast, are accountable to their districts, which most often have more limited interests.

Congress performs three major functions: representation of interests, making of laws, and overseeing of government operations. The legitimacy of government derives in great measure from its representational character. Similarly, the authority of Congress is based on the understanding that legislators represent their constituents' interests. Thus, it has generally been assumed that a major responsibility of senators and representatives is to protect and maximize the interests of their states and congressional districts.

The extent to which congressmen act in their constituents' behalf is open to much doubt. First, the American voter does not seem to be aware of or interested in the decisions of Congress. Studies have shown that only a small portion of the electorate is aware of the central issues in Congress or the positions taken by their legislators.[15] Second, even if a congressman knew how his constituents felt about issues, it would be difficult to determine the nature and level of support for such concerns. Not only are constituents generally divided on public policies, they also tend to differ in the intensity with which they support or oppose issues. Third, studies have shown that numerous factors affect a congressman's voting behavior. In a recent survey of representatives, the most important determinant of voting behavior was the influence of House and Senate colleagues. This was followed closely by the impact of constituents (Table 10.1)

The second major function of Congress is to make laws. In order for a bill to become law, it must pass both chambers in identical form. Since the Senate and House often amend proposed legislation, there is often a need to reconcile divergent bills. This is done in a *conference committee,* a group of senators and representatives who helped pass the proposed legislation in their respective chambers. After a compromise has been reached, the bill goes back to the two legislative bodies for final approval. The last stage of the law-making process is submission of the bill to the president. He can sign it into

TABLE 10.1   Significance of Influences on Representatives

REPORTED IMPORTANCE	CONSTITUENCY	FELLOW CONGRESSMEN	INTEREST GROUPS	PRESIDENCY
Determinative	7	5	1	4
Major importance	31	42	25	14
Minor importance	51	28	40	21
Unimportant	12	25	35	62
Total	101%	100%	101%	100%

SOURCE: After Table 1-2 "Actor Importance" (p.9) from CONGRESSMEN'S VOTING DECISIONS, 2nd Edition by John W. Kingdon. Copyright ©1981 by Harper & Row, Publishers, Inc. Reprinted by permission of the publisher.

law, let it become law without his signature, or return it to Congress for reconsideration. Congress may override the president's veto with a two-thirds vote in each chamber.

Since congressmen have different values, political orientations, and representational commitments, the deliberations of Congress are characterized by much conflict. Laws, however, can be passed only if there is a majority consensus. One of the important functions of Congress is to represent incompatible and conflicting interests and then to resolve the disharmony when decisions need to be made. There are two ways by which legislative conflict is resolved. The first is compromise, which occurs when two opposing groups accept a middle ground alternative. The second approach is logrolling. This involves gaining support from those opposing an action either by promising support for actions they will initiate or by including appropriation of public funds for programs in their districts. This latter type of legislation is called *pork barrel;* it usually involves establishing numerous public works benefitting constituents from areas where legislative support is desired.

The third function of Congress is to oversee the work of government. This is an increasingly important function because Congress has delegated many legislative responsibilities to bureaucratic agencies and departments of government. As a result, Congress does not seek to design policies and programs in their entirety but to hold agencies and departments accountable for effectively carrying out the goals and objectives established by Congress. Since Congress holds the power of the purse, the continued funding of programs depends on the extent to which Congress is satisfied with the performance of the bureaucracy. The continuation, expansion, or reduction of programs is thus in the hands of Congress.

Closely associated with this last function is the informational contribution of Congress. When important issues are being considered, debates and hearings within the Senate and the House provide a means for educating the American people. For example, the Senate debate over the Panama Canal Treaty helped inform the people about an important foreign-policy issue. Hearings in the Senate Foreign Relations Committee in the last half of 1979 on the proposed SALT II Treaty significantly heightened awareness of growing imbalances in American-Soviet military forces.

In order for Congress to carry out its many tasks, it is supported by numerous committees and subcommittees. In 1978, there were eighteen standing (or permanent) committees in the Senate and twenty-two in the House. Each of these committees is supported by a host of subcommittees, numbering close to 120 in each chamber. Each of the committees and subcommittees is headed by a chairman selected by the majority party. Ordinarily the most senior party member (seniority is determined in terms of continuous, unbroken service) is selected chairman. During the 92nd Congress (from 1970 until 1972) House committee chairmen averaged twenty-eight years of service and Senate chairmen averaged twenty-one years.

The Judiciary

The federal judicial system is composed of three levels of courts. At the highest level is the U.S. Supreme Court, a body of nine justices appointed by the president and confirmed by the Senate. The Supreme Court's judicial jurisdiction extends to both original cases and cases of appeal. It may review a judicial case heard in a lower court, or it may examine a case that has not been examined previously. The intermediate level consists of eleven Courts of Appeal. Established by Congress in 1891, these courts have from three to nine judges and ordinarily hear only cases appealing decisions of lower federal courts. The third judicial level consits of some eighty-nine district courts whose jurisdiction involves hearing original cases involving violations of federal statutes.

Federal courts perform at least two main important functions. First, they interpret federal laws, including the Constitution itself. Legal interpretation is normally undertaken on the basis of the principle of *stare decisis,* which means that laws must be interpreted in the light of precedent unless there is a clear and compelling reason not to do so. American courts (including the Supreme Court) never offer advisory opinions on the meaning of laws. Federal courts examine only substantive issues, and their interpretations of federal law are issued in terms of concrete disputes. The function of *judicial review*—the power to declare an act of Congress unconstitutional—is thus always undertaken within the context of specific laws.

The second important function of federal courts is to hear and settle disputes involving federal law. Most of the work of the district and appeals courts involves hearing cases on violations of federal law. In some cases, these violations may involve private parties; most of the time, however, the government is one of the parties to the dispute as it tries to prosecute alleged violations of federal statutes. The major responsibility for prosecuting federal violations is in the hands of the Justice Department, headed by the Attorney General and supported by assistant attorneys located in each of the federal districts. Their responsibility is to prosecute federal criminals. When sufficient evidence is accumulated, the alleged criminal is indicted (accused) and brought to trial at one of the district courts. There, federal prosecutors present their evidence, and the defendant's lawyer presents his defense against the alleged violations. The function of the federal judge is to ensure that the court remains a neutral arena so that the jury may determine the guilt or innocence of the accused. If a party loses its case, it may appeal the decision of the district court to the appropriate U.S. Court of Appeals and eventually to the Supreme Court itself. (Figure 10.3 presents the major relationships among the three branches of government. The diagram obviously covers only the major relationships among the central components of American national government.)

Figure 10.3   Major Components of the American Political System and their Interrelationships

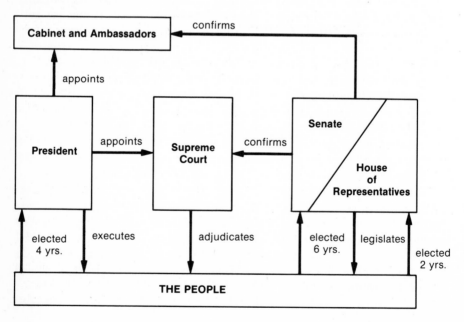

PROCESSES OF CONFLICT MANAGEMENT

As noted earlier, the development of community consensus is carried out largely through nongovernmental means. The task of government is not to create order and harmony out of a totally chaotic society but rather to refine and strengthen social harmony. This is done by guiding and directing American society through government decisions and by maintaining a framework for selecting officials for positions of political leadership.

The government's capacity to lead and direct society and to manage and resolve social conflict depends upon the continuing support of a large segment of the American people. This support is channeled to a significant degree through *interest groups* and *political parties,* political institutions that provide the connecting link between the people and the government. Interest groups provide an informal method by which people can organize and express common concerns to public officials. Political parties, by contrast, are much larger, more influential institutions that seek to gain control of government offices through competitive elections. In order to understand how American parties and interest groups conribute to the building of national consensus and to the management of social and political conflict, we first need to examine briefly the nature of politics in the United States.

The Character of American Politics

The development of national consensus does not result automatically from political competition among interest groups and political parties. Political conflict cannot always be managed and resolved by the interaction of competing political groups. Sometimes, conflict can become so intense that maintenance of social harmony becomes difficult, and the making and implementation of laws and policies by the government is significantly impaired. When society becomes deeply polarized and competing groups are unwilling to reconcile their incompatible goals through compromise, the development of a stable, harmonious society becomes difficult, if not impossible.

Fortunately, American society has rarely been deeply polarized along social classes, geographical boundaries, or dominant political issues. With the exception of the nineteenth-century Civil War, American conflict has generally been diffuse and focused on numerous, relatively minor issues. Occasionally, political cleavages have become significant, as in the mid 1960s on civil rights issues. But most groups have generally been able to work out their incompatible interests within the framework of party structures or governmental institutions.

The development of national consensus and the resolution of political conflict are greatly facilitated by the pluralistic character of the American electorate. Americans are a highly heterogeneous people who live in a vast country where political diversity is not only tolerated but encouraged. Although Americans are divided on the major social, political, and economic issues in society and on how government should cope with the dominant problems of the country, there are no dominant cleavages in the nation. Neither social class, economic profession, nor geographical location is a significant source of political conflict. Unlike British politics, which is based significantly on class cleavages, economic and social differences in the United States do not result in dominant political cleavages. As the data in Table 10.2 indicate, public opinion does not vary significantly between the professional or managerial classes and those in manual or clerical positions. Moreover, political opinion does not appear to be affected greatly by regional considerations. As Table 10.3 suggests, public opinion is virtually the same throughout the nation. Since there are no dominant differences on public policy issues among social classes or territorial regions, there is little basis for the development of significant political cleavages.

TABLE 10.2   Public Opinion on Selected Issues (1974)

ISSUES	PROFESSIONAL AND BUSINESS	CLERICAL AND SALES	MANUAL
1. Favors busing to achieve racial balance	25	30	41
2. Favors diplomatic relations with Cuba	71	72	61
3. Favors reduction of military spending	56	62	55
4. Favors reduction of social programs	33	38	30
5. Favors the Equal Rights Amendment	80	87	77

Source: The Gallup Opinion Index, *Report No. 113, November 1974.*

One of the major reasons for the lack of significant political divisions along territorial, class, or ideological dimensions is the existence of a pluralistic political culture that inhibits single-issue political divisions. Most Americans belong to a number of interest groups but seldom belong to the same ones as their neighbors and friends. Moreover, people often agree on many social, political, and economic issues, but seldom agree on all issues of public concern or on which ones are most significant politically. Because of the diversity of interests and the variety with which group interests are expressed in society,

TABLE 10.3 Public Opinions on Selected Issues by Region (1974)

ISSUES	EAST	MIDWEST	SOUTH	WEST
1. Favors busing to achieve racial balance	36	30	37	35
2. Favors the death penalty for persons convicted of murder	63	63	66	63
3. Favors reduction of social programs	32	36	39	29
4. Favors diplomatic relations with Cuba	68	64	55	67
5. Favors reduction of military spending	59	56	52	54

Source: The Gallup Opinion Index, *Report No. 113, November 1974.*

single-issue politics is seldom the basis of American political conflict and consensus. Rather, the foundation of American political harmony is the multitude of conflicting group interests that encourage flexibility and and pragmatic adjustment.

The Nature of Political Parties

National consensus is also facilitated by the two major American parties. They have contributed to the building of national unity because of their large size and broad political orientation. In comparison to European parties, American parties play a less significant role in directing and organizing public opinion, managing electoral campaigns, and guiding the decisions and politics of government after they have successfully competed for power. American interest groups, by contrast, have more influence than do their European counterparts. The relative strength of interest groups and the comparative weakness of political parties in the United States derives in great measure from the nature of American political parties.

American party structures share three significant characteristics: first, they are not ideological in orientation; second, they are not administered by strong central offices; and third, party leaders have limited control over the actions of their members once they are elected to office.

1. U. S. political parties have historically been pragmatic rather than ideological in character. Unlike European parties, which are based on well-defined principles and goals, American institutions are usually guided by general but concrete programmatic interests. The major objective of

American parties is to maximize popular support and political influence over government policy. Parties therefore maintain a flexible and pragmatic orientation to maximize popular appeal. But the major reason for the absence of a strong ideological focus is that the American electorate itself is not divided along clear ideological positions. Most Americans hold moderate political views, i.e., ideas that are at neither extreme of the political spectrum. While studies show that party leaders hold more extreme positions than party followers,[16] these differences have always been kept in check by the people who hold ultimate control over the direction and aims of the Democratic and Republican parties. The lack of significant political differences between Democrats and Republicans is illustrated in Table 10.4. While party officials rank key issues differently, the data suggest substantial agreement among both political organizations.

TABLE 10.4   Party Officials' Ranking of Issues in Terms of Overall Importance

REPUBLICANS	DEMOCRATS
1. Curbing Inflation	1. Reducing unemployment
2. Reducing role of government	2. Curbing inflation
3. Maintaining a strong military	3. Protecting freedom of speech
4. Developing energy sources	4. Developing energy sources
5. Reducing crime	5. Achieving equality for blacks
6. Reducing unemployment	6. Reducing crime
7. Protecting freedom of speech	7. Giving people more to say in government decisions
8. Giving people more say in government decisions	8. Achieving equality for women
9. Achieving equality for blacks	9. Maintaining a strong military defense
10. Achieving equality for women	10. Reducing the role of government

Source: Survey by The Washington Post *and the Harvard University Center for International Affairs.*
The Washington Post, *September 27, 1976.*

Figure 10.4 provides a general description of the political distribution of the American electorate. Since most Americans consider themselves political moderates, the members of the Democratic and Republican parties tend to overlap within the political center. Individuals who do not consistently support either party but tend to split their electoral support are called *independents*; they represent a growing political force in American politics. In 1952, for example, only 22 percent of American voters considered themselves independents, but by 1976 this number had increased to 36 percent. The growth of political independents comes at the expense of both major parties. The Democratic party declined in electoral strength during the 1952–1976 period by 8 percent (from 47 to 39 percent), while the Republican party declined by 4 percent (from 27 to 23 percent).[17]

Figure 10.4 Political Distribution of the American Electorate

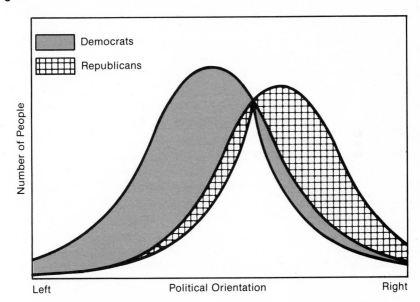

2. Another characteristic of American political parties is weak central organization. The lack of national party cohesion derives largely from the decentralized structure of the parties. Although both Democratic and Republican parties are coordinated by national committees, party power is not in the national headquarters but in the state party organizations. State institutions not only control state politics but also play a major role in selecting delegates to the quadrennial national party convention and to the national party committee. While national party committees are (in principle) the head of the two parties, the effective power of the institutions lies in the states. American parties are thus local and state organizations that become national every four years for presidential elections. In the interim, national party offices are largely confined to fund raising and public relations.

3. A final significant characteristic of American parties is their lack of internal discipline. Since political parties are loosely organized both at state and national levels, party leaders are unable to effectively control

governmental activities of their party's elected officials. While party organizations contribute significantly to the selection and election of political candidates, they are relatively ineffective in directing the course of public policy development. Unlike the discipline of European parliamentary parties, state and national legislators rarely vote along party considerations alone. Party officials often vote similarly on issues, but no party organization has the influence and strength (as in the English political system) to ensure that party positions are supported by legislators. As a result, American legislative politics is not only unpredictable but also characterized by intense conflicts between bicameral legislative chambers and between the legislature and the executive, even though the same party may control each of these political institutions.

Because of their nonideological nature, weak cohesion, and lack of organizational discipline, American political parties are able to generate broad electoral support. Since the two major parties have no clear ideological orientation or commitment to well-defined goals, the intensity of public support toward each of the parties is modest — at least when it is compared with the fervent support generated by ideological parties. On the other hand, American parties are able to develop support from a broader and more diffuse political constituency. The scope of support is therefore significant, but the level of commitment toward party objectives is limited. As a result, American parties are able to win elections and gain control of government positions but are then unable to provide a well-defined set of goals and priorities to elected officials. Given the absence of clear party goals and the lack of party discipline, elected officials are subject to political influence from their constituents, bureaucratic officers, and interest groups. Indeed, the political vacuum created by the lack of clear party goals has most often been filled by interest groups, which compete for influence in the policy-making process.

As noted at the beginning of this chapter, the United States is characterized by a high degree of conflict when compared with other developed democratic countries. Although such conflict challenges the American political system, it also ensures that changing values and interests of the people are not inhibited. The open toleration of diversity and conflict is one of the strengths of American government. Such freedom and openness not only permits continual change within political institutions but also helps ensure a dynamic and vigorous society.

SUMMARY

The United States is a large, heterogeneous nation. Despite the diversity of its people and the frequency of political conflict among parties, interests groups, and individuals, the American nation enjoys a substantial amount of unity and social consensus. This cohesion derives partly from shared social and political values, effective networks of economic and social integration, and the wide acceptance of the instituions of government. With few exceptions, when major tensions and conflict develop within the American political system, the institutions of government adapt to the changing values and interests of the people.

The foundation of American government lies in the idealism of the Declaration of Independence and the realism of the Constitution. The Declaration provides the aims and aspirations of the nation; the Constitution provides the structural rules by which those aims are realized.

The United States is a presidential democracy. The Founding Fathers established a constitutional (or limited) system of government by partitioning political power yet allowing different branches of government to interact to ensure energetic and vigorous policy making. The primary means of partitioning government authority include separation of powers and federalism.

The main institutions of conflict management in the United States are the three national institutions of government — the presidency, Congress, and the courts. The effectiveness of these institutions, particularly of the executive and legislative branches, depends significantly upon the nature and role of political parties and interests groups. These two political organizations provide the primary instruments for building national consensus, which is the base of government authority. American parties are effective organizations for building a broad political consensus, although they have been ineffective in developing specific and widely accepted goals that can be implemented by government. As a result, policy making is not as strongly controlled by party organizations as it is in other Western European states.

KEY TERMS

confederal	bicameralism
federal	federalism
political equality	checks and balances
individualism	conference committee
popular sovereignty	judicial review
counterpoise	pluralistic
separation of powers	independent

NOTES

1. U.S. Bureau of the Census, *Historical Statistics of the U.S.,* Part 1 (Washington D.C.: U.S. Government Printing Office, 1975), p. 11.
2. Alexis de Tocqueville, *Democracy in America* (New York: New American Library, 1956), p. 26.

3. Gabriel A. Almond and Sidney Verba, *The Civic Culture* (Boston: Little, Brown & Co., 1965), pp. 64, 108, and 173.

4. Robert A. Dahl, *Democracy in the United States: Promise and Performance,* 4th ed. (Boston: Houghton Mifflin Co., 1981), pp. 42–43. Used with permission.

5. Ted Robert Gurr, "A Comparative Study of Civil Strife" in *The History of Violence in America,* ed. Hugh Davis Graham and Ted Robert Gurr (New York: Frederick A. Praeger, 1969), p. 629.

6. Ivo K. Feierabend et al., "Social Change and Political Violence: Cross-National Patterns" in *The History of Violence in America,* ed. Hugh Davis Graham and Ted Robert Gurr (New York: Frederick A. Praeger, 1969), p. 652.

7. Charles Lewis Taylor and Michael C. Hudson, *World Handbook of Political and Social Indicators,* 2nd ed. (New Haven: Yale University Press, 1975), pp. 114–115.

8. Peter H. Rossi, Richard A. Berk, and Bettye K. Eidson, *The Roots of Urban Discontent* (New York: John Wiley and Sons, 1974), p. 4.

9. Arthur H. Miller, "Political Issues and Trust in Government, 1964–1970," *American Political Science Review* 68 (September 1974), p. 953.

10. James Bryce, *The American Commonwealth,* 3rd ed. (New York: Macmillan Co., 1893), vol. I, p. 306.

11. Richard Hofstadter, *The American Political Tradition and the Men Who Made It* (New York: A.A. Knopf, 1948), p. 1.

12. The idea of counterbalancing centers of powers is analyzed by James Madison in *The Federalist No. 51.*

13. The electoral college is comprised of individuals selected by the winning party in each state. The number of electors from each state is equal to the combined number of senators and representatives.

14. U.S. Bureau of the Census, *Historical Statistics of the U.S.,* Part 2 (Washington D.C.: U.S. Government Printing Office, 1975), p. 1085.

15. See Angus Campbell, Philip E. Converse, Warren E. Miller, and Donald E. Stokes, *Elections and the Political Order* (New York: John Wiley & Sons, 1966), pp. 204–207.

16. Herbert McClosky, Paul J. Hoffman, and Rosemary O'Hara, "Issue Conflict and Consensus among Party Leaders and Followers," *American Political Science Review* 54 (June 1960), pp. 406–427.

17. William H. Flanigan and Nancy H. Zingale, *Political Behavior of the American Electorate,* 4th ed. (Boston: Allyn and Bacon, 1979), p. 54.

SUGGESTED READING

BARBER, JAMES DAVID. *The Presidential Character: Predicting Performance in the White House.* Englewood Cliffs, N.J.: Prentice-Hall, 1972. A pioneering psychobiographical study of the American presidency from Taft to Nixon. Seeks to develop a psychological typology in order to explain and predict presidential performance.

CAMPBELL, ANGUS, et al., *The American Voter.* New York: John Wiley & Sons, 1960. A landmark study of American voting behavior. Although the conclusions are based on survey data from the 1952 and 1956 presidential elections, most of the insights and conclusions are still valid. An abridged edition is available.

CLAUSEN, AAGE R. *How Congressmen Decide: A Policy Focus.* New York: St. Martin's Press, 1973. A detailed analysis of how Congressmen vote, based on selected roll call votes from 1953 to 1964 and 1969 to 1970.

DAHL, ROBERT A. *Who Governs?* New Haven: Yale University Press, 1961. A detailed examination of the decision-making process of the town of New Haven, Conn. The study found that power is shared by numerous different groups in New Haven and therefore tends to support the pluralistic conception of American politics.

FENNO, RICHARD F., JR. *Congressmen in Committees.* Boston: Little, Brown & Co. 1973. An important study of the nature, organization, and operation of congressional committees. The study is based on a detailed study of six House committees and their Senate counterparts.

LEWIS, ANTHONY. *Gideon's Trumpet.* New York: Random House, 1964. A lucid and interesting account of the Supreme Court case establishing the right of a defendant to legal assistance, even if a person does not have funds for a lawyer.

LOWI, THEODORE J. *The End of Liberalism: Ideology, Policy, and the Crisis of Public Authority.* New York: W.W. Norton, 1969. An insightful but controversial study of the impact of interest group politics on the American political system. Argues that the interest group approach to policy making is unable to solve society's problems and meet its basic needs.

NEUSTADT, RICHARD E. *Presidential Power: The Politics of Leadership from FDR to Carter.* 2nd ed. New York: John Wiley and Sons, 1980. An influential study of how presidents gain and maintain power. Neustadt argues that a president's effectiveness is determined ultimately by his capacity to persuade.

ROSSITER, CLINTON. *Seedtime of the Republic.* New York: Harcourt, Brace, Jovanovich, 1953. A penetrating study of the ideas and practices of the colonial and revolutionary periods, which served as the foundation for the American governmental system.

TOCQUEVILLE, ALEXIS DE. *Democracy in America.* Abridged edition. New York: New American Library, 1956. A classic commentary on American social and political institutions by a distinguished nineteenth-century French political observer.

VERBA, SIDNEY, and NIE, NORMAN H. *Participation in America: Political Democracy and Social Equality.* New York: Harper & Row, 1972. An exhaustive empirical study of who participates in American politics and why.

WILDAVSKY, AARON. *The Politics of the Budgetary Process.* 2nd ed. Boston: Little, Brown & Co. 1974. An insightful study of how federal departments and agencies formulate the U.S. national budget.

11 / CONFLICT MANAGEMENT IN GREAT BRITAIN

The purpose of this chapter is to examine the major institutions and processes involved in managing political conflict and building political consensus in Great Britain. As one of the oldest parliamentary systems, Great Britain provides a vivid illustration of the political dynamics of parliamentary government and an interesting comparison to the presidential politics of the United States. Moreover, unlike most political systems in the world, British governmental institutions are ancient, having been developed through slow, incremental change over the past eight centuries. Largely because of its evolutionary political development, British politics is characterized by flexibility and adaptability and a high level of peace and stability. Whereas violence and revolution are common features of the twentieth-century domestic politics of many developed and developing countries, British domestic politics is generally peaceful and nonviolent. The high degree of harmony and consensus is not the result of the absence of domestic political differences but a consequence of social values and political structures that facilitate compromise and flexibility. In this chapter we shall seek to explore some of the conditions that have helped encourage consensus and facilitate peaceful conflict management. Our objective is to describe some of the major dimensions of the British political system and to suggest some factors contributing to societal consensus.

THE NATURE OF THE BRITISH STATE

The formal title of the British community is the United Kingdom of Great Britain and Northern Ireland. The United Kingdom, with a population of about 56 million people, is a multinational state comprised of four peoples; the Welsh, the Scots, the English, and the Ulstermen. The dominant nationality is the English, who are responsible for conquering the surrounding territories and creating the modern political institutions that govern the British state.

The rise of the contemporary British state began around the tenth century with the establishment of the kingdom of England. Subsequently, England conquered Wales and in 1536 both territories were integrated formally into the United Kingdom. Beginning in 1603, the United Kingdom and the Kingdom of Scotland (located to the north of England) were ruled by Scottish kings; this combined rule eventually led to the union of both states with the formal creation of Great Britain in 1707. In 1801, Ireland was added to Great Britain, thus establishing the United Kingdom of Great Britain and Ireland. In 1922, however, southern Ireland (a highly Catholic region) regained political autonomy, while Ulster, the northern, Protestant portion of the island, refused to accept political independence. Thus, the United Kingdom currently comprises four territories—Wales, Scotland, England, and Northern Ireland—with some 2.5 million Welshmen, 5 million Scots, 47 million English, and 1.5 million Ulstermen.

The territory of the United Kingdom is about ninety-four thousand square miles, or roughly the size of Oregon. England, which is slightly over fifty thousand square miles, is slightly smaller than Illinois or Wisconsin. Although Scotland, Wales, and Northern Ireland are not highly populated, England is one of the most densely populated areas in the world and is one of the most urbanized countries (nearly 80 percent of all Englishmen live in towns or cities). London, the center of England, has almost one-sixth of the total population. Economically, the United Kingdom is one of the more developed nations in the world. In 1976 average GNP per capita income in the United Kingdom was $4,180 (English average income was well above that level). Educationally, the British are one of the most highly literate people in the world. The law requires children to attend school until they are sixteen years of age; nearly 30 percent of the students continue with some form of professional or higher education. Great Britain has forty-four state-financed universities. Culturally, Britain contributes immensely to the arts, music, and literature. In short, Great Britain is a modern, urban, sophisticated, and economically developed nation.

THE DEVELOPMENT OF CONSENSUS

As already noted, Britain is a highly harmonious, peaceful state. Whereas many major continental European states (such as France, Russia, Poland, Spain, and Italy) have experienced domestic violence and revolution in the twentieth century, Britain—and England in particular—has maintained a high degree of domestic harmony. Apart from the brief political turmoil surrounding Ireland's separation from the United Kingdom in the early twentieth century, England has experienced only one domestic war since the Middle Ages—the civil war of the mid-seventeenth century.

**THE UNITED KINGDOM
OF GREAT BRITAIN AND
NORTHERN IRELAND**

*ATLANTIC
OCEAN*

*North
Sea*

Scotland

Edinburgh

**No.
Ireland**

Belfast

*Irish
Sea*

REPUBLIC
OF
IRELAND

Dublin

England

Wales

Cardiff

London

English Channel

Recent studies of violence and conflict further document the comparatively high level of peace and consensus within Britain. One study by Ted Gurr, for example, shows that the United Kingdom ranked seventy-fourth out of 114 nations in terms of level of civil strife during the 1961–1965 period.[1] Another study, based on political violence during the 1948–1965 period, shows that the United Kingdom ranked sixty-fifth out of eighty-four nations.[2] Moreover, from 1948 until 1967 there were only nine deaths attributed to domestic political violence, while the median number of deaths for other countries was 131.[3] Although Northern Ireland became deeply polarized in the early 1970s, most social scientists continue to regard the United Kingdom as a highly consensual society.

The Nature of British Consensus

British consensus derives in part from the strong agreement about the fundamental norms of conflict management, as well as from the general consensus about substantive political, economic, and social concerns of the state. The British, in other words, have a high degree of harmony over procedural and substantive issues.

The high degree of procedural consensus is well documented by a study comparing the "civic culture" of five countries — the United States, the United Kingdom, France, Italy, Germany, and Mexico. The public opinion–survey data gathered for this study indicates that the British people are strongly supportive of their governmental institutions and political processes. When people were asked if the national government improves conditions, more than two-thirds of the British people responded in the affirmative. (This figure was greater than for any of the other four countries.) Similarly, when people were asked what they were most proud of in their country, almost 50 percent of the British respondents indicated their political institutions, while only 7 percent of the Germans and 3 percent of the Italians did so. Furthermore, more than half of the British people surveyed felt that they could do something to change an unjust law at either the national or local level (a response that was only greater in the United States). Finally, more than one half believed that civil servants would give their individual problems serious consideration, and nearly three-fourths thought that the police would. These data reinforce one of the commonly accepted generalizations about British society — that it is a highly consensual and harmonious society and that this consensus is most deeply embedded in the broad acceptance of its political institutions.[4]

Britain is also characterized by a high level of agreement about the content of politics. This agreement is partly the result of the pragmatic, nonideological approach to political decision-making processes and the management of societal conflict. Whereas the French and the Italian political systems are divided along ideological lines, the British system is far more concerned about practical, programmatic issues. There is, of course, a major cleavage between social classes. But this tension, dramatized continually by labor-management disputes, is seldom over ideological issues but rather over the allocation and distribution of economic resources. For this reason and for maximum popular support, the two major political parties try to be concrete but flexible in developing party platforms.

Sources of Consensus

A number of factors contribute to the establishment and maintenance of political consensus in Britain. One important source is the homogeneity of its people. While the United Kingdom is a multinational state, no significant racial, religious, or linguistic cleavages impede domestic consensus. Unlike the United States, for example, there are no significant ethnic minorities. In 1950 the percentage of non-white people in England was less than one-fourth of one percent. Even with the substantial immigration of non-white people from former British colonies during the postwar years, English society still remains highly homogeneous (the non-white population is slightly more than one million, or about 2.3 percent of the total English population). Linguistically, English is the dominant language throughout the nation. It has been estimated that only one-fourth of the Welsh can speak their native language, and less than 2 percent of the Scots can speak Scottish Gaelic. As for religion, Britain is a Protestant nation, and nearly 90 percent of the people claim that religion. The official Church of England is the Anglican Church, headed by the monarch; the official church of Scotland is the Presbyterian Church. Wales and Northern Ireland do not have an established church.

A second important source of domestic consensus is the geographical insularity of the state. According to Finer, Great Britain's insularity has had three important consequences for its development. First, British political development was carried out over many centuries completely insulated from the turmoil and conflict of the European continent. Moreover, at no time during the past nine hundred years were English institutions ever subjected to radical transformation or reconstruction as were the French, German, or Russian institutions. The development of the State was therefore carried out in the absence of foreign, revolutionary control. Second, insularity encouraged and facilitated the political integration of Scotland, Wales and England. Since there were no major natural barriers within the island, the natural boundary of the state was the sea. Finally, insularity helped develop the tradition of constitutionalism in Britain. Because the major military threat to the state came from a foreign naval invasion, the great need was for a strong navy to protect the British coastline. Unlike standing armies, which have historically posed a continuing threat to civilian political authority, British naval forces were much less of a threat to civilian governmental institutions because they were comparatively small and spent a large portion of time away from the mainland. The absence of large domestic military forces thus contributed to and facilitated the growth of civilian government in England.[5]

A third source of British consensus is the high level of social and economic moderanization. As noted in Chapter 5, one of the important results of economic development is a tendency to increase the level of national integration. As transportation and communications networks expand, the various areas of a country tend to become far more interdependent. One of the important results of the British Industrial Revolution during the early nineteenth century was the breakdown of traditional agrarian patterns of society and the development of new traditions and customs as people moved in increasing numbers to urban, industrial centers. Moreover, as the number and size of these new urban clusters increased, more efficient transportation systems were developed to facilitate production and distribution of goods. The rise of urbanization and interdependence thus became a source for challenging traditional, parochial values of isolated agrarian communities and for encouraging the development of a homogeneous, cosmopolitan culture. If the British have one of the most homogeneous cultures, it is greatly due to the high level of urbanization and to effective communications and transportation systems in contemporary Britain.

Ironically, while economic development tends to bring about a more homogeneous culture, it also encourages political cleavage. One of the important results of the Industrial Revolution was the development of economic classes—more particularly the division of society into the working class and the managerial or professional class. Although there are virtually no significant cultural or social differences among the regions, class conflict remains a dominant cleavage in British society. To a significant extent this tension is perpetuated by the present two-party system—the working class is represented by the Labour party, and the middle and upper classes are represented by the Conservative party. Because of the importance of this tension, we shall examine it in greater detail in the concluding section of this chapter.

A final source of British consensus is the media. Unlike those of the United States and other Western European countries, the media in Britain is highly centralized. Radio and television are controlled by the British Broadcasting Company (BBC), which provides two network television services and four radio stations throughout the United Kingdom. In addition, the government controls the Independent Broadcasting Authority (IBA), which licenses some fifteen companies to produce programs of regional interest. Although the press is completely private, newspaper publishing is also centralized. Most major newspapers are published in London and distributed nationally by evening rail. There are eight major London dailies, and their circulation accounts for about two-thirds of the total newspaper circulation in Britain.

CHARACTERISTICS OF THE POLITICAL SYSTEM

The British political system has three distinctive characteristics: first, the management of political conflict is guided by an unwritten constitution; second, the structure of government is unitary; and third, the representative institutions of government are parliamentary in form.

No Written Constitution

All political systems operate in terms of fundamental norms and rules that guide conflict-management processes in society. Unlike most contemporary democracies, however, the principles and rules of Great Britain's government are not found in a single, written constitution but are rather a collection of fundamental acts and customs associated with the rise of modern Britain. Great Britain has a constitution, but it is an unwritten, uncodified system of principles, statutes, parliamentary law, judicial decisions, conventions, and customs. There is no explicit delineation of duties of government, nor is there an explicit description of all major human liberties guaranteed to citizens. However imprecise the content and boundaries of Britain's constitution, though, there can be little doubt that British constitutional traditions, laws, and conventions effectively guide conflict-management processes in Britain. This is demonstrated by the fact that England has been and remains one of the most stable and free political systems in the world, while numerous countries with written constitutions have been unable to operate in accordance with their explicit constitutional provisions.

Although no single document sets forth the powers of Britain's government, there is a broad consensus as to the content of constitutional traditions, conventions, and laws that should guide the operations of government. These general principles derive from the long evolutionary history of British political development. Throughout a large period of English history, the British government was considered a "mixed constitution" because the monarch and the Parliament shared responsibilities and held each other's power in check. Gradually, however, all power was transferred to Parliament and then eventually to the House of Commons itself. Today, the supreme authority of the state is vested in that representative body.

In the process of development of the modern governmental institutions, Parliament has passed many significant acts that play a determinative role in contemporary politics. Some of the great sources of Britain's unwritten constitution include:

1. the Magna Carta (1215), the charter of English liberties, which guaranteed protection against arbitrary punishment;
2. the Act of Supremacy (1534), which declared the monarch as supreme head of the Church of England;

3. the Petition of Right (1628), in which the House of Commons condemned forced loans, arbitrary imprisonment, and compulsory billeting of soldiers;

4. the Habeas Corpus Act (1679), which protected accused individuals from indefinite imprisonment without trial;

5. the Bill of Rights (1689), by which the monarch was forbidden to suspend a law, levy a tax, or maintain an army without parliamentary consent;

6. the Act of Settlement (1701), which set forth the procedures for succession to the throne;

7. the Reform Acts of 1832, 1867, 1884, 1918, and 1928, all of which eliminated barriers to suffrage; and

8. the Parliamentary Act (1911), which effectively curtailed the power of the House of Lords and established the House of Commons as the supreme legislative body of England.

Thus, while there is no single statement of fundamental governmental principles, English history does provide many important conventions and parliamentary acts that are the basis of the British constitutional tradition. This tradition can be modified, and the history of England suggests that the constitution of Britain has been continually revised through minor incremental changes. The supreme authority of the state is in the hands of the House of Commons, and there is theoretically no limit to its powers. In practice, however, the laws of Parliament are guided by principles that ensure a limited government and help preserve and protect individual rights from government encroachment.

Unitary Government

The second important characteristic of British government is its unitary structure. Unlike the decentralized federal system in the United States, political power and decision-making authority are located in the central government. This does not mean that all significant governmental activities are carried out by the British Parliament. The supreme and final authority, however, to deal with issues and concerns of the state is in the hands of the central government. In practice, however, there is a good deal of governmental decentralization.

For one thing, the British Parliament grants limited political autonomy to each of the other regions of the United Kingdom — Wales, Scotland, and Northern Ireland. Historically, the most independent region has been Northern Ireland, which until 1972 had its own elected parliament and crown governor. When civil strife erupted in the early 1970s, the British Parliament abolished the Stormont Parliament and established direct rule over the region. As of 1980, Northern Ireland continues to be ruled directly through the Northern Ireland Office of the British government.

Wales and Scotland also have regional autonomy, although less than that enjoyed previously by Ulster. Their domestic affairs are represented in London through their elected members of Parliament, who combine to form Welsh and Scottish grand committees to take care of the particular interests of each region. In addition, cabinet ministers head the central government's Scottish and Welsh Offices, which oversee Parliament's programs and policies in each region. It is the responsibility of the minister for each region to ensure that the interests and welfare of the people are protected.

In the 1970s Scottish and Welsh nationalism increased, resulting in growing demands for national autonomy. In response to rising political nationalism, the British Parliament in 1978 agreed to "devolve" some internal governmental responsibilities to elected assemblies in Scotland and Wales (as had previously been the case in Northern Ireland), provided the *devolution* acts were approved in national referendums. Both Scottish and Welsh voters, however, failed to give the required approval to devolve authority to regional parliaments.

Local government units also play an important role in the United Kingdom. While there can be no doubt that local government is a creature of the central government, local administrative agencies play a significant role in the lives of the British people. As in relations between American state and local authorities, the central government may, and often does, use local government units to carry out programs and policies of the central government. Important programs such as tax collection, pensions, national insurance, and welfare are, however, handled directly by the local offices of the central government. Perhaps the most significant activity of local government is education, which is paid largely out of property taxes collected by the local units themselves.

While local government continues to play an important role in Britain, its relative scope and responsibilities have declined significantly this century as the scope of the central government has increased. In 1905, for example, local governments accounted for about 51 percent of total government expenditures, while in 1968 this percentage fell to 24 percent. In addition, the source of local government funding has also shifted, giving the central government far more control over the allocation of local funds. In 1905 only 25 percent of local government funds were received from central government grants, but by 1968 this percentage increased to 38 percent.[6] While local government institutions continue to play an important function in Britain, it is clear that the relative influence of local units has declined as the control of fiscal resources has shifted to London.

Parliamentary Structure

The third and most important feature of the British political system is its parliamentary form. One expression of this type of government is that the functions of chief of state and head of government are carried out by separate persons—a monarch and a prime minister, respectively. The other major expression of parliamentarianism is that all power is centralized in a parliament. Unlike the American system of separation of powers, British parliamentary institutions do not provide for the separation of executive, legislative, and judicial responsibilities. All authority ultimately resides in the Parliament in London.

Legally, Parliament consists of the Crown, the House of Lords, and the House of Commons. Normally, the consent of each is required before legislation is legally binding. This is indicated by the usual enacting clause of a statute: "Be it enacted by the Queen's most excellent Majesty, by and with the advice and consent of the Lords Spiritual and Temporal, and Commons, in this present Parliament assembled, and by authority of the same." In practice, however, political power resides in the House of Commons; the Crown and House of Lords play a largely symbolic role.

The power of the monarch was effectively curtailed following the Bloodless Revolution of 1688, which brought to the throne William and Mary, who readily acknowledged the supremacy of Parliament over the Crown. Since then, elections have been held regularly, and since 1707 no monarch has failed to give his assent to legislation passed by the two legislative chambers. The power of the House of Lords was also significantly curtailed early in the twentieth century by the Parliamentary Act of 1911, which established that money bills could be delayed but not stopped by the Lords. Because political power resides chiefly in the House of Commons, the term *Parliament* generally refers only to the lower house, or to the combined lower and upper houses.

Unlike the United States, whose Constitution sets specific limits on the power and authority of its legislative branch, the British unwritten constitution sets no a priori boundaries to the powers of Parliament. Since no court of law may override the acts of Parliament, there is no judicial review as is found in presidential systems. Only Parliament itself can limit or alter its own decisions. In the United States, by contrast, laws passed by Congress and signed by the president may be declared unconstitutional by the Supreme Court.

Although the power of Parliament is theoretically unlimited, in practice its authority is restricted by the cabinet and prime minister. Since the cabinet has the responsibility for developing policies and initiating programs, the leadership of Parliament is not within the legislature itself but within the executive. The cabinet directs, leads, and controls the business of Parliament. The actions and initiatives of the cabinet depend greatly upon Parliament itself—

for the government's ability to govern rests on the willingness of majority party legislators to continue to support the inititives of the prime minister and cabinet. Thus, it may be said that while the cabinet *leads* and Parliament *follows,* the cabinet's ability to lead is based on Parliament's willingness to follow.

INSTITUTIONS OF CONFLICT MANAGEMENT

There are four major institutions of conflict management within the United Kingdom: the Crown, the Cabinet and Prime Minister, the House of Commons, and the House of Lords. We shall examine the role each institution plays in developing national consensus and managing political conflict.

The Crown

Although the concept of the Crown (Sovereign) is most often associated with the monarch, its meaning is broader than that of the royal office. The Crown is the symbol of supreme executive authority. Indeed, the Crown, as figurehead leader of the state, is the symbolic representative of the state, and more particularly, of the sovereignty of the state. While the Crown has been divested of real political authority, the monarch continues to serve as the symbolic fountainhead of power. It is the Crown that establishes the government. The Crown also dissolves government and calls for new elections. The monarch also opens Parliament annually by reading a short speech (ordinarily drafted by the prime minister), in which the major programs and goals of the government are set forth. While the political influence of the prime minister and his cabinet are derived from an electoral victory, formal authority to govern is granted by the Sovereign. The prime minister rules because the Crown asks him or her to govern; people obey laws because the Sovereign enacts them; and elections are held because the Crown decrees them. Moreover, the Sovereign establishes or charters all government departments and agencies and often bestows a special blessing on business firms, which proudly boast this favor by the sign "By Royal Appointment." Furthermore, since 1534, the Crown has served as the temporal leader of the Church of England.

The British political system has no constitutional document that clearly delineates all the functions of the monarch. Indeed, since many of the duties of the monarch are carried out on the basis of convention, there is often ambiguity and uncertainty as to responsibilities of the Crown. But as Bagehot points out in his classic nineteenth-century study of English government, this ambiguity, far from weakening the British royal office, tends to strengthen it. "Its mystery is its life."[7] Through its ambiguity and mystery, the Crown inspires awe, dignity, and reverence for the state and its royal family, and

The opening of Parliament in the House of Lords.
Pictorial Parade, Inc.

thereby strengthens the unity of the nation. Since the monarch does not become involved in politics, the king or queen can encourage community consensus by providing strong symbolic leadership for all groups within the state.

The Cabinet and Prime Minister

The agencies of the executive branch of government are generally referred to as "The Government" or simply "Whitehall," which is the London street where most buildings of the central government are found. Off Whitehall is

Downing Street, where the prime minister lives, and at the end of Whitehall is Parliament, home of the House of Commons and the House of Lords. *White-hall* is therefore used to denote the prime minister and cabinet along with the supporting British civil service, while *Westminster* refers to the Whitehall executive machine plus Parliament.

The structure of the parliamentary executive is significantly different from that of the American executive. Unlike the American president, who gets his office through a national mandate, the prime minister gets and retains his position because, as leader of the majority party, he can ensure that his government's program will be passed by the House of Commons. In other words, the prime minister holds office because he can govern. The prime minister's programs may be defeated in the House of Commons if some members of the majority party refuse to support the government or defect to another party. The prime minister would then no longer have the required support of the Commons and would be forced to resign.

Theoretically, the prime minister can lose his position if a major government proposal is defeated in the House of Commons. If a resolution of "no confidence" is passed, he may also lose his position. In either case the majority support needed to maintain a government is no longer present. The third way a prime minister can lose office occurs when the majority party is defeated in an election. According to British law, parliamentary elections must be held at least every five years. Should the government's popularity decline and lead to loss of its control in the Commons, it would not be able to govern the nation.

Since the decision as to when an election is held is largely in the hands of the prime minister, the governing political party attempts to schedule an election (within the five-year period) at a time when it is most likely to maintain or increase its majority in the House of Commons. Since a government's popularity is generally highest around the middle of its term, prime ministers often try to capitalize on this favorable public opinion by calling elections earlier than the five-year requirement. The elections, which are formally promulgated by the Sovereign on the request of the prime minister, are short (generally less than five weeks) and involve a debate over party programs rather than competition over personalities. When an election is called, Parliament is dissolved; the prime minister and cabinet continue, at the request of the Sovereign, to serve as an interim (or caretaker) government.

The responsibility for creating a government lies with the Crown. By convention, the Crown always selects the leader of the House of Commons' majority party. When a party leader is a member of the House of Lords (this was the case in 1963 when Lord Home was head of the Conservative party), British law provides that a peer may renounce his peerage and run for office in the House of Commons.

Once the Crown appoints the prime minister, he or she in turn must select the members of his cabinet and other ministers who will form his government.

The most important positions to be filled are those on the cabinet. Numbering about twenty ministries, the cabinet and prime minister share the state's executive power collectively and provide leadership by initiating proposals, directing policies, and managing programs. In addition to cabinet posts, there are some 10 senior ministers who head major departments not represented on the cabinet. Supporting each of the cabinet and senior ministers are parliamentary private secretaries (PPSs), who assist ministers in keeping in touch with developments in the House of Commons. Finally, the prime minister selects some 50 to 60 junior ministers to head up less important agencies. The formation of the government thus involves the selection of some 100 to 120 political leaders to help guide and direct the programs and policies of the government. Of course, the most significant appointments are the cabinet ministers. The British cabinet plays a far more significant role in the development and execution of government policy than does its American counterpart. Indeed, its role has been so dominant in English history that the British system is often referred to as a "cabinet" government.

Cabinet posts are generally given to leaders within the majority party who have demonstrated the required managerial skills to head up a major department. In addition, with the exception of the Lord Chancellor (who serves as ex officio Speaker of the House of Lords and is the recognized political leader in that chamber), cabinet ministers are almost always members of the House of Commons. Indeed, virtually all junior and senior ministers and the PPSs are members of the Commons. The reason for this is obvious: since the government's authority derives from Parliament, the leaders of government must themselves be leading members in the House of Commons' majority party if they are to effectively maintain majority support for cabinet decisions.

Unlike the presidential system, where executive and legislative branches may be controlled by different political parties, the British parliamentary system inhibits cabinet-Parliament tensions. Since the prime minister and the cabinet are the leaders of the government's parliamentary party, the executive and the House of Commons are integrally interconnected. As Bagehot long ago noted, the "efficient secret" of British government is the almost complete fusion of the executive and legislative power.[8] Thus, a government's capacity to govern depends upon continuing harmony between the cabinet and the House of Commons. When such harmony vanishes, the government ceases to hold the confidence to govern and must resign.

The major function of the prime minister and the cabinet is to lead and direct the nation. As the government, the task of the cabinet is to initiate proposals, to establish programs, and to manage the ongoing activities of the central government. The cabinet meets two or three times each week to discuss issues and to develop the government's policies and programs. Although a significant number of cabinet proposals come from the prime minister himself, cabinet members are responsible for their own departments and must represent their department's particular concerns to the whole cabinet. When necessary, they help draft proposals that will strengthen their operation. Although full cabinet meetings play an important role in the development and execution of policy, an increasing amount of work is handled by the prime minister's "inner cabinet," which is a small group of trusted ministers and selected specialized cabinet committees that undertake preliminary work in such areas as foreign affairs, defense, trade, economic welfare, etc. The use of smaller groups enables a few ministers to undertake a good deal of preparatory work before full cabinet meetings.

A cabinet minister has two major responsibilities. On the one hand, he is head of a department or agency and must ensure that it is managed effectively. On the other hand, the minister is part of the plural executive and shares in the development and execution of government policies and programs. Ministers are therefore responsible individually and collectively to Parliament. As head of a government department the minister is personally accountable for the management of his department. Cabinet members are regularly called on to explain and defend their agencies' policies and programs in Parliament. By regularly calling ministers to explain their department's activities, Parliament is able to continually monitor the operations of government and hold ministers individually accountable for their leadership. If a minister is unable to manage his agency or if a major scandal or problem develops within his department, Parliament loses confidence in the minister and he will be forced to resign.

Ministers are also held collectively accountable for the actions of all other cabinet ministers. *Collective responsibility* means that a minister, as member of a plural executive, must publicly support all government programs and policies and share responsibility for their implementation. If he is unable to support some of the policies of the cabinet or if he is unwilling to defend policies relating to other ministries, he must resign. By the same token, a challenge to a department minister must be viewed (under the doctrine of collective responsibility) as a challenge to the whole government. The defeat of one minister ultimately impairs, if not defeats, the government. In short, the effectiveness of the British cabinet rests on consensus. Unlike in the United States, where cabinet members often operate quite independently of the president and where there may be open dissension on policies, the effectiveness and survival of the British cabinet depends on unity and public harmony.

Departments are the backbone of British government. Each agency or department is staffed by civil servants who are expected to implement programs of the government. Their task is not to become involved in political debates or in the selection of programs but rather to implement policies and programs developed by the government and legislated by Parliament. Since civil-service leaders remain in their particular departments for long periods of time, they provide the needed continuity and the expertise to run the departments. As a result, the appointed departmental ministers rely heavily on the advice and assistance of their bureaucratic subordinates.

One of the important issues in discussing contemporary British government is whether executive leadership is provided by the cabinet or by the prime minister. The traditional view holds that final executive responsibility is in the hands of the cabinet, with the prime minister serving as "first among equals."[9] According to this view, while the leadership of the cabinet itself is in the hands of the prime minister, the influence and power of government rest collectively on the cabinet's ability to manage and direct Parliament. Since the prime minister's time is limited and because of the relatively small administrative staff supporting him, the executive branch of government is highly decentralized. Individual ministers dominate and control their departments much more than is done in the United States, where the president, supported by a staff of about five hundred, can help lead and direct the operations of each major government agency.

More recently, however, some observers have suggested that British government has evolved to a prime-ministerial government because of the increased centralization of political and administrative authority.[10] The influence of the prime minister has always been significant — at least far greater than other party or cabinet leaders. For one thing, it is the prime minister who forms, maintains, and dissolves the government. Since ministers are chosen by him and serve at his pleasure, he may request at any time the resignation of any one of them or may even replace a group of them if he so chooses. In addition, the prime minister, like the President of the United States, is the political and governmental leader of the nation. As chief spokesman for the government and as leader of the people, the prime minister gets much publicity and press coverage, which allows him to influence public opinion far more than others. Moreover, as leader of the majority party, the prime minister not only directs the majority party within Parliament but also leads the national party organization as well.

Besides these formal powers, the prime minister's influence is further enhanced by the centralization of the structure of political parties and by the centralization of government bureaucracy. Whereas a group of party leaders may have provided effective fusion of the cabinet with the House of Commons in the past, some scholars believe that that contemporary fusion is largely carried out individually by the prime minister. Whether or not the British system has been transformed from a "cabinet" to a "prime-ministerial" government is debatable. There can be little doubt, however, that the prime minister plays a more important role now in British politics than he did during the nineteenth century.

The House of Commons

The House of Commons, the lower legslative chamber, is composed of 635 members of Parliament (MPs), each one representing one of the United Kingdom's 635 constituencies. Membership for the four regions of the United Kingdom is as follows: 516 seats for England; 71 seats for Scotland; 36 seats for Wales; and 12 seats for Northern Ireland. Although MPs need not be residents from the constituencies they represent, about one-half of them generally come from and live in their territories.

The presiding officer in the Commons is the Speaker, who sits at the head of the chamber and between the major groups of MPs. The Speaker is chosen by Parliament and is generally reelected continuously until he dies or chooses to retire. The major function of the Speaker is to control debate and guide the proceedings of Parliament. Since he is expected to remain impartial in all political debates, his constituency responsibilities are normally assumed by another MP, who can more effectively represent his constituencies' interests and needs. The Speaker never gets involved in a debate, and the only time he votes is when there is a tie.

Seating arrangements in the Commons clearly indicate the status of each party. On the right hand of the Speaker is the majority party, or what is often called *Her Majesty's Loyal Government.* The front seats are used by the prime minister and cabinet, along with other senior and junior ministers, to present and defend the government's programs. Senior government leaders sitting in the first row of seats are generally referred to as *front-benchers* and are generally expected to lead and guide the *back-benchers,* i.e., newer and less influential party members.

On the opposite side of the center aisle is the political opposition, or what is often called *Her Majesty's Loyal Opposition.* Like the Government, the front benches of the opposition party are used by senior party officials, who themselves are organized into a "shadow cabinet." The function of the shadow cabinet is to lead and direct parliamentary actions of the opposition party and be prepared to assume office should the majority party lose the confidence of the House of Commons. As with the government party, opposition front-benchers help ensure that back-benchers vote in accordance with the interests and policies of the party. The task of ensuring *party discipline* within each party is in the hands of the party whip and assistant whip, who attempt to secure attendance, supply information, survey parliamentary opinion, and above all, guide voting.

The most important function of the House of Commons is to enact legislation, a function it shares with the Crown and the House of Lords. But since the power of the Crown and the Lords is chiefly symbolic, the enactment of laws is primarily the function of the Commons. Virtually all major legislation is prepared by Whitehall civil servants and initiated by cabinet ministers. Although it is possible for the opposition party to present major legislation, only the government has the adequate resources to carefully prepare bills that will be supported by a majority of Parliament's members. Individual MPs may also prepare and introduce *private bills* dealing with concerns of their own constituents. While the number of such bills introduced into Parliament is much greater than the number of *public bills* initiated by the government, most legislative debates focus on government proposals.

A second function of the House of Commons is to oversee the work of government departments. As noted earlier, cabinet members are individually and collectively responsible to Parliament. Cabinet ministers are regularly asked to defend the management of their departments and to explain (either orally or in writing) issues that may be of concern to some members of the Commons. In addition, the general policies and programs undertaken by the government are continuously monitored by Parliament. Unlike the Presidential system, which provides for little accountability of the executive to the legislature, the underlying assumption of the parliamentary system is that the most effective and responsible administration of government results from continuous parliamentary review of executive activities.

In comparison with their American counterparts, MP salaries are modest. In 1980, the annual salary was £10,755 (or about $24,000) plus a limited additional allowance for secretarial and living expenses. As a result many MPs supplement their incomes by holding other jobs. It has been estimated that about one-fourth of the Labour MPs and about two-thirds of the Conservative MPs have outside employment.

House of Lords

The upper legislative chamber of the British Parliament is the House of Lords. Membership in the Lords is not gained through election but through hereditary title or Crown appointment. Of the 1,150 peers in 1979, about 770 were hereditary peers (dukes, marquesses, earls, vicounts, and barons) and about 320 were life peers, of whom 9 were members of the Court of Appeal, the highest judicial body in England. In addition, the 26 representatives of the Church of England (two archbishops—from Canterbury and York—and 24 bishops) are a part of the House of Lords as long as they hold their church positions. Life peers are created by the Crown, upon recommendation of the prime minister, in accordance with the Peerages Act of 1958. No hereditary peerages have been created since 1965.

The leader of the House of Lords is the Lord Chancellor. As member of the cabinet, he is the government's representative in the upper chamber and serves as its official political leader. Politically, the House of Lords tends to identify with the Conservative party, although there has been a declining commitment to the Party's concerns in recent years. Since the creation of life peers in the 1960s, most of the new members tend to be politically more moderate than the strongly conservative hereditary peers who have dominated the House of Lords for centuries. It has been estimated that in the 1970s Conservative peers outnumbered Labour peers by about three to one.

The major role of the House of Lords is in the enactment of legislation. Normally, bills need the consent of the Lords to become law, although since 1911 important legislation passed twice by the House of Commons may become law without the assent of the Lords. Moreover, a money bill dealing with expenditures or taxation that is passed by the House of Commons may be delayed up to one month but automatically becomes law after that. As a result, the effective political power of the upper house has declined significantly. As with the House of Commons, the House of Lords can introduce new legislation and can discuss, revise, and amend bills. Ordinarily, less than one-fourth of the peers participate in legislative debates at any time and these debates are generally dominated by life peers who have had previous government service. In addition to legislative functions, judicial responsibilities are handled by the nine peers who form the Lords' Court of Appeal. Peers are paid a modest sum for each day's work.

Figure 11.1 summarizes the most important relationships between the major governmental institutions of the British political system.

Figure 11.1   Major Governmental Institutions in the British Political System

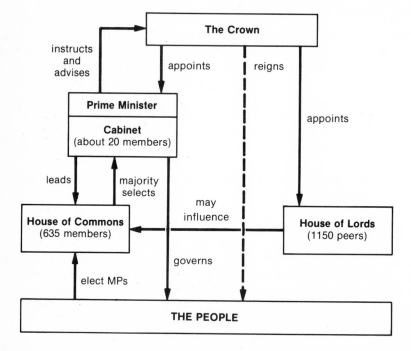

PROCESSES OF CONFLICT MANAGEMENT

The Role of Political Parties

The most important institutions in building and maintaining British consensus are political parties. While governmental institutions play a central role in the management of societal conflict, British parties are the primary vehicles by which private interests are transformed into general, public concerns. Parties therefore provide the fuel and energy for the operation of government.

One of the central features of the British political system is that it is dominated by two political parties. Although several party organizations compete for political power in Britain, since the nineteenth century political power has (with few exceptions) been controlled by two political parties. During the nineteenth century, political power was shared by the Whigs (liberals) and Tories (conservatives) and then gradually shifted to the Liberal and Conservative parties. The Liberal party, which grew out of the nineteenth-century Whig party, played a dominant role in the early twentieth century but then lost virtually all influence as the Labour party expanded precipitously with the growth of organized labor. As Table 11.1 suggests, during the postwar years the Conservative and Labour parties consistently received between 75 and 90 percent of the popular electoral vote. As a result, with the exception of the ten to fifteen Liberal members elected to Parliament, virtually all 635 members are affiliated with one of the two leading parties.

TABLE 11.1 Popular Vote in British General Elections, 1950–1979

YEAR	CONSERVATIVE	LABOUR	LIBERAL
1950	43.5	46.1	9.1
1951	48.0	48.8	2.5
1955	49.7	46.4	2.7
1959	49.4	43.8	5.9
1964	43.4	44.1	11.2
1966	41.9	47.9	8.5
1970	46.4	43.0	7.5
1974 (Feb.)	37.9	37.1	19.3
1974 (Oct.)	35.8	39.2	18.3
1979	43.9	36.9	13.8

Sources: David Butler and Anne Sloman, eds., British Political Facts, 1900–1975, *4th ed. (London: The Macmillan Press, 1975), pp. 184–186;* The Stateman's Yearbook, 1979–1980 *(London: The Macmillan Press, 1979), p. 1298.*

One of the reasons for the two-party system in Britain is that the electoral system discriminates against third parties. Since the British system is based (like that in the United States), on a winner-take-all basis, candidates who receive a plurality of votes become the representatives of individual constituencies. If a party is to have its popular support represented in Parliament, it is essential that its strength be concentrated in a number of districts that will ensure parliamentary victory. If party support is distributed broadly (as has been the case for the Liberal Party), it is possible to receive moderate support in numerous districts but win few seats in the House of Commons. This is what happened in the October 10, 1974, election, when the Liberals received 18.3 percent of the total vote but only 13 of the 635 seats in Parliament.

Another important consequence of the winner-take-all method is that an electoral victory will not necessarily result in a political victory. It is possible for a party to receive a majority of the popular vote and still not be asked to form the government. For example, in the February 28, 1974, election the Conservative party received more than 1 percent more of the popular vote than the Labour party, yet it received only 296 seats to Labour's 301. As a result, the monarch asked Labour leaders to form a new government.

A more important reason for the British two-party system lies in the social structure. The dominant cleavage in contemporary Britain is between social classes — between the working class, on the one hand, and the professional, managerial class, on the other. The political system has not created this national division. Rather, political parties develop their strength by aligning themselves with the interests of a particular social class — the Conservative party is the spokesman for the middle and upper-middle classes, and the Labour party is associated with the economic and political concerns of the working man. The inability of the Liberal party to play a more significant role in contemporary British politics stems in part from its inability to gather substantial support from either the managerial or the labor class. Of course, the division between parties is not completely symmetrical. Were this so, the Labour party would continuously dominate the British political system, since the working class outnumbers the middle and upper classes two to one. What can be affirmed, however, is that British parties are closely linked to social class. As one political scientist observes: "Class is the basis of British politics; all else is embellishment and detail."[11]

Table 11.2 presents survey data that tend to support this generalization. The data indicate that the British labor class tends to identify much more strongly with the Labour party, while the middle and upper-middle classes are linked far more with the Conservative party. Support for the Liberal party tends to be distributed rather evenly among social groups. If one examines the relationship between occupation and party identification, the results are largely the same: British manual workers tend to identify more strongly with the Labour party than do nonmanual workers. One study found that almost three-fourths of the nonmanual workers prefer the Conservative party, whereas only about one-fourth prefer the Labour party. On the other hand, about three-fifths of the manual workers tend to identify with the Labour party, while about one-fifth identify themselves with the Conservative party.[12]

TABLE 11.2   Party Vote and Class Identification (In percentages)

	UPPER MIDDLE CLASS		MIDDLE CLASS		WORKING CLASS		VERY POOR	
	1950	*1966*	*1950*	*1966*	*1950*	*1966*	*1950*	*1966*
Conservative	79	79	69	66	36	34	24	19
Labour	9	5	17	14	53	46	64	51
Liberal	10	6	14	7	11	5	12	5

Source: Samuel Beer, "The British Political System" in Patterns of Government, *ed. Samuel Beer and Adam B. Ulam (New York: Random House, 1973), p. 307.*

As one might expect, the Labour party is strongly identified with the British labor movement. It has been estimated that there were approximately 1.5 million union members at the turn of the century, or 11 percent of the total number of the British labor force. But by the mid-twentieth century, this number increased to 9.5 million members, or roughly 42 percent of the total work force. Since the strength of the Labour party is based on organized labor, as the number and size of unions increased in the twentieth century, so did the political influence of the Labour party. Given the increasingly powerful role of labor unions in the British postwar economy, it is not surprising that during the 1945–1980 period the Labour party has been in control of the House of Commons nearly half of the time.

British labor unions are highly integrated into the Labour party organization. Trade unions provide about 90 percent of the Party's membership and nearly 85 percent of its operating income, and sponsor more than one-third of the Labour MPs. In addition, more than half of the seats on the Party's National Executive Committee—the governing council of the extraparliamentary party—are held by union representatives. The organization that coordinates most trade union activity for the Labour party is the Trades Union Congress (TUC). In 1977, the TUC included more than 150 union affiliates representing nearly 10 million members. Although the TUC is not directly in control of unions, it plays an important role in developing cohesion among various trade union groups.

In contrast to the close relationship between trade unions and the Labour party hierarchy, the Conservative party is much less dependent on organized interest groups. Whereas a large part of the political strength of the Labour party derives from its union organizations, membership in the Conservative party is wholly individual. The strength of the Conservatives does not depend directly upon the work of interest groups but on the commitment of many individuals concerned with a more restrictive role of government in British society. Although numerous professional and business groups are associated with the party organization, few of them have much influence on its goals and policies. Given the limited impact of interest groups on the party's ruling bodies, power tends to be more diffuse than in the Labour party hierarchy. As a result, Conservative party leaders and MPs have much more independent influence than the Labour leaders, who must regularly be accountable to their powerful councils and conferences.

The effectiveness of British parties in aggregating and articulating public interests is due greatly to well-organized and highly centralized party structures. Unlike the decentralized organization of American parties, British parties are strongly cohesive and well-disciplined institutions. This is especially the case for the party organizations in Parliament (the parliamentary parties, as they are called in Britain). The strong national organization not only facilitates internal decision making but also helps bring about British consensus within the party membership as well as within the parliamentary party in the House of Commons.

Since the party organization controls the use of its party label, no political leader can run for office under the name of a party without first getting the approval of the party leadership. This is only granted once a person demonstrates his commitment to the party in previous political activities and agrees to support the principles and programs of the party. Since election to office is virtually impossible without party affiliation, party organizations exercise virtually complete control over the selection of MPs.

After winning a seat in the House of Commons an MP must continue to serve the interests of the party organization if he expects to continue in office. To be sure, party leaders and whips do not instruct their members how to vote on every parliamentary issue. Indeed, the opposition party is often careful not to oppose all actions of government, particularly those that may be popular with constituents, lest its own popular influence decline. But when the party leadership agrees to support or oppose a particular program or policy, it is generally expected that the back-benchers will support the front-benchers. This practice of voting party line (called *party discipline*) is not only one of the most important sources of party consensus, but also enables the British parliamentary system to operate smoothly and orderly.

As party discipline has increased with the institutionalization of the two-party system, it has tended to transform the open, flexible parliamentary system of the nineteenth century into a more organized, predictable, and even rigid political machine. R.H.S. Crossman, a former Labour minister, suggests a number of important changes that have resulted from the increasing power and influence of political parties in British politics. First, individual MPs no longer have the liberty and independence to vote as they once did. If they are to rise within the party hierarchy of Parliament, they must defend and support the party programs and policies. Second, parliamentary control of the executive has declined significantly with the increasing influence of party leadership over the majority party membership. Since government ministers exert strong influence over their party, there is little likelihood that majority party MPs will defy party discipline and seek to alter and modify government proposals. As a result, opposition to government programs has shifted from Parliament as a whole to the opposition party. Another important consequence of party discipline is that major power struggles are no longer open-party debates but are within parties themselves. The principle struggles are not between the government and the opposition but within the government or the shadow cabinet, where loyalty and political influence is rewarded by promotion within the party structure. Fourth, ministerial responsibility has shifted from the full Parliament to the prime minister and cabinet. As a result, resignation and dismissal of ministers is possible only when the prime minister and his party leaders support such action. Finally, party discipline has brought a decline in the role of Parliament. Since MPs are expected to abide by the party line on major issues, the function of Parliament is primarily to support and ratify the proposals and initiatives of government.[13]

Political Parties and Conflict Management

British political parties have historically been effective institutions for building national consensus. Because of their tight organization and centralized control, the Conservative and Labour parties are generally effective in aggregating the major public interests within the state and funneling them into limited but workable proposals. By limiting the range and scope of political diversity, parties thus contribute significantly to the development of a political consensus on which government policies can be developed and executed. Of course, the reduction of political diversity to two major party alternatives may facilitate the management of national conflict, but it does not automatically ensure peace and stability. Two-party systems can and have experienced deep cleavage. If national consensus is to develop, more than just effective consensus-building parties is needed.

Two factors have facilitated national consensus-building in Britain. The first of these is the programmatic character of British parties. Unlike the strongly ideological parties of some Western European states, the Labour and Conservative parties are concerned predominantly with pragmatic implementation of policies and programs and are much less concerned with the development of highly philosophical or rigidly ideological party platforms. During postwar years the Labour party was guided by socialistic ideals as it sought to construct a collectivist, welfare state. But unlike the rigid and theoretical orientation of radical socialist parties in Communist states, Labour was concerned primarily with altering concrete working and living conditions for the working class.

The second factor that has facilitated national consensus is the flexibility and adaptability of British parties, which result from the continuing need to adapt to changing political concerns of different sectors of British society. Given the fluid nature of British politics, parties must constantly avoid unpopular positions and try to maintain the support of the British political center. The continuing competition for the support of the political center thus helps ensure party flexibility. For example, the Conservative party was strongly opposed to the collectivist policies when they were first established in the late 1940s and early 1950s. By the 1960s the party's leadership, recognizing that the majority of British citizens were supportive of the welfare state, accepted the fundamental notions of the collectivist state and became chiefly concerned with the practical expression of those fundamental norms. The Labour party, for its part, was no longer pressing for more socialism but was becoming increasingly concerned with greater economic efficiency and national economic productivity.

Historically, Britain's manner of resolving conflict among its political parties is characterized by a high degree of flexibility and compromise. The tendency of British parties to work out their differences harmoniously and to cooperate in the achievement of common national goals depends greatly upon the values of British political culture, including the norms of moderation, incremental political change, and adaptability, and on the ability of the two parties to continue to share political power. Since electoral defeat does not mean a permanent loss of power, parties have historically accepted the temporary loss of political power with the hope of regaining political leadership in a subsequent election. To the extent that a nation's style of conflict management can be described, the British approach is characterized by its flexibility, pragmatism, and nonideological orientation. Unlike the rigid and ideological orientations found in countries like France and Italy, British politics exhibits flexibility and moderation — qualities that have made British politics an inspiration for so many decades and even centuries.

During the early 1970s, the peace and order that prevailed for much of the nineteenth and twentieth centuries became threatened by the increasing polarization of society. This rise in social class conflict was in great measure heightened by the relative slow economic growth of the British economy. Unlike most Western European countries, which had annual economic growth rates of 3.5 to 4 percent per year during the 1960s and early 1970s, the British average per capita annual growth rate during the 1960–1976 period was 2.7 percent — the lowest rate of any Western European nation.[14] The comparatively low level of economic growth along with the rising rate of inflation thus contributed to the increasing economic cleavage between unions and management and to the belligerence of the claims of each party.

The absence of national economic consensus contributed to a decline in international confidence in the British economy and brought about a precipitous decline in the relative value of the pound. As competition over the distribution of economic goods increased, the traditional compromising approach of resolving conflict appeared to lose ground gradually as parties became more inflexible in pursuing their particular objectives. Whereas national consensus had historically been resolved through flexible compromise between labor and management interests, the increasing intransigence of economic interest groups posed a major threat to the order and stability of the British political system. Fortunately, the economic problems that gave rise to the acute political tensions during the 1973-1975 period were partially relieved in subsequent years. Despite the lowering of the inflation rate and the reestablishment of greater confidence in the British pound, Britain's economic problems are by no means over.

The fundamental problem still remains: how to maintain a high level of social services and still ensure a high rate of investment and growing national productivity. For some, the cause of Britain's contemporary economic ills is the reduction of the private sector as the major producer and consumer in society. The radical transformation in the British economy during the postwar years has helped create a public sector that now accounts for more than 52 percent of the GNP and nearly half of the domestic capital investment. In terms of employment the government now employs more than 25 percent of the total labor force, or roughly 6.3 million workers out of a total labor force of 25 million.[15] According to some Conservatives, the major reason for British economic difficulties lies in the overextension of government programs and the inadequate encouragement of private investment. Others argue that Britain's problems result fom the increasing politicization of unions, which continue to press for higher wages without a commensurate rise in productivity. Labour and union leaders, on the other hand, argue that British management is not effective in guiding British enterprise and making it internationally competitive. Whatever the source of Britain's economic problems, it was clear in the late 1970s that there were no easy, quick solutions and that if the country was to regain its vigor and dynamism it must develop a political consensus about how to encourage economic growth and still provide extensive public services. This remains the major dilemma of contemporary British politics.

SUMMARY

Great Britain is a stable and consensual nation. Although an increasing number of tensions developed in the 1970s, the country remains one of the most developed political systems in the world. The high level of social and political harmony is the result of many factors, including the homogeneity of its people, the geographical insularity of the state, and well-developed economic and social institutions, and the centralized media. In addition, British political consensus is possible because of a large degree of agreement about rules of conflict management and goals to be pursued by the state.

The British government is characterized by its unwritten constitution, a unitary division of government authority, and a parliamentary structure of government. Formally, all laws of Britain require the assent of the monarch and the two chambers of Parliament. In practice, the authority of government is vested in the House of Commons. Both the Crown and the House of Lords play a largely symbolic role in the decisions of government.

The leadership of the British state is in the hands of a prime minister and cabinet, who collectively lead and direct the work of Parliament and ensure implementation of government policies and programs through the bureaus and departments of the state. Since the authority of the cabinet derives from the House of Commons, the government's ability to govern depends upon continuing harmony between the executive and legislative branches. When a majority of MPs no longer have confidence in the prime minister and cabinet—i.e., no longer support the goals and aims they are pursuing—then the cabinet must resign, and new parliamentary elections must establish a new government.

British politics has historically been dominated by two political parties. During the postwar period, the two groups controlling the House of Commons have been the Conservative and Labour parties. Both parties are well organized and directed by strong ruling bodies. If the British parliamentary system has enjoyed stability during the nineteenth and twentieth centuries, a significant reason for this lies in the discipline and strong organization of each party. In addition, the flexible and nonideological character of British parties facilitates continuing adjustment of political institutions to changing conditions and problems of society.

KEY TERMS

unitary government	inner cabinet
devolution	collective responsibility
parliamentary system	party discipline
the Crown	peers
Whitehall	parliamentary private secretary
cabinet	

NOTES

1. Ted Robert Gurr, "A Comparative Study of Civil Strife," in *The History of Violence in America,* ed. Hugh Davis Graham and Ted Robert Gurr (New York: Frederick A. Praeger, 1969), p. 629.
2. Ivo K. Feierabend et al., "Social Change and Political Violence: Cross-National Patterns," in *The History of Violence in America,* ed. Hugh Davis Graham and Ted Robert Gurr (New York: Frederick A. Praeger, 1969), p. 652.
3. Charles Lewis Taylor and Michael C. Hudson, *World Handbook of Political and Social Indicators* (New Haven: Yale University Press, 1975), pp. 114–115.
4. Gabriel A. Almond and Sidney Verba, *The Civic Culture* (Boston: Little, Brown & Co., 1965), *passim.*

5. S. E. Finer, *Comparitive Government* (Harmondsworth, England: Penguin Press, 1970), pp. 135–136.

6. Samuel H. Beer, "The British Political System," in *Patterns of Government,* 3rd ed., ed. Samuel H. Beer and Adam B. Ulam (New York: Random House, 1973), p. 174.

7. Walter Bagehot, *The English Constitution* (Ithaca: Cornell University Press, 1971), p. 100.

8. *Ibid.,* p. 65.

9. For a discussion of this view see G. W. Jones, "The Prime Minister's Power" in *The British Prime Minister,* ed. Anthony King (London: Macmillan & Co., 1969).

10. For a discussion of this view see R. H. S. Crossman, *The Myths of Cabinet Government* (Cambridge: Harvard University Press, 1972) and John P. Mackintosh, *The British Cabinet,* 2nd ed. (London: Stevens and Sons, 1968).

11. Peter G. J. Pulzer, *Political Representation and Elections in Britain* (London: Allen and Unwin, 1967), p. 98.

12. Robert Alford, *Party and Society* (Chicago: Rand McNally, 1963), 352.

13. R. H. S. Crossman, "Introduction" in Walter Bagehot, *The English Constitution* (Ithaca: Cornell University Press, 1971), pp. 26–42.

14. World Bank, *Atlas: Population, Per Capita Product, and Growth Rates* (Washington, D. C.: World Bank, 1977), p. 18.

15. Beer, "British Political System", p. 163.

SUGGESTED READING

BAGEHOT, WALTER. *The English Constitution.* Introduction by R.H.S. Crossman. Ithaca: Cornell University Press, 1971. Although written more than one hundred years ago, this volume remains the classic commentary on the British structure of government.

BEER, SAMUEL H. *British Politics in the Collectivist Age.* 2nd ed. New York: Vintage Books, 1969. Examines the institutions and processes of the British political system, focusing on the major society changes brought about by the socialist Labour movement during the postwar period.

BUTLER, DAVID, and STOKES, DONALD. *Political Change in Britain.* 2nd ed. New York: St. Martin's Press, 1976. The most sophisticated and detailed study of British political behavior.

———— and Sloman, Anne, eds. *British Political Facts, 1900–1975.* 4th ed. London: Macmillan & Co., 1975. A useful handbook on British government and politics during the twentieth century.

CROSSMAN, R. H. S. *The Myths of Cabinet Government.* Cambridge: Harvard University Press, 1972. Crossman, an MP, analyzes the structure and function of the British executive and seeks to show that the prime minister plays a dominant role within the cabinet.

MACKINTOSH, JOHN P. *The British Cabinet.* 2nd ed. London: Stevens and Sons, 1968. A comprehensive account of the structure and function of the British cabinet. Argues that the executive responsibility is centralized in the prime minister.

MCKENZIE, ROBERT T. *British Politial Parties.* 2nd ed. New York: Praeger Publishers, 1964. A standard introduction to British political parties.

MOODIE, GRAEME C. *The Government of Great Britain.* London: Methuen & Co., 1971. A short, lucid introduction to British politics; highly recommended for the student not acquainted with British government and politics.

MORRISON, HERBERT. *Government and Parliament: A Survey from the Inside.* 3rd ed. London: Oxford University Press, 1964. A standard, comprehensive text on the structure of British government. The approach is institutional.

ROSE, RICHARD, ed. *Policy-Making in Britain: A Reader in Government.* New York: The Free Press, 1969. This anthology includes numerous, interesting case studies on the operation of the British political system.

_____. *Politics in England.* 2nd ed. Boston: Little, Brown & Co., 1974. Applies the structural-functional approach to the English political system. The study focuses on the processes and dynamics of decision making.

VERNEY, DOUGLAS V. *British Government and Politics: Life Without a Declaration of Independence.* 3rd ed. New York: Harper & Row, 1976. Provides a clear discussion of the principles and ideals by which the British political system operates.

12 / CONFLICT MANAGEMENT IN THE SOVIET UNION

The Soviet Union presents a dramatically different approach to the building of national consensus and the management and resolution of political conflict from that found in the United States and Great Britain. Since 1917 the Soviet political system has been under the control of a single, monolithic organization — the Communist Party of the Soviet Union (CPSU) — which has sought to create a political community in accordance with the principles of Marxism-Leninism. The Communists are convinced that their ideals are the only valid and legitimate goals; they therefore do not tolerate any opposition to the government's policies and programs. To be sure, Communist leaders do not always agree on national goals and objectives. But the debates and discussions that go on are usually within the structure of the CPSU, the dominant and controlling organization in the state.

In this chapter we shall examine the major features of the Soviet political system. We shall first analyze the nature of the state and then examine some of the chief characteristics of Soviet society. We shall also examine the processes and institutions involved in the building of national consensus and in managing political conflict. Since the CPSU is the major political actor in the Soviet Union, we shall focus attention on the role and organization of that institution.

THE NATURE OF THE STATE

The Soviet Union is the largest territorial state in the world. An area of nearly 8 million square miles, it is more than twice the size of the United States. Its population was estimated in 1977 to be close to 258 million, of which almost 160 million lived in urban areas and 98 million were in rural areas. During the

1960s and 1970s the population of the Soviet Union increased at approximately 1.1 percent per year, or roughly at the same rate as the population of the United States.

The Multiplicity of Nationalities

The Soviet Union is made up of more than one hundred ethnic nationalities. By far, the largest group is the Slavic people, who comprise nearly three-fourths of the total population and are represented by three major groups: Russians (129 million), Ukrainians (40.7 million), and Byelorussians (9 million). The development of the multinational Soviet state began with the establishment of the Russian state in the sixteenth century and continued over the next four centuries. As the Russian tsars expanded their control from Moscow (the political center), they increasingly absorbed different ethnic groups to the west and the south. The five major nationalities incorporated in the south include: Kazakhs, Kirghiz, Turkmen, Uzbeks, and Tatars. Unlike the Slavs, who were historically associated with the Christian Orthodox Church, the southern ethnic groups are of Turkic and Muslim background and tend to follow the Islamic religion. In 1940 the Soviet Union expanded its territory by forcibly incorporating three Baltic states — Lithuania, Latvia, and Estonia. The contemporary Soviet state is thus a multinational country with numerous ethnic peoples, each with its own customs and habits. Of these many nationalities, the dominant group is the Russians, whose language is spoken by nearly three-fourths of the Soviet people.

The formal title of the Soviet Union is the "Union of Soviet Socialist Republics" (USSR). Like the federal structure of government in the United States, the Soviet Union is composed of fifteen union republics, each of which has its own constitution and governmental institutions. To a large extent the boundaries of the republics are based on the distribution of the major nationalities. The largest union republic is the Russian Soviet Federal Socialist Republic (RSFSR), which contains about 134 million persons and covers more than two-thirds of the country's territory. Although nearly 85 percent of the people of the RSFSR are Russians, there are also some thirty-eight ethnic groups that are also a part of this republic. In most union republics, the dominant nationality comprises 60 to 80 percent of the total population. Thus, Estonia is made up primarily of Estonians, Moldavia of Moldavians, Lithuania of Lithuanians, Georgia of Georgians, etc. Only Kazakhstan has a minority population, with 33 percent of its people claiming Kazakhian nationality.

The ethnic diversity of the Soviet Union poses a major challenge to the development of a consensual, homogeneous society. Aware of the potential for division and conflict, the Soviet government has historically pursued a policy of strong central control of the various republics' political institutions while tolerating the diversity of customs and traditions unique to each ethnic group. Even before the Communists took control in 1917, the Russian central

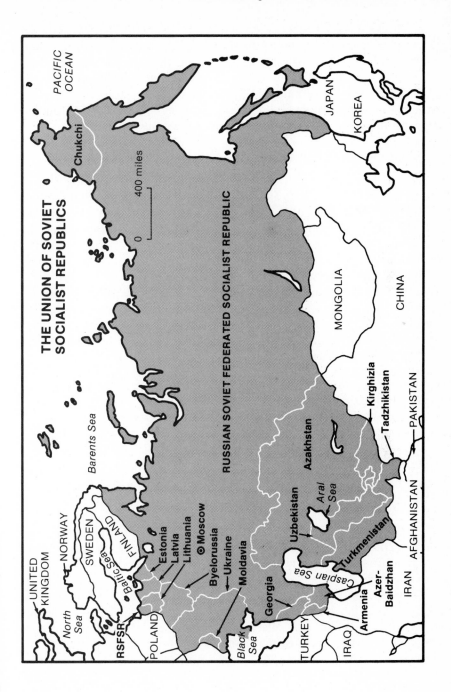

THE UNION OF SOVIET
SOCIALIST REPUBLICS

RUSSIAN SOVIET FEDERATED SOCIALIST REPUBLIC

PACIFIC
OCEAN

Chukchi

400 miles

0

JAPAN

KOREA

MONGOLIA

CHINA

Kirghizia

Tadzhikistan

PAKISTAN

Azakhstan

Aral
Sea

Uzbekistan

Turkmenistan

AFGHANISTAN

Caspian Sea

IRAN

Azer-
Baidzhan

Armenia

IRAQ

TURKEY

Georgia

Black
Sea

Moldavia

Ukraine

Byelorussia

◎ Moscow

Lithuania

Latvia

Estonia

Barents Sea

FINLAND

SWEDEN

NORWAY

UNITED
KINGDOM

North
Sea

Baltic Sea

RSFSR

POLAND

government dominated the federation of separate republics. This was done not only to ensure continued unity of the state but also to ensure that the union republics, which are strategically located along the western and southern fronts, would continue to serve as buffer states for the Russian Republic. Since 1917 the Communist government in Moscow has continued to dominate the other union republics, although the means for doing so have shifted from the regular institutions of government to those of the party organization.

Economic Development

One of the major objectives of the Communists since they took control of the government is to create a classless society. As Lenin and Stalin found out, however, the problem of creating such a society is far more difficult than Marx (the father of communism) may have realized. The establishment of communism (or of its preliminary stage—socialism) involves not only the redistribution of wealth but also the more difficult problem of creating wealth.

Shortly after the Bolsheviks took power following the October 1917 Revolution, the Communist regime began to dismantle the private enterprise system and to establish state socialism. Lenin, who led the government until his death in 1924, began the process of transforming the economy by nationalizing banks, industries, land, and the other major means of production. The immediate effect of these changes was a dramatic fall in production. As economic dislocations and production shortfalls increased, Lenin responded by instituting in 1921 the New Economic Policy (NEP) to help restore pre-1917 levels of production.

Shortly after becoming undisputed leader of the CPSU, Stalin established a new planning apparatus to provide further government control over the production and distribution of goods. The First Five-Year Plan was introduced in 1928; its major objectives included collectivization of farmland and further modernization of industries. Stalin assumed that as long as capitalist countries continued to develop economically, they would threaten the Soviet Union's effort to establish communism domestically and internationally. As a result, Stalin believed that the Soviet Union should become a major industrial power that could protect itself from foreign, capitalist aggression. His solution was to industrialize as quickly as possible by shifting resources from agriculture to industry.

To do this, agricultural production had to be completely in the hands of the state. In 1929 the state began to forcibly collectivize farm land—a program that the peasants, and particularly the richer peasants *(kulaks)*, deeply opposed. It has been estimated that hundreds of thousands of peasants were killed and that nearly a million died from starvation during this transitional phase. Moreover, nearly one-half of the Soviet Union's horses and oxen and nearly two-thirds of its sheep and goats were lost. Despite the human and material cost to the collectivization of agriculture, Stalin's will prevailed. By the end of the First Five-Year Plan (1932), some 60 percent of peasant holdings were taken over by the state. The process of collectivization of land continued, and by 1940 private land ownership was virtually eliminated.[1]

The transfer of land ownership to the state brought a concentration of farm management into larger, more mechanized farm units. By 1940 the 25 million peasant holdings were absorbed into some 237,000 state farms; by 1960 these were further reduced to about forty-three thousand units. The purpose of these large farming units was to facilitate application of capital-intensive methods to large-scale farming in order to increase agricultural productivity and to decrease the proportion of the population in the agrarian sector. Although the human cost in realizing these changes was enormous, the two objectives were partially realized. Agricultural productivity increased (although it still remains highly inefficient by Western standards), and the proportion of the population in the agrarian sector decreased remarkably. In 1928 nearly 80 percent of the Soviet work force was involved in agriculture. By the time Stalin died in 1953 the proportion had declined to less than 45 percent.

The dramatic shift in the composition of the Soviet work force is illustrated in Table 12.1. In 1939 the total number of white-collar employees was about 11.6 million, or about 16 percent of the total work force. By 1970 this group of employees had increased two and one-half times to 30.8 million, or about 21 percent of the total work force. During the 1939–1970 period, however, the number of agricultural workers declined both absolutely (from about 35 million to 22.5 million) and relatively (from about 48 percent of the total work force to about 21 percent). As Deutsch observes, "Never before was so agrarian a country transformed into so industrial a state in so few years."[2]

TABLE 12.1 Classification of Soviet Labor (1939 and 1970)

TYPE OF LABOR GROUP	SIZE IN 1939 (thousands)	PERCENT OF TOTAL WORK FORCE	SIZE IN 1970 (thousands)	PERCENT OF TOTAL WORK FORCE
White Collar	11,580	16	30,820	29
Skilled Labor	9,595	13	33,485	31
Moderately Skilled Labor	16,485	23	20,050	19
Agricultural Labor	34,765	48	22,605	21
TOTALS	72,425	100	106,960	100

Source: Data is adapted from Jerry F. Hough and Merle Fainsod, How the Soviet Union is Governed *(Cambridge: Harvard University Press, 1979), p. 564.*

The development of a strong industrial economy has made possible the creation of the second-most-powerful economy in the world. The World Bank estimates the 1975 GNP of the United States at about 1.5 trillion dollars and the Soviet economy at about 649 billion dollars, or roughly 43 percent of the size of the American economy. If per capita income in the two countries is compared, the economic differences are even more noticeable. In 1975, per capita income of the USSR was $2,550, while that of the United States was $7,120, or nearly three times the income of the Soviet Union. Although there are uncertainties about these comparative figures, it is clear that the Soviet economy has grown enormously over the past fifty years. When the Communists took control, the wealth of the Soviet Union was under one hundred dollars per person, while the wealth of the average American was nearly ten times that. By 1928 this ratio shrank to about 5 to 1, and by the early 1970s the ratio further declined to about 2.5 to 1. The reason for this is simple: the Soviet economy has been growing at a faster rate than has the American economy. In the 1960–1970 period, for example, the average annual economic growth rate for the Soviet Union was 3.8 percent, while the growth rate for the United States was 2.5 percent.[3]

If instituting a command economy has strengthened economic production, it has not facilitated the establishment of a socialistic system of distribution. In 1936 Stalin proclaimed that a new society had been created in the Soviet Union, where former competitive tensions between exploiters and exploited were replaced by the friendly and peaceful relations of peasants and workers. But there is little evidence that the Soviet Union has made significant progress toward establishing a classless society, where income levels have little relation to social class and professional work. Highly trained professionals tend to earn substantially more than peasants, while party officials enjoy a substantially higher standard of living than the average workers. Although income may be more equally distributed in the Soviet Union than in Western nations, the inequality of wealth in the USSR is not radically different from that found in the West.[4]

THE DEVELOPMENT OF CONSENSUS

Despite the heterogeneous character of its people, the Soviet Union is a highly orderly and consensual society. This harmony is evidenced by the high level of agreement about the ideals and goals of the Soviet system and the relatively low level of overt conflict and turmoil. A comparative study of civil strife during the 1961–1965 period indicates that the Soviet Union ranked eighty-ninth in total magnitude of conflict, while the United States ranked forty-first.[5]

The high level of order and stability and the low level of conflict do not mean that the Soviet Union is managing conflict more effectively than the United States or other Western democratic countries. The goal of a political community, after all, is not to establish order and consensus by any means or at any cost. As was suggested in Chapter 1, what is needed in any mature and healthy political community is a *balance* between freedom and government authority. What distinguishes the Soviet system from Western democratic systems found in the United States and Great Britain is not just a higher level of consensus and order but the forceful means used to achieve that order. Whereas the United States and Great Britain seek to develop domestic harmony out of competing and conflicting interests (pluralism), the Soviet Union seeks to develop order by the imposition of a single, monolithic world view. Whereas democratic systems attempt to develop harmony by managing and resolving conflicting claims, the monolithic Soviet system seeks to impose a dominant set of values and interests that ensure order and stability.

Political consensus has been developed and is maintained largely by two general approaches. First, the ruling party seeks to create common values and ideals through direct control of the socialization process, and more particularly, through programs of indoctrination. The purpose of these programs is to define the legitimate ends of the Soviet state and to articulate specific policies and programs to realize those ends. Second, Soviet rulers have created a noncompetitive political environment in which opposition to the party's goals is prohibited. By limiting freedom of expression, freedom of assembly and freedom of the press, the Soviet Union makes it virtually impossible for opposition groups to develop and challenge the authority of the Communist party. Because there is no "loyal opposition" (as in democratic states), the Soviet political culture is characterized by a monolithic world view.

Soviet Political Culture: Marxism-Leninism

There is only one acceptable political culture in the Soviet Union — communist ideology, or what is commonly called Marxism-Leninism. The content of the Communist world view, however, is not a synthesis of the ideas of Karl Marx and Vladimir Lenin. Since both leaders were prolific writers, it would be an impossible task to synthesize and reconcile all of their views into a few central ideas. As a result, what is called Marxism-Leninism is what the Communist party leaders define at any given time as the central ideas of communism. For example, Joseph Stalin's ideas played an enormously significant role during the time when he was in power (from 1928 until 1953). A more accurate description of Communism during these years would have been Marxism-Leninism-Stalinism. But when Nikita Khrushchev assumed power, he began a de-Stalinization program to eliminate the emphasis on the ruthless tactics used for implementing party goals and to deemphasize the cult of personality, which had dominated the party organization. Contemporary Communism is still heavily based on the ideas of Marx and Lenin, although the emphasis on the means to achieve communism (Leninism) seems to have had greater impact than the communist goals of an ideal "communitarian" society (Marxism).

What are the essential doctrines of contemporary Soviet Communism? The following eight ideas are generally considered fundamental to the communist ideology:

1. History is a record of class struggles. In the present civilization, the dominant system of exploitation is capitalism, a system in which the bourgeoisie (owners of the means of production) are able to exploit the proletariat (workers).

2. The ideal political community is a communist (or classless) society, where no exploitation can occur. According to Marx, such a society is characterized by the fact that people contribute according to their abilities and receive according to their needs.

3. All values, ideals, and interests are the product of the socio-economic environment. Metaphysical and ethical notions are the result of the material environment, and more particularly, of the productive relations in society. If new values and ideals are established (a necessity for changing to communism), the relations and institutions of production must first be altered.

4. Although the shift from capitalism to communism is inevitable, a group of leaders (the vanguard of the proletariat) is needed to lead and direct the change. The replacement of capitalism with communism will either come by force or may involve parliamentary procedures in the more industrially advanced states.

5. After the Communist party has won power in a capitalist system, it must establish a dictatorial regime in which proletarian values are imposed on society. In this transitional stage, communist leaders must eliminate private property and establish state socialism.

6. In the establishment of socialism, the Communist party organization can use any means necessary to accomplish its objectives. The Party must not allow individuals and groups to oppose the goals of the proletarian revolution.

7. Following the establishment of socialism, the Communist party begins to create conditions that will make a voluntary, classless society possible. In this first phase of communism class consciousness disappears, but production is still related to incentives.

8. Since capitalist systems continue to increase in economic and military strength, it is imperative that socialist countries be capable of protecting themselves from capitalist aggression. This can best be accomplished by cooperative ties among other Communist states and by maintaining an alert military defense.

Socialization: The Selling of Marxism-Leninism

How are the values of the communist ideology to be communicated to the masses so that they will be accepted in theory and will result in common action? Like other political systems, the Soviet Union needs to ensure that its members are socialized, i.e., that they learn and adopt the values and ideals of the political system in operation. Unlike democratic systems, however, the Soviet government plays a major role in directing and controlling the socialization process. The responsibility for ensuring that children and adults are developing acceptable values is, of course, in the hands of the CPSU. Not only does party leadership define the content of its Marxist-Leninist ideology, but it also ensures that citizens are learning and practicing the truths of the communist world view.

Socialization of Children and Young Adults   Communist systems have historically placed great emphasis on the political education of children. They have assumed what research has documented—that childhood provides the greatest opportunity for developing values and attitudes that are supportive of existing political institutions. Soviet party leaders stress the use of educational institutions for inculcating norms and values that support the proletarian revolution. These values include: development of a "scientific and materialistic" outlook on life, knowledge and appreciation of political economy (i.e., the relationship between economic and political processes and institutions), positive attitude toward manual labor, concern for community welfare as opposed to individual success, strong sense of public duty, and intolerance for attitudes and actions assumed to be harmful to the public interest. The goal is not to teach Marxism-Leninism as a theory or set of abstract values but to develop values and attitudes that affect everyday existence.

Formal educational institutions are one of the major ways in which the CPSU carries out its socialization program among children, adolescents, and young adults. As in the West, children in the Soviet Union learn early to support the system of which they are a part. In the early grades, they do this by practicing symbolic rituals expressing allegiance to the Soviet state. As children grow older, the socialization program begins to provide political and historical content and culminates with a political science course ("Fundamentals of Political Knowledge") taken in the last year of secondary education. In addition to formal learning of politics, political socialization takes place informally within and outside the classroom.[6] For example, children are taught to compete for group rewards rather than for individual achievement. By emphasizing group performance, students learn to identify their own welfare with that of their classmates. In addition, schools emphasize a strongly authoritarian mode of education. Barghoorn observes that pedagogical techniques used by Soviet teachers are designed to foster discipline and respect for those in authority.[7] Since success in the Soviet educational system is associated with group performance and with obedience to those in authority, the socialization that occurs from these informal social processes can have a powerful influence on political values and attitudes.

Formal study of political issues is also an important aspect of higher education in the Soviet Union. The typical university student may spend up to 10 percent of his work load on political education dealing with such themes as the history of the Communist party, historical materialism, political economy, and so on. Political instruction in universities is generally given by members of the CPSU. Since knowledge of Marxist-Leninist principles is assumed to be a necessary requirement for professional success, all higher education includes some political education to ensure a balance between technical and political knowledge.

In addition to political instruction, university students are also influenced by peer associations. A particularly significant institution for young adults is the Komsomol (Communist Party Youth League). The Komsomol, which in 1976 had about 35 million members from the ages of fifteen to twenty-six, is the major political association by which party indoctrination takes place during the adolescent and early adult years. Nearly all young adults are associated with the organization. As an agency of the CPSU, the Komsomol supports the party's socialization program in schools and universities in numerous ways and plays a major role in screening prospective party members. Since CPSU membership is limited to adults who have demonstrated skills, knowledge, and commitment, the Komsomol provides a means by which young adults can demonstrate their leadership qualities and zeal for the party's goals.

Socialization of Adults The objective of the Soviet Union's political-socialization program is to create political consensus among adults that leads to continuous support for the policies and programs of the Communist government. The CPSU program of political socialization has two major dimensions—"agitation" and "propaganda." *Propaganda* involves political instruction to increase people's awareness about political, economic, and social realities from a communist perspective. The goal of propaganda is to provide knowledge that will increase the level of commitment toward the CPSU's objectives and goals. *Agitation,* by contrast, is the process by which the CPSU mobilizes people to action. Whereas propaganda is chiefly an educational program, agitation seeks to gain public support for the goals of the government and to encourage direct action in bringing about the desired actions.

Since the development of ideological understanding is a complex and time-consuming process, the CPSU has established various types of programs by which people can increase in political knowledge. These programs last from several months to several years and are available to both members and non-members of the CPSU. In 1961 it was estimated that nearly 22.5 million persons were involved in some form of Soviet propaganda, of which 7 million were party members.[8]

Agitation, the other important method of political socialization, is carried out through the media and through oral persuasion. All newspapers and radio and television stations are responsible to the CPSU leadership. *Pravda* ("truth"), the leading Soviet newspaper, is published by the Party's Central Committee, the top party organ. *Izvestiya* ("news"), the second most important daily, is published by the Supreme Soviet, the national legislature. Both papers are distributed nationally and have a circulation of about 8.5 million. In addition there are some twenty other national newspapers and some 150 regional dailies. The leading newspaper of each republic is published jointly by party members and representatives of the regional government. The central news agency TASS, which serves as the major source of domestic and international news, is also in the hands of the CPSU. Finally, radio and television are also controlled by the Party organization.

Oral persuasion is a distinctively Soviet means of mobilizing people to action. The direct personal approach to political action was developed early in the twentieth century in order to reach relatively illiterate and unsophisticated laborers and peasants. Direct personal communication by party agitators offered the advantage of giving more control over the communication process and of observing and reporting to superiors the general responses and moods of people. As the Soviet people have become more sophisticated and better informed, the means of agitation have likewise become more refined. But even in the 1970s, party leaders continued to insist that direct, face-to-face contact with groups and large audiences is an essential means of conveying urgent political messages and of providing a two-way means of communication between the masses and the party cadre.

In conclusion, the CPSU is not concerned with the aggregation of interests (as in Western democratic states) but with the development of common ideals and goals that will uphold the Soviet political system. The major goal of the CPSU is to build a political harmony of values on which the government can act.

INSTITUTIONS OF CONFLICT MANAGEMENT

Since 1917 the Soviet Union has had four major political leaders. The first, Vladimir Lenin, ruled from the time the Bolsheviks successfully took power in 1917 from the Provisional Parliamentary Government of Alexander Kerensky until Lenin's death in 1924. The second ruler was Joseph Stalin, who assumed unquestioned control in 1928 and ruled until his sudden death in 1953. The third leader was Nikita Khrushchev, who ruled from 1953 until he was ousted from office in 1964. The fourth (and current) political leader is Leonid Brezhnev, who has ruled since 1964.

What has made each of these political figures the undisputed leader of the Soviet political community is their dominant position within the CPSU. In each case the road to power has been through the Communist party organization. The twentieth-century political history of the Soviet Union clearly indicates that he who leads the CPSU also leads and dominates the politics and government of the country and has the ultimate voice in the management of domestic conflict. The reason for this, of course, is that in Soviet society the CPSU is recognized as the only legitimate source of leadership and guidance for the nation. ARTICLE 6 of the 1977 Soviet Constitution says: "The Communist Party of the Soviet Union is the leading and guiding force of Soviet society, the nucleus of its political system and of all state and public organizations. The CPSU exists for the people and serves the people. Armed with the Marxist-Leninist teaching, the Communist Party determines general prospects for the development of society and the lines of the USSR's domestic and foreign policy, directs the great creative activity of the Soviet people, and gives their struggle for the victory of communism a planned, scientifically substantiated nature."

But to say that Party leaders govern Soviet society is an accurate but incomplete assessment. The Soviet Union does have a well-organized party, but it also has a well-organized government and bureaucracy. To say that the party alone governs obscures the fact that the Soviet political system has formal governmental institutions and informal party structures with overlapping authority. Although ultimate authority rests in the party organization, any assessment of conflict-management institutions in the Soviet Union must examine not only the party structures and their respective functions but also the governmental institutions through which party goals and policies are developed and implemented.

Formal Conflict-Management Structures

The formal institutions of the Soviet Union have two significant features. First, the organization of government is federal (as in the United States); and second, the institutions are parliamentary (as in the British political system).

Soviet Federalism   The official title of the Soviet Union is the Union of Soviet Socialist Republics. Theoretically, the Soviet political system is comprised of a "union" of some fifteen *union republics,* each of them recognized by the Soviet Constitution[9] as a "sovereign" state with the capacity to carry out independent foreign relations (ARTICLE 76) and with the formal right of seceding from the union (ARTICLE 72). Each of the republics has a constitution and its own executive, legislative, and judicial governmental institutions. Soviet citizens are therefore subject to two levels of government simultaneously — the national institutions in Moscow and the regional institutions in their republic.

Within the union republics there are a number of other territorial subdivisions. The most important of these is the *autonomous republic.* In the Soviet Union there are 20 of these republics, of which 16 are in the Russian Soviet Federal Socialist Republic (RSFSR), the largest and most ethnically heterogeneous union republic. Each autonomous republic is subordinate to the union republic in which it is located, but it also enjoys a level of autonomy similar to the union republic's relation to the central government. Like the union republics, autonomous republics have their own constitutions and independent government structures.

Two other territorial subdivisions are the *oblasts* (regions) and the *krais* (areas). Both the *oblasts* and the *krais* are based on relatively small nationalities within rather large territories. In 1971 there were 122 *oblasts* (8 of which had political autonomy like the republics) and 6 *krais.* Finally, within republics and *oblasts* there are certain administrative units called *raions,* which are equivalent to American counties. In the late 1960s there were close to 1500 of these districts, of which 300 were urban and 1200 were rural.

Soviet Parliamentary Structures   According to the Constitution, the highest organ of the Soviet government is the Supreme Soviet, the national parliament of the country. The Soviet Union is, theoretically at least, a parliamentary system because final executive, legislative, and judicial authority resides in this institution. The Supreme Soviet does not make and implement all laws, nor does it serve directly as the highest judicial body. The Soviet parliament does, however, "elect" persons responsible for executive and legislative decisions and also elects members to the State's Supreme Court. Constitutionally, then, there is no formal separation of powers within the Soviet government. Like the British system, the responsibility to make, enforce, and interpret laws are in one source — the parliament.

1. *The Supreme Soviet.* The Supreme Soviet consists of two legislative chambers — the *Council of the Union* and the *Council of Nationalities.* The Council of the Union (lower house) is composed of deputies elected from territorial districts of approximately equal size. In 1974 there were

767 deputies, or roughly one for every three hundred thousand citizens. The Council of Nationalities (upper house) is composed of 750 deputies elected from each of the major autonomous government territories, apportioned as follows: thirty-two from each of the fifteen union republics, eleven from each of the twenty autonomous republics, five from each of the eight autonomous regions *(oblasts),* and one from each of the ten national districts *(okrugs).* Representation in the upper chamber is thus based on equal membership for each type of political unit regardless of size of membership. Deputies in each chamber serve a five-year term of office.

Supreme Soviet deputies are not full-time legislators but perform their duties in connection with other professional work. Since the CPSU controls the "election" process (by allowing only one candidate to run for each position), all members of the Supreme Soviet have been "elected" with the tacit approval of the party. Not surprisingly, nearly three-fourths of the deputies in 1974 were members of the CPSU. In terms of professional composition, the Soviet parliament generally has a high proportion of party and government officials along with many planners, managers, and scientists. Professional composition, however, has changed significantly over the past two decades as the number of peasants and workers has increased significantly. For example, in 1950, labor and peasant deputies comprised about 7 percent and 0.2 percent of the Supreme Soviet; in 1974 these proportions rose to approximately 18 percent each. Meanwhile, regional party and government officials have declined from a total of about 42 percent in 1950 to about 20 percent in 1974.[10]

With more than fifteen hundred members, the Supreme Soviet is the largest parliament in the world. Perhaps because of this, and partly because its members hold full-time jobs elsewhere, the parliament meets only twice each year for two or three days at a time. As a result the Supreme Soviet is unable to carry out any significant amount of work, nor is it effective in monitoring and supervising other agencies of government. Most of the six or seven days that the Supreme Soviet is in session each year are devoted to hearing speeches and approving recommendations that have been prepared elsewhere. There is seldom open political discussion and debate within each chamber. Most of its work is devoted to rubber-stamping projects and proposals that have been prepared for its approval. The work of the Supreme Soviet is thus symbolic, ceremonial, and ornamental. Like the figurehead role of the British monarch, the Supreme Soviet functions as a noticeable government institution but with little authority and influence. Its role in conflict management is relatively insignificant.

2. *The Presidium of the Supreme Soviet.* To ensure continuity in its work, the Supreme Soviet "elects" a Presidium of thirty-nine members at the beginning of its five-year term. As with all elections in the Soviet Union, the selection of Presidium members is carried out by the CPSU leadership and then presented to the parliament for its automatic approval. Thus, the authority of the Presidium derives less from its relationship to the legislative body than to the party organization.

   The primary function of the Presidium of the Supreme Soviet is to carry out the responsibilities of the parliament when it is not in session. Its tasks are to provide leadership and direction to the work of that body and to coordinate the activities of its committees. Perhaps the most important task of the Presidium is to issue legislative decrees — decisions that have the effect of laws. Nonetheless, the Presidium's role in governmental decision making cannot be considered significant, in part because of the infrequency of its meetings. Since the Presidium meets only once every two or three months, the limited schedule does not allow it either to direct the work of the Supreme Soviet or to serve as an effective legislative organ.

   Another function of the Presidium is to carry out the symbolic and ceremonial functions of chief of state, such as the sending of diplomatic representatives, the receiving of foreign dignitaries, and the signing of international treaties. In practice, this function is carried out by the chairman of the Supreme Soviet's Presidium, who is generally regarded as the president of the nation and a figurehead chief of state. It is the chairman who (like the monarch of Great Britain) serves as the ceremonial leader of the state. In 1980 Leonid Brezhnev held this position.

3. *The Council of Ministers.* The third institution of the Soviet Union's parliamentary government is the Council of Ministers, a collective body of some one hundred junior and senior ministers and heads of administrative agencies.[11] According to the Soviet Constitution, the Council of Ministers is the "highest executive and administrative organ of state power." Since its members include all the heads of the most important executive departments as well as the chairmen of the fifteen councils of ministers in each of the union republics, the council serves as the major executive agency of government. Constitutionally, the council's authority derives from its "election" by the Supreme Soviet; as in the selection of the Supreme Soviet's Presidium, the appointment of council members is controlled by the party organization. Authority is therefore tied to the CPSU, not to the Supreme Soviet.

   As the chief executive body in the Soviet Union, the Council of Ministers performs many of the same functions carried out by the "governments" constituted by the majority party (or parties) in Western parliamentary systems. Those functions include initiation of legislation, establishment of programs, management of the bureaucracy, and most importantly, coordination of policies among the various ministries of the government. Since the Soviet Union has a command economy, the establishment of centrally developed plans is an all-important activity of the council.

In 1978 the council had sixty-two ministries and sixteen state comittees. The ministries in the Soviet government are much like those in Western nations — covering such areas as energy, agriculture, trade, foreign affairs, social welfare, etc. The state committees, on the other hand, are collective agencies that seek to coordinate the work of various ministries, and do not have a direct counterpart in the West. The most important state committees deal with planning (the *Gosplan*), science and technology, agriculture, construction, and economic resources. Because of its important role in economic and social planning, the Council of Ministers is considered the most important governmental institution. During the 1964–76 period, when the Supreme Soviet and its Presidium issued twenty-one laws and eighty-six decrees, the Council of Ministers implemented some 207 major decisions alone and another 139 with the cooperation of other agencies.[12]

Despite its relatively significant role in decision making, the effectiveness of the Council of Ministers is impaired by its size and, to a lesser degree, by the lack of frequent meetings. In 1978 the Council of Ministers had 108 members, and press reports suggest that meetings are held only three to five times per year. Under these conditions it is not surprising that the Council of Ministers elects its own Presidium, a small "inner cabinet," to provide continuity and leadership to the larger body. The members of the Presidium of the Council of Ministers are the leaders of the council. The chairmanship of the Presidium of the Council of Ministers is held by the Soviet premier, who serves as the head of government. The position resembles somewhat the position of prime minister in Western parliamentary systems. The Soviet Union's premier for sixteen years (1964–1980) was Alexei Kosygin. Following Kosygin's death late in 1980, Nikolai A. Tikhonov assumed the position of premier.

In summary, the 1977 Soviet Constitution (like its earlier versions) provides for conflict-management institutions that are federal and parliamentary in character. In practice, however, the formal institutions do not operate in accordance with constitutional provisions. Since the CPSU is the only legitimate political party, CPSU officials are able to ensure control of both national and regional governmental institutions. The actual operation of the Soviet political system appears more unitary than federal.

Figure 12.1   Major Institutions of the Government of the Soviet Union

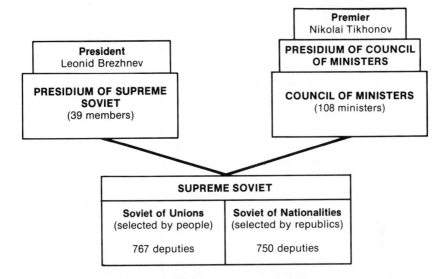

The Soviet parliament does not play as significant a role as do the parliaments of West European systems. In these systems, the elected lower house plays a major role in the formation, continuation, and demise of governments. In the Soviet system, the Supreme Soviet does not have a comparable position to, say, the House of Commons in England or the Bundestag of West Germany. This is clearly evident when the position of head of government is compared with other parliamentary systems. In West European countries the premier or prime minister is ordinarily the head of government and receives his position by being leader of the majority party in the parliament. In the Soviet Union, however, the premier's position—chairman of the Presidium of the Council of Ministers—is essentially a figurehead position; the real duties of head of government are carried out by the leader of the Communist party. The Soviet system is a parliamentary systems of sorts in that there is no effective separation of executive, legislative, and judicial responsibilities. The parliament of the Soviet Union is not the Supreme Soviet; it is the party's Central Committee. The effective cabinet is not the Council of Ministers but the party's Politburo. In functional terms, the head of government is the general secretary of the Party and the leader of its Politburo.

Informal Institutions of Conflict Management

The formal institutions of government outlined above obviously play a role in the decision-making process of the Soviet Union, although scholars tend to disagree on the exact nature and extent to which these institutions participate in the governing of Soviet society. It is clear, however, that (unlike Western political systems) the formal governmental institutions of the Soviet Union do not have the final authority for resolving conflict. Rather, that authority is in the hands of the ruling Communist party. Thus, the Soviet Union's "elected" parliament, the Supreme Soviet, and its subsidiary bodies (the Presidium of the Supreme Soviet and the Council of Ministers) do not have the supreme authority commonly vested in parliaments of Western democratic states. The organization that holds final authority is the CPSU; it controls the selection of deputies to the Supreme Soviet and to the other agencies and bureaus of government. Since the CPSU influences the selection of government officials, the formal institutions have historically been instruments through which the CPSU has been able to lead and direct the Soviet Union. The Presidium of the Supreme Soviet and the Council of Ministers do, of course, play an important role in the planning and execution of policies, but their role always depends upon the party.

That the Communist party is the ultimate decision-making authority is a well-accepted fact. ARTICLE 6 of the 1977 Constitution states that the CPSU is "the leading and guiding force of Soviet society." Yet, the Soviet charter fails to explain how the party is to lead and direct the Soviet Union or how it is to be organized in carrying out its duties. The government of the informal party institutions thus operates on the basis of extraconstitutional provisions — i.e., regulations and decisions created by the party organization.

Party Organization   The strength and influence of the CPSU in the Soviet political system is due, above all, to the disciplined and hierarchical organization of the party. The impact of the party does not rest on numbers. Indeed, the 1977 CPSU membership was estimated at 16 million, or about 9 percent of the adult population. Although the size of the party's membership is relatively small, the CPSU is a strong, dominant institution in great measure because of its organization and internal cohesion.

Vladimir Lenin, founder of the party, first set forth the principles on which party organization was to be established. The success of communism throughout the world bears the results of Lenin's theory of organization. To a large extent, the success of communism in the world is not because Marxism has been proven valid but because Leninism has proven to be a successful means of organizing political authority. The success of the CPSU derives less from Marxist goals and ideals and more from Leninist tactics and methods of organization used to implement Marxist ideals. Given the growth of communism in the world, the creation and development of the CPSU and of other Communist parties is one of the major political inventions of the twentieth century.

How is the CPSU organized? At the lowest level there are some 390,000 basic party organizations, or what until 1939 were called party cells. The primary party organizations (PPOs) vary in size from three to five members to

The opening of the 25th All-Party Congress in the Kremlin in February, 1976.
Tass from Sovfoto

The Soviet of Unions in session.
United Press International Photo

as many as three hundred (average size is thirty-five to forty). PPOs are normally constituted in either residential or employment areas to facilitate regular participation. They are found in such areas as neighborhoods, collective farms, factories, universities, government agencies, and schools. Each PPO has an "elected" bureau or committee to provide leadership for the organization for one year. Ordinarily, the chairman of the committee is a party secretary who serves as a part-time or full-time paid party official.

The PPO plays a major role in the CPSU, for it provides the means by which Marxist-Leninist propaganda and political agitation is carried to the Soviet people. As the lowest level of political organization, the PPO is the key institution by which the Soviet people are mobilized in accordance with the aims of the CPSU; it is the level at which party members and citizens make contact. Since the number of CPSU members is less than 10 percent of the adult Soviet population, members of the PPO have a major responsibility in guiding, directing, encouraging, and stimulating the interests of people. Most importantly, the PPO must ensure that the values and opinions of the common citizens are supportive of the aims of the Communist party.

The PPO has the responsibility for admitting new members to the Party. To be admitted, a citizen must submit a life history and have the support of three party members who have been in the organization for not less than five years. If the applicant has shown a strong commitment toward the ideals of the communist cause and has participated in the Komsomol or some other relevant political activities, PPO members are likely to approve the application and give the applicant a one-year probationary term. If successful, after a year of candidate membership a person is eligible for full membership in the party.[13]

Above the PPO is the *raion* party conference — the party organizations for some 4,243 cities and districts of the country. The members of these party organs are ordinarily "elected" by the PPOs and help provide coordination and direction among party activities within cities and districts. Above the *raion* conferences are the *oblast* or provincial party conferences, and above them are the fourteen Union republic congresses. As with the *raion* party conference, members of *oblast* conferences and republic congresses are selected by each of the party organizations at the level just below them.

The highest party organization is the All-Union Party Congress, which (theoretically) is the supreme party organ. The Congress is ordinarily convened every five years in Moscow, and the number of delegates is now close to five thousand. Although the All-Party Congress is supposed to be the ultimate parliament of political decision making, in actual fact the organization is more of a political convention in which party representatives listen to speeches and reports and then give their automatic approval to what has been said and done.

As indicated in Figure 12.2, each party committee is directed by a bureaucratic secretariat. With the exception of the local party committee (which is generally staffed by only one secretary), city, regional, and national party committees are supported by three or more secretaries and a well-staffed

Figure 12.2   Structure of the Soviet Communist Party

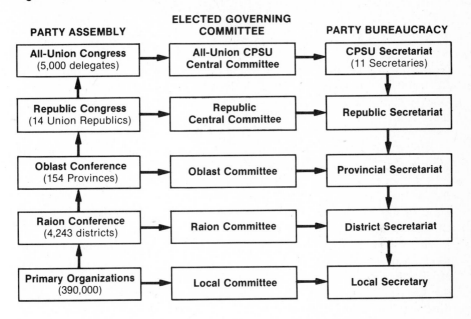

PARTY ASSEMBLY	ELECTED GOVERNING COMMITTEE	PARTY BUREAUCRACY
All-Union Congress (5,000 delegates)	**All-Union CPSU Central Committee**	**CPSU Secretariat** (11 Secretaries)
Republic Congress (14 Union Republics)	**Republic Central Committee**	**Republic Secretariat**
Oblast Conference (154 Provinces)	**Oblast Committee**	**Provincial Secretariat**
Raion Conference (4,243 districts)	**Raion Committee**	**District Secretariat**
Primary Organizations (390,000)	**Local Committee**	**Local Secretary**

office of party functionaries. These full-time party officials are generally referred to as the party apparatus (the *aparatchiki*) and play a critical role in directing and coordinating the activities of the CPSU. The chief party official in each city, district, or republic is the first secretary,[14] who directs the work of the party machinery in his area. It has been estimated that the total number of full-time party functionaries in the Soviet Union is between one hundred thousand and one hundred fifty thousand members.[15] The party apparatus is ultimately responsible to the Secretariat of the Central Committee, a bureau of 11 secretaries headed by the general secretary of the party. Because of the enormous influence wielded by the general secretary through the intricate party apparatus, it has long been considered the top party post along with the chairmanship of the Politburo. The power of the last two political leaders of the Soviet Union—Nikita Khrushchev and Leonid Brezhnev—has derived largely from the holding of this position.

Party Leadership   The leadership of the CPSU is in the hands of three organizations: the Central Committee, the Politburo, and the Secretariat. The Central Committee, as noted earlier, is constituted to carry out the work of the All-Party Congress when it is not in session. Since the Congress is the highest party organ in theory, the supreme decision-making authority of that body is placed in the hands of the Central Committee, which is the effective parliament of the Soviet Union. The Central Committee is composed of some 426 members—287 full members and 139 candidate or nonvoting members. Most of these are either party officials or government leaders. Some 40 percent are full-time party officials of the central, regional, or local levels, while another 30 percent are government leaders who serve as members of the Council of Ministers or in other high offices of the bureaucracy.[16] In 1976 nearly 90 percent of the voting members were in the Supreme Soviet. The persons on the Central Committee are thus highly influential party and government leaders. One student of Soviet affairs summarizes the position of the Central Committee as follows: "Except for the fifteen or twenty members whose inclusion has more symbolic meaning, the Central Committee is basically a collection of the approximately 250 most powerful individuals in the country—or at least the occupants of the 250 most powerful posts in the Soviet system.[17]

Although most students of Soviet affairs consider the Central Committee the principal party organ, its influence is limited by the infrequency of its meetings and by its large size. Since Brezhnev took office in 1964, the Central Committee has met in plenary session an average of about twice a year for one to three days each time. In addition, the large size of the committee (close to three hundred voting members) makes it difficult to resolve issues quickly and efficiently. Much of the ongoing work of the party is therefore carried out by the Central Committee's specialized subcommittees and other subsidiary organizations and by its Politburo, the ultimate repository of political authority in the Soviet political system.[18]

According to party statutes, the Central Committee "elects" members to a Politburo (or political committee) to direct its work between plenary sessions. The Politburo, generally regarded as the effective cabinet or collective executive of the Soviet Union, is composed of some twelve to fifteen members (in addition, there may be six to eight nonvoting or candidate members) who provide the overall direction and leadership of the CPSU. The Politburo generally meets weekly and provides the continuing direction to the party apparatus through its Secretariat. The Politburo, in other words, is the chief decision-making authority in the Soviet political system. During the Cuban Missile Crisis of 1962, for example, the major institutional actor for the Soviet Union was the Politburo, with its head, Nikita Khrushchev, serving as the main spokesman. The enormous political influence of the Politburo derives largely from the fact that its members have always been the top party and government leaders of the nation. In 1979 some of its members included the following: Leonid Brezhnev, party leader; Andrei Grechko, defense minister; Alexei Kosygin, prime minister; Mikhail Suslov and Andrei Kirilenko, both party secretaries; and Andrei Gromyko, foreign minister.

The instrument by which the Central Committee and the Politburo carry out their decisions and implement them in society is through the CPSU *aparat-chiki* (apparatus), which is directed by the national CPSU Secretariat. As noted already, the Secretariat is administered by eleven party secretaries who have responsibility for directing and supervising the work of some one hundred thousand to one hundred fifty thousand full-time party employees.[19] Since most of the members of the party apparatus are highly trained professionals, they provide administrative support not only to the Central Committee and its Politburo but also to party and government agencies at the national, regional, and local levels.

Figure 12.3   Principal Institutions of the CPSU

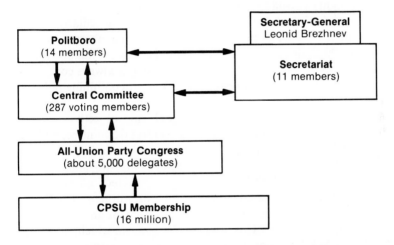

Above all, the purpose of the party apparatus is to supervise and monitor all significant governmental and nongovernmental agencies and institutions in order to ensure that the party's objectives are implemented. In addition to its administrative support and monitoring activities, the party seeks to influence decision making by influencing selection of personnel to key positions in society. From its many years of government experience, party personnel have developed a listing of positions *(nomenklatura)* they consider significant in society. When vacancies occur, the CPSU organization exercises its enormous influence to fill those positions with individuals supportive of party goals.

Party Functions   In carrying out its direction and leadership of Soviet society, the CPSU performs three major functions: first, it directs the program of political education in society; second, it determines the specific goals and objectives for the state; and third, it ensures that the goals and objectives are implemented in society.

In order to ensure that the CPSU is an effective instrument of political indoctrination, it must itself be comprised of personnel who are politically knowledgeable. One of the major requirements of CPSU membership is a basic knowledge of Marxism-Leninism and a commitment to continue learning the principles of communism. The statutes of the CPSU state that a member's duties are to "master Marxist-Leninist theory, to raise his ideological level, and to contribute to the molding and rearing of the man of communist society; to combat resolutely any manifestations of bourgeois ideology, remnants of a private-property psychology, religious prejudices, and other survivals of the past; to observe the principles of communist morality; and to place public interests above personal ones."[20] A major assumption of Leninist organization is that before the party can effectively guide and mold public values its members must be thoroughly persuaded of the goals of communism. To this end, one of the major activities of party organizations (and particularly of the PPO) is the offering of political-education programs for members as well as nonmembers. Since the major responsibility for transferring communist values to society is with the local party unit, the party leadership is always concerned that local units have a strong commitment to programs of continuing political education.

The second function—the articulation of goals and objectives for the state—is carried out by the CPSU leadership, the Central Committee, and the Politburo. Unlike Western democratic states, which seek to aggregate public interests, the CPSU does not develop its goals out of competing and conflicting interests of its members. Rather, it seeks to use "elected" governmental organizations to support decisions taken by the top party organs. The Soviet Constitution and the Party Statutes require that government and party positions be filled through "elections." This term is a euphemism, which, in reality, means that the public has the opportunity to offer public support for the single candidate selected by the CPSU. Leadership positions, in short, derive their legitimacy not from consent but from the party organization.

One of the guiding principles of the CPSU is *democratic centralism,* which (in practice) has meant two things: (1) that some discussion and debate is tolerated before a decision is made but that unquestioning support must be given after a decision is reached; and (2) that decisions of higher bodies must be unconditionally binding on lower ones. Although discussion and debate do occur about policies and programs to be carried out by the Soviet government, the development of goals and objectives is always under CPSU control.

Finally, the party ensures that its articulated goals are implemented in society. Implementation of policies and programs is facilitated by the disciplined organization of the CPSU and also by the general attitudes in society in support of individuals in authority. More significantly, the government and the party are closely interrelated at all governmental levels; the higher the level of government, the greater the participation of the party (Figure 12.4). Since ultimate political authority lies in the CPSU, participation in the Supreme Soviet, Council of Ministers, or their respective Presidiums has historically required a commensurate leadership position within the party organization. Election to the Council of Ministers or the Presidium of the Supreme Soviet is based on participation in top party organs in a republic or in the nation. Conversely, significant party posts generally ensure positions of responsibility within the government. Jerry Hough estimates that in 1976, 88 percent of the voting members of the Central Committee were also deputies of the Supreme Soviet.[21] The overlapping nature of governmental and party authority is perhaps best illustrated by the positions of the two top leaders of the nation. In 1980 Leonid Brezhnev was chairman of the Presidium of the Supreme Soviet, chairman of the Politburo, and general secretary of the party; Nikolai Tikhonov was chairman of the Presidium of the Council of Ministers (premier of the state) and a member of the Politburo.

Figure 12.4 Interrelationship of Party and Government Institutions*

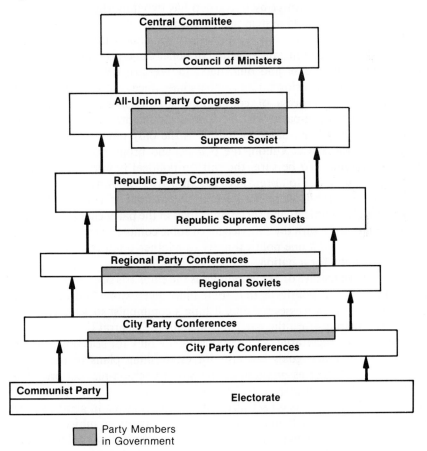

Regional organizations include autonomous republics, oblasts, and krais; city organizations include raions, cities, and boroughs.

Since elected and appointed government positions are filled by individuals who are either party members or those who have demonstrated a commitment toward party objectives, the government and its bureaucratic agencies can be expected to publicly support the goals of the CPSU and to implement the desired programs. As the "vanguard of the proletariat," the party elite selects the social, economic, cultural, and political objectives that it believes will encourage the establishment of a communist society. The task of government is to realize these goals. In Great Britain and other European parliamentary systems, the majority party (or parties) is responsible for establishing the government and creating programs and policies to achieve desired goals. But unlike European democratic systems, Soviet politics is noncompetitive. The task of setting goals, therefore, never alternates among different groups; it is concentrated in the leadership of one party.

The monopoly of power by one group has two important results. First, the Soviet monolithic party system has established an efficient system for the selection of goals and objectives. Since decision-making authority is vested in the top CPSU organizations, the selection of policies and programs can be carried out with relative ease and quickness. In Western democratic systems, decision making is much slower and cumbersome, since goal selection involves the time-consuming process of compromise among interested groups. A second result of the one-party Soviet system is the maintenance of continuity in policies and programs. Since the CPSU is the only political organization that can direct the Soviet Union, the policies and programs exhibit a high degree of continuity. To be sure, the shift in political power from Stalin to Khrushchev and then to Brezhnev has involved important new party emphases. Nevertheless, there has been a high degree of continuity in the overall economic, political, and social objectives in the party elite. This continuity contrasts sharply with the experiences of some competitive systems, where transfer of power from one political party to another often results in significant new directions for a nation.

A distinctive feature of Soviet politics is the emphasis on *planning*. A key assumption of Soviet politics is that some individuals know and understand the goals of and the processes for establishing a communist society. The leaders of the proletariat—i.e., the party members in the Central Committee, the Politburo, and the Secretariat—are responsible not only for selecting economic, social, and political goals but also for establishing plans to realize the desired ends. A further assumption of the Soviet decision-making process is that the establishment of plans is to be carried out through scientific and technical means. The emphasis on scientific methodology stems in great measure from Marxism itself, which views the unfolding of history as subject to scientific laws of historical change. Since Marxism views science as a tool for understanding and controlling the course of human events, it is not surprising that communist ideology encourages the application of scientific methods in Soviet planning.

Although planning is applied mostly to important spheres of Soviet society, it is most visibly demonstrated in the economic realm. Beginning shortly after the Communists took control of the Soviet government, Lenin instituted the first economic-planning efforts with the creation of the New Economic Policy (NEP). The purpose of the NEP was to allow the government a direct role in allocating resources and in setting production goals. Subsequently, Stalin established a number of Five-Year Plans to increase agricultural productivity through collectivization of farms and to develop a strong industrial economy. To carry out the economic goals, Stalin created a bureaucratic organization with responsibility for planning and coordinating all major economic activities. This economic-planning organization *(Gosplan)* still functions today in much the same manner as it did in the 1930s and 1940s, although the planning procedures themselves are increasingly more technical.

EVALUATION OF SOVIET CONFLICT MANAGEMENT

How well have Soviet political institutions managed conflict? How well have they governed? One of the strengths of the Soviet political system is that it is efficient. Since only one political party can participate in the development of public policies and since party leadership is in the hands of a small elite group, determination of goals is generally carried out with quickness, simplicity, and a large degree of continuity. Moreover, since the government is the servant of the powerful CPSU organization, implementation of the party's programs and proposals is generally carried out with a high degree of effectiveness. In short, goal setting and goal implementation are not affected with some of the problems found in Western democratic societies, which delay decision making and complicate implementation.

The Soviet system pays a high cost for this efficiency in the public sector. This high cost is in the form of a lack of ingenuity, creativity, and vitality, which can only result from an open and free society. If the search for the appropriate policies and programs is carried out by a small group of individuals with limited freedom of expression and debate, the resulting solutions may not be as effective as they might have been if the search had been conducted in a free and competitive environment. There is little doubt that the Soviet political system can make and implement decisions more easily. But the fundamental question remains: are the goals and policies selected by the party elite the best ones? Are the gains in government efficiency worth the loss of human freedom?

To a significant extent the Soviet system seeks to avoid the problem of managing conflict altogether. It does so by seeking to create a political culture that is strongly homogeneous and that inhibits the development of significant political cleavages. The fundamental purpose of the Communist party is not to manage conflict by reconciling competing and diverse interests but to create a society that is strongly committed to a common body of values and beliefs and that accepts the CPSU as the only legitimate guide for society. Its major purpose is to create political consensus. As has been noted earlier, this is carried out by a widespread program of socialization and by a well-organized party that endures effective control throughout Soviet society. The political system of the USSR thus avoids (to a large degree) the problem of politics altogether. If a precondition of politics is conflict, the effort to eliminate conflict from society suggests that the goal of the CPSU is to make politics unnecessary in a nation. What the party seeks is to direct human energies not toward the search for the creation of appropriate public goals and objectives (a task it has left to itself) but toward the implementation of the selected policies and programs.

By emphasizing the implementation of goals, the energies of Soviet citizens are directed toward economic and social development. One of the major achievements of the Soviet system is the transformation of a relatively backward agrarian society into the second-most-powerful industrial state in the world. Despite its economic achievements, the Soviet system continues to pursue authoritarian practices inimical to the development of a creative and innovative society.

James Madison long ago alluded (in the *Federalist No. 10*) to the fundamental problem facing the Soviet Union. The basic problem in all societies, according to Madison, is the problem of group conflict (faction), which would make societal harmony and productivity impossible. One approach to deal with the problem (the easiest way of coping with conflict and disharmony) is to eliminate its permissive cause—human freedom. Madison objected to this solution because he felt that the solution was worse than the problem. The only valid solution is to manage competing group interests—a less efficient and less effective means of controlling the detrimental effects of faction but one that ensures a vital and innovative society.

Perhaps the party elite has begun to recognize the need for greater diversity within society. Over the past two decades there has been a slow but noticeable growth toward a more pluralistic society. To be sure, this pluralism is well-controlled by the party organization. But the CPSU is less monolithic than it was in the 1950s, and many of the totalitarian practices of the Stalin era have gradually disappeared. The overall result is that the Soviet citizen enjoys more freedom today than in the previous decades of Communist rule. This increasing level of freedom and the declining level of authoritarianism is expressed in Figure 12.5.

Despite the relaxation of some political controls over the people, the Soviet system remains a one-party state. Competitive politics are anathema to the goals and purposes of the Communist elite. Thus, while specialization and modernization has resulted in a moderation of the totalitarian practices of the early part of the century, the Soviet system remains strongly committed to the principle of one-party government.

Figure 12.5   Changing Levels of Government Regulation and Individual Freedom in Selected Periods

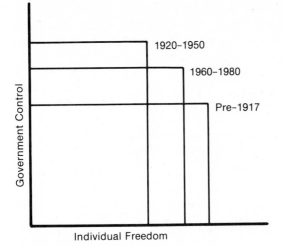

SUMMARY

The Soviet Union, the largest territorial state, is a one-party political system. Formally titled the Union of Soviet Socialist Republics, this country is a federal state comprised of fifteen union republics, the largest being the Russian Soviet Federal Socialist Republic. The RSFSR covers nearly two-thirds of the country and holds more than one-half of the Soviet population (more than 260 million).

Although the USSR is one of the most heterogeneous states, it is a highly consensual and orderly society. This harmony derives in great measure from the deeply ingrained Marxist political culture and the efficient and effective political institutions that implement CPSU policies. The creation and mainte-nance of a Marxist culture has not been achieved by accident but by systematic programs of political socialization for children and adults.

Although the CPSU membership represents less than 10 percent of the adult population, the party is unusually effective in carrying out its policies and programs. The ability to implement goals derives in great part from well-developed party institutions at the local, regional, and national levels. The two highest party institutions are the Central Committee and the Politburo, which together set goals and objectives to be carried out by lower-level party organs and formal institutions of government.

The Soviet political system is formally a parliamentary system, with final authority (theoretically) in the hands of the Soviet parliament, the Supreme Soviet. Since the Soviet parliament is large and meets only a few days each year, the legislature's power is effectively vested in the Supreme Soviet's Presidium, and more particularly, in the Council of Ministers. The Council of Ministers includes heads of all ministries and government agencies and thus serves as a collective executive for the Soviet system. The Presidium of the Council of Ministers is generally considered to be the Soviet cabinet, although the effective executive authority resides in the party's supreme organization, the Politburo.

KEY TERMS

CPSU
RSFSR
agitation
propaganda
union republic
autonomous republic
raion
oblast
Supreme Soviet
Council of Nationalities

Council of Ministers
primary party organization
All-Union Party Congress
Central Committee
Politburo
Secretariat
democratic centralism
planning
Council of Unions
Presidium of the Supreme Soviet

NOTES

1. Stanley Rothman and George W. Breslauer, *Soviet Politics and Society* (New York: West Publishing Co., 1978), p. 92.

2. Karl Deutsch, *Politics and Government: How People Decide Their Fate* (Boston: Houghton Mifflin Co., 1974), p. 358.

3. World Bank, *Atlas: Population, Per Capita Product, and Growth Rates* (Washington, D.C.: World Bank, 1977), p. 18.

4. For a short discussion of income inequality in the Soviet Union see Deutsch, *Politics and Government: How People Decide Their Fate,* pp. 362–5.

5. Ted Robert Gurr, "A Comparative Study of Civil Strife," in *The History of Violence in America,* ed. Hugh Davis Graham and Ted Robert Gurr (New York: Frederick A. Praeger, 1969), p. 629.

6. For a comparative analysis of Soviet and American schools and their impact on children see Urie Bronfenbrenner, *Two Worlds of Childhood: U.S. and U.S.S.R.* (New York: Russell Sage, 1970).

7. Frederick C. Barghoorn, *Politics in the USSR* (Boston: Little, Brown & Co., 1966), p. 97.

8. *Ibid.,* p. 126.

9. Since 1917 the Soviet Union has had four constitutions—those of 1918, 1924, 1938, and 1977.

10. Jerry F. Hough and Merle Fainsod, *How the Soviet Union is Governed* (Cambridge: Harvard University Press, 1979), p. 364.

11. In theory, the Council of Ministers is collectively responsible to the Supreme Soviet. The council is elected by the parliament and must resign at the first session of a newly elected Supreme Soviet. This is not unlike Western parliamentary practices, where the cabinet holds its position as long as it maintains the confidence of the parliament.

12. Hough, *How the Soviet Union is Governed,* p. 381.

13. For a more complete description of the role of the PPO, see "The Statutes of the Communist Party of the Soviet Union," in *Man, State, and Society in the Soviet Union,* ed. Joseph L. Nogee (New York: Praeger Publishers, 1973), pp. 92–112.

14. The term *secretary* in the Soviet Union does not mean a clerical position as in the West. Rather, party secretary is the highest level of political office. The first secretary is generally the most powerful person in a community.

15. Hough, *How the Soviet Union is Governed,* pp. 495–6.

16. Rothman, *Soviet Politics and Society,* p. 174.

17. Hough, *How the Soviet Union is Governed,* p. 458.

18. For an excellent analysis of the organization and functions of the Central Committee, see Hough, *ibid.,* pp. 455–66.

19. Hough, *How the Soviet Union is Governed,* pp. 495–6.

20. Nogee, *Man, State, and Society,* p. 93.

21. Hough, *How the Soviet Union is Governed,* p. 456.

SUGGESTED READING

ASPATURIAN, VERNON V. *Process and Power in Soviet Foreign Policy.* Boston: Little, Brown & Co., 1971. A comprehensive analysis of the Soviet Union's foreign-policy institutions and processes.

BARGHOORN, FREDERICK C. *Politics in the USSR.* 2nd ed. Boston: Little, Brown & Co., 1972. Applies systems analysis to the politics and government of the Soviet Union. Excellent overview of political culture, socialization, and public opinion in the Soviet political system.

BRZEZINSKI, ZBIGNIEW, and HUNTINGTON, SAMUEL P. *Political Power: USA/USSR.* New York: The Viking Press, 1965. An insightful comparison of the American and Soviet political systems, noting the strengths and weaknesses of each.

HOLLANDER, GAYLE D. *Soviet Political Indoctrination: Developments in Mass Media and Propaganda Since Stalin.* New York: Praeger Publishers, 1972. Examines the role of the media in Soviet political socialization during the 1950s and 1960s.

HOUGH, JERRY F. *The Soviet Prefects: The Local Party Organs in Industrial Decision Making.* Cambridge: Harvard University Press, 1969. A detailed account of how the party and state governmental institutions interact at the *oblast* level.

_____ and Fainsod, Merle. *How the Soviet Union Is Governed.* Cambridge: Harvard University Press, 1979. This is an extensively revised and enlarged edition of Fainsod's classic study *How Russia is Ruled.* This new, up-to-date, and comprehensive analysis of Soviet government and politics is clearly the most thorough account of how the Soviet political system operates.

INKELES, ALEX. *Public Opinion in Soviet Russia.* 2nd ed. Cambridge: Harvard University Press, 1950. A dated but still informative examination of the role of the Communist party in molding Soviet public opinion.

MOORE, BARRINGTON. *Soviet Politics: The Dilemma of Power.* Cambridge: Harvard University Press, 1950. A brilliant analysis of how communist ideology changed to cope with the problems of governing a large nation.

NOGEE, JOSEPH L., ed. *Man, State, and Society in the Soviet Union.* New York: Praeger Publishers, 1972. An excellent collection of introductory readings on the politics and society of the USSR.

ROTHMAN, STANLEY, and BRESLAUER, GEORGE W. *Soviet Politics and Society.* New York: West Publishing Co., 1978. A lucid, up-to-date introductory text on Soviet politics and government. Highly recommended for the student with little familiarity with Soviet affairs.

SHARLET, ROBERT. *The New Soviet Constitution of 1977: Analysis and Text.* Brunswick, Ohio: King's Court Communications, Inc., 1978. An analysis of the major changes in the new Soviet constitution.

SKILLING, H. GORDON, and GRIFFITHS, FRANKLYN, eds. *Interest Groups in Soviet Politics.* Princeton: Princeton University Press, 1971. An excellent collection of studies on the role of professional and government groups in the Soviet political system. The most significant volume presenting the pluralistic perspective of Soviet politics.

ULAM, ADAM B. *Expansion and Coexistence: Soviet Foreign Policy 1917–1973.* 2nd ed. New York: Praeger Publishers, 1974. The most comprehensive account of Soviet foreign affairs.

13 / CONFLICT MANAGEMENT IN THE DEVELOPING COUNTRIES

In this chapter we are concerned with the process of conflict management in the developing nations, or Third World. These countries, which are also referred to as transitional, underdeveloped, or less developed (LDC), include some eighty nations in Asia, Africa, Latin America, and the Middle East and hold nearly 3 billion people, or roughly 70 percent of the world's total population. While there are significant social and economic differences among the developing nations, we shall treat these countries as a group.

The goal of this chapter is to examine the major governmental institutions and the dominant political processes in Third World states. A central assumption is that, despite the many political and governmental differences among them, the Third World nations share many significant features in their political systems. We shall first examine some of the common socioeconomic problems facing most of these states and the means used to respond to them. We shall be particularly concerned with the challenges of creating domestic consensus in the emerging states. In the last part of the chapter we shall review a number of significant theories of political development. These prescriptive theories of political growth have been developed as a means of highlighting ways in which Third World political processes can be strengthened.

SOME CHARACTERISTICS OF DEVELOPING COUNTRIES

One feature of Third World states is that they are relatively young. With the exception of Latin American nations, which received their independence in the early part of the nineteenth century, most LDCs became independent during the postwar decades (in Africa alone, more than forty states declared political independence from their European colonial powers). The significance of the relative youth of the LDCs is that their political systems are still in the process of development.

A second significant characteristic of developing nations is their high population-growth rate. Growth rates in Asia, Africa, and Latin America were 2.5 or higher during the 1960s (Figure 13.1). Although growth rates vary significantly among the Third World, the average estimated growth rate for this group of states during the 1960s and early 1970s was more than twice that of the developed countries (DCs). The result of these differing growth rates is a gradual increase in the population of the western industrial states but a population explosion in the developing nations. As the data in Figure 13.2 suggest, if past trends continue, the total population of the Third World countries is expected to total nearly 5 billion persons by the end of the twentieth century. This means that from 1950 to 2000 the population of the Third World nations will have increased by nearly 3.5 billion, while the population of the DCs will have increased by only 600 million.

Figure 13.1   Population-Growth Rates for Selected Areas of the Third World, 1961–1970 (Percentages)

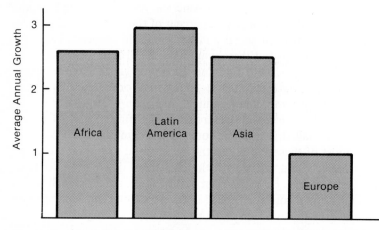

Source: World Bank, Trends in Developing Countries *(Washington, D. C.: World Bank, 1973), p. 3.*

The primary cause of the population explosion in the developing nations is the declining death rate made possible by the introduction of medical care. In the early 1950s the death rate in the developing nations was estimated at twenty-four deaths per thousand; by the end of the 1970s the death rate declined to eleven deaths per thousand, or less than one-half the earlier rate. In addition to the declining death rate, LDCs have historically had higher birth rates than those of the DCs. In the 1965–1969 period, for example, the birth rate in the DCs was estimated at nineteen per thousand, while the rate of the Third World was estimated at thirty-nine per thousand.[1] Despite declining birth rates for nearly all countries, the LDCs continue to have a birth rate nearly twice that of the DCs.

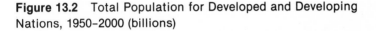

Figure 13.2 Total Population for Developed and Developing Nations, 1950–2000 (billions)

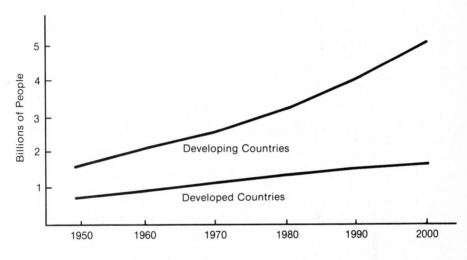

Source: World Bank, Trends in Developing Countries *(Washington, D. C.: World Bank, 1963), p. 11.*

One of the significant implications of the population explosion is the high proportion of young people. According to World Bank estimates, in 1970 about 42 percent of the total Third World was under ten years of age (Figure 13.3). The high proportion of children and young people in a political system can place heavy social and political burdens on a nation, for the government must provide a significant portion of resources for health and education. At the same time, there is a proportionately smaller labor force from which the government may extract taxes and other resources. Finally, the large proportion of young people places heavy burdens in terms of political socialization. Since young people are often the most likely to question and challenge the values and institutions of a state, it is important for children to develop a strong commitment toward the states.

Figure 13.3   Age Structure for Developed and Developing Regions

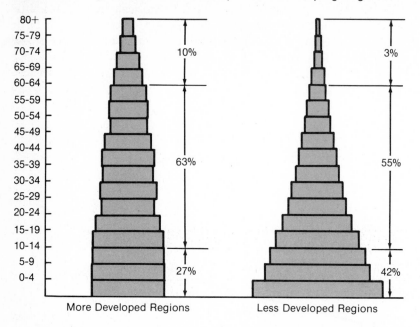

More Developed Regions   Less Developed Regions

Source: World Bank, Trends in Developing Countries *(Washington, D. C.: World Bank, 1973), p. 20.*

    The third characteristic of developing countries is their relative poverty. In 1976 the total GNP of the DCs was estimated at 5,499 billion dollars; the LDCs' GNP was estimated at one-fourth that amount, or 1,321 billion dollars. Since there are nearly three times as many people in the LDCs as in the DCs, the economic comparisons between the two groups of states become all the more striking when per capita income is compared (Figure 13.4). Although average personal income in the Third World remains at about one-tenth of that of modern, developed states, the growth rates have led to a widening economic gap between the rich and the poor nations. While per capita economic growth rates between the DCs and LDCs during the late 1960s and early 1970s were roughly the same, the absolute increases in income in the industrial countries led to huge international economic inequities. From 1960 to 1970, per capita income in the Third World increased by $65 per person, while the per capita income in the developed countries increased by $740 per person.

    A fourth trait of the developing nations is the growth of the urban sector. The urbanization movement is, of course, affecting all nations, LDCs and DCs alike. What makes this development of particular significance for the Third World, however, is the enormous challenge posed by the demands of increasing urban populations. The World Bank estimates that between 1970 and 1985 the urban population of the DCs will grow by 229 million; during this

Figure 13.4 GNP per Capita by Region, 1960, 1970, and 1976 (thousands of dollars)

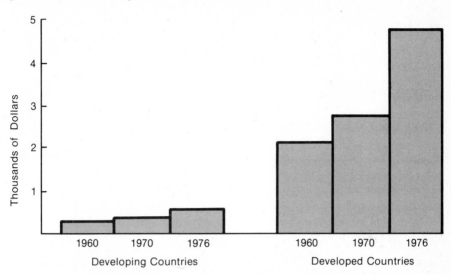

Source: *World Bank,* Trends in Developing Nations *(Washington, D. C.: World Bank, 1973) and 1978* World Bank Atlas *(Washington, D. C.: World Bank), p. 12.*

period the LDCs' urban population will grow by 611 million (Figure 13.5). The challenge for Third World countries is thus to direct and control increasing urbanization so that adequate water, sewage, transportation, employment, and other requirements can be provided for those who migrate to the cities. But to do this, enormous funds for city planning are required. While urbanization may be a desirable aspect of the modernization of states, the dramatic increases in urban populations pose a major challenge to the health, well-being, and political stability of countries that do not have adequate resources to support significant demographic changes.

Closely related to the problem of urbanization in the Third World is the scarcity of resources available for meeting social and economic needs. One indicator of the level of government support for the public welfare is the level of funds allocated for health and education. In 1976, for example, the total annual government expenditures for health and education in the LDCs were estimated at 12 and 35.6 billion dollars, respectively, or roughly $3.82 per person for health and $11.30 per person for education. In the DCs, on the other hand, health and education expenditures totaled 144.5 and 307.2 billion dollars, respectively, or about $137.60 per person for health and $292.60 per person for education.[2]

Although developing nations have many other common features, the above characteristics are listed because they help explain some of the important social and economic changes affecting the political systems of the Third

Figure 13.5   Urban and Rural Population of DCs and LDCs for 1960, 1970, and 1985 estimate (billions)

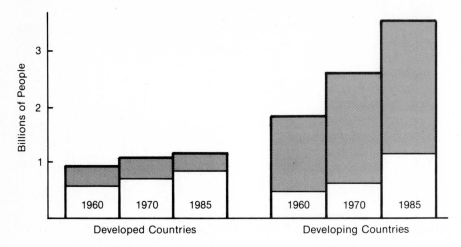

Source: World Bank, Trends in Developing Countries *(Washington, D. C.: World Bank, 1973), p. 23.*

World. Moreover, the problems and challenges in the LDCs should not be regarded as a sign of inferiority or weakness. We list these conditions not to characterize the many countries of Asia, Africa, and Latin America as backward or poor but rather to seek to understand the dynamic developments occurring in those regions and to appreciate the difficult challenges facing the governments of the Third World states.

THE DEVELOPMENT OF CONSENSUS

Conflict in the LDCs

One of the noticeable traits of the political systems of the Third World is the higher level of conflict over fundamental societal concerns. Unlike the frequent conflict and competition in developed democratic systems — where conflict occurs continuously within and among political institutions like interest groups, political parties, and governmental agencies — conflict in the Third World often arises from lack of a homogeneous, consensual society. This lack of unity is often rooted in heterogeneity of culture, linguistic diversity, and absence of social and economic integration within the nation. In Table 13.1, for example, the countries that tend to be the most culturally heterogeneous are those of the Third World. Developed, industrial states tend to be more homogeneous (although there are exceptions, such as Canada, Belgium, and the Soviet Union).

TABLE 13.1 Countries Classified According to Level of Ethnic Heterogeneity

INDEX OF ETHNIC HETEROGENEITY SCORE (0 – HIGHLY HOMOGENEOUS – TO 8 – HIGHLY HETEROGENEOUS)

0	1	2	3	4	5	6	7	8
Argentina	Cuba	Australia	Albania	Algeria	Belgium	Afghanistan	Chad	Sudan
Austria	Dominican R.	Bulgaria	Colombia	Brazil	Bolivia	Burma	Congo (Lco.)	
Chile	France	Buruandi	Israel	Cambodia	Cyprus	Canada	Ecuador	
Costa Rica	Germany, E.	El Salvado	Jamaica	Cent. Afr. R.	Czech'kia	Cameroun	Ethiopia	
Denmark	Finland	Germany, W.	Libya	Haiti	Guatemala	Ceylon	Laos	
Greece	Hungary	Honduras	Spain	Jordan	Ivory Coast	Congo (Bra.)	Malaya	
Iceland	Italy	Japan	U.K.	Lebanon	Liberia	Dahomey	Nigeria	
Ireland	New Zealand	Korea, N.	U.S.	Somalia	Malagasy	Gabon	S. Africa	
Luxembourg	Venezuela	Korea, S.	Vietnam, N.	Syria	Morocco	Ghana	Uganda	
Norway		Mexico	Vietnam, S.	Thailand	Nepal	Guinea		
Paraguay		Mongolia		Trinidad	Philippines	India		
Poland		Netherlands		Yemen	Senegal	Indonesia		
Portugal		Nicaragua			Tanganyika	Iran		
Sweden		Panama			U.S.S.R.	Iraq		
Tunisia		Rumania			Upper Volta	Mali		
U.A.R.		Rwanda				Mauritania		
Uruguay		Saudi Arabia				Niger		
		Turkey				Pakistan		
						Peru		
						Sierra Leone		
						Switzerland		
						Togo		
						Yugoslavia		
N = 17	N = 9	N = 18	N = 10	N = 12	N = 15	N = 23	N = 9	N = 1

Source: Marie R. Haug, "Social and Cultural Pluralism as a Concept in Social System Analysis," *American Journal of Sociology, 73* (1967), p. 299. Used with permission of the University of Chicago Press.

Some common manifestations of disunity are revolts and strikes against a government, military coup d'etats, and severe conflict between the government and such groups as the intelligentsia, labor unions, peasants, and religious organizations. Where the authority of government is weak, the dominant groups in society compete intensively for the privilege of making rules and decrees for a nation. As countries become more modern, one of the results is a growth in national unity, based not so much on a more effective government as much as on a more socially homogeneous culture and a more economically integrated society. As the data in Table 13.2 suggest, modern countries tend to enjoy a lower level of political conflict in contrast to either traditional or transitional states. Although it might be reasonable to expect that the shift from a traditional to a modern society would lead to greater concensus, the process of change itself is a highly destabilizing and conflictual one. Indeed, numerous social scientists suggest that the most disorderly and conflictual societies are likely to be those undergoing modernization.[3]

TABLE 13.2   Political Conflict and Level of Socioeconomic Development, 84 Countries, 1948-1965

LEVEL OF SOCIOECONOMIC DEVELOPMENT	LOW %	HIGH %	TOTAL (N)
Traditional	43	57	23
Transitional	32	68	37
Modern	83	17	24
Total: (N)	42	42	84

Source: Ivo K. Feierabend, Rosalind L. Feierabend, and Betty A. Nesvold, "Social Change and Political Violence; Cross-National Patterns," in The History of Violence in America: A Report to the National Commission on the Causes and Prevention of Violence, ed. Hugh Davis Graham and Ted Robert Gurr (New York: Bantam Books, 1969), p. 655.

One indicator of the level of political instability is the frequency of illegal government takeovers. S.E. Finer has examined the number of coups during the 1958–1978 period and found that of the 157 coups during these two decades all but six were in the LDCs. The 151 LDC coups affected fifty-five countries and were distributed as follows: Africa, sixty-five, Asia, fifty, and Latin America, thirty-six.[4] Although many Third World countries had three or more coups, the fact that more than half of the LDCs had at least one coup suggests that political instability resulting from military-civilian incompatibilities is rather pervasive.

Impediments to Consensus

Why do developing nations have a higher level of conflict and disorder than the DCs? Some nonpolitical reasons include: lack of national unity, presence of a dualistic social structure, challenge of Western ideas, absence of economic integration, and gaps between expectations and fulfillment of desires.

Lack of National Unity   One explanation for the political instability of the Third World is that most states are composed of numerous tribal, religious, linguistic, and cultural groups that have not been fully integrated within the nation. Although nationalism is a powerful force in unifying nations to achieve political independence, the movement of nationalism is not nearly as effective in bringing domestic political cohesion. Thus, following the strong unity achieved during the period of independence (during the 1950s and 1960s) many Asian and African countries have become less unified as tribal and regional conflicts have surfaced. The domestic conflicts within countries like Angola, Burundi, and Sudan have in great measure resulted from the lack of an integrated society.

Social Dualism   Social dualism is the existence of a modern and a traditional culture and society within a nation. Since social change is generally associated with urban life, most developing countries tend to have relatively modern societies within their major cities but relatively traditional cultural and social patterns in the rural and semirural areas. A result of the imbalance between rural and urban areas is a significant tension between the values and practices of the traditional and modern sectors of society.

Another manifestation of social dualism is the tension between the aristocratic elite and the masses. This tension is found especially in Latin America, and to a lesser extent, in the former colonies of Asia and Africa.[5] Latin American tensions over social dualism have their roots in the nature of Spain's conquest and colonization. Because the Spanish came to America to conquer and control the land and the peoples of the continent, the three centuries of colonial rule led to the development of two different societies — one culture representing the indigenous values and interests of the Spanish elite and the other representing the values and interests of the masses. Unlike the relatively homogeneous culture that resulted in the United States and Canada, Latin America developed a dual society with limited interaction between rich and poor, privileged and less privileged. This lack of unity between the two sectors of society has resulted in significant tensions between the traditional elite, who have tried to use military force to hold on to their privileged status, and the masses. Mexico is one of the most stable and developed Latin American countries, due largely to its revolution (1910) in which the masses revolted and eventually paved the way for a more homogeneous society.

The External Challenge of the West   Closely associated to social dualism is the conflict created by the impact of Western ideas, practices, and products. As people in developing nations become more aware of the ideas and commodities associated with developed societies, this increases social, political, and economic expectations. The problem with a "revolution of rising expectations" is that political systems often are unable to meet the demands of the people;

the result is frustration and eventual revolution. One of the influential explanations of revolution is James Davies's *J*-curve theory. In his words, "Revolution is most likely to take place when a prolonged period of rising expectations and rising gratifications is followed by a short period of sharp reversal, during which the gap between expectations and gratifications quickly widens and becomes intolerable."[6] Although Davies's theory is primarily concerned with major political revolt, his idea that instability arises from unfulfilled expectations is valid not only for major revolutions but also for less dramatic forms of domestic disturbances. In most political communities there is some gap between society's wants and its ability to meet those wants. As long as the gap between aspirations and fulfillment is not significant, however, a political system may anticipate a reasonable level of order and harmony. When the gap becomes significant, as is often the case in transitional societies (Figure 13.6), then a political system may experience increased levels of domestic conflict and tension. Developing nations in which the modernization process is creating significantly higher levels of popular aspirations are often unable to meet the demands of the people.

Figure 13.6   Need Satisfaction and Level of Socioeconomic Development

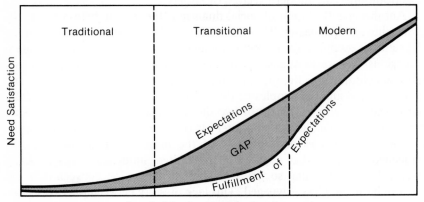

Level of Socioeconomic Development

Perhaps even more important than the external challenge of economic modernity is the challenge of Western ideas. In *The Rich Nations and the Poor Nations,* Barbara Ward suggests that a major explanation for the difference between the LDCs and the DCs lies in the extent to which Western ideas of equality, progress, and materialism are incorporated into society. The rich, industrial societies are those in which the social, political, and economic life of the nation is regulated by these ideas; the LDCs are those states in which these ideas have not fully taken hold. Although political equality is an ideal articulated by leaders and statesmen from all nations, in practice traditional hierarchical patterns and caste systems still prevail in many LDCs. Similarly, the idea of progress—the notion that a person's position in society is not determined at birth but can be changed through individual effort—is a common aspiration among the peoples of the LDCs. For most poor people in the developing states, however, there is little hope of altering social position because of national economic conditions and the existence of norms and values inhibiting social mobility.

Finally, the Western notion of materialism is a challenge to the traditional, religious cultures of numerous Asian and African states. Whereas many of the developing nations have historically been based on other-worldly values, the process of modernization emphasizes temporal, material concerns. A modern society is, by definition, a secular, pragmatic, commercial society. Although coins in the United States bear the words "In God we trust," American culture is essentially secular and materialistic in comparison to Islamic, Hindu, or Confucian societies. Western countries are modern precisely because they focus on the achievement of temporal goods by the application of technology and science. The LDCs are not as modern because they have not made the effort nor have they succeeded in making national production an all-consuming passion. For many of them the fundamental goals of life are religious and ascriptive, not technical and commercial. When the Western emphasis on materialism and secularism comes in contact with the religious orientations of traditional cultures, the outcome is conflict. The revolt of the Islamic leaders against the Shah of Iran in 1978 and 1979 was partly motivated by the increasing emphasis on economic growth at the expense of the traditional Islamic values of Iran. The result was a revolution in which the Shah was deposed and the Ayatollah Khomeini assumed power.

Lack of Economic Integration   One of the characteristics of a modern, developed nation is a high level of national unity. One of the ways by which such states build and maintain national cohesion is through modern communications and transportation systems. A modern communications system involves a large number of telephones, radios, and television; an effective system involves a network in which all parts of a nation are effectively connected by highways, railways, or air. Karl Deutsch observes that a nation is a people, and a people are a group of individuals who understand each other.[7] The development of a common understanding among people, however, is dependent on continued, frequent interaction. People who do not speak to each other or interact in any significant way become dissimilar; individuals who regularly interact and communicate with each other become more alike. Thus, Deutsch suggests that the foundation of a strongly integrated society is a network of interdependent communication and action. If this is to occur within the boundaries of a nation, this requires the modern instruments of communication and transportation.

The importance of integrative systems can be illustrated by comparing two countries, Peru and the United States. In the United States virtually all people have a radio and a television and have access to newspapers and weeklies to keep them informed of public affairs. Almost all homes and businesses have telephones, and mail delivery is quick and inexpensive. Transportation, whether by car, airplane, or rail is also inexpensive and efficient. Goods are shipped efficiently and cheaply throughout the country either by truck, rail, or airplane. In Peru, by contrast, the communications networks are much more limited. Telegraphic service is adequate, but telephone service is far more limited and expensive. Communicating within the country poses major difficulties. Because of the geographical barrier of the Andes Mountains, there are few modern highways and railroads in Peru. Those that do exist provide a slow, cumbersome means of transporting goods within the nation. Cuzco (the ancient Inca capital) is located some three hundred miles from Lima (the capital), but because of inadequate roads, the trip is a three-day ordeal by bus. Shipping goods between Cuzco and Lima is thus a slow, expensive process. In some cases the only efficient method of traveling and transporting goods is by airplane.

One country that has sought to accept the challenge of developing modern transportation networks is Brazil. Until the 1960s most transportation systems were limited to the coastal areas of Brazil. Indeed, the vast majority of Brazilians live within two hundred miles of the Atlantic Ocean, with major population centers located in the southern regions of São Paulo and Minas Gerais. But in 1958 Brazil founded a new capital city, Brazilia, in the interior of the jungles. The goal for such a dramatic move was to shift resources from the coast toward the interior. Along with the establishment of a new capital, Brazil began to establish many new highways to seek to integrate the formerly abandoned Amazonian jungle with the highly populated coastal areas. The result of the growing transportation networks in Brazil is that national unity is significantly strengthened.

One of the most effective ways of building national cohesion is by encouraging interdependent action and communication among the peoples of a state. This requires effective networks of communication and transportation. The difficulty in developing modern integrative systems, however, is not only the lack of resources and technology but also geographical barriers. Many LDCs are in the tropics; establishing roads and railways in jungle or mountainous areas presents a major difficulty. Increasing use of the airplane, however, is an effective means by which to communicate with various regions of a state, although it is not an adequate means by which to transport goods for export. But the development of national consensus requires the presence of effective mechanisms by which towns, villages, and cities of a nation can interact with each other.

In addition to these socioeconomic impediments to consensus, two political factors help explain the higher level of conflict and disorder in the LDCs. The first is the absence of organized public opinion; the second is the weakness of government.

The Absence of Organized Public Opinion   We observed that long-term government rule requires broad popular support. Stable, effective government cannot be based on coercion but must have the voluntary support of substantial numbers of people — it must be recognized as legitimate by a large proportion of the population. What this means is that public opinion must be organized so that it can support, sustain, and uphold the government and the decisions it makes. If public opinion is to provide a broad foundation for political action, political parties must be able to direct and organize the interests of people. Only through well-developed parties and interest groups can public order be created and sustained.

The instability of Third World governments results, in great measure, from an absence of organized public opinion. The lack of consensual public opinion is partly the result of three weaknesses: an ineffective media, a low literacy rate, and the weakness of political parties. We have already emphasized the importance of communications networks. In the Third World the development of an informed populace is made difficult by relatively high illiteracy rates and by limited means by which to communicate with the people. Although the level of illiteracy in the LDCs has been declining in the past decade (Figure 13.7), the number of illiterate persons has increased in a number of regions. In Africa, for example, illiteracy increased from 124 million to 143 million from 1960 to 1970, while in Asia the number increased from 542 million to 579 million. Despite increasing numbers of radios, televisions, and newspapers in the LDCs, the availability of the media is still limited. For example, whereas average newspaper circulation in the DCs was estimated at about three hundred copies per one thousand persons in the late 1960s, the rate of distribution in the Third World was less than forty copies per one thousand persons. Similarly, the number of radios in the DCs was about 320 per one thousand persons, while the LDCs had less than ninety per one thousand persons. Television-ownership comparisons are even more significant — 150 sets per one thousand persons in the DCs to less than twenty sets per one thousand persons in the LDCs. In short, the instruments by which a people become aware and informed about domestic and international issues are far more limited in the developing world.

The more significant cause of unorganized public opinion is the weakness or absence of political parties in the LDCs. Blondel estimates that in 1969 thirty LDCs had no political parties and thirty-four had only one ruling party.[8] Political parties are significant because they are the major instruments by

Figure 13.7   Illiteracy in Third World Regions, 1960–1970

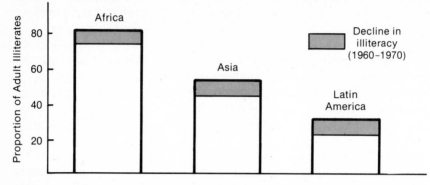

Source: *John W. Sewell and the staff of the Overseas Development Council,* The United States and World Development: Agenda 1977 *(New York: Praeger for the Overseas Development Council, 1977), p. 177.*

which public opinion can be developed, directed, and used to support the actions of government. One political scientist observes that "the capacity to create political institutions is the capacity to create public interests."[9] Public opinion, on which government rests, needs to be generated; if there is no consensus, the only other method by which government can rule is coercion.

According to Huntington, the effectiveness of political parties in building public opinion depends upon their level of public support and the extent of institutionalization. The level of institutionalization is the extent to which an organization gains acceptance and stability within a political community. The seniority system, for example, is an institutionalized procedure in the U.S. Senate because it is an accepted, recurring pattern of behavior in that chamber. When a political party becomes part of an ongoing political process and follows regular patterns and procedures, it becomes institutionalized. The extent of party institutionalization, according to Huntington, depends in great measure on four indicators—the adaptibility, complexity, autonomy, and unity of the party organization.[10] As a party increases in these qualities, the level of institutionalization likewise increases because of its increasing ability to lead and direct public opinion. If a political system is to govern effectively, it needs institutionalized parties; on the other hand, popular support is needed if the party organization is to effectively support government rule. High levels of political participation without effective parties results in unstable government and even violence and disorder.

The major political shortcoming in the LDCs is the absence of institutionalized political parties. As modernization and social change increase the level of awareness and the interest in political affairs, political participation tends to increase. But many countries do not have effective institutions to direct the rising levels of mass participation. The most common type of political party is the personalistic party — an organization built around the personality and charisma of one leader, such as Juan Domingo Peron in Argentina, Fidel Castro in Cuba, Kwame Nkrumah in Ghana, Juan Velasco Ibarra in Ecuador, and Julius Nyerere in Tanzania. The weakness of the personalistic party is that its effectiveness depends upon the leader. Thus, when the leader becomes ill or dies, the party organization is jeopardized.

In short, the stability of government depends upon the strength of organized public opinion. If political parties are to effectively lead and direct public opinion, they have to be well-institutionalized to provide continuous direction to the masses.

Weakness of Government The capacity to govern depends directly on the extent of the regime's authority — i.e., on the level of voluntary support for those in power and for the actions they take. Authority is an economical way of influencing behavior. When public opinion is not organized, the only way by which a government may be able to rule is through coercion.

At least two factors impair the effectiveness of Third World governments: overemphasis on bureaucracy, and lack of national integration to effectively support implementation of government decisions throughout the nation. The overemphasis on bureaucracy is in great measure the result of a colonial heritage left by the British and the French. When these two imperial powers colonized African and Asian nations, they established modern bureaucratic systems by which they could maintain effective control, but little emphasis was placed on politics. The chief concern was with administration. Development of an elaborate bureaucracy is clearly evident in the British legacy to India. But while colonial powers provided their colonies with excellent tools for governing, they failed to develop indigenous political forces to buttress the government. Where development of such forces was encouraged, it was often done without reference to the bureaucracy. Thus, one political scientist remarks that the role of the bureaucrat was established and maintained in almost complete isolation from the politician.[11] As a result, when colonies became independent in the 1960s and 1970s, few of them had the political preparation to govern effectively. The colonies had institutionalized bureaucracies but limited experience in maintenance of political parties.

Closely associated with overemphasis on bureaucracy is the relatively weak role of courts and legislatures among many of the LDCs. The dominant government institution in the Third World is the executive — that is, the president, prime minister and his cabinet, or a military *junta* (council). Because of the weakness of parties, government authority is most often centralized in the hands of the elected or self-appointed leader. The making of laws by the legislature or the interpretation of laws by courts is significant in only those countries that have developed political forces to organize popular interests. In the absence of an elected legislature or an independent court system, the executive branch itself seeks to make and interpret laws.

The second reason for the weakness of Third World governments is the lack of national integration. We have already observed that a common feature of LDCs is the weakness of their transportation and communications networks. When nations are not well-integrated because of geographical impediments or inadequate communications and transportation systems, the government's ability to rule is impaired. If the decisions of government are to be carried out uniformly throughout the state, there needs to be efficient and effective means by which those decisions can be implemented. The absence of national cohesion can thus be a major barrier to the implementation of the government's actions.

When a government is unable to enforce its decisions effectively, differing patterns of government compliance develop that can lead to a disregard for the law. Nowhere is the contradiction between law and political behavior more evident than in Latin America. The weakness of law in the region can perhaps be traced to the colonial period, when Spanish monarchs sought to impose their rules and regulation on their colonies. But geographic distances between the colonies and Spain (as well as internal barriers between the capital and the surrounding towns and villages) resulted in a general disregard for the laws of the king. Theoretically, the viceroy and his deputies sought to implement the laws made for the colonies, but in practice it was much easier to disregard them. Similarly, decisions of the viceroy himself were difficult to implement away from the centers of power. The result of this colonial tradition of theoretically supporting the law but of disregarding it when it is convenient to do so leads to a general contradiction between legal theory and practice.

Duplicity between goals and results of law are most dramatically illustrated by the weak role of constitutions in Latin American governments. For example, Bolivia, the Dominican Republic, and Venezuela have each had more than twenty constitutions since they became independent in the early nineteenth century. The reason for this is that constitutions are not viewed as regulatory documents but as statements of ideals. When political realities are obstructed by constitutions, political leaders find it convenient to change or disregard constitutions rather than seek to abide by the stated principles.

THE MANAGEMENT OF CONFLICT

Since most developing nations do not have strongly integrated societies or mature political institutions, the nature and performance of government in those states tends to differ from that of the more advanced nations. There are two characteristics of Third World governments that illustrate their different role in managing societal conflict and in building consensus. These two features are militarism and the absence of democracy.

The Role of the Military

One of the common occurrences in the LDCs is the coup d'etat. Although the involvement of the military in government is not limited to the Third World, the vast majority of military regimes are in the LDCs. Finer estimates that between 1958 and 1973 fifty-one countries experienced military rule; of these, forty-nine were from the Third World.[12] Since 1973 the number of LDCs that have had military rule has increased to more than fifty-five. Militarism is particularly prevalent in Latin America, where the armed forces have historically been involved directly or indirectly in government. From 1951 to 1970, only four (Chile, Costa Rica, Mexico, and Uruguay) of the eighteen Latin American states did not have military governments. Since then, two (Chile and Uruguay) have succumbed to military rule.

What causes a military government? First, military institutions themselves are not the basic cause. Although military officers are ambitious and play a respected role in many LDCs, their own interests cannot account for the significant impact of military power in the governments of the Third World. Similarly, foreign military-assistance programs cannot be blamed for the lack of civilian rule. One of the common criticisms against the U.S. military-assistance program is that it encourages authoritarian regimes in Asia, Africa, and Latin America. But research does not seem to support this view.[13] Similarly, the size and expenditures of the LDCs for the military would not seem to justify the view that military rule is caused by a misallocation of resources. In 1976 the average per capita expenditure for military defense in the LDCs was $26 (as compared to $279 in the DCs). The proportion of the GNP devoted to the military is only slightly higher in the LDCs than in the DCs (6.3 percent versus 5.6 percent).[14] Clearly, military explanations do not explain military intervention in politics.

To understand why the military becomes involved in government, we need to examine the different patterns of military regimes in the LDCs. In the past two decades, three types have been particularly dominant. First, some military regimes are only *transitional*. Their objective is not to shift political power from normal civilian institutions to military organizations but rather to intervene temporarily to halt or alter the course of public policy. When the military intervenes to stop the goals of a civilian regime, it carries out a "veto" coup. Once it helps civilian authorities to reorganize in order to carry out programs that are acceptable to it, it withdraws its forces. One of the dangers of the "veto" approach, however, is that what is intended to be a brief period of military rule results in an extended period of military government. When the Brazilian military intervened in 1964 to stop some of the radical programs of President Goulart, it was assumed that the military would reestablish a civilian government within a short time. Yet, in 1980 the military was still in control of politics in Brazil.

Another type of transitional intervention may occur when civilian authorities are unable to resolve their different aims and goals. This outcome is often associated with inconclusive election results — where there is no clear mandate for one party or group to assume power. Thus, when elections are inconclusive or when losing parties are unwilling to accept defeat, the armed forces may decide to intervene to bring temporary stability and order.

A second type of military government is the permanent *programmatic* regime. Unlike the transitional regime, a permanent military government assumes power in order to carry out a particular political and economic program. Such programs may involve radical social and economic changes (as was the case in the early 1970s in Peru), or it may involve a conservative program of economic stabilization with limited concern for social change. This latter pattern has been followed by Brazilian and Argentine military governments in the 1970s. It has also been the pattern followed by the Chilean military junta, which toppled the Socialist regime of Salvador Allende in 1973.

A third type of military rule is the *dictatorial* regimes led by charismatic leaders such as Idi Amin of Uganda, Fidel Castro of Cuba, and Alfredo Stroessner of Paraguay. Unlike institutionalized military regimes, which govern most often through a council of representatives of each of the branches of the armed forces, the charismatic military regime is dependent on the strength of a single military official. The goals and directions of the military government are determined to a large degree by the leader himself. Since the power of the military is controlled by the dictator, the role of military institutions in policy making is limited. The function of military organizations is not to assist in the decision-making process but to provide support for the dictator's regime. It is the military that helps maintain the dictator in power and implement his goals.

Given the different types of regimes, military intervention can be explained partly by the following three factors: (1) the desire to limit or stop the policies and programs of the ruling civilian government; (2) the desire to establish and implement a program supportive of the aims of the military institutions; and (3) the attempt by military dictators to maximize their political influence by consolidating power and eliminating political opposition.

More fundamentally, the intervention of the military into politics is caused by a vacuum of civilian authority. All nations need to regulate the tensions and conflicts among their citizens, groups, and parties. When civilian institutions are unable to develop the authority required to manage and resolve domestic conflict, the military may fill the vacuum of authority in order to preserve the integrity of the country. The military, in other words, intervenes to ensure the order and stability that cannot be realized through normal civilian institutions. When public opinion is highly consensual, civilian authority is able to govern effectively, and the threat of military rule is unlikely. But as public opinion becomes less organized, the likelihood of militarism increases.

Finer summarizes the relationship of civilian authority to military government as follows: "The greater the degree of consensus in society and the width and organization of this opinion, the less the likelihood of a military intervention and the less likely, in the event, of its success."[15]

Democracy in the Developing Countries

Figure 13.8 illustrates the different levels of democracy among the countries of the world. Among the developing nations it is clear that democratic government and political freedom are not common. What is perhaps even more significant is that the level of political freedom does not increase with the processes of modernity and economic development. Rather, LDCs increasingly resorted to authoritarian means during the 1970s.

Following the independence of numerous Asian and African states in the late 1950s and 1960s, most of these countries attempted to rule through parliamentary institutions (as had been the pattern under colonialism). But few countries were able to develop the political institutions required to support and maintain representative governmental institutions. As a result, many developing states experienced increasing factionalism based on regional, social, tribal, and economic considerations. That led countries to create a parliamentary consensus based on single-party rule or military government. In the case of Latin American countries (most of which have been independent since the early nineteenth century), the absence of democracy is due chiefly to the lack of social, cultural, and economic cohesion within the nations and not to insufficient knowledge or experience with democracy.

In order to understand the scarcity of democracy in the LDCs, it is necessary to recognize that democracy is a means of governing, not a means of building community. Democracy can be an effective means of acquiring political authority and of using it to make societywide decisions. But when no firm community consensus exists, there is little likelihood that democratic procedures can lead to the establishment of a government that can act authoritatively. There is more to democracy than counting votes and supporting the principle of political equality. Democracy presupposes community. More specifically, the successful implementation of democracy requires a number of preconditions.

One essential requirement of democracy is a literate and informed society. Democracy is based on the principle of popular sovereignty, which means that the ultimate authority of government is vested in community members. But if people are to act intelligently, they need to be literate and informed about the issues. Daniel Lerner points out (in a study of the politics of the Middle East) that a precondition for participant politics is a modern society. More particularly, he argues that before the masses can be significantly involved in political affairs, society needs to experience growth in urbanization, literacy, and the mass media.[16] Building on Lerner's study, we may

Figure 13.8   Map of Freedom in the World (1980)

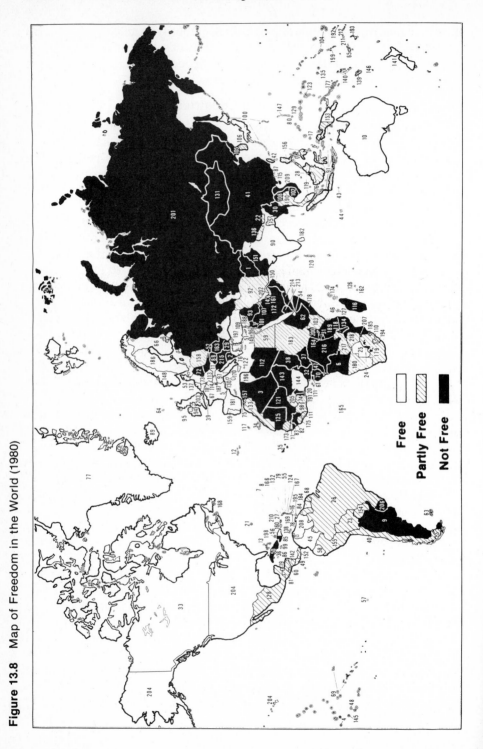

Free Nations

- 10 Australia
- 11 Austria
- 13 Bahamas
- 16 Barbados
- 18 Belgium
- 25 Botswana
- 33 Canada
- 45 Colombia
- 49 Costa Rica
- 53 Denmark
- 55 Dominica
- 56 Dominican Republic
- 58 Ecuador
- 65 Fiji
- 66 Finland
- 67 France
- 71 Gambia
- 73 Germany, West
- 76 Greece
- 89 Iceland
- 90 India
- 94 Ireland
- 96 Israel
- 97 Italy
- 99 Jamaica
- 100 Japan
- 104 Kiribati
- 114 Luxembourg
- 122 Malta
- 135 Nauru
- 137 Netherlands
- 141 New Zealand
- 144 Nigeria
- 148 Norway
- 153 Papua New Guinea
- 159 Portugal
- 167 St. Lucia
- 169 St. Vincent
- 177 Solomon Islands
- 181 Spain
- 182 Sri Lanka
- 184 Surinam
- 186 Sweden
- 187 Switzerland
- 195 Trinidad & Tobago
- 197 Turkey
- 199 Tuvalu
- 203 United Kingdom
- 204 United States
- 205 Upper Volta
- 208 Venezuela

Related Territories

- 7 Anguilla (U.K.)
- 8 Antigua and Barbuda (U.K.)
- 12 Azores (Port.)
- 19 Belize (U.K.)
- 21 Bermuda (U.K.)
- 34 Canary Islands (Sp.)
- 36 Cayman Islands (U.K.)
- 39 Channel Islands (U.K.)
- 48 Cook Islands (N.Z.)
- 63 Falkland Islands (U.K.)
- 64 Faroe Islands (Den.)
- 75 Gibraltar (U.K.)
- 77 Greenland (Den.)
- 95 Isle of Man (U.K.)
- 117 Madeira (Port.)
- 123 Marshall Islands (U.S.)
- 127 Mayotte (Fr.)
- 129 Micronesia, Federated States of (U.S.)
- 130 Monaco (Fr.)
- 132 Montserrat (U.K.)
- 138 Netherlands Antilles (Neth.)
- 139 New Caledonia (Fr.)
- 140 New Hebrides (Fr.-U.K.)
- 145 Niue (N.Z.)
- 146 Norfolk Island (Aus.)
- 147 Northern Marianas (U.S.)
- 149 Occupied Territories (Isr.)
- 157 Places of Sovereignty in North Africa (Sp.)
- 160 Puerto Rico (U.S.)
- 162 Reunion (Fr.)
- 165 St. Helena (U.K.)
- 166 St. Kitts and Nevis (U.K.)
- 168 Saint Pierre & Miquelon (Fr.)
- 170 San Marino (It.)
- 180 South West Africa—Namibia (S. Afr.)
- 192 Tokelau Islands (N.Z.)
- 198 Turks and Caicos (U.K.)
- 210 Virgin Islands (U.S.)
- 211 Wallis and Futuna (Fr.)

Partly Free Nations

- 14 Bahrain
- 15 Bangladesh
- 22 Bhutan
- 23 Bolivia
- 26 Brazil
- 40 Chile
- 42 China, Taiwan
- 46 Comoro Islands
- 51 Cyprus
- 54 Djibouti
- 59 Egypt
- 60 El Salvador
- 74 Ghana
- 78 Grenada
- 81 Guatemala
- 84 Guyana
- 86 Honduras
- 91 Indonesia
- 92 Iran
- 98 Ivory Coast
- 103 Kenya
- 106 Korea, South
- 107 Kuwait
- 109 Lebanon
- 110 Lesotho
- 111 Liberia
- 119 Malaysia
- 120 Maldives
- 126 Mauritius
- 128 Mexico
- 133 Morocco
- 136 Nepal
- 142 Nicaragua
- 152 Panama
- 154 Paraguay
- 155 Peru
- 156 Philippines
- 158 Poland
- 161 Qatar
- 173 Senegal
- 174 Seychelles
- 175 Sierra Leone
- 176 Singapore
- 179 South Africa
- 183 Sudan
- 185 Swaziland
- 188 Syria
- 190 Thailand
- 193 Tonga
- 194 Transkei
- 196 Tunisia
- 202 United Arab Emirates
- 212 Western Samoa
- 217 Zambia
- 218 Zimbabwe Rhodesia

Related Territories

- 4 American Samoa (U.S.)
- 5 Andorra (Fr.-Sp.)
- 17 Belau (U.S.)
- 27 British Virgin Islands (U.K.)
- 43 Christmas Island (Aus.)
- 44 Cocos Islands (Aus.)
- 68 French Guiana (Fr.)
- 69 French Polynesia (Fr.)
- 79 Guadeloupe (Fr.)
- 80 Guam (U.S.)
- 87 Hong Kong (U.K.)
- 113 Liechtenstein (Switz.)
- 115 Macao (Port.)
- 124 Martinique (Fr.)

Not Free Nations

- 1 Afghanistan
- 2 Albania
- 3 Algeria
- 6 Angola
- 9 Argentina
- 20 Benin
- 29 Bulgaria
- 30 Burma
- 31 Burundi
- 32 Cameroon
- 35 Cape Verde Islands
- 37 Central African Republic
- 38 Chad
- 41 China, Mainland
- 47 Congo
- 50 Cuba
- 52 Czechoslovakia
- 61 Equatorial Guinea
- 62 Ethiopia
- 70 Gabon
- 72 Germany, East
- 82 Guinea
- 83 Guinea-Bissau
- 85 Haiti
- 88 Hungary
- 93 Iraq
- 101 Jordan
- 102 Kampuchea
- 105 Korea, North
- 108 Laos
- 112 Libya
- 116 Madagascar
- 118 Malawi
- 121 Mali
- 125 Mauritania
- 131 Mongolia
- 134 Mozambique
- 143 Niger
- 150 Oman
- 151 Pakistan
- 163 Rumania
- 164 Rwanda
- 171 Sao Tome and Principe
- 172 Saudi Arabia
- 178 Somalia
- 189 Tanzania
- 191 Togo
- 200 Uganda
- 201 USSR
- 206 Uruguay
- 209 Vietnam
- 213 Yemen, North
- 214 Yemen, South
- 215 Yugoslavia
- 216 Zaire

Related Territories

- 24 Bophuthatswana (S. Afr.)
- 28 Brunei (U.K.)
- 57 Easter Island (Chile)
- 207 Venda (S. Afr.)

Source: Freedom House, Map of Freedom (New York, 1980). Used by Permission of Freedom House, Inc.

suggest that before democracy can become a viable method of governing an LDC, the people and the institutions must have a "modern" outlook.

Another important precondition of democracy is a viable economy. Lipset and others[17] draw attention to the importance of economic development in the establishment and maintenance of democracy. Although Lipset does not suggest a direct causal link between economic development and democracy, he indicates that a relatively well-developed economy is a necessary condition for long-term representative government. The data in Table 13.3, which indicate a positive relationship between levels of political freedom and levels of per capita income among selected countries, tend to support such

TABLE 13.3   Classification of Selected Countries by Level of Political Freedom and Rank in Per Capita Income

RANK IN PER CAPITA INCOME	LEVEL OF POLITICAL FREEDOM		
	Free	*Partly Free*	*Not Free*
1	Switzerland		
2	United States		
3	West Germany		
4	France		
5	Netherlands		
6	Japan		
7	United Kingdom		
8			USSR
9	Greece		
10	Venezuela		
11			Argentina
12			Iraq
13		Brazil	
14		Mexico	
15		Peru	
16			Congo
17		Bolivia	
18		Zambia	
19		Nigeria	
20			China
21			Uganda
22			Haiti
23			Zaire
24			Cambodia (Kampuchea)

Sources: Per capita income data taken from 1978 World Bank Atlas (Washington, D. C.: World Bank), p. 6; political data taken from Map of Freedom (New York: Freedom House, 1979).

a conclusion. The significance of economic development for a viable democratic system is not that a high GNP per capita or a highly industrialized economy are requirements for representative government. Money itself cannot buy democracy, and high productivity does not help establish representative government. (The experience of Nazi Germany clearly demonstrates this.) The significance of economic development is that it requires education, communication, a modern media, and other related qualities that are also essential for democracy. Economic development may not cause democracy, but it helps bring about those conditions that help develop an informed and organized public.

A third precondition for democracy is a consensual society. To be sure, all societies have some regional, social, and ethnic conflict. But if democratic processes are to work, substantial consensus is needed as to the goals and methods to realize these goals. Democracy is not a method for creating a politically and socially integrated society. Rather, it is a means for making decisions in a nation when there is substantial agreement about community aims and rules of conflict resolution. Democracy does not create community order; it presupposes it. Thus, when there is no national consensus, the operation of democratic institutions and procedures becomes difficult, if not impossible. Moreover, since democratic institutions can operate only when there is substantial national harmony, some countries may need nondemocratic procedures to establish political preconditions on which democracy can be subsequently established.

Because democracy requires preconditions of modernity, any effort to encourage the development of representative government must seek to ensure that the social, economic, and political preconditions are at least partly fulfilled. The failure to understand that democracy requires a modern, cohesive society often results in unjustified expectation for democratic rule in the Third World.

Nation-building is the concept used to describe the development of a modern consensual nation. *State-building,* on the other hand, is the concept representing the development of political and governmental institutions. Since the societal preconditions listed above are primarily aspects of nation-building (the establishment of democratic institutions and procedures are chiefly aspects of state-building), we can summarize our argument by suggesting that democracy requires that nation-building precede state-building.

THE STRENGTHENING OF THIRD WORLD GOVERNMENTS

After the Second World War a growing literature developed in economics on the subject of economic growth. The assumption of much of the literature was that an increase in economic welfare (generally defined in terms of GNP per capita) is a desirable goal and that the task of economics is to devise different theories and models by which to realize this goal. Following the work of economists, political scientists began to examine the process of political change, leading to numerous theories about the growth and development of political systems. Although the concept of *political development* may be defined in several ways, research on the theory and practice of political development is based on two assumptions: it is possible to distinguish between countries that are politically developed and those that are not; and it is possible to design models and strategies by which the desired conditions can be realized. We shall briefly examine five influential theories or approaches to political development.

Theories of Political Development

Development as Modernity   In 1961, before the term *political development* had become fashionable in the social sciences, Karl Deutsch published a seminal article entitled "Social Mobilization and Political Development." The thesis of the article is that political development is a direct consequence of *social mobilization,* the socioeconomic processes by which traditional societies become modern. Although Deutsch does not define the concept of political development, he assumes that an increasing number of politically relevant people will bring about greater popular demands on the government and that these increased expectations will lead to a growth in the public sector (the proportion of the GNP accounted for by government). In short, the changes associated with modernization — increase in literacy, growth of media, increasing urbanization, declining labor force in agriculture, and increasing GNP per capita, etc — would have an automatic, beneficial spillover effect in the political realm. Socioeconomic change would lead to political development.[18]

Another political scientist who sets forth a similar thesis is A.F.K. Organski in *The States of Political Development,* a study patterned after W.W. Rostow's *The Stages of Economic Growth.* According to Organski, development involves "increasing governmental efficiency in utilizing human and material resources of the nation for national goals."[19] Building on Rostow's four stages, Organski argues that the development of states proceeds through four stages: the politics of unification, the politics of industrialization, the politics of national welfare, and the politics of abundance. In the first stage the basic task of government is to establish order and control over the nation. In the second stage the government seeks to encourage the processes of economic change and development. In the third stage, the fundamental concern of government is to maximize the national welfare for all citizens, (this is done by strengthening social and economic institutions by which goods and services can be equitably distributed). In the final stage—the politics of abundance—the task of government is to encourage structural changes to protect the people and the environment from the negative effects of industrialization. Although Organski focuses on the changing functions of government as political systems become more developed, the real engine of growth in Organski's theory is economic and social change. The development of government is not an isolated change; rather, the development of the political system is in direct response to the socioeconomic processes of modernization. Like Deutsch, Organski associates the processes of social and economic change with those of politics.

One of the reasons for the popularity of this perspective during the 1960s was that it coincided with the thinking of many intellectuals and policy makers in the United States. Since a major concern of the U. S. government is the promotion of democratic institutions, the assumption that social and economic development would encourage the growth of participant politics provided an easy method by which the United States could utilize its resources to assist other nations economically and politically. Unfortunately, as others were to point out subsequently, the process of socioeconomic development does not automatically lead to stable participatory government. Indeed, a rapidly growing economy can be a destabilizing force.

Development as the Institutionalization of Politics According to Samuel Huntington,[20] political development involves the increasing capacity of the state to govern and regulate the behavior of citizens. Unlike Deutsch, who argues that development automatically results from social and economic changes, Huntington suggests that economic development may not only inhibit political development but may also bring about political decay in the form of instability and domestic violence. The reason why socioeconomic change may result in disorder and violence is that the processes of social mobilization bring about rising expectations that LDC governments may not be able to satisfy. When popular demands exceed the government's capacity to fulfill those demands, the result of the imbalance is often political instability and violence.

Since socioeconomic change does not automatically strengthen political institutions, the preservation of order in the LDCs results only when there is a deliberate attempt to control the social, economic, and political forces in society. There are two means by which social order can be maintained: first, countries can regulate the extent to which the processes of social mobilization are tolerated within society; and second, a nation can deliberately seek to strengthen the institutions and procedures of government. It is this last method that Huntington believes is most effective in the development of political systems.

Political institutions are important in creating and maintaining order because they are the most effective instruments by which interests can be organized and directed. Of the various types of institutions and organizations within a political system, the party is the most important. Political parties play a critical role because they are the organizations that relate government to the people. It is through them that interests are aggregated and articulated. Of course, if parties are to be effective in development consensus, parties have to be "institutionalized"—that is, they need to be flexible, complex, independent, and unified. In addition, parties need to have broad public support if they are to serve as effective instruments of government support or opposition.

Although Huntington obviously prefers a democratic type of government, this theory of development is chiefly concerned with the development of institutional effectiveness, i.e., government institutions that can carry out the task of governing a state. It is for this reason that Huntington admires the organizational effectiveness of Communist regimes. "The real challenge which the Communists pose to modernizing countries," he writes, "is not that they are so good at overthrowing governments (which is easy), but that they are so good at making governments (which is a far more difficult task). They may not provide liberty, but they do provide authority; they do create governments that can govern."[21] In short, the process of political development involves the creation of effective institutions that can govern a nation. The extent to which a government can govern is a function not only of the modernity of its political institutions but also of the socioeconomic pressures brought about by social mobilization.

Development as Specialization and Secularization   One of the most influential studies in comparative politics is *Comparative Politics: A Developmental Approach* by Gabriel Almond and G. Bingham Powell. Building on David Easton's systems analysis, the authors seek to develop a framework by which political processes and institutions of states can be compared and evaluated. The authors list six major functions that all political systems carry out: the articulation of interests, the aggregation of interests, political communication within society (such as the media), the making of rules (legislatures), the application of rules (executives), and adjudication of rules (courts). The effectiveness with which these tasks are carried out within a nation can be determined by the outputs or capabilities of a political system. Almond and Powell suggest five major capabilities by which performance may be compared:[22]

1. the regulatory capability—the ability to enforce laws and decisions;
2. the extractive capability—the capacity to tax people and corporations;
3. the distributive capability—the capability to redistribute resources through welfare or other similar programs;

4. the responsive capability — the ability to fulfill popular demands and expectations; and

5. the symbolic capability — the ability to create and maintain unity through symbols and myths.

Political systems that can effectively carry out these tasks of regulating, extracting, and distributing resources and of responding to changing demands are more effective and therefore more developed than those that are not able to do so.

What countries are likely to be most able to carry out the functions of government? According to Almond and Powell, three qualities are essential for effective and efficient government: first, political institutions need to be specialized (differentiated); second, governmental institutions need to be independent from each other (subsystem autonomy); and third, the culture of society must be secular — that is, the prevalent norms and values of society must focus on relativistic, materialistic, pragmatic, and temporal concerns, not on other-worldly, future-oriented religious values.[23] Thus, Almond and Powell assume that as the social and political institutions become more specialized, secular, and bureaucratic and as the culture becomes more secular, the prospects for political development tend to increase. But development also requires the strengthening of institutional independence among the different levels and branches of government. A strong, central government is needed to direct and coordinate the work of the state, but a developed polity (according to the model) must possess institutions capable of acting independently from the central administration. In effect, Almond and Powell assume that the decentralized democratic institutions of Europe and North America are better prepared to govern than are the centralized monolithic institutions in Communist countries.

Figure 13.9 compares a number of selected countries in terms of the three variables of the Almond and Powell theory. Role differentiation and secularization are included together, since they are parallel processes associated with modernization. Subsystem autonomy, on the other hand, is a change unrelated to modernization. Some modern states may or may not have institutions with a high level of political autonomy among regulatory institutions. In addition, the level of secularization obviously differs among modern political systems. It may be possible to have highly differentiated and autonomous political institutions in a culture where religious and ascriptive values still have an important role. This is, of course, the situation in Israel, where Judaism plays a dominant role, and in Colombia and Italy, where Catholic values and institutions are deeply imbedded in the culture. As a general rule, however, the processes by which societies become modern and efficient are associated with an increasing secularization of norms.

Figure 13.9   Selected Countries Compared in Terms of Institutional
Specialization, Secularization, and Independence

LEVEL OF SUBSYSTEM AUTONOMY

	Limited	Significant
Significant	Albania China Cuba Rumania Soviet Union	Great Britain Denmark Japan Netherlands Sweden
Limited	Haiti Iran Libya Saudi Arabia	

SPECIALIZATION AND SECULARIZATION

Development as Economic Independence   One of the most widely accepted explanations for underdevelopment in the LDCs is the theory of dependency *(dependencia)*. Although originally formulated as a theory to explain the economic poverty of the Third World, the theory is also used to explain the weaknesses of social and political institutions as well. Building on Marxist perspectives on the international economy, the formulators of the theory—Andre Gunder Frank, John Galtung, Theotonio Dos Santos and others[24]—assume that the poverty and backwardness of the LDCs is chiefly the result of an exploitative and discriminatory international economic system. But whereas Marxists assumed that the tools of exploitation were colonies and, more recently, the large multinational corporations, the dependency theorists argue that the responsibility for poverty and backwardness lies in the formal and informal interrelationships between the rich and the poor states.

According to the theory of dependency, the world is divided into two distinct areas—the *center* and the *periphery,* the *metropolis* and the *satellites.* Each developed area or center is further subdivided into areas that are developed and those that are not. Thus, metropolitan countries have areas that can be classified as centers of the center and peripheries of the center; less developed countries are similarly divided in centers and peripheries of the periphery. According to the theory, whenever trade occurs between nations and areas, the benefits from such interaction are always assumed to flow from the satellites to the metropolises, from the peripheries to the centers. Since the gains from trade are assumed to be unequal, any domestic or international interaction between centers and peripheries leads to *uneven development*. According to dependency theorists, the division of the world into modern and traditional countries and, within the LDCs, into the rich elite and the poor masses, is explained by the processes of uneven economic and social growth.

According to Frank, one of the influential writers on dependency theory, before Western modernity spread to Asia, Africa, and Latin America, these areas were poor and *undeveloped*. But with the establishment of exploitative international economic structures, these areas became unevenly developed, resulting in areas and countries that were *overdeveloped* and those that were *underdeveloped*.[25] Since the underdevelopment of the Third World is assumed to be a direct consequence of the spread of a capitalistic international framework, the development of the Third World can only occur when the satellite areas can break the exploitative ties to the metropolitan countries. Development requires the creation of new relationships.

Development as a Moral Issue   In contrast to the social, economic, and political theories on development, a number of writers examine the nature of social and political change from a humanistic or moral perspective. Representative of this concerned group of Western intellectuals is Dennis Goulet.

In his study on *The Cruel Choice* (subtitled "A New Concept in the Theory of Development"), Goulet suggests that the process of development does not involve increasing economic productivity or developing more modern social and political institutions. Rather, development is chiefly the means by which opportunities are created by which people can become "more human." Development is not simply measured by increasing economic benefits or by making transportation and communications networks more efficient. While visible benefits are undoubtedly desired, the major objective in development, says Goulet, is to encourage an autonomous and authentic development of individuals and states.[26]

What does "authentic" development entail? According to Goulet, three central principles must govern this never-ending process: first, essential human needs must be met. But unlike the traditional approaches of development, which have focused on the consumption of goods, authentic development needs to provide only those goods that are essential to human fulfillment. The emphasis must be on the moral dimensions of the person. Development must be concerned with "being" and not "having." Second, global relationships must be strengthened. This should not be done through nations but should be directly carried out through people. Indeed, the strengthening of international bonds will only be accomplished by deemphasising the nation-state as an international actor. Finally, government must carry out decision making with broad public support. Goulet believes that what is needed is the creation of "popular elites," through which the interests and concerns of the underprivileged masses can be communicated and eventually fulfilled.[27]

Although Goulet suggests that these principles are essential for the creation of an environment in which development can occur, he does not believe that their application leads to the automatic realization of specific goals. Indeed, the process of development is not the fulfillment of well-defined goals but the creation of an environment where peoples, groups, and nations can realize their own goals in their own way. Authentic development requires that the process and end of development be unique to each community. Goulet states the individualistic character of development in the following way:

> *A developed world is one in which each person's and each group's sound potentialities find societal encouragement and structural support. What this means in concrete terms for different peoples, heirs to a variety of cultures, values, and aspirations, no one can as yet say. But this is precisely what development means: to keep exploring such possibilities and inventing ways of actualizing them. Development, like true politics, is the art of creating new possibilities.*[28]

For Goulet, then, political development is not a linear process of change—a process by which political growth proceeds through several well-defined sequential stages. On the contrary, the ends and the process of development cannot be defined *a priori* because each group must determine and create its own development conditions. One thing, however, is certain: the development of society does not occur through increasing tangible resources but by creating a supportive environment where people can express their individual potentialities.

Ideologies of the LDCs

An ideology is a set of ideas and values that guide and direct the actions of states. As such, an ideology can be regarded as a theory of political development that has gained acceptance among the political leaders and masses within countries. To be sure, ideologies are much broader than political development theories, since they cover economic, social, cultural, religious, and other dimensions of life. Nonetheless, ideologies are ultimately concerned with the realization of particular ideals and the creation of political instruments to achieve those ideals. It is in this sense that political development may be viewed as one of the central aspects of ideologies.

Although all ideologies are to a certain degree unique, the ideologies of the LDCs have a number of common traits that express widely shared aspirations of Third World states. Some of the most important of these are the emphasis on political and economic independence, the revival of indigenous culture, the preference for nonalignment in international relations, and the emphasis on socialism. We shall briefly examine each of these.

1. The concern with political and economic independence among Third World countries is largely due to long experience with colonialism. Because of the dependent status of Asian and African countries, the movement of nationalism that swept those states in the 1960s was predominantly concerned with gaining political freedom and independence. Once that objective was realized, however, the Third World states became increasingly concerned with achieving economic independence from the rich, industrial states. The prevailing view in the Third World was that the wealth of the DCs and the poverty of the LDCs was the result of discriminatory and inequitable international economic relations. Thus, if economic development was to be encouraged, the LDCs needed to alter the domestic and international economic conditions that had contributed toward their exploitation.

   In practice, the LDCs have tried to achieve economic independence in two ways: first, they have tried as a group within the United Nations to alter the international economic order; and second, they have tried to regulate and control the role of foreign investment in their national economies. The efforts to regulate foreign capital, and more particularly the multinational corporation, have not been accepted throughout the LDCs; the cost of limiting foreign capital often leads to a lower rate of economic growth. The rapid economic development of the 1960s and 1970s in countries like Brazil, South Korea, and Taiwan was achieved in great measure with the support of foreign capital. The rapid growth in national income in these states serves to remind developing nations seeking to become economically free that the process of economic development usually involves foreign capital and stable trading relationships for exporting and importing goods and services.

2. Another dimension of Third World ideologies is the emphasis on indigenous cultural norms. The revival of traditional culture has come about in part by the search for ideals and values that could inspire and direct the new nations following their independence. This revival has been expressed in many different forms throughout the Third World. In Africa, for example, the revival has emphasized "negritude"[29] or the social, religious, and cultural norms of black civilization. In the Middle East, the revival of traditional norms has focused on Islamic values and practices. While there has been much modernization in this area, governments in Egypt, Iraq, and Turkey have sought to ensure that planned social and economic changes were in accord with traditional Islamic values. In some cases, when political and economic change was considered a challenge to Islam, the result has been revolution. This occurred in Indonesia in 1965 when the masses revolted against the Communist party and in 1979 in Iran when the Shah was forced into exile by Islamic

radicals. In Latin America, too, there has been a rebirth of native culture. Called *indigenismo,* this movement has sought to esteem the pre-
Columbian civilizations and to extol the virtues of the Indians and
mestizos who fought oppression and helped bring about political and
economic independence to the poor masses. In addition, the emphasis on
indigenous values has been expressed through art, literature, music, and
architecture. The concern with traditional religious and cultural norms
has not given much specific guidance to the developing nations, but it has
served as a symbolic source of consensus. By drawing attention to the
unique contribution of their native peoples, the LDCs have found a
fountain of inspiration and motivation.

3. A third common trait of the ideologies of the LDCs is the attempt to
   forge a foreign policy independent from both the Communist and
   Western states. The desire for *nonalignment* is, of course, partly due to
   the attempt to become economically independent from the DCs. In addition, Third World states may prefer nonalignment because it has allowed
   them to focus on economic development rather than to become em-
   broiled in political disputes over communist and democratic procedures
   and values. As the East-West tensions have subsided and have been
   replaced by those between the North and South (the rich vs. the poor
   states), the practice of nonalignment has become increasingly irrelevant
   in the international system. Since the key issues within the international
   system are considered to be economic and not ideological, Third World
   states have tried to maximize their interests by remaining politically neutral between the Eastern and Western powers.

   One important development in connection with nonalignment has
   been the growth of regionalism. As LDCs have tried to achieve economic
   and political independence from the First and Second Worlds, they have
   sought to strengthen regional economic and political ties. In Africa this
   has been accomplished through the Organization of African Unity
   (OAU) and other smaller economic regional arrangements and in Latin
   America by the Organization of American States (OAS). The strengthening of regional ties within the Western Hemisphere has been complicated, however, by the fact that the United States is a member of the
   OAS. Nevertheless, Latin American states have used the OAS and
   regional economic organizations (such as the Latin American Free Trade
   Association and its Andean Group) to encourage regional economic and
   political interdependence.

4. The final trait of Third World ideologies is the popularity of socialism as
   a vehicle for economic development. As suggested above, development
   in the Third World is defined primarily in terms of social and economic
   change. The predilection for socialism as a system of achieving economic
   development derives in part from the perceived success of the economic

growth of the Soviet Union. The ability of the government to plan and direct a massive economic transformation in those states has led many leaders to assume that state planning is essential for rapid economic growth. But the appeal of socialism is based on more than the successful transformation of an agrarian economy into an industrial power. What has made socialism appealing, above all, is that it is concerned with achieving an equitable distribution of the economic resources of society. Daniel Moynihan observes that the popularity of distribution is derived largely from the influence of British socialism — that is, from the distributive policies of the British welfare state created in the mid-twentieth century.[30] Whereas the influence of Soviet planning tended to encourage production through state planning, British socialism tended to encourage government redistribution of wealth. While state planning and welfare policies are popular among the LDCs, the welfare policies are more influential. With the exception of Cuba (and Chile during the Allende regime of 1970-73), no LDC has established state planning as found in Communist states. Rather, the goal is to realize distributive justice. Not surprisingly, LDCs are exceedingly critical of capitalist policies, which they believe have contributed toward their own poverty and the extreme economic inequities within their own states.

The debate over socialism versus capitalism in the Third World is largely concerned with stereotypes, not with actual economic and political systems. All developing countries have some economic planning, have some restrictions on foreign investment and international trade, and provide some services toward the poor, elderly, and the sick. The difference in the government's role in producing and distributing goods is relatively small. Virtually all countries, whether they espouse socialistic or nonsocialistic values, have a mixed economy — a system where the public and private sectors work cooperatively. Indeed, one of the ironies of the socialist-antisocialist debate is that the difference in policies pursued by countries avowedly socialist and those that are not is insignificant. The differences in ideological rhetoric are often extreme, yet the economic practices of states are largely alike.[31]

In conclusion, the model for Third World development is chiefly concerned with socioeconomic changes. The LDCs are concerned with improving health and medical care and with strengthening institutions by which economic growth can be encouraged. Political structures and dynamics are significant insofar as they assist in realizing basic human needs. The institutions of conflict management have an important role, but only in bringing about the strengthening and the improvement of the quality of life. Whether states should have one, two, or many political parties is not a central concern. Moreover, whether the state is governed by military or civilian forces is not as important as whether the governing authorities, whatever their legitimacy, carry out effective economic and social policies—i.e., policies that lead to economic growth and that strengthen and improve social and economic conditions for the masses.

SUMMARY

The Third World is the largest group of states in the modern world, comprising some eighty nations in Africa, Asia, and Latin America. Although each of these states is partly unique, the developing nations share many common social, economic, and political traits. Some of these similarities include:

1. Most developing nations are relatively new, having achieved political independence since the Second World War;
2. The population-growth rate of the LDCs is more than twice that of the DCs, resulting in a high proportion of young people in their societies;
3. The developing nations are poor and have an average per capita income of about one-tenth that of the DCs;
4. Although the rate of urbanization is about the same in developed and developing nations, the total number of people moving from the countryside to cities is much greater in the Third World;
5. Most developing nations have a higher level of political conflict than the mature Western democracies.

While the lack of political experience, high population-growth rates, national poverty, and high urbanization levels help explain the continuing political tensions and conflicts in the Third World, other significant factors contribute to the political instability of these countries. Some of the conditions that contribute to social and political conflict include: lack of national cohesion, social dualism, challenge of modern ideas and practices to traditional culture, absence of a well-integrated economy, absence of organized public opinion, and lack of authority of the institutions of government.

The Third World tends to be characterized politically by militarism and an absence of democratic practices. The significant role of the military in the politics of LDCs results primarily from the inability of civilian institutions to effectively regulate social and political conflict and build national consensus. Similarly, the absence of democracy is due primarily to the lack of national consensus, not to a lack of knowledge of or experience with the procedures and techniques of democracy.

The challenge posed by Third World political problems has led social scientists to formulate theories of political development. These theories present different definitions of a politically mature state and identify processes by which the conditions of "development" can be realized.

The leaders of countries are not guided by theories of development, however, but by their national ideologies. Four common features of Third World ideologies are: emphasis on political and economic independence, revival of indigenous culture, a preference for nonalignment in international relations, and an economic orientation towards socialism rather than capitalism.

KEY TERMS

traditional society
transitional society
social dualism
military government
junta
national integration
coup d'etat
nation-building
state-building

political development
social mobilization
subsystem autonomy
secularization
dependency theory
uneven development
authentic development
nonalignment

NOTES

1. World Bank, *Trends in Developing Countries* (Washington, D.C.: World Bank, 1973), p. 13.
2. U.S. Arms Control and Disarmament Agency, *World Military Expenditures and Arms Transfers, 1967–1976* (Washington, D.C.: Government Printing Office, 1978), p. 28.
3. See, for example, Mancur Olson, Jr., "Rapid Growth as a Destabilizing Force," *Journal of Economic History* 23 (December 1963), pp. 529–552; and Samuel P. Huntington, *Political Order in Changing Societies* (New Haven: Yale University Press, 1968), Chapter 1.
4. S.E. Finer, "The Military and Politics in the Third World," in *The Third World: Premises of U.S. Policy,* W. Scott Thompson (San Francisco: Institute for Contemporary Studies, 1978), pp. 66–67.
5. For an excellent analysis of social dualism in Latin America, see Jacques Lambert, *Latin America: Social Structures and Political Institutions,* trans. by Helen Katel (Berkeley: University of California Press, 1967), passim.
6. James C. Davies, "Toward a Theory of Revolution," *American Sociological Review* 27 (January 1962), p. 6. See also Ivo K. Feierabend, Rosaline L. Feierabend, and Betty A. Nesvold, "Social Change and Political Violence: Cross-National Patterns" in *Violence in America: Historical and Comparative Perspectives,* ed. Hugh Davis Graham and Ted Robert Gurr (New York: The New American Library, 1969), Chapter 18.
7. Karl W. Deutsch, *Nationalism and Its Alternatives* (New York: Alfred A. Knopf, 1969), pp. 14–16.

8. Jean Blondel, *An Introduction to Comparative Government* (New York: Praeger Publishers, 1969), p. 140.

9. Samuel P. Huntington, *Political Order in Changing Societies* (New Haven: Yale University Press, 1968), p. 24.

10. *Ibid.,* pp. 12–23.

11. Lucian W. Pye, *Aspects of Political Development* (Boston: Little, Brown & Co., 1966), pp. 19–23.

12. S.E. Finer, *The Man on Horseback: The Role of the Military in Politics* (Baltimore: Penguin Books, 1976), p. 274.

13. See, for example, Charles Wolf, Jr., *United States Policy and the Third World: Problems and Analysis* (Boston: Little, Brown & Co., 1967), Chapter 5.

14. U.S. Arms Control and Disarmament Agency, *World Military Expenditures and Arms Transfers, 1967–1976,* p. 72.

15. S.E. Finer, *Comparative Government* (Harmondsworth, England: Penguin Books, 1970), p. 536.

16. Daniel Lerner, *The Passing of Traditional Society: Modernizing the Middle East* (Glencoe, Ill.: The Free Press, 1958), passim.

17. Seymour M. Lipset, "Some Social Requisites of Democracy: Economic Development and Political Legitimacy," *American Political Science Review* 53 (March 1959), pp. 69–105. See also Gabriel A. Almond and James S. Coleman, eds. *The Politics of the Developing Areas* (Princeton: Princeton University Press, 1960, pp. 540–542.

18. Karl W. Deutsch, "Social Mobilization and Political Development," *American Political Science Review* 55 (September 1961), pp. 493–514.

19. A.F.K. Organski, *The Stages of Political Development* (New York: Alfred A. Knopf, 1965), p. 7.

20. Huntington, *Political Order in Changing Societies,* pp. 1–11.

21. *Ibid.,* p. 8.

22. Gabriel A. Almond and G. Bingham Powell, Jr., *Comparative Politics: A Developmental Approach* (Boston: Little, Brown & Co., 1966), pp. 16–41.

23. *Ibid.,* pp. 299–314.

24. Andre Gunder Frank, *Capitalism and Underdevelopment in Latin America: Historical Studies of Chile and Brazil* (New York: Monthly Review Press, 1967); Johan Galtung, "A Structural Theory of Imperialism," *Journal of Peace Research* 8 (1971), pp. 81–118; Theotonio Dos Santos, "The Structure of Dependence," *American Economic Review: Papers and Proceedings* 60 (May 1970), pp. 321–336; and Susanne Bodenheimer, "Dependency and Imperialism: The Roots of Latin American Underdevelopment" in *Readings in U.S. Imperialism,* eds. K.T. Fann and Donald C. Hodges (Boston: Porter Sargent Publisher, An Extending Horizons Book, 1971).

25. Andre Gunder Frank, *Latin America: Underdevelopment or Revolution* (New York: Monthly Review Press), Chapter 1.

26. Denis Goulet, *The Cruel Choice: A New Concept in the Theory of Development* (New York: Atheneum, 1975), Chapter 3.

27. *Ibid.,* Chapter 6.

28. Denis Goulet, "The World of Underdevelopment: A Crisis in Values," *The Christian Century* (April 24, 1974), p. 454.

29. For an explanation of African "negritude," see excerpts from a speech delivered by Leopold Sedar Senghor in Paul E. Sigmund, *Ideologies of the Developing Nations,* 2nd rev. ed. (New York: Praeger Publishers, 1972), pp. 250–252.

30. Daniel P. Moynihan, "The United States in Opposition," *Commentary* (March 1975), p. 34.

31. For an excellent analysis of the impact of socialism on the practices of Third World countries, see Chapter 11 of Charles W. Anderson, Fred R. von der Mehden, and Crawford Young, *Issues of Political Development,* 2nd ed. (Englewood Cliffs, N.J.: Prentice-Hall, 1974).

SUGGESTED READING

ALMOND, GABRIEL, and POWELL, G. BINGHAM, JR. *Comparative Politics: Systems, Process, and Policy.* 2nd ed. Boston: Little, Brown & Co., 1978. Presents the structural-functional approach to comparative politics. Although not concerned with Third World politics *per se,* this study includes a theory of political development.

ANDERSON, CHARLES W., et al. *Issues of Political Development.* 2nd ed. Englewood Cliffs, N. J.: Prentice-Hall, 1974. An examination of some issues in building and maintaining political order in the Third World. Chapters 11 and 12 examine the nature and role of ideologies.

BANFIELD, EDWARD C. *The Moral Basis of a Backward Society.* New York: The Free Press, 1958. An analysis of the backwardness and political development of a small Italian village. Although the book is dated, this work remains an insightful study of the cultural, psychological, sociological, and economic sources of political underdevelopment.

BINDER, LEONARD, et al. *Crises and Sequences in Political Development.* Princeton: Princeton University Press, 1971. This study, the seventh in a series on political development, examines the process and some key aspects of political development, including political culture, participation, and governmental regulation. Some of the previous volumes in the series include: *Bureaucracy and Political Development,* ed. Lucian W. Pye (1963); *Political Culture and Political Development,* ed. Lucian W. Pye and Sidney Verba (1965); and *Political Parties and Political Development,* ed. Joseph LaPalombara and Myron Weiner (1966).

BLACK, C.E. *The Dynamics of Modernization: A Study in Comparative History.* New York: Harper & Row, 1966. A lucid and stimulating historical account of the nature and process of modernization. This volume is essential reading for any student interested in understanding the relationship of modernization to political development.

CLARK, ROBERT P. JR. *Development and Instability: Political Change in the Non-Western World.* Hinsdale, Ill.: The Dryden Press, 1974. A useful synthesis of much of the significant literature on political change and development.

FINER, S.E. *The Man on Horseback: The Role of the Military in Politics.* 2nd ed., enlarged. Baltimore: Penguin Books, 1975. Generally regarded as the definitive study on the role of the military in politics, this study examines the motives, causes, and results of military intervention. The new, enlarged edition includes an up-to-date overview of the military in the Third World.

FINKLE, JASON L., and GABLE, RICHARD W., eds. *Political Development and Social Change.* 2nd ed. New York: John Wiley & Sons, 1971. This comprehensive reader on political and social change in the Third World is particularly useful to the more advanced student of politics. Includes many significant theoretical essays on political development.

HUNTINGTON, SAMUEL P. *Political Order in Changing Societies*. New Haven: Yale University Press, 1969. In this highly influential study, Huntington argues that social and economic modernization does not automatically lead to political development. Whether or not one agrees with the author's thesis that the preeminent need in developing nations is for the creation of order, this volume is required reading for any student of Third World politics.

KAUTSKY, JOHN H. *The Political Consequences of Modernization*. New York: John Wiley & Sons, 1972. Examines the impact of modernization on traditional societies and the political responses to it by various social groups.

PYE, LUCIAN W. *Aspects of Political Development*. Boston: Little, Brown & Co., 1966. A highly useful introduction to selected issues relating to political development. Chapter 1 provides an historical overview of Third World development and Chapter 2 sketches ten different ways in which the concept of political development is used. Other areas covered include culture, bureaucracy, democracy, the military, the media, and insurgent rebellion.

SIGMUND, PAUL E. *The Ideologies of the Developing Nations*. 2nd rev. ed. New York: Praeger Publishers, 1972. Selected readings on the political thought of the leaders of developing nations. The introduction provides a general overview of some of the common features of the ideologies of the Third World.

TULLIS, F. LAMOND. *Politics and Social Change in Third World Countries*. New York: John Wiley & Sons, 1973. An introductory study of Third World politics using the tools and methods of contemporary political-science research. Tullis analyses the impact of modernization on political and governmental institutions in three countries — Brazil, Libya, and Peru.

14 / CONFLICT IN THE
INTERNATIONAL SYSTEM

In previous chapters we examined the nature of conflict and the role of political institutions within the nation-state. Our analysis suggested that states tend to have a high level of domestic order and consensus. This peace results, in great measure, from a cohesive and homogeneous society, which is made possible by such factors as a common language, territorial proximity, common values and habits, integrated communications and transportation networks, and nationalism. Above all, domestic consensus is made possible by well-developed governmental institutions backed by a monopoly of force that can effectively regulate and resolve community conflict. In the international system, however, there are no common customs, values, language, and integrated economic and social systems to strengthen the development of a common world culture. Most importantly, the international system does not have the institutions that can regulate the behavior of states and resolve conflict in a final and authoritative manner.

The purpose of this chapter is to examine the nature of the international community by focusing on the nature of and the reasons for interstate conflict and the means available for its management and resolution. We shall first examine the major differences between domestic and international politics and then analyze the nature of the foreign-policy-making process. Finally, we shall analyze the nature and extent of international conflict, briefly noting some of the common explanations for war. In the following chapter we shall examine the methods and institutions available for managing interstate conflict.

THE NATURE OF THE INTERNATIONAL COMMUNITY

International politics is qualitatively different from domestic politics. Whereas the freedom of individuals and groups is restricted within states, the international system has no central authority that can limit the freedom of nation-

369

states. The result of this overabundance of state liberty is disorder and conflict. In addition, the international system does not have any well-developed
governmental institutions to manage and resolve interstate conflicts. The only
way to resolve them is for the parties themselves to try to reconcile their incompatible interests; this can be done either through peaceful means or through
force. Given the absence of effective conflict-management institutions, the
international system is generally viewed as a primitive, undeveloped political
community.

The Sovereignty of States

One of the most significant features of the international community is
the decentralized organization. Since the seventeenth century, the world has
been divided into territorial units called nation-states, each of which considers
itself free and independent from other states. States came into being as a result
of the efforts of princes, monarchs, and other rulers to gain authority to
govern within specific territories. As their power became unchallengeable both
from within and without the country, the ruler's ability to rule independently
was gradually accepted within the land and by the rulers of other territories.
Within the contemporary world, there are some 150 nation-states, each of
which claims to have ultimate authority over all domestic issues and to be
therefore totally free from the regulatory power of other states.

The concept that is used to denote the freedom and independence of
nation-states is *sovereignty.* As expressed by Jean Bodin in his *Six Books of
the Republic,* the first systematic explanation of the term *sovereignty* is "the
absolute and perpetual power of a State."[1] It is the capacity of the state to be
able to carry out any action, subject to the laws of God. The centralization of
power was needed, Bodin thought, because in the absence of a central governmental authority there would be continuous conflict among individuals and
groups within society. The state, in other words, not only needed developed
governmental institutions but also needed to have a monopoly of force
through which the decisions of government could be enforced. Although a
government could be divided into separate agencies or departments, the ultimate authority within the state should always be centralized.

When Bodin wrote about the need for sovereign authority in the seventeenth century, continuous conflicts and turmoil existed in France and other
continental states. Some of these tensions were religious, others were political
and economic. What was therefore needed was a superior power that could use
its monopoly of force to bring a halt to the violent and destructive conflict
among the various factions within the new states. As monarchs consolidated
their power and effectively became sovereign rulers (i.e., rulers with supreme
power within their states), order began to return to the European continent.

But whereas the centralization of political authority tended to encourage
peace and harmony within the state, the development of sovereign states
tended to create a major barrier to world order. As states increased their

sovereign authority to regulate domestic affairs, states increasingly became more independent and reluctant to be influenced by the interests and concerns of other states. The result of sovereignty was ironic: it encouraged domestic peace and tranquility but produced anarchy and disorder in the international community.

State sovereignty is a matter of degree. No state is totally free and independent from other states or from the general social, economic, and political forces within the world system. For example, as states become more economically developed, they also become more dependent upon other states for vital raw materials. The United States and other Western European Countries depend on other states for primary products such as oil, tin, and copper, while the developing nations are highly dependent on the industrial states for technology and agricultural produce. This mutual interdependence tends to place restrictions on the amount of freedom of action that states have within the world.

Another development that tends to restrict the freedom of states is the increasing number of new actors in the world system. These actors include new nation-states and numerous large public international organizations such as the United Nations Conference on Trade and Development (UNCTAD), the International Monetary Fund (IMF), the World Health Organization (WHO), and regional organizations like the Organization of American States (OAS), the European Economic Community (EEC), and the North Atlantic Treaty Organization (NATO). In addition, the increasing role of the large, private multinational corporations (MNCs) similarly tends to restrict the freedom of states, particularly that of the less powerful Third World nations.

Finally, the doctrine of sovereignty is qualified by moral principles generally accepted within the international environment. The Charter of the United Nations affirms, for example, the notion of fundamental human rights based on the dignity and worth of each person, while other international organizations give expression to universal human standards and rights. Although there is much disagreement about the specific meaning of these basic human values, the expression of such moral norms tends to place public-opinion pressure on those states that try to disregard them. In short, sovereignty represents the ability to act freely, independently, and forcefully. But sovereignty is never totally absolute; there are always restrictions that inhibit and influence a state's behavior.

A Primitive Political System

Roger Masters suggests that the international system is an undeveloped political community similar to primitive, stateless societies, such as the Nuer people of southern Sudan. Masters suggests that the international system shares a number of characteristics with undeveloped political communities that have no organized political activity. First, the international system, like primitive societies, has no formal governmental institutions to judge and punish violators of the law. Second, both international and primitive communities are unable to enforce community obligations and protect legitimate individual interests except through methods of "self-help." Third, the international system and the stateless communities do not have institutions that can make laws. Rather, laws are developed through bargaining relationships or gradually evolve from the customs and practices of the community.[2]

In 1956 Secretary of State John Foster Dulles listed six means by which nation-states maintain domestic peace and prevent violent conflict. The six instruments were:

1. laws reflecting a broad moral consensus within the community;
2. political machinery available for changing laws;
3. an executive institution to enforce and apply the law;
4. courts to resolve legal disputes;
5. superior public force by which to apprehend and punish those who violate the law and thereby to inhibit community violence; and
6. economic well-being so that people are sufficiently satisfied and do not resort to violence.

Dulles then went on to suggest that one of the major reasons for the lack of order within the international system is that these institutions and processes are largely absent in the world.[3]

In comparing the international community with the nation-state, it becomes clear that the major difference between the two communities is not that governmental institutions are entirely absent in the international system, but rather that processes and regulatory functions of the nation-state are undeveloped in the world system. Nations tend to have codified laws based on general approval of the community; the international system has some written laws (international law) and unwritten principles. But neither is supported by legal institutions like those found in nation-states. Moreover, states generally have appointed or elected legislatures that make and change laws; the international system, on the other hand, has no formal legislature to carry out this task, although the United Nations General Assembly and its subsidiary organizations have occasionally served as a forum for discussing issues of common concern.

The executive authority of the international system is similarly weak. While the U.N. Security Council has the responsibility of keeping peace within the world, its responsibilities do not extend to the general administration of international law. The judicial institutions of the world order are also weak when compared with domestic courts. The principal international court, The International Court of Justice of The Hague, is a formal part of the United Nations. But it has no compulsory jurisdiction except that given it by the states themselves. Perhaps most importantly, there is no central authority with a monopoly of force to ensure implementation of international law. The only transnational forces within the world are those established under the auspices of the United Nations, but the military power of these forces is limited and the scope of operations is generally restricted to particular areas of tension. The international system thus lacks the regulatory institutions found in the nation-state. If order is to be increased within the world, the primitive and undeveloped institutions and processes of conflict management must be strengthened.

Since the institutions regulating conflict are relatively weak and undeveloped in the international system, interstate conflict tends to be frequent and often violent. Unlike domestic politics, where formal governmental institutions are available for directing and resolving conflict, the international system has no institutions to manage conflict effectively. As a result, states resort to peaceful and nonpeaceful means to preserve their own interests. When vital interests are at stake, nations do not hesitate to use military force to maximize their particular interests within the world. Not surprisingly, the ultimate means of conflict management is war. Whereas international politics tends to have a high level of conflict and a low level of order, domestic politics is much more orderly (Figure 14.1). The only method of fundamentally altering the anarchy of the world community is to establish the preconditions on which domestic order is based.

Figure 14.1 Levels of Freedom and Order in Domestic and International Politics

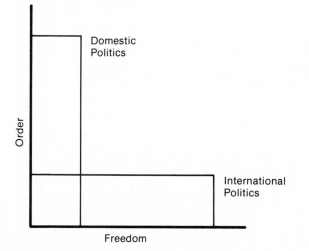

A Hobbesian Political Community

Given its primitive and undeveloped nature, the international community is often viewed as the anarchic, disorderly state of nature depicted in Hobbes's *Leviathan*. Recall that, according to Hobbes, the state of nature is an environment with much freedom but little order. Because conflict was frequent and violent, Hobbes believed that life apart from governmental order was unproductive and uncertain. The fundamental problem posed by Hobbes is thus similar to the central issue facing the international system: how can the intense conflict and disorder of the state of nature be transformed into harmony and peace? The solution proposed by Hobbes is that every member give up the liberty and freedom found in the state of nature in return for the order and peace created by a supreme sovereign power. What is needed, in essence, is to centralize power in a single authority.

But states are unwilling to sacrifice their individual freedom and liberty in return for world peace. Although all states claim to be concerned with the problem of war, they continue to focus on their national interests rather than on the general interests of the international community. The world is still a primitive community with power divided into some 150 pieces of different sizes and states free to act largely as they please. The world community is thus a Hobbesian state of nature — an environment with no common sovereign authority. Since there is no central institution to effectively manage and resolve interstate disputes, each nation must depend upon its own capabilities to protect its interests. The result of this highly uncertain, unstable, and disorderly environment is that members of the international community are unwilling to find security apart from their individual efforts. Like the state of nature, the international community remains an environment where there is little trust.

The unwillingness of nations to trust other states or the rudimentary institutions of international organization is dramatically illustrated by the significant amounts of resources nations devote to national defense. In 1976 the United States and the Soviet Union spent more than 200 billion dollars on military defense, while total military expenditure for all nations was more than 380 billion. Of this amount nearly 87 billion, or 23 percent of total military expenditures was spent by the Third World.[4] In terms of personnel, in 1976 the armed forces occupied nearly 26.2 million persons, of whom 10.6 million were employed by the developed nations and 15.6 were employed in the developing nations. Total military expenditures per capita in all states was estimated at $90 in 1976. Table 14.1 illustrates the level of material resources allocated to national defense for selected nations.

The importance that states attach to military defense is even more evident when defense costs are compared with other areas of major government concern. In 1976 the single largest budgetary expense for all states was military defense, followed by education and health (Figure 14.2). Military expenses

TABLE 14.1 Military Expenditures for Selected Countries (1976)

COUNTRY	MILITARY EXPENDITURES AS A PERCENTAGE OF GNP	PER CAPITA MILITARY EXPENDITURES (IN DOLLARS)
Argentina	2.4	33
Belgium	3.1	204
Bolivia	2.7	11
China (PRC)	10.7	34
Czechoslovakia	5.6	207
Egypt	10.5	28
France	3.8	256
Germany, Dem. Republic	6.5	245
Iran	12.2	207
Iraq	10.6	134
Israel	32.2	1,141
Jordan	9.4	56
North Korea	9.6	56
Nigeria	5.3	23
Oman	40.1	1,020
Panama	.7	8
Peru	5.2	42
Saudi Arabia	19.4	932
Soviet Union	12.6	471
Switzerland	2.0	171
United States	5.4	400

Source: U.S. Arms Control and Disarmament Agency, World Military Expenditures and Arms Transfers, 1967–76 (Washington, D.C.: Government Printing Office, 1978).

account for approximately 25.3 percent of central governmental expenditures, while education and health accounted for 22.7 percent and 10.4 percent, respectively.[5] Although developed nations spent more than three times what the developing nations did on military defense, Third World countries spent a slightly higher proportion. A significant development is that the proportion of funds devoted to military defense as a percentage of GNP declined from 36.7 percent in 1967 to 25.3 percent in 1976. This relative decline, however, occurred during a decade when total military expenditures increased by some 20 percent, even after an adjustment is made for inflation.

Although political leaders and statesmen from all continents continue to deplore exorbitant financial commitments to military defense, arms expenditures nonetheless continue to increase. During the 1967–76 decade, total military expenditures, for example, increased in real terms by approximately

Figure 14.2 Total World Expenditures for Military Forces, Education, and Health, 1976 (billions of dollars)

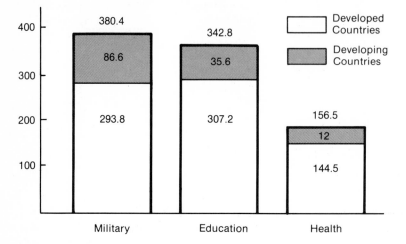

Source: U. S. Arms Control and Disarmament Agency, World Military Expenditures and Arms Transfers, 1967–76 (Washington, D.C.: Government Printing Office, 1978).

20 percent.[6] The basic cause of continued growth in military resources is not to be found, as some have supposed, in the economic interests of the military-industrial complex or in the perverse ambitions of government rulers. Rather, the continuing escalation in military armaments is itself a symptom of a more fundamental problem—the decentralized and uncertain international environment, in which national security can only be secured through individual initiative. So long as states must ensure their own security and protection in an anarchic world, political leaders will be unwilling to alter the fundamental pattern of national-resource allocation. Thus, in the absence of a moderation of state sovereignty and the establishment of more effective international governmental institutions, states will continue to mistrust other states and will depend primarily on their own military, economic, and political capabilities to achieve their national interests.

The difficulty of moderating arms expenditures is illustrated by the long and difficult process by which the United States and the Soviet Union have sought to limit the nuclear arms race. The first series of Strategic Arms Limitations Talks (SALT) resulted in a Treaty and Agreement in 1972. The Treaty limited both countries to two ABM (antiballistic missile) sites (this was later reduced to one), and the interim agreement placed a five-year limit on strategic offensive weapons. On the surface, the limitation of ABM sites and strategic missiles and bombers appears to have been a significant milestone in curbing the arms race. In fact, however, both the Soviet Union and the United States continued to improve and refine their strategic nuclear weapons. The overall result of the 1972 interim agreement was therefore not a reduction but a diversion of military resources. The negotiations for SALT II, the subsequent arms-limitations talks, have been far more difficult than those that led to SALT I. From 1972 through 1979, American and Soviet statesmen continually bargained and negotiated over an acceptable treaty to further limit strategic nuclear weapons. The results of seven years of negotiation, however, give little hope to the arms-reduction process, for the new proposed SALT treaty places few major limitations on the two superpowers.

The irony of the arms race is that military armaments are acquired in order to preserve peace and order. Yet, continued expenditures for military defense itself makes the search for security within the international system more elusive and perilous as the possibility of accidental war increases and as the destructive capacities of states continue to grow. The search for peace and justice within the world cannot be solved simply by refusing to participate in the arms race. The fundamental fact of the international system is that the national interests of each state are protected not by a central authority but by the government of each state. Refusal to acquire military armaments may be a noble act, but only prudent insofar as other states agree to follow it. While spending large sums of money on weapons and military forces may be foolish, it may be even more foolish to channel those resources elsewhere if the integrity of the community cannot be protected. In short, states prepare for war in order to maintain peace. The object of military might is not to conquer and destroy but to protect the interests of states, an objective that is most often realized not by direct use of military force but by the deterrent power resulting from their possible use.

In summary, the distinctive quality of the international environment is an ordered anarchy. Because there is no international sovereign, states resolve disputes in the final analysis only by relying upon their own resources. It is for this reason that students of international politics suggest that the distinctive trait of world politics is war, for it alone can ultimately settle interstate disputes.

THE NATURE OF FOREIGN POLICY

All governments pursue general and specific goals. Some of these can be realized within the state's boundaries, while others can be fulfilled only within the context of the international system. *Foreign policy* is the process by which a country seeks to fulfill its national interests within the world. Since the tangible and intangible resources of the world are limited and the interests of states unlimited, states are in continuous competition and conflict over the world's scarce resources. As a result, an effective foreign policy is not merely the expression of national aims but the articulation and implementation of goals in the light of other states' interests.

The development and implementation of foreign policy requires two steps. First, states need to delineate the goals they wish to pursue within the international system. This first task — determination of the fundamental interests of states — is complex and difficult, for there is no easy way of ranking the major interests of a nation. The second task involves the implementation of foreign policy. To be effective, a state needs to be able to influence the behavior of other states if it is to accomplish its major goals. The ability to influence other states depends on national power and the quality of diplomacy. *National power* is the overall capacity to affect other states by virtue of superior tangible and intangible factors. *Diplomacy,* by contrast, is the process by which diplomats use national power to maximize foreign-policy goals within the international community. In the section below we shall examine in greater detail the nature of national interests and the role of power and diplomacy in implementing those objectives.

National Interests

Determining what a nation's fundamental interests are is a difficult and uncertain task. For one thing, a state is not a clearly defined entity but a fictitious body composed of elements such as people, government, territory, and common heritage. The state itself does not have interests; only its people do. As a result, foreign-policy goals must be based on the values, habits, customs, historical traditions, and moral commitments (i.e., on the national character of a state) and must be concretely supported by its people if they are to be effectively implemented in the world. One of the difficulties in determining national interests is that states rarely have systematic procedures for developing goals and priorities for their people. Moreover, states are often reluctant to make their national interests explicit, lest continued changes in the world make implementation of such aims impossible.

National interests can be differentiated in terms of their importance, specificity, permanence, and nature. Since some goals are obviously more important than others, statesmen find it useful to differentiate between vital and nonvital interests. Those that are essential generally involve preservation of the political, territorial, economic, and social integrity of the state. The preservation of Hawaii and Alaska from foreign attack is obviously a much more important concern to the United States than is the protection of American business interests in Chile, Bolivia, or Iran.

Interests may also differ in terms of the level of generality. The American goals of peace and preservation of human rights, for example, are broad, general concerns, while American interests in foreign investment in Africa or in shipping legislation are much more limited in scope. Generally, the more specific a policy becomes, the more likely it will require modifications in the future as conditions change.

Goals can also be distinguished in terms of their permanence. Early in the nineteenth century the United States developed the Monroe Doctrine, by which it claimed that the Western Hemisphere is to be viewed as a sphere of North American interests. From the time this doctrine was first articulated in 1823 until the present, it has continued to serve as a general guiding foreign-policy principle. But sometimes foreign-policy interests change. This was the case during the early 1970s when the United States began to establish friendlier relations with the People's Republic of China—a development that ultimately led to the establishment of full diplomatic relations in 1979.

Finally, national interests may be either competitive or absolute. Competitive goals, such as the desire to maximize military power, are pursued because of unlimited wants of states in an environment where resources are limited. Absolute interests, by contrast, are concerned with fulfilling specific aims or conditions regardless of how other states behave. Examples of absolute interests include the maintenance of a particular level of economic growth, the establishment of a specific level of economic welfare, the protection of fishing rights in territorial waters, and the control of aliens entering a state.

One of the most challenging and influential theories of international politics is the one advanced by Hans Morgenthau. Morgenthau believes that it is possible to reduce foreign-policy interests of states to one fundamental national interest—power. He suggests that whether states are weak or strong, rich or poor, large or small, the basic goal is always to maximize national power. "We assume," writes Morgenthau, "that statesmen think and act in terms of interests defined as power."[7] Morgenthau does not deny that states pursue a variety of goals, but he suggests that the fundamental drive is always toward increasing national power. Power is the means by which other goals can be realized. Although power may be regarded primarily as a means to achieve social, political, cultural, and economic objectives, power is always the immediate end. No interests can be effectively realized if a state is unable to influence other states in accordance with its aims.

The Role of Power

In Chapter 3 we defined *influence* as the capacity of one party to affect or alter the behavior of another without using or threatening to use sanctions. Influence, we noted, could be brought about through manipulation, persuasion, argumentation, or other peaceful means but could not use (or threaten to use) resources in a coercive manner.

Power, by contrast, is defined as a specific form of influence in which an individual, group, or state seeks to alter the behavior of another party by using (or threatening to use) positive or negative sanctions. In order for a state to have power over another state, direct coercive action is not required. All that is needed is that people assume or perceive that one state has more power than another, i.e., that it has the resources and abilities by which it can effectively alter behavior. Tangible and intangible resources are important in creating an impression of power, but ultimately the ability to influence behavior rests not on resources and capabilities per se but on the perception of the ability to use them in realizing the desired goals.

Force is defined as the direct use of military and police power in order to achieve political influence. A war between states represents the application of force to the settling of an international dispute that could not be settled through less extreme methods of influence. As a specific form of power, force is the most violent and costly method of seeking political influence. It is violent because it involves the use of military and police power to achieve goals; it is costly because it consumes money and energy that could be used for other community concerns.

Although all political systems involve some influence, power, and force, the proportion of each tends to vary. Domestic politics is generally far more harmonious and stable than is international politics; as a result, it requires less coercive influence. Since there are no effective institutions of conflict resolution in the world, states seek to maximize their interests by relying primarily on their national power, backed by substantial military force. Whereas legitimate power (voluntary influence) is the basic means by which domestic political systems establish order and harmony, coercive power is the commonly accepted method of conflict management in the international system. Although noncoercive influence is used in interstate relations, the ultimate capacity to alter the behavior of another state is dependent upon the perception of power—the perception that a state can threaten to use its resources to protect and maximize its national interests. Because of the important role of power in the world system, international politics is commonly defined as an environment where states struggle for power.

Organski suggests that states can use power in the international system in at least four ways. First, states can attempt to *persuade* others to do something they might not otherwise do. Second, states may seek to use their resources to *reward* other states for doing what they want. Third, states may threaten other states with *punishment* if they do not act in accordance with expressed desires. Fourth, states may use direct military or economic *force* to try to get a state to behave in accordance with the expressed wishes.[8] Whether a state uses persuasion, reward, punishment, or force to influence the behavior of another state, the effectiveness to alter behavior ultimately depends upon the military capabilities to force another state to comply with the desired goals.

Since power is an important element in international relations, how do states acquire power to implement their foreign policies? How do states develop the reputation that they can effectively protect their national interests and carry out their foreign-policy goals? Developing an understanding of the sources of national power is a most difficult and elusive task, for power is not an entity that can be acquired. Capabilities themselves do not ensure power. Although objective abilities and resources are important in establishing power relationships, power is ultimately based on a subjective perception. In developing that perception, two qualities are required: first, a state must possess tangible resources and capabilities, such as people, military forces, a large territory, etc.; and second, a state must possess intangible resources, such as leadership and high morale, which ensure that the tangible capabilities are used effectively.

Tangible Elements of Power   One significant tangible resource is a nation's *territory*. Morgenthau believes that a nation's location is "the most stable factor upon which power of a nation depends."⁹ He suggests that the separation from other continents by large bodies of water to the east and the west is a major determinant of U.S. power. The location of a nation's territory affects industrial development, agricultural productivity, and the strategic defense of a state. The size of a territory is also important insofar as it may provide a source of abundant raw materials and advantages for military defense. Large countries like the Soviet Union, Canada, and the United States benefit not only from an abundance of material resources but also from extensive land in which they can mobilize their military forces. Topography, too, can influence a country's ability to develop economically and to protect its borders. A mountainous terrain (such as that found in the Andean countries of Ecuador, Peru, and Bolivia) can be a major barrier to economic and political unification of the state; at the same time it may serve as a deterrent to foreign aggression.

During the late nineteenth century and early twentieth century, students of geopolitics tended to give territorial issues a central position in the study of national power. Sir Halford Mackinder, for example, believed that control of Eastern Europe is the central determinant of international power. Mackinder's thesis was, "He who rules Eastern Europe commands the Heartland of Eurasia; who rules the Heartland, commands the World Island of Europe, Asia, and Africa; and who rules the World Island commands the World."¹⁰ Alfred T. Mahan, on the other hand, believed that the most important determinant of power was the ability to control the oceans.¹¹ Although the size, location, and topography of a state's territory remain important in any consideration of national power, the value that geopoliticians of the early twentieth century applied to territorial concerns no longer seems warranted in the age of nuclear weapons and increasing economic interdependence.

Another tangible factor affecting national power is *population*. It determines a nation's degree of unity and cohesion, its level of economic development, its morale and purposefulness, and its ability to respond militarily to foreign acts of aggression. Although the size of the population is important, the number of people itself does not guarantee power. India, the world's second most-populous state, has not developed the perception of power partly because of the poverty of its people. If a population is to be a source of power, the population needs to be healthy, educated, well-organized, and able to enjoy at least a moderate standard of living. Israel, for example, has a population of less than 5 million, yet the strong cohesion and high morale of its people gives Israel a perception of power generally associated with much larger states.

National resources are another tangible element of power. Raw materials are important because they provide the resources necessary for economic development and for ensuring a high degree of independence in the world environment. The importance of raw materials was dramatically illustrated in 1973 when the oil-producing states (OPEC) organized a cartel and increased the price of crude oil fourfold. Since then, OPEC has continued to exert economic pressure on the oil-consuming nations. Their oil expenditures have placed major burdens on their balance of payments. To be sure, there are limits to the pressures that raw-materials-exporting countries can exert on the major industrial powers. But access to strategic resources such as oil, copper, bauxite, tin, and uranium cannot only facilitate the process of economic growth but can also make a state less vulnerable to the interests of other nations.

The *level of economic development* is also a significant element of a nation's power. It is possible to develop substantial national wealth by exporting raw materials, as has been done by the Middle East oil-exporting states. But the perception of power requires more than substantial reserves within banks. If wealth is to serve as an indicator of power, it must be based on the overall productive capacity of a nation. What is needed is a modern industrial infrastructure to provide the material and technical needs of society and a modern and efficient agricultural sector to produce enough food for its people. Of the five major powers (the United States, the Soviet Union, the People's Republic of China, France, and the United Kingdom), all have well-developed industrial foundations, although one of them (China) is still a relatively poor country with an average annual per capita income of only $380.

A final tangible element of power is *military strength*. Military power is based on both conventional and nuclear forces. In terms of conventional forces, the tangible indicators are the size and mobility of forces as well as the number and quality of weapons. Perhaps even more important than these quantitative measures are the intangible elements of training, readiness, organization, and morale. The Israeli armed forces, for example, are numerically smaller than those of other Arab states, yet the Israeli forces have developed a reputation of strength in part because of discipline and *esprit de corps*.

The other aspect of military capability deals with nuclear forces. Because of the enormous destructive force associated with nuclear weapons, it is impossible to be a major power in the contemporary atomic age and not to possess nuclear weapons. It is estimated that the total destructive power of all bombs dropped by the U.S. Air Force during the Second World War amounted to about two megatons (or the equivalent of two million tons of TNT). Yet the larger missiles of both the United States and the Soviet Union

TABLE 14.2   Military and Economic Indicators for Selected Countries (1976)

COUNTRY	TOTAL POPULATION (millions)	TOTAL GNP (billions of dollars)	TOTAL ARMED FORCES (thousands)	MILITARY EXPENDITURES (billions of dollars)
Canada	23	159	77	3.2
China (PRC)	966	309	4,300	32.8
France	53	353	585	13.6
Germany, Fed. Rep.	62	447	495	15.3
India	646	88	1,440	3.0
Israel	3.6	13	190	4.1
Italy	56	174	432	4.7
Japan	112	517	236	4.8
Soviet Union	257	960	4,600	121.0
United States	217	1,611	2,000	86.7
United Kingdom	56	231	344	12.0

Source: U.S. Arms Control and Disarmament Agency, World Military Expenditures and Arms Transfers, 1967–1976 *(Washington, D. C.: Government Printing Office, 1978), passim.*

can now carry strategic nuclear bombs with an even greater destructive capability. It is estimated that the nuclear destructive power of two major superpowers (the United States and the Soviet Union) is the equivalent of fifteen tons of TNT for every living person. In 1977 the effective destructive power of the United States and the Soviet Union was estimated at 2,887 megatons and at 7,491 megatons, respectively. The destructive capabilities of each of the other nuclear nations was assumed to be substantially less than one hundred megatons.[12]

In addition to total destructive power, the effectiveness and flexibility of delivery vehicles for nuclear weapons is also a major consideration in nuclear forces. Since nuclear power is so destructive, both superpowers tend to emphasize development of flexible and dependable means of delivering nuclear weapons. Both the Soviet Union and the United States possess three major types of delivery vehicles: intercontinental ballistic missiles (ICBMs), a submarine-launched missiles (SLBMs), and bombers. As Figure 14.3 suggests, in 1978 the Soviet Union was estimated to have about four hundred fifty more nuclear delivery vehicles than did the United States. On the other hand, U.S. missiles are considered technically superior. One advantage of American missiles is that they are considered more accurate. Another advantage is the flexibility resulting from the ability to target multiple positions from one missile. The multiple independent-reentry vehicles (MIRVs) permit one missile to target from three to fifteen separate nuclear warheads on different targets. As of 1978, it was estimated that the United States had MIRVed 550 ICBMs and

496 SLBMs (with about nine thousand warheads), while the Soviet Union had MIRVed 455 ICBMs (with approximately five thousand warheads). Thus, while the Soviet Union is assumed to have a much greater destructive potential, the United States is assumed to have a numerical advantage in nuclear warheads.

Figure 14.3   Nuclear Delivery Vehicles for the United States and the Soviet Union (1978)

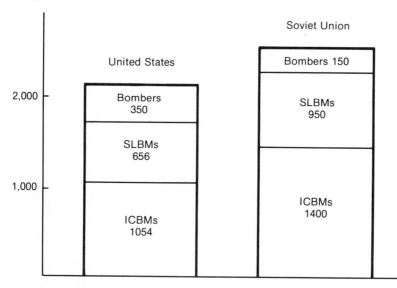

Source: Department of State, SALT and American Security *(Washington, D. C.: Government Printing Office, 1978), p. 3.*

Intangible Elements of Power   As important as military force may be in developing a reputation of power, tangible elements of power themselves won't guarantee power. Power, to repeat, is the ability to influence the probability of behavioral outcomes through the threat or use of coercion. To be able to affect the behavior of people requires many subtle, intangible qualities. One important intangible element is the *cohesion and morale of a country*. A nation deeply divided or lacking a sense of national mission will obviously find it difficult mobilizing its tangible resources. One of the major reasons for the inability of the United States to fully realize its objectives in Vietnam was the disunity and dissension about America's Southeast Asian policies. This division of purpose sharply contrasts with the strong cohesion and high morale of the North Vietnamese.

Leadership is also an important intangible element of power. Although it is difficult to describe the exact nature and function of political leadership, a brief examination of international relations of the twentieth century suggests that leaders such as Roosevelt, Churchill, Stalin, Mao, de Gaulle, and Castro played a critical role in their countries and within the international system. Because of their leadership skills they were able to mobilize their people and direct them toward particular national objectives; the result was greater domestic unity and a more vigorous expression of the national interest within the international community. Morgenthau suggests that the most important element of power is diplomacy, i.e., the quality of leadership in the making and implementation of foreign policy. Diplomacy is considered the preeminent element, because the diplomat has the function of using all other tangible and intangible resources to maximize the state's national interests. Diplomats, in other words, need to be superior leaders who can bring unity to various disparate elements of society and can articulate the nation's aims and goals with clarity and forcefulness.

The Measurement of Power   Given the importance of power in world affairs, numerous attempts have been made to quantify the power of nations. One of the recent interesting efforts is by Ray Cline, a former CIA official.[13] According to Cline, power can be measured by adding the value of tangible elements of power and multiplying them by an assumed value representing the intangible elements. His equation is:

$$Pp = (C + E + M) \times (S + W)^* \text{ where}$$

Pp = Perceived power;

C = Critical Mass (population + territory);

E = Economic Capability (GNP + the sum of energy sufficiency, raw materials, industrial capacity, agricultural production, and the proportion of world trade);

M = Military Capability (conventional and nuclear);

S = Strategic Purpose (a coefficient subjectively measuring the clarity of national goals and purposes); and

W = Will to Pursue National Strategy (a coefficient subjectively measuring leadership, unity, and the determination to carry out national goals).

*Reprinted by permission of Westview Press from WORLD POWER ASSESSMENT by Ray S. Cline. Copyright © 1977 by Westview Press, Boulder, Colorado.

Using this equation, Cline found that the perceived power of the Soviet Union is a little higher than that of the United States, while the perceived power of

West Germany and Japan is higher than that of the People's Republic of China. Table 14.3 summarizes Cline's findings for some of the major nations of the world.

TABLE 14.3   Perceived Power Based on Tangible and Intangible Elements for Selected States (1977)

COUNTRY	TANGIBLE ELEMENTS POWER (C + E + M)	INTANGIBLE ELEMENTS POWER (S + W)	TOTAL PERCEIVED POWER
U.S.	468	.9	421
USSR	402	1.3	523
China (PRC)	171	.7	120
France	112	.9	101
United Kingdom	99	1.0	99
Germany, Fed. Rep.	112	1.5	168
Italy	71	.8	57
Japan	111	1.3	144
India	97	.6	58
Indonesia	85	1.0	85

Source: Reprinted by permission of Westview Press, from WORLD POWER ASSESSMENT by Ray S. Cline. Copyright © 1977 by Westview Press, Boulder, Colorado.

Attempts to quantitatively measure national power are useful because they make explicit assumptions about the role of tangible and intangible factors. Ultimately, however, we must recognize that power is not the sum of a state's tangible and intangible elements but is a tentative and often elusive relationship between two or more states. Power does not reside within a state. Rather, a state becomes powerful by being able to influence the behavior of other states. To the extent that resources enable the state to do this, power is based on those visible and invisible elements discussed above.

Diplomacy

States use both peaceful and nonpeaceful methods in pursuing their national interests in the international system. *Diplomacy* is the process by which states implement their foreign-policy objectives through peaceful procedures. When states are unable to accomplish their aims through peaceful negotiation, they often resort to nonpeaceful methods. The use of force may help to realize national interests within the international system, but it is a slow, costly, and highly destructive method of implementing foreign policy.

The ideal approach to maximizing the national interest within the world is through the peaceful procedures of diplomacy. The art of diplomatic negotiation is essential for creation of a relatively stable and harmonious international environment.

Diplomatic Functions   Morgenthau suggests that there are four tasks of diplomacy. First, diplomacy needs to determine national objectives in the light of the power available for implementing those objectives. Second, diplomacy must assess the goals of other nations and the actual or potential power available for pursuing those goals. Third, diplomacy must determine to what extent the foreign-policy goals of states are compatible with each other. Finally, diplomacy must use appropriate means to implement foreign-policy objectives. The basic responsibility of the diplomat is to know his nation's interests and to develop appropriate tactics and strategies by which those interests can be fulfilled in the international system.

An essential requirement of a diplomat is that he be an effective negotiator. The international system is an environment of some 150 separate, free, and independent states, each of which seeks to maximize its individual interests. Since the foreign-policy interests of states are seldom complementary, the simultaneous expression of divergent foreign policies creates continuous and often intense interstate conflict. As a result, diplomats need to know how to negotiate and compromise — in effect, how to manage and resolve international conflicts — so that national objectives can be realized as much as possible without resorting to war. Because of the importance of negotiation and compromise in the international system, diplomacy is often defined as the implementation of foreign policy through negotiation.

Diplomacy is carried out between states on the basis of mutual consent. When states wish to establish diplomatic relations, they grant permission to the foreign government to be represented either through a mission or an embassy. The chiefs of missions or embassies are generally ambassadors or ministers who are chosen to represent the head of state of the sending country and are received by the head of state of the host country. A minister or ambassador begins to represent his government in the host state only when he has been properly credentialed, i.e., given formal permission to act as the sending government's emissary. The minister (or ambassador) continues to serve in the host country as long as the host government finds him an acceptable representative. When a chief of mission or an officer of an embassy is no longer desired, the host government may declare the diplomat *persona non grata* — that is, no longer acceptable to government leaders.

In the eighteenth and nineteenth centuries, diplomats generally had significant amounts of discretionary authority in representing their countries. With the advent of sophisticated communications systems and advanced methods of travel, diplomacy is more centralized in the foreign-affairs ministry of the home state or in the central government itself. The result is that major foreign-policy negotiation is no longer carried out within embassies, but at "summit" meetings. (The centralization of the diplomatic process is most evident in the "shuttle" diplomacy of Henry Kissinger. As Secretary of State he made numerous trips to China to assist in the normalization of East-West relations and carried out untold number of trips to various Middle East states in an effort to bring peace.)

As diplomatic responsibilities have shifted toward the home government, the most important function of contemporary embassies has become the reporting of social, cultural, economic, and military developments in the host country. By providing accurate estimates of foreign conditions, the ministry of foreign affairs is given the information on which it can carry out major decisions and instruct its mission staff on how to implement those decisions. In addition to the reporting function, embassies also assist, guide, and protect their foreign nationals and their property.

What kind of person should be a diplomat? Harold Nicolson, the most respected contemporary student of diplomacy, observes that the effective diplomat needs the following qualities: truthfulness, precision, calmness, good temper, patience, modesty, and loyalty. Nicolson also suggests that diplomats should possess such traits as intelligence, imagination, discernment, prudence, courage, and industry. The qualities needed for diplomacy are those of detachment, equanimity, and flexibility, qualities not necessarily developed in domestic politics. Politics is generally a conflictual and combative activity, and in order to be successful in politics a person needs to have a high profile, enjoy publicity, and thrive on conflict. The qualities required of the diplomat, however, are different, says Nicolson. An effective negotiator must shy away from controversy, must avoid publicity, must be flexible and discreet, and maintain a low profile. His objective must be maintenance of peace while tenaciously pursuing the long-term national interests of the state. An effective diplomat is a person who can apply reason to the conflict-management process.[14]

Ethics and Diplomacy   One of the important but difficult issues in international relations is the place of morality in diplomacy. Should the moral standards of individuals apply to states, for example? Should the foreign-policy aims of states be fixed on moral standards, or should they be based on the changing and more immediate, pragmatic interests of states? How should diplomacy be evaluated—by its intentions or by its consequences? As statesmen try to relate moral values to the foreign-policy process, two general approaches are followed. One approach emphasizes the application of ideals and moral norms to international relations. This approach, termed *idealism,* assumes that the basic function of politics is to search for moral purposes and to seek to realize those moral ends in the political realm. The other approach, termed *realism,* assumes that the basic objective of politics is to deal with the facts (the realities of international politics) and to carry out foreign affairs in light of those facts. Politics should not be concerned with the expressed moral aspirations of government leaders but with the observed behavior of states.

The idealist tradition in foreign affairs is based on an underlying optimism about the international system in general, and people in particular. Idealistic diplomats assume that the world is fundamentally a harmonious environment; the diplomat's task is to eliminate barriers that impede the international good will of states and to increase interaction among nations. During the mid-nineteenth century, some idealists assumed that there was an essential harmony of economic interests among states and that it could be realized through free trade. The assumption was that an increasingly free economic environment would benefit all peoples of the world, strengthen the world community, and make war less likely. In the twentieth century, Woodrow Wilson perhaps best exemplifies this tradition with his optimism about world peace. Wilson believed that the people of all nations wanted peace and that the most effective way to achieve this goal was to abolish the secretive diplomacy of states. What was needed was to make international politics the servant of world public opinion; this could best be realized by "open covenants, openly arrived at." Wilson's optimism was also expressed in his dream of creating an international organization (the League of Nations) to help regulate the behavior of states and to punish those states that pursued international aggression.

The *realist tradition* emphasizes the inherently selfish and conflictual nature of interpersonal and interstate relations. Politics is assumed to be a continuous struggle for scarce resources, and the most that can be achieved is a temporary, tenuous peace based on a realistic assessment of the perceived power of states. Hans Morgenthau, the most influential defender of realism, suggests that international politics cannot be based on ethical and moral aspirations of people but on actual behavior of states. Since power and influence are given facts of the international system, states that attempt to disregard the behavior of states and to place their security in the moral ideals of mankind fall fictim to those states who refuse to alter their nationalistic policies. "If the desire for power cannot be abolished everywhere in the world," writes Morgenthau, "those who might be cured would simply fall victims to the power of others."[15] Defenders of the tradition of realism (or *realpolitik*) believe that the only way to seek peace and harmony in the world is through policies of prudence—that is, policies based on an empirical assessment of what people and states will do in the light of previous actions.

Comparing the traditions of idealism and realism in foreign affairs highlights several important differences. First, idealists tend to assume that foreign policy should be judged chiefly by intentions; realists, on the other hand, assume that foreign policy should be judged primarily by consequences. The emphasis that idealists place on intentions and motives derives partly from the concern with ideals and moral norms. Realists, however, are aware that good intentions won't necessarily ensure desirable consequences. Since much of foreign policy requires balancing and reconciling of numerous conflicting moral ends, the task of diplomacy is often not to choose between a good and evil end but to select a policy minimizing evil, undesirable results.

The moral ambiguity of foreign policy is clearly illustrated in President Carter's efforts to seek minimum human rights. Although the U.S. policy of human rights was inspired with the noblest of intentions, the application of the doctrine to American foreign relations antagonized numerous states, including the Soviet Union, Brazil, Argentina, and Chile. It led to counterproductive results in a number of countries (such as increasingly cool and hostile relations) and increased military and economic dependence on other states and greater measures of repression and political control. The inadequacy of intentions is also demonstrated by the policies of then British Prime Minister Neville Chamberlain, who sought to appease the Germans in the late 1930s. While those policies were probably inspired with the highest motives and ethical ideals, the results inexorably led to war and an enormous human and economic cost to England. Winston Churchill, by contrast, was probably far less humane and moral and pursued policies based on an inferior morality. Yet the results of his World War II policies ultimately brought victory and peace — results that were morally superior to those of Chamberlain.

A second important distinction deals with the role of personal ethics in foreign policy. Idealists tend to assume that the virtues and ethical values that apply to individuals also apply to statesmen as they act on behalf of nations. Realists assume that the ethical standards of individuals are not applicable to corporate behavior. Reinhold Niebuhr, theologian and eloquent Christian realist, observes that the individual must always be guided and judged by the "law of love" but that states cannot be guided by the unselfish and altruistic standards of persons. George Kennan, noted American diplomat, writes:

> *Moral principles have their place in the heart of the individual and in the shaping of his own conduct, whether as citizen or as a government official...But when the individual's behavior passes through the machinery of political organization and merges with that of millions of other individuals to find its expression in the actions of government, then it undergoes a general transformation, and the same moral concepts are no longer relevant to it. A government is an agent, not a principal, and no more than any other agent may it attempt to be the conscience of its principal.*[16]

As a trustee, a state must seek to protect the interests of its people. In doing so, it may have to reconcile conflicting moral claims.

A third difference between realism and idealism relates to the place of moral and ethical values in defining the national interest. Idealists believe that fixed and universal moral standards should be the foundation of any expressed foreign-policy goals. Realists, on the contrary, have suggested that the articulation of national interests in terms of ideal, moral norms tends to make foreign policy inflexible and impedes the process of international negotiation. As a result, they believe that national interests should be defined primarily in terms of concrete political and economic wants of states. The advantage of a foreign policy based on ideal norms is that it sets standards that can enlighten a people's vision and mobilize their energies toward a common end. The disadvantage of viewing national interests as a group of selfish interests with no standards to evaluate the legitimacy of various competing claims is that foreign policy leads to a swamp of relativism.

When the foreign-policy process is examined in detail, it becomes clear that the simple dichotomy between idealism and realism is inadequate. Foreign policy cannot be based either on naive idealism or on unchecked realism. A pure policy of realism could only be practiced by a Machiavellian dictator, while an idealistic policy could only be applied by a religious saint. Foreign-policy objectives need to be informed by ideals if the claims of justice are to be partially realized in the international system. At the same time statesmen need to be realistic in their assessment of interstate relations. They need to understand that, while moral values are essential in avoiding the abyss of relativism in foreign affairs, moral values themselves can and have been used to clothe and hide the self-interest of states.

What is therefore needed is a pragmatic idealism in foreign affairs to integrate values with power. Diplomats need power in order to protect the legitimate interests of their peoples and to ensure international peace. At the same time they need moral values to help guide and direct the foreign-policy aims of states.[17] The function of moral norms, however, is not to prescribe general principles that lead to rigid, fanatical policies. Rather, the function of ethics should be to clarify, inform, and qualify the national interest. The task of integrating the claims of morality with the claims of power is a difficult and often hazardous responsibility.[18] The difficulty of making a wise, ethical, and prudent foreign policy is described by Morgenthau:

> *We have no choice between power and the common good. To act successfully, that is according to the rules of political art, is political wisdom. To know with despair that the political act is inevitably evil, and to act nevertheless, is moral courage. To choose among several expedient actions the least evil one is moral judgment. In the combination of political wisdom, moral courage and moral judgment, man reconciles his political nature with his moral destiny.[19]*

THE PROBLEM OF WAR

A distinctive quality of international politics is the high level of conflict and tension. Because of the absence of any effective procedures for resolving disputes, peace is difficult to maintain within the international system. Quincy Wright, who has carried out the most exhaustive research on war, found that from the end of the fifteenth century to the middle of the twentieth century there have been about 278 wars (an average of one war every two years).[20] Pitirim Sorokin examined the number of years some of the major European states had been at war and found that war appeared to be more common than peace. For example, he found that Russia (his homeland) had experienced only one peaceful quarter in the previous one thousand years, and that since the tenth century it had been at war forty-six of every one hundred years. He also found that England had been at war fifty-six of every one hundred years since the early eleventh century.[21]

If wars have been frequent throughout the history of Western civilization, their intensity and destructiveness has not remained constant. Indeed, the application of modern technology to warfare has resulted in a dramatic alteration in the nature of war. Sorokin estimates that European war casualties in the fourteenth, fifteenth, and sixteenth centuries were 167,000, 285,000, and 863,000, respectively; casualties from the seventeenth, eighteenth, and nineteenth centuries were 3.4, 4.6 and 3.8 million.[22] The twentieth century has been by far the most destructive, involving more deaths than in the previous ten centuries combined. It is estimated that civilian and military casualties for the First World War were approximately 26 million and for the Second World War, 64 million.

War and Foreign Policy

War is the ultimate means for carrying out foreign-policy objectives. It is the final instrument by which states can get something or keep other states from obtaining what they desire. As von Clausewitz, noted nineteenth-century student of wars, observes, war is "a political instrument, a continuation of political activity by other means."[23] Wars occur because states cannot satisfy all their wants. Since the demand for political, economic, social, and cultural resources exceeds their supply in their international systems, states inevitably become involved in competition and conflict over scarce resources. When such tensions and disputes involve nonvital or secondary interests, states are generally willing and able to peacefully reconcile their conflicting objectives. Compromise, however, becomes difficult (if not impossible) when vital interests are at stake. The result of conflict over essential stakes is that countries would rather go to war to preserve their interests than to maintain peace.

Since there is no final, authoritative instrument for the reconciliation of conflict, states must depend on their own abilities and resources to maximize their own national interests in the international environment. The result is that war plays a decisive role in settling interstate disputes. Indeed, Clausewitz argues that the map of the world is determined largely on the battlefield. In his view, war is the instrument by which most of the great facts of national history are settled and maintained.

However ridiculous it may seem, states prepare for war to maintain peace. The object of military might is to ensure that peace and justice, defined in terms of the interests of individual nations, are maintained within the international system. Nuclear weapons are not developed in order that they might be used to decimate the people of the world but rather to prevent another nuclear power from using its weapons. The fundamental purpose of military armaments, and in particular of nuclear weapons, is to make their use unnecessary. But to achieve this condition where military might is neutralized, states assume that they must be capable of defending themselves against possible aggression. The maintenance of an effective deterrent is the basic requirement for self-protection. While spending large sums of money on weapons and military forces may be considered foolish, statesmen generally agree that it may be even more foolish if those resources are not channeled into the defense budget. Until the structure of the international system is transformed, states continue to assume that their preservation ultimately depends on their ability to influence other states. To do this effectively, states need military capabilities, on which the concept of power ultimately rests.

Causes of War

Why do wars occur? Why do states resort to armed violence to settle disputes? Obviously, any effort to explain interstate conflict from a single source is bound to be incomplete and ultimately futile. There have been numerous efforts to explain the causes of war, however. An examination of some of these can provide valuable insights into understanding the source of interstate aggression. The brief review that follows does not attempt to cover all perspectives on war but seeks to highlight some of those theories most widely accepted in this century. The perspectives focus on the following factors as causes of war: perception, human aggression, cultural values, imperialism, the military-industrial complex, and the interstate system.

Perception   A number of political scientists have examined the process of communication among statesmen prior to major international conflicts and conclude that perception can be a major factor in causing war. John Stoessinger, in his study on why nations have gone to war in the major conflicts of the twentieth century, found that misperception of political leaders was the most important factor.[24] According to Stoessinger, misperception is revealed in four ways: in a leader's image of himself; in a leader's view of his adversary's character; in a leader's view of his adversary's intentions toward himself; and in a leader's view of his adversary's capabilities and power. Of these four types of misperception the most significant is the last — the tendency of statesmen to misjudge the opponent's military strength. Most twentieth-century wars, Stoessinger suggests, began when nations disagreed over their perceived relative strength and went to war to test the reality of those perceptions. Peace becomes possible only when misperceptions give way to a realistic assessment of the relative balance of power among states. Stoessinger's central finding is cogently expressed in his international relations text, *The Might of Nations:*

> *...the beginning of each war is a misperception or an accident.*
> *The war itself then slowly, and in agony, teaches men about*
> *reality. And peace is made when reality has won. The outbreak*
> *of war and the coming of peace are separated by a road that*
> *leads from mispreception to reality. The most tragic aspect of*
> *this truth is that war has continued to remain the best teacher of*
> *reality and thus has been the most effective cure for war.*[25]

Holsti, North, and Brody examined the outbreak of the First World War and the Missile Crisis of 1962 and found that diplomatic perceptions played a central role in both crises. In their study on the outbreak of the First World War, the three political scientists found that a major source of the escalating hostilities could be traced to misperception among major European statesmen. In their analysis of the Missile Crisis, on the other hand, they found that the peaceful resolution of the American-Soviet conflict was facilitated by the low level of misperception of each other's statements and actions.[26]

Human aggression   Sigmund Freud believed that the fundamental source of conflict is in the human psychological propensity toward aggression. Freud believed that within all people two drives were in continuous tension — the life impulse *(Eros),* which provides excitement, creativity, and vitality, and the death impulse *(Thanatos),* which directs behavior toward destruction, extinction, and disintegration. Since the destructive impulse cannot be eliminated, the health of the individual depends upon the channeling of this drive toward others. In his essay "Why War," written in 1933 in response to a request by Albert Einstein to analyze the problem of war, Freud applied the psychoanalytic method to the international system and suggested that the fundamental source of war is within people.[27] Just as individual health requires that people direct their innate aggressive impulses toward external sources, so nations need to direct their destructive impulses toward other states. International aggression is a means by which the state can preserve its vitality and life. The periodic recurrence of interstate conflict is simply a symptom of the basic human drive to direct destructive energies toward external environments. Although Freud believed that it is virtually impossible to suppress the tendencies of human aggression, he was not entirely pessimistic about the establishment of a peaceful world. According to Freud, civilization can learn to tame the destructive impulse by developing a more rational society. This can be accomplished through continued development of cultural values and mores that further channel and direct the behavior of people. Peace can be realized if people become sufficiently enlightened to alter their militaristic values and institutions.

The instinctivist argument for war has more recently been popularized by Konrad Lorenz and Robert Ardrey, who suggest that international conflict has its source in human biological drives.[28] Both Lorenz and Ardrey, whose theories of warfare are based chiefly on animal research, believe that human beings, like animals, have an innate biological drive toward aggression. This drive is the result of human genetic evolution conditioned through the principle of natural selection. Warfare exists, Lorenz and Ardrey believe, because survival has depended on the development of aggressive, combative behavior. Human aggression is thus not simply the result of learned behavior but of human genetic endowment. If war is to be managed and eliminated, therefore, human instincts must be modified. Like Freud, Lorenz is optimistic that through human reason people will be able to further develop civilization so that the inward traits of people are gradually modified toward more peaceful and harmonious behavior.

Cultural Values Comparative anthropological studies demonstrate that warfare is not equally present in all cultures; historical data indicate that primitive man may have been more peaceful and cooperative than modern man. As a result, some anthropologists conclude that war is not based on an innate impulse toward aggression but is the product of human development. This view was propounded most convincingly by Margaret Meade. "Warfare," she wrote, "is an invention like any other of the inventions in terms of which we order our lives, such as writing, marriage, cooking our food instead of eating it raw, trial by jury, or burial of the dead, and so on."[29] Human nature has a potential for both order and peace and conflict and destruction, and whether a civilization is peaceful or warlike depends wholly on the cultural traditions within each community. Whether children learn to delight in violence and murder or to pursue agriculture, trade, or knowledge is directly related to the cultural values learned by the children. To prove her point that warfare is simply a sanctioned form of social behavior, Meade observed that there are human communities, such as the Eskimos of North America and the Lepchas of Sikkim, where warfare is unknown. Since warfare is a human invention whose detrimental effects are perpetrated through culture, Meade was optimistic that a poor invention eventually gives way to a better invention. In order for this to occur, however, civilization must first recognize the evils of the old invention (warfare) and then create a new one. For Meade, then, the creation of a peaceful world lies principally in the establishment of cultural norms that promote cooperative, peaceful behavior and inhibit aggression and violence.

Economic Imperialism   Karl Marx believed that the basic cause of war lay not in human nature but in the socioeconomic structures of capitalism. Capitalism is not only the cause of continued domestic conflict between the rich and the poor but is also the basis for international conflict as well. Although Marx alluded to the relationship of capitalism to war, the development of the Marxist explanation of war was left to V.I. Lenin, whose study *Imperialism: The Highest Stage of Capitalism* attempts to explain a number of phenomena that were not consistent with the theory that Marx exposed some fifty years earlier.

According to Lenin, imperialism—that is, the practice by major world powers of extending their dominion over other territories—is caused chiefly by economic forces associated with the development of capitalism. Capitalism is not dying, however, as Marx's theory had predicted, but is becoming a more vigorous institution in the world. The reason for this is that in the more developed stages of capitalism, wealth becomes increasingly unevenly distributed not only between the proletariat and the bourgeoisie but also among the rich capitalists themselves. Lenin believed that as capitalism becomes more developed, production becomes increasingly concentrated and eventually leads to intense competition among major industries. This intense competition for profits eventually spills over into the international system; business firms try to establish control over foreign territories that can provide markets for surplus goods and can serve as a source of cheap labor and raw materials.

Lenin believed that capitalist countries are dominated by a business class whose chief interest is to protect and increase investment earnings. As a result, the foreign policies of industrial states are assumed to be chiefly concerned with the maximization of profit—a goal that can be accomplished most thoroughly through imperialism. Because of the intensity of competition for economic interests, Lenin believed that capitalist states do not hesitate to use force to accomplish their ends, whether it involves a small foreign colony or a major confrontation with another imperialistic state. Although wars can develop over a variety of issues, the fundamental source of interstate conflicts is the intense and violent competition among capitalist states for scarce economic interests. Following Marx, Lenin believed that as capitalism becomes more developed, capital becomes increasingly concentrated among a few firms within the major industrial states. This increasing concentration of wealth leads, of course, to frequent, intense international wars.

In short, the phenomenon of war in the world is basically the result of imperialistic policies originating from the advanced development of capitalism. The root cause of war is not human nature but the socioeconomic structures of capitalist society. As long as class consciousness prevails within countries, conflict will continue not only within states but also between states. The only way to a peaceful world, according to Lenin, is to establish a classless society worldwide. As class structures are eliminated, the nation-state becomes less important and is gradually replaced by a universal brotherhood of workers. In the new, universal community, peace and harmony will reign.

The Military-Industrial Complex   A variant of the Leninist explanation is the view that war is the product of specific elite groups that profit from military spending and international conflicts. The groups having an interest in military expenditures are generally referred to as the military-industrial complex and include such groups as the armed forces, the major firms manufacturing military hardware, and the government officials concerned with the making of defense and foreign policy. In his study *The Causes of World War III,* C. Wright Mills suggests that a military-industrial complex can exist in both capitalist and socialist societies. The most common view is that which associates war making with only the Western Industrial system. This is the view taken by Richard Barnet in his study *Roots of War.* According to Barnet, the source of war is found in the domestic structures of developed, industrial societies. "War," he writes, "is primarily the product of domestic social and economic institutions."[30] American wars will cease, argues Barnet, only when the military, political, and economic institutions of society are transformed so that the basic goal is peace and not war. As so long as it is profitable for major industrial companies to have war or to prepare for war, wars will continue to develop. Barnet singles out three major roots of war in the United States: (1) concentration of power in a national security bureaucracy that is not sensitive to long-term national and international interests; (2) continued need for economic growth in a capitalist system significantly influenced by military expenditures; and (3) vulnerability of the public to manipulation by governmental and business institutions when dealing with foreign-policy issues. If peace is to become more likely, capitalist countries need to restructure their economies and political system in such a manner that powerful business and defense groups no longer can control the foreign-policy process.

Institutional Lag   Another explanation for war is the inability of political and legal institutions to adapt rapidly enough to the continuing social, economic, and technological change associated with the modern world. This view is expressed by Quincy Wright in his monumental work *A Study of War.* Although he argues that there is no single cause of war, he suggests that one of the most important sources of war is the lag in the adjustment of political and legal institutions to the technological changes in society, particularly those relating to military armaments. In his view, society has four major dimensions — technological, legal, social, and cultural — and peace can occur only when there is equilibrium among the various parts. Changes in any one area requires compensating changes in others. Of particular significance, however, is the relationship of politics to technology, for the possibility of war tends to increase when political institutions are unable to effectively control technology. War can be attributed, says Wright, "either to the intelligence of man manifested in his inventions, which increase the number of contacts and speed of change, or to the unintelligence of man, which retards his perception of the instruments of regulation and adjustment necessary to prevent these contacts and changes from generating serious conflicts."[31] Whether or not the world becomes more harmonious or not depends in great measure on the ability of political leaders to govern society and ensure that the various societal forces are balanced.

International System   The most basic and perhaps most widely accepted thesis about war is that it is caused by the system itself. Wars occur because there is nothing to stop them. Unlike nation-states, which have a government to control violence, the international system is anarchic. Since no institution can prohibit aggression or punish states that violate the rights of other states, the foundation of world order is national power. The paradox of the international system is this: on the one hand, a state must trust other states if peace is to be maintained; on the other hand, a state must learn to distrust other states if it is not to be surprised by foreign aggression.

The paradoxical nature of the international anarchy is illustrated by Rousseau. According to him, five men come together at a time when all are suffering from extreme hunger. Since the hunger of each can be satisfied by a one-fifth part of a stag, they all agree that they will cooperate and trap one. But the hunger of any one of them is also satisfied by a hare. As they go hunting, a hare comes within reach of one of the hunters and he grabs it. The defector, obtaining the means to satisfy his hunger, in so doing permits the stag to escape. His immediate interests thus prevail over the common concerns of the group of hunters.[32]

This story, which illustrates the dilemma of rational activity in an anarchic community, has significant implications for the international system. Since the common concern of all states is peace, states should reduce their stockpile of military armaments. But the success of international disarmament depends not only on the will of a few states but also on the will of all. Total cooperation is required if the plan is to succeed. As with the stag hunt, the particular interests of one or two states may prevail over the common good if some states refuse to disarm. Rational action in an anarchic environment is complex and difficult; not only must a state pursue peace and disarmament, but it must also assume that all other states will do likewise. Rational action in the international system is thus *conditional* — that is, what is good for one state can only be determined in the light of the assumed action of another state.

The nature of conditional action can best be illustrated by a prisoner's dilemma from game theory. The essentials of the problem are diagrammed in Figure 14.4. Two prisoners, A and B, have been captured because of a crime. The sheriff admits that he does not have sufficient evidence to convict either person without their confessions. He tells them, however, that if neither one confesses, they can be released from prison within one week. He also tells them that if one of them confesses and the other does not, the confessor will go free, while the other will be hanged. If both confess on the same day, both will get a prison term of at least one year. What should either prisoner A or prisoner B do? What is important to recognize from the payoffs in Figure 14.4 is that the best action for either prisoner is to know what the other prisoner will do. Rational action, in other words, is conditional on the behavior of the other party.

Figure 14.4 The Prisoners' Dilemma

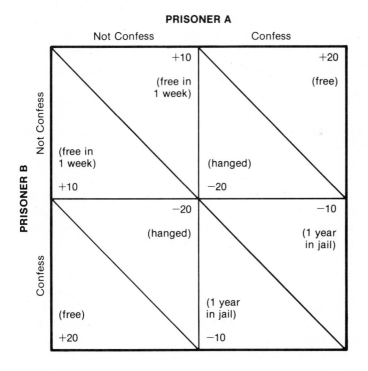

PRISONER A

In a decentralized, anarchic system where rational action is conditional on the action of all parties, disarmament may or may not be the best policy. Whether or not states should dramatically reduce their military resources depends upon what other states do.

Wars, in short, can be explained in terms of many factors. Some theories emphasize intrinsic sources of conflict, while others emphasize extrinsic conditions. In his study *Man, the State, and War,* Kenneth Waltz presents a pluralistic explanation for war. According to him, the immediate cause of war is the aggression of man and the aggression of states, while the permissive cause is the international system. Individuals and states are the major instigators of war, but no matter how good individuals and states become, peace is always impossible within the anarchic world system. If peace and harmony are to prevail, human nature, the state, and the international system must be transformed. But the inability to fundamentally alter any one factor suggests that the problem of war is far more intractable than many have supposed.

SUMMARY

The international community is a primitive or underdeveloped political community. It is primitive because there are no governmental institutions to manage social conflict. Unlike domestic politics, where governmental institutions are sovereign, the international community has no institutions that can make, implement, and interpret laws authoritatively. In the international community, sovereign authority rests not in international organizations but in each state's government.

The international community is Hobbesian because there is too much conflict. The excess of interstate conflict results from the absence of a common sovereign as well as from the lack of common understanding among different cultures. Since each state depends upon its own resources to protect and maximize its national interests, governments spend large amounts of money for military armaments in order to maintain a credible deterrent.

Every state has national interests that it seeks to maximize within the world. The expression of these interests in terms of the interests of other states constitutes a nation's foreign policy. Since the desires of states are greater than the supply of resources and goods, states compete and engage in conflict over the distribution of the world's scarce resources, whether real or symbolic.

Diplomacy is the process by which statesmen seek to maximize national interests without resorting to war. To be effective, statesmen need to have power – that is, the capacity to alter the behavior of other states through the threat or use of coercive action. Although power is based on numerous tangible and intangible resources, it is ultimately a subjective assessment of the potential to bring about coercive action on another state.

An important issue in foreign affairs is the place of moral norms in the making and implementation of foreign policy. One tradition, idealism, emphasizes the importance of ethics in establishing national interests. The other tradition, realism, is far more pessimistic about the possibility of international harmony and therefore places much less emphasis on the role of morality in carrying out foreign policy.

The fundamental problem of the international system is war. Nearly 100 million persons have died in this century from interstate conflict. In seeking to understand and explain the frequency and intensity of war, theorists have emphasized numerous factors contributing to interstate conflict. These include the following: human biological and psychological instincts, cultural patterns, economic practices and institutions, the military-industrial complex, the lag in political and social institutions' ability to regulate the technological developments facilitating war, and the anarchic international system. Obviously, no single factor is sufficient to explain war—it is a product of numerous conditions. These must include, at a minimum, those relating to the individual, the state, and the international system itself.

KEY TERMS

sovereignty	idealism
foreign policy	realism
national interests	imperialism
power	influence
force	diplomacy

NOTES

1. Jean Bodin, *Six Books on the State* in William Ebenstein, *Great Political Thinkers: Plato to the Present,* 4th ed. (Hinsdale, Ill.: The Dryden Press, 1969), p. 354.
2. Rogers Masters, "World Politics as a Primitive Political System," *World Politics* XVI (July 1964), pp. 594-619.
3. John Foster Dulles, "Institutionalizing Peace," *The Department of State Bulletin* 43 (May 7, 1956), p.740.
4. U. S. Arms Control and Disarmament Agency, *World Military Expenditures and Arms Transfers, 1967-76* (Washington D. C.: Government Printing Office, 1978), pp. 6-7.
5. *Ibid.,* p. 28.
6. *Ibid.,* p. 1.
7. Hans Morgenthau, *Politics Among Nations: The Struggle for Power and Peace,* 5th ed. rev. (New York: Random House, 1978), p. 5.
8. A. F. K. Organski, *World Politics* (New York: Alfred A. Knopf, 1958), pp. 105-107.
9. Morgenthau, *Politics Among Nations,* p. 117.
10. Sir Halford Mackinder, *Democratic Ideals and Reality* (New York: Holt, 1919), p. 150.
11. See Alfred T. Mahan, *The Influence of Sea Power upon History* (Boston: Little, Brown & Co., 1890).
12. Paul H. Nitze, James E. Dougherty, and Francis X. Kane, *The Fateful Ends and Shades of SALT* (New York: Crane, Russak & Co., 1979), p. 83.
13. Ray S. Kline, *World Power Assessment, 1977* (Boulder, Colorado: Westview Press, 1977).

14. Sir Harold Nicolson, *Diplomacy,* 3rd ed. (New York: Oxford University Press, 1973), p. 55–67.

15. Morgenthau, *Politics Among Nations,* p. 36.

16. George F. Kennan, *Realities of American Foreign Policy* (New York: W. W. Norton, 1966), p. 48.

17. See Chapters 2–9 of E. H. Carr, *The Twenty Years' Crisis, 1919–1939* (New York: Harper & Row, 1964) for an invaluable discussion of the role of ideals and power in international affairs.

18. See Arthur Schlesinger, Jr., "The Necessary Amorality of Foreign Affairs," *Harper's Magazine,* August 1971, pp. 72–77.

19. Hans Morgenthau, *Scientific Man Versus Power Politics* (Chicago: University of Chicago Press, 1952), p. 203.

20. Quincy Wright, *A Study of War,* vol. I (Chicago: University of Chicago Press, 1942), p. 651.

21. Geoffrey Blainey, *The Causes of War* (New York: The Free Press, 1973), p. 3.

22. Wright, *A Study of War,* p. 656.

23. Carl von Clausewitz, *On War,* ed. and trans. Michael Howard and Peter Paret (Princeton: Princeton University Press, 1976), p. 87.

24. John G. Stoessinger, *Why Nations Go to War,* 2nd ed. (New York: St. Martin's Press, 1978), passim.

25. John G. Stoessinger, *The Might of Nations: World Politics in Our Time,* 5th ed. (New York: Random House, 1975), p. 212.

26. Ole R. Holsti, Richard A. Brody, and Robert C. North, "Measuring Affect and Action in International Reaction Models: Empirical Materials from the 1962 Cuban Crisis," in James N. Rosenau, ed., *International Politics and Foreign Policy* (New York: The Free Press, 1969), pp. 691–4.

27. Sigmund Freud, "Why War?" in William Ebenstein, *Great Political Thinkers: Plato to the Present,* 4th ed. (Hinsdale: The Dryden Press, 1969), pp. 857–60.

28. See Robert Ardrey, *The Territorial Imperative* (New York: Atheneum Publishers, 1966) and Konrad Lorenz, *On Aggression,* trans. Marjorie Kerr Wilson (New York: Bantam Books, 1967).

29. Margaret Mead, "Warfare Is Only an Invention—Not a Biological Necessity," *Asia* 40 (August 1940), pp. 402–5.

30. Richard Barnet, *Roots of War* (Baltimore: Penguin Books, 1973), p. 337.

31. Quincy Wright, *A Study of War,* abridged ed. (Chicago: The University of Chicago Press, 1964), p. 352.

32. Kenneth N. Waltz, *Man, The State, and War* (New York: Columbia University Press, 1965), pp. 167–168.

SUGGESTED READING

BROWN, SEYOM. *New Forces in World Politics.* Washington, D.C.: Brookings Institution, 1974. A useful account of the growing impact of social and economic forces in world politics.

CARR, E. H. *The Twenty Years' Crisis: 1919–1939.* New York: Harper & Row, 1964. An excellent theoretical introduction to the field of international politics, focusing on the role of power and moral norms in foreign affairs.

COULOUMBIS, THEODORE A., and WOLFE, JAMES H. *Introduction to International Relations: Power and Justice.* Englewood Cliffs, N.J.: Prentice-Hall, 1978. This recent text combines traditional and behavioral perspectives in introducing the field of international relations. Good discussion of the role of international law and organization in world affairs.

FISHER, ROGER. *International Conflict for Beginners.* New York: Harper & Row, 1969. An insightful and creative volume on the processes and institutions involved in the resolution of interstate conflicts.

KENNAN, GEORGE F. *American Diplomacy, 1900–1950.* New York: Mentor Books, 1963. One of the most insightful accounts of American foreign relations of the first half of the twentieth century by a noted U.S. diplomat and student of Soviet affairs.

KENNEDY, ROBERT. *Thirteen Days: A Memoir of the Cuban Missile Crisis.* New York: W.W. Norton & Co., 1969. A short, lucid account of one of the most dramatic international conflicts of the postwar years. The afterword by Richard Neustadt and Graham Allison is particularly helpful in understanding this event.

MORGENTHAU, HANS J. *Politics Among Nations: The Struggle for Power and Peace.* 5th ed. rev. New York: Random House, 1978. This is the classic introductory international-relations text from a realist perspective.

SPANIER, JOHN, and USLANER, ERIC M. *How American Foreign Policy is Made.* New York: Praeger Publishers, 1974. A short introductory volume on U. S. foreign policy, with emphasis on the process and the major actors.

STOESSINGER, JOHN G. *Why Nations Go to War.* 2nd ed. New York: St. Martin's Press, 1978. Examines the major wars of the twentieth century in order to develop generalizations about major causes of interstate warfare.

WALTZ, KENNETH N. *Man, The State, and War.* New York: Columbia University Press, 1965. A theoretical examiniation of the causes of war focusing on human nature, the state, and the international system.

WALZER, MICHAEL. *Just and Unjust Wars: A Moral Argument with Historical Illustrations.* New York: Basic Books, 1977. Using historical illustrations from the Athenian attack on Melos to the My Lai Massacre, Walzer examines the major moral issues of modern warfare.

WRIGHT, QUINCY. *A Study of War.* Abridged ed. Chicago: University of Chicago Press, 1969. This is an edited version of the classic study on war. Although it does not include the valuable appendices of the unabridged edition, all of the narrative sections are included.

15 / THE MANAGEMENT OF INTERNATIONAL CONFLICT

Our analysis of international relations in the previous chapter led us to the conclusion that the international system is a disorderly, anarchic environment where war is the ultimate instrument by which interstate disputes can be resolved. While the causes of war are complex and the structural inadequacies of the international system enormous, a basic premise of this text is that an understanding of the methods and instruments of conflict management can significantly aid people in improving the domestic and international political environment. Conflict is a fact of life, but if the world is to become safer and more humane, it will only happen through the intelligible efforts of people.

The purpose of this chapter is to examine the primary approaches and methods of managing conflict in the international system. We shall first examine six general theories about the development of a more orderly international environment. We shall then examine the role of international law and world organizations in building international harmony and consensus. Although the role of law and governmental institutions is not as significant in the international system as in the nation-state, law and organizations can and do play an important role in the development of world order. The important challenge of our time is to determine how such processes and institutions can play an even more significant role than they have to date.

It should be noted at the outset that the role assigned to law and institutions in the search for world order depends greatly upon assumptions of how community order is established. One school, the realists, believes that the only effective way of building community consensus is by establishing the underlying factors on which order can be based. As a result, they tend to emphasize the need for accommodation and compromise among states and the need for a high level of transnational relations to foster common values, interests, and practices. Order, they believe, is not caused by law and governmental institutions; rather, law and government are expressions of a deep, fundamental consensus manifested by the outward institutions of government and the common regulations of law. The other school, the idealists, assume that government can create community consensus. Rather than wait until the conditions of world order are well-established, idealists believe that the creation of common laws and rudimentary international organizations can foster world community. As a result, they tend to place much emphasis on legal and institutional means of peace keeping. Perhaps the truth of the matter is that community consensus requires simultaneous development of laws and institutions as well as cultivation of those underlying conditions on which such an order is based.

METHODS OF MANAGING INTERNATIONAL CONFLICT

Methods of conflict management can be divided according to three general perspectives toward power. The first perspective assumes that power is a reality of the international system and that it needs to be *managed* if peace is to be maximized; the second assumes that international harmony among states can be maximized by *avoiding* power; and the third assumes that peace will be encouraged when international power is *reduced* or *eliminated*.

The perspective of managing power is expressed by three classic theories of peace keeping: balance of power, collective security, and world government. The first method assumes that international peace is obtained when a general equilibrium of power is maintained among states; the other two assume that peace is obtained through a disequilibrium of power so that the preponderance of power is available to resolve conflict, if not to deter aggression. Collective security achieves the required superiority of power by creating a voluntary association in which states pledge their commitment toward peace and their automatic opposition to aggression. World government involves a fundamental transformation in the world system so that final authority and power are in the hands of a central government institution.

The approach of power avoidance is expressed by two peace-keeping methods — pacific settlement of disputes, which involves the efforts of a third party in resolving international conflicts, and functionalism, which seeks to avoid politics and encourage international socioeconomic interdependence. Pacific settlement assumes that peace can be encouraged among states by avoiding direct competition for power and by encouraging the role of reason and law in the development of harmonious international relationships. Functionalism assumes that international harmony can best be encouraged by avoiding international politics and fostering transnational cooperation.

The third approach—the reduction or elimination of power—is best expressed in disarmament. This method does not attempt to alter the decentralized international system but rather seeks to reduce the war-making capacity of states by controlling, reducing, and even eliminating military power within the world.

There are six primary methods of peace keeping. We shall briefly examine the central characteristics of each of these.

TABLE 15.1   Perspectives and Methods of Peace Keeping

PERSPECTIVES ON POWER	METHODS OF PEACE KEEPING
I. *Managing Power*	
Through Balanced Power	Balance of Power
Through Imbalanced Power	Collective Security
	World Government
II. *Avoiding Power*	Pacific Settlement of Disputes
	Functionalism
III. *Reducing and Eliminating Power*	Disarmament

Balance of Power

This method of peace keeping assumes that states, like people, are inherently selfish and concerned primarily with the maximization of their own national interests. This approach, therefore, does not attempt to transform the imperfect drives of states, but rather seeks to build order and harmony out of the greed and ambitions of states. The fundamental assumption of the balance of power is that peace can be achieved most effectively by maintaining a general equilibrium of power among states. The balance of power within the international system is not established or created by any single state or group of states but results inevitably from the competitive drives of states. Much like the "invisible hand" of Adam Smith's economic theory (a theory that assumed that as each individual maximized his own economic interests the general welfare would also be maximized), the balance-of-power approach likewise assumes that as states pursue their own interests they automatically pursue the general interests of peace. The balance of power that results from the selfish drives of states thus creates the foundation on which peace and order can be established.

It is important to recognize that the balance-of-power approach does not describe the foreign policies of states but only the resulting condition from these foreign policies. States attempt to maximize their national interests, and they do so by maximizing their power capabilities. As a result, the process by which states establish the conditions of general equilibrium involves peaceful negotiation as well as nonpeaceful struggles. Balance of power, in short, does not describe the intentions and goals of states but the consequences resulting from the competitive struggles among states.

The validity of this approach depends in great measure on two assumptions—that as states pursue their own interests an automatic byproduct is a general equilibrium of power and that a balance of power is an effective means of establishing and maintaining peace. Although a general balance might result from the continuous conflicts and competitions among states, it is difficult to assume that local, regional, and international struggles for power always led to a general balance among states. There are some 150 states continuously maximizing their specific interests within the international system. The requirements of establishing bilateral and multilateral equilibria are too complex to assume that balanced power always results automatically. Moreover, the assumption that balance leads to peace has also been criticized. Organski, for example, challenges this assumption as follows: "The relationship between peace and the balance of power appears to be exactly the opposite of what has been claimed. The periods of balance, real or imagined, are periods of warfare, while the periods of known preponderance are periods of peace."[1] Claude, too, suggests that there is no necessary correlation between peace and balance and that the preponderance of power may serve to keep harmony if the "right" state has the superiority of force.[2] Even if the assumptions of balance of power are proven valid, the approach itself is a highly uncertain and tentative method of developing international peace. Since states are continuously in competition with other states, the pattern of interstate relations is in continuous flux.

Despite its shortcomings, the balance-of-power method is perhaps the most widely practiced approach of peace keeping. Since its operation is based on the existing realities of the international system, this method provides a theory by which states can justify the continued protection and maximization of national interests. The balance-of-power approach provides statesmen, in effect, with a means by which they can equate the cause of peace with their own struggle for superiority of military force.

Contemporary international relations provide examples of peace being maintained through an apparent "balance" of power. During the postwar years both the United States and the Soviet Union have had sufficient conventional and nuclear armaments to effectively deter the other from any assumed aggressive behavior. Although the Soviet Union has noticeably increased its military power vis-à-vis the United States in the 1970s, there is still a "rough equivalence" of power between the two superpowers that contributes to the stability of the international system. Another example is the continued Middle East tensions between the Israelis and the Arabs. Although Israel has been in five wars since it became an independent state in 1948, a dominant assumption in

American foreign policy toward that region has been that peace would be maximized by ensuring a general balance of power between the two opposing parties. As a result, during the 1970s the United States supplied both Egypt and Israel with weapons.

Collective Security

Collective security involves the creation of a voluntary association of states in which states pledge themselves to use their power against any other member state that commits aggression. The fundamental idea of this peacekeeping method is summarized in the phrase "an attack on one is an attack on all." Like the balance of power, collective security operates within the existing decentralized international system. Unlike it, this method uses the superior military forces of all states within the community to repel aggression.

If collective security is to operate effectively, the international system must be harmonious and peaceful. Collective security does not attempt to build international harmony; rather, it seeks to provide a conflict-management method that can be utilized in a relatively peaceful environment. What collective security attempts to do is to systematize and institutionalize procedures for dealing with unacceptable international behavior.

There are two requirements for operating collective security: first, a community of states must be able to identify a state committing aggression; and second, states must be willing and able to automatically punish the aggressor state. Both conditions are often difficult to meet. Identifying aggression is difficult because states differ in their understanding of aggression and also because the facts surrounding alleged conflicts are not clear. It is often difficult to know who began an interpersonal quarrel; so, too, it is often difficult to know which state is responsible for international violence. In addition, states are generally not prepared to identify their particular national interests with the interests of other states. Whereas balance of power assumes that countries automatically defend their own interests when they are threatened, collective security goes a step further by assuming that states will act when other states are victims of aggression.

The League of Nations and its successor, the United Nations, have both attempted to partially implement this method of conflict management. The League, created at the end of World War I, established a system whereby all member states were responsible for protecting victims of aggression. ARTICLE 16 of its charter states: "Should any Member of the League resort to war in disregard of its covenants under ARTICLES 12, 13 or 15, it should *ipso facto* be deemed to have committed an act of war against all other Members of the League." The League's Charter also placed the responsibility for determining when aggression had been committed in the hands of each member, although the League's council had the task of directing the collective forces against the aggressor state. Despite its commitment to collective peace keeping, the League was not effective in preventing wars. As a result, the United Nations was established on less optimistic assumptions. Instead of allowing each of its members to determine when aggression had been committed, the United Nations centralized the peace-keeping function in the hands of the Security Council, and more particularly in the five major powers of the world. The result of the centralization of the collective-security function in the big five states, however, meant that collective security could be applied only to the smaller states since the major powers could veto any Security Council action they opposed.

Collective security has not worked well under either the League of Nations or (in its modified form) under the United Nations. The major reason for this is that states are unwilling to equate the general interests with their own particular concerns. While states may strongly defend peace, justice, and international cooperation, the common good is not as important as the immediate interests of states. Peace is not the most important value of states. Were this so, no wars would occur and there would be no need to manage power. The problem of implementing collective security thus boils down to the fact that the conditions on which this peace-keeping method is to operate have not been fully realized under either the League or the United Nation. Until the general interests of the international system take precedence over the individual interests of state — that is, until international organization is effectively reconciled with national sovereignty — collective security will remain a relatively unimportant peace-keeping method.

World Government

The third and most radical method of managing power is world government. This approach assumes that in order to establish and maintain peace in the world, political power must be centralized. But unlike collective security, which seeks to create a voluntary monopoly of force within the present international system, world government assumes that the interstate system must be fundamentally transformed. States must be completely disarmed, and sovereignty must be transferred to a single international agency responsible for managing interstate conflict. What world government attempts to do, in effect, is to duplicate the national state in the world. The underlying premise is that the possession of a monopoly of force by an international enforcement agency is sufficient to manage and resolve disputes. Unlike collective security, which requires partial and periodic centralization of power, world government attempts to establish a permanent and complete monopoly of force.

Two different models have been discussed as potential types of world government. Some think that the international system should have a unitary structure, where political power is centralized in one international office.

Based on this model, world government would look much like an international empire (such as the Roman civilization). The second and more popular model is the federal structure, where power is divided between a central authority and the 150 states. Under such a system, the world government would have ultimate authority. States would continue to play an important conflict-management function, even as provinces and states do in domestic federal systems such as Canada, Switzerland, and the United States.

Most observers agree that a world government, whether unitary or federal, would reduce, if not eliminate, the problem of war. But much disagreement exists about how to achieve the required structural changes. Some believe that the problem of state sovereignty is so difficult and complex that the only effective way of creating a world government is to do so in a single, quick change. This view was expressed by Robert Hutchins, who once said that "the only real step toward world government is world government itself."[3] Other theorists, such as Greenville Clark and Louis Sohn, suggest a gradual process for shifting sovereignty and military power from the states to a central government.[4] The process they suggest, however, is chiefly concerned with legal, military, and political institutions, and provides little role-altering values, ideals, and political goals of the people.

Those who emphasize the primacy of law and politics in creating a world community often use the federal system of the United States as a model for the establishment of world government. The Philadelphia Convention of 1787, it will be recalled, created a constitution that changed the U.S. political structure from a confederal system, where sovereignty was in the hands of thirteen separate states, to a federal system, where sovereignty was in the hands of a national government. Some exponents of world government therefore suggest that a similar transfer of sovereignty needs to occur in the international system. The emphasis on legal and political institutions, however, fails to appreciate the role of nonpolitical factors in the creation of the American community. The American community was not established in 1776 or in 1787 but was the outgrowth of continued development throughout the seventeenth and eighteenth centuries. The United States was not created by the political and legal acts of 1787; rather, the development and ratification of a constitution was made possible because of the presence of a formative, if undeveloped, American community. (The creation of a national government, therefore, was not the beginning but the ending of a process of community-building.) If the American experience is to serve as a model for creating a world government, we need to remember that the development of a world community requires both political changes in the form of new government institutions and nonpolitical changes in the form of new loyalties and values. The dilemma is this: the world needs world government to reduce the threat of war, but the precondition for a world government is world community, which can only be developed and solidified through world government.

Pacific Settlement of Disputes

This method of peace keeping, unlike the first three, seeks to manage and resolve international conflicts by avoiding international power. Pacific settlement is the attempt to encourage peace and harmony within the existing decentralized international system by emphasizing legal, moral, and factual issues of a dispute. The central premise of this approach is that war results when there is misunderstanding or misperception between states or when emotional passions get in the way of rational comprehension of issues. The objective of this approach, therefore, is to provide a mechanism whereby passion, ignorance, and misperception can be eliminated. This is done by establishing a cooling-off period — a time when reason is able to overcome passion and emotion — to encourage statesmen to talk rather than fight, to compromise rather than challenge. It is also done through the services of an outside or third party. The advantage of an external party is that it is not emotionally involved in the dispute and can thus help clarify communication, assist in determining the facts regarding the conflict, and select possible alternative solutions.

There are two methods of third-party involvement in disputes — one political and the other nonpolitical. Three of the most popular political techniques include good offices, mediation, and arbitration. *Good offices* involve the assistance of an outside party in clarifying communication between disputants, gathering relevant facts, and highlighting central issues of the conflict. The function of the third party is to be a facilitator. *Mediation* is a more formal technique in which the outside party not only seeks to clarify the issues but also presents alternative solutions to the problem. In some cases a compromise solution may be recommended, although the recommendation is not binding. *Arbitration,* the most systematic and well-developed political technique, involves the analysis of a conflict and the presentation of a binding decision. States, of course, need not accept the jurisdiction of a panel of arbitrators, but once they have committed themselves to arbitration, states are expected to abide by the arbitrators' decision. A major source of international arbitrators is the Permanent Court of Arbitration, created by the Hague Peace Conference of 1899 and now located in the Peace Palace of The Hague. The court is not a judicial body concerned with settling international legal disputes, nor is it permanent in its operation. The court is essentially a list of distinguished persons who have indicated their willingness to serve on an arbitration board to settle international disputes as the need arises.

The nonpolitical technique of pacific settlements is adjudication, which is the settling of international legal disputes through a court of law. This method of peace keeping is used when a conflict involves a question of international law. The primary court for resolving international legal conflicts is the International Court of Justice (ICJ), an international tribunal that is a formal part of the United Nations. The ICJ, located in The Hague, was preceded by the Permanent Court of International Justice, which operated from 1921 until 1945. Another important court is the European Court of Justice, which adjudicates disputes within the European community. We shall examine this approach more fully later on in the chapter.

Functionalism

Another approach that seeks to avoid power is functionalism, the most recently developed theory of peace keeping. The functional method assumes that since international conflicts are frequent, difficult, and complex, the most effective means of dealing with international incompatibilities is to avoid politics altogether and focus on social and economic issues. Rather than try to manage and resolve interstate disputes, functionalism tries to encourage international economic and social interdependence and cooperation, with the hope that such ties encourage more harmonious political relationships and displace hostilities. "The problem of our time," observes David Mitrany, the father of functionalism, "is not how to keep the nations peacefully apart but how to bring them actively together."[5]

Functionalists do not try to alter the international system; rather, they believe that by establishing strong economic and social ties among states, international conflicts will become less likely. This results partly from an increasing cooperation among states and a higher level of understanding among different cultures, but also from the growing role of transnational organizations as they seek to facilitate social and economic international relations. The hope is that, as these organizations become institutionalized, they will develop sufficient influence to be able to affect the political relations of states. The key assumption of functionalism, then, is that social and economic cooperation has a beneficial "spillover" effect in the sphere of international politics.

The dominant expression of the functional approach of peace keeping is *neofunctionalism* — an approach that combines elements of world organization with socioeconomic interdependence. Whereas functionalism seeks to make the world more peaceful through nonpolitical transactions, neofunctionalism assumes that international organizations must lead, direct, and coordinate the growth of functional relationships. Neofunctionalism combines, in other words, elements of managing power (federalism) and avoiding power (functionalism).

The most explicit implementation of the neofunctional approach is the European Economic Community (EEC), a common economic union of nine Western European states. The basic premise of the EEC is that war will be less likely if the European nations become more economically and socially interdependent. This premise is stated in the treaty creating the European Coal and

Steel Community, the organization that served as the catalyst for the larger EEC. The treaty expresses the functional assumptions by calling European states "to substitute for historical rivalries a fusion of their essential interests," and "to establish, by creating an economic community, the foundation of a wider and deeper community among peoples long divided by bloody conflicts." Since the creation of a common coal and steel community, European interdependence has grown enormously. This functional growth has not resulted automatically but has been encouraged and directed by the governmental institutions of the community, in particular the EEC's council and commission. The development of greater European unity has thus resulted both from growing socioeconomic interdependence as well as from expansion of authority by EEC institutions.

Disarmament

This method of peace keeping can be defined as the reduction or elimination of military armaments. Closely associated with disarmament is arms control, which is primarily concerned with regulating the testing, production, and deployment of military armaments. Although both disarmament and arms control are concerned with controlling the proliferation of destructive military hardware, the primary difference between the two methods is that disarmament is primarily concerned with significant *reductions* or total *elimination* of military instruments for war, while arms control is far more concerned with managing the expansion of military capabilities. The Limited Nuclear Test Ban Treaty of 1963, which prohibited atmospheric nuclear testing, and SALT I, which placed restrictions on the offensive and defensive strategic capabilities of the United States and the Soviet Union, are examples of arms control. The Washington Treaty of 1922, which called for significant reductions in naval weapons among the five major powers, is an example of disarmament.

The goal of disarmament is to reduce and possibly eliminate the instruments with which states go to war. The basic premise of this approach is that the arms race is not just a symptom of the decentralized, anarchic world system but is itself a cause of international conflicts. The competition for military superiority is a major cause of contemporary political tensions and of war itself. This view is expressed by Lewis Richardson, the father of mathematical peace research, in his pioneering study *Arms and Insecurity*. In that work Richardson argues that states increase their military expenditures in an exponential fashion and that if such expenditures are not regulated, the long-term result will be war.[6] Thus, the goal of disarmament is to seek to control a specific aspect of the international system—the escalating military capabilities of states. This approach does not seek to alter the decentralized political structure of the world, nor does it attempt to deal directly with the political imcompatibilities of states. Rather, the goal of disarmament is to deal with the military potential of states and thereby to reduce the risk of war.

There are a number of difficult issues involved in any scheme to implement disarmament theory. One of these is whether disarmament should proceed unilaterally, bilaterally, or multilaterally. If the process is to be mutual, as has always been the case in history, then there is the further problem of determining the type and quantity of military armaments that should be eliminated. Determining what ratio of military armaments should be reduced is a most difficult question, for the power of states cannot be easily measured. As a result, any effort to carry out bilateral or multilateral reductions of armaments is a slow and difficult process. The Strategic Arms Limitations Talks between the United States and the Soviet Union, for example, clearly demonstrates this, for the negotiations for the second phase of SALT required more than seven years. Even after an agreement is reached on the quantitative and qualitative reductions, there is the problem of verification — the requirement of monitoring the disarmament process to ensure that no violations occur. Since there is mutual suspicion among states, governments are often anxious to have effective means of inspection and control. Yet, the very suspicion and distrust among states often inhibits the possibility of effective verification. Finally, an important shortcoming of disarmament is that it is inherently static in nature in that it tends to freeze existing power relationships. This static bias occurs because disarmament is based on the balance of power at a particular time in history but does not provide for change resulting from the dynamic character of international relations. The result, of course, is that until there is complete and universal disarmament, disarmament schemes must be regarded as temporary, short-term instruments for controlling the arms race.

If the purpose of disarmament is to make war less likely, the history of disarmament does not provide much encouragement for the effectiveness of this approach. With the exception perhaps of the Rush-Bagot Agreement of 1817 (which limited U.S. and Canadian naval forces in the Great Lakes) and the Washington Treaty of 1922 (which resulted in the reduction and control of capital ships for the United States, Great Britain, Japan, Italy, and France), most disarmament attempts have not been effective in either eliminating significant numbers of weapons or in decreasing the possibilities of war. The discouraging record of disarmament is proof that international conflicts are not fundamentally the result of the arms race. Disarmament, like functionalism, attempts to skirt the chief cause of conflict (the political ambitions of states). Until the underlying tensions and insecurities of states are resolved, disarmament can contribute minimally to the establishment of a peaceful and harmonious world. As Morgenthau aptly puts it: "Men do not fight because they have arms. They have arms because they deem it necessary to fight. Take away their arms, and they will either fight with their bare fists or get themselves new arms with which to fight."[7]

INTERNATIONAL LAW AND CONFLICT MANAGEMENT

International law is the body of rules, customs, and principles that states accept as binding obligations. Since there is no sovereign authority over states, international law is a set of regulations voluntarily accepted by states. Although most international law is concerned with the rights, duties, and responsibilities of nation-states, there is a growing body of international rules that deal with international organization, corporations, and individuals.

Sources of International Law

The basic source of domestic laws is a legislature empowered to make and change legislation. In the international community there is no sovereign legislature to make and change law. As a result, there is no well-defined source of international law as in domestic law. According to ARTICLE 38 of the Statute of the International Court of Justice, international law has its roots in five areas: international treaties, customs, general principles, judicial decisions, and the teachings of major academic writers on international law. We shall briefly discuss each of these sources.

1. *Treaties,* which are contractual obligations between two or more states, are a major source of international law. They set forth the accepted standards for a vast array of common international concerns and thus facilitate international cooperation in such areas as extradition of criminals, copyrights, environmental protection, nuclear energy, international economic relations, trade agreements, and registration of vessels. Since treaties are the most explicit expression of international law, Akehurst suggests that they are the "maids of all work" in international law. Although most treaties involve only two states (bilateral), the most important treaties are those that involve numerous signatories (multilateral), such as the Covenant of the League of Nations, the United Nations Charter, the Inter-American Treaty of Reciprocal Assistance (Rio Pact), and the Nuclear Nonproliferation Treaty. Generally, the provisions of a bilateral treaty are binding on the signatory states only. A multilateral treaty can take on the force of general international law and eventually can create principles that are regarded as binding even on non-signatory states.

2. *Customs* are also an important source of international law. When customary practices are accepted by a large number of states and no state expressly rejects them, they can become a part of the rules of international law. An example of such a custom is the three-mile limit of territorial waters — a custom accepted in the seventeenth century up until the mid-twentieth century. This custom, based on the assumed distance of a cannonball shot, has been superceded as states have expanded their territorial boundaries for military and economic purposes. Another example is the international custom of exempting unarmed fishing vessels from war booty.

3. *General Principles* that are internationally accepted can also serve as a source of international law. Such principles may include moral issues such as the establishment of minimal standards of human dignity, the abolition of the slave trade, the right to wage war for just moral ends, and so on. Principles may also include procedural issues such as *pacta sunt servanda* and *rebus sic standibus.* The first principle means that treaties should be observed; the second means that when the original conditions of an agreement have changed, the agreement itself is no longer in force. If general principles are to serve as law, they need to be widely accepted and specific enough to be applied in concrete situations.

4. *Judicial Decisions* of domestic and international courts are also an important source of international law. Although domestic cases have no force beyond the territorial limits of a state, the principles, arguments, and decisions of domestic courts can contribute to the development of international law. A more important source are the decisions of international and regional tribunals, such as the International Court of Justice in The Hague or the European Court of Justice of the European Economic Community. Although decisions of international tribunals have no binding effect on other legal cases, the precedents of previous international cases almost always play a significant role in the adjudication of subsequent disputes.

5. *Publications* of leading international lawyers have influenced international law. Hugo Grotius, regarded as the father of international law, is generally recognized as a major contributor of a number of key principles of international law, such as the notion of diplomatic immunity, the principle of extraterritoriality, the rights of noncombatants in war, etc. Grotius's fame rests, in great measure, on his classic work *De Jure Belli ac Pacis (The Law of War and Peace),* published in 1625 as an exposition of the rights and duties of newly emerging states during the revolutionary period of the Thirty Years' War. Other leading contributors to the early development of international law include Samuel Pufendorf, author of *The Law of Nature and of Nations* (1672); Cornelius van Bynkershoek,

author of *Forum of Ambassadors* (1721) and *Questions of Public Law* (1737); and Emerich de Vattel, author of *The Law of Nations* (1758). While it would be incorrect to suggest that writers such as these created international law, their ideas have been a significant source of law insofar as they have summarized and codified the customary behavior of states or have influenced the values and ideas governing the behavior of states.

The Nature of International Law

One of the continuing debates in international relations is whether international law is really law or simply a general community expectation or a moral aspiration. Those who raise the question generally assume that law requires force in order to ensure compliance. There are others, however, who believe that force may be a requirement for obeying the law but that other factors are even more important in ensuring compliance. If law is defined as a command backed by force, then it is clear that the international community has little law, for there is no superior force in the international system. On the other hand, if law is defined as a set of obligations that people and states accept (whether backed by force or not), then international law can be considered a form of law.

In his study *International Conflict for Beginners,* Roger Fisher, a professor of international law, argues that the idea that law requires force is based on a number of misconceptions.[9] First, law does not work solely because it is a command backed by force. There are times, he argues, when governments obey the decisions of courts, even though they possess superior force to disregard such legal action. For example, when steel workers went on strike in 1950 and forced the steel mills to close, President Truman used executive power to open the mills and keep them functioning. The Supreme Court, however, ruled that Truman's action was illegal and ordered him to cease running the companies. He complied with the action, even though he could have used the military forces at his disposal to defy the court. A second misconception is that force is necessary to influence the behavior of other states. As suggested in the previous chapter, there are numerous elements of power. States may utilize a combination of factors to try to influence the behavior of states. Strong military forces are important, but they alone will not ensure international influence. A third misconception is that law only restrains, but does not affect, the choices and interests of states. Law, however, is not only a set of rules prohibiting actions but also a series of principles and guidelines directing the aims and goals of states. Law is concerned with restraining selfish behavior of states, but it also plays a major role in guiding the development of foreign-policy aims and goals. In short, a major function of law is to lead and direct — a task that does not require force.

If force is not essential for compliance with international law, why do states voluntarily abide by the rules and principles of international law? One reason, of course, is that states are in the habit of obeying law. It will be recalled from Chapter 3 that we suggested that the foundation of political community is the voluntary habits of compliance. Force is used to ensure order, but it is used marginally and intermittently. In the international system the role of voluntary compliance is even more important than in domestic political systems, for the instruments of enforcement available in the state are not available in the international system. It is for this reason that the customary practices of states are an important source of international law.

The voluntaristic foundation of international law can pose major drawbacks. Since only the practices that states support will become a part of the law, international law tends to represent a low common denominator of interstate behavior. On the other hand, a major strength of international law is that it is based not on the wishes of a legislative body but on the generally accepted values and practices of states. This means that the law that is established will be one that is favored by most states and will receive a high level of compliance. One of the difficulties of domestic legislation is that laws may be enacted that are fundamentally at variance with the practices of people (such as the U.S. amendment prohibiting alcoholic beverages and the recent federal law imposing a fifty-five mile-an-hour speed limit).

The second reason statesmen obey international law is that they may prefer the long-term gains resulting from compliance to the short-term gains resulting from noncompliance. For example, all states benefit from a peaceful and stable international system. Since international law is a major source of world order, states benefit by obeying international law. The major difficulty with this source of compliance, however, is that it assumes that statesmen are able to determine what their long-term and short-term interests are. This is not always the case. Even if statesmen could distinguish between their essential and their peripheral interests, compliance with the law may not always benefit all parties alike. As a result, some states may be tempted to disobey the law and attempt to maximize their short-term interests in an effort to limit perceived gains to other states.

If a domestic or international legal system is to be effective, both *force* and *voluntary compliance* are essential, although the exact proportions of each tend to vary with the circumstances of the law. Ideally, of course, voluntary compliance should be the cornerstone of all law; on the other hand, if law is to set a standard above the common norm of behavior, it must represent more than the actual practices of states. But if the law is to serve as a schoolmaster, some force will be required. The force that is available to implement international law, however, is relatively insignificant, particularly when compared to domestic systems. Since there is no common sovereign in the world, the only force that can be generated in the international system must come from the states themselves. The common methods available for the enforcement of international law include methods of self-help, such as diplomatic protests, rupture of diplomatic relations, economic sanctions, etc., and measures of collective enforcement through regional and international organizations. In addition, international public opinion can be brought to bear on states, as has been done against Rhodesia and South Africa in the 1970s for the racial policies of segregation pursued by both states.

In conclusion, we can accept international law as a legitimate form of law. Although it uses less force than does domestic legislation, international law nonetheless guides, regulates, and directs the behavior of states and thus serves as an important force in world order.

International Law and Interstate Conflicts

Over the centuries a rather substantial body of rules and principles of international law have been developed that play an important role in facilitating international relations. Such laws cover the rights and duties of states, procedures for determining jurisdiction over citizens and aliens, rules for recognizing states and governments, acquisition of territory, rules governing the sea and air space, procedures for pacific settlement of disputes, and rules of warfare. The following principles represent some typical areas covered by international law:

1. *due diligence*—states have a responsibility for apprehending and punishing criminals who have injured resident aliens; when states fail to show diligence in carrying out justice, they may be sued by aliens through their governments.

2. *genuine link*—in order for a person to enjoy the full privileges and protection associated with citizenship, there must be a legitimate relationship between the person and the state, including such factors as residency, family ties, etc. Citizenship cannot provide economic protection if that is the only justification for it.

3. *innocent passage*—ships have a right to navigate through the territorial waters of another state provided such waters (straits or channels) connect two bodies of international sea and the passage is carried out in a peaceful manner.

4. *diplomatic immunity*—the ambassador and his senior diplomatic officers are immune from prosecution by foreign governments, even when they may have violated the laws of the host government.

5. *act-of-state doctrine*—governments may not question the legality of the acts of foreign governments, even when the acts of those states would be contrary to the rules and values of the home state.
6. *jurisdiction by flag*—when a crime is committed on a vessel on the high seas, the flag-state has jurisdiction over the crime.
7. *self-defense*—states have the right to use military force in order to defend themselves from foreign aggression.

Although each one of these principles is significant, none of them alone can be assumed to be absolute. In most international conflicts, there are often two or more legal principles at issue; the task is to resolve different legal claims. For example, if a French citizen kills a Japanese citizen on board a Panamanian vessel in American territorial waters, four different states may claim jurisdiction in such a criminal dispute. Similarly, while states generally accept the principle of nonintervention in the domestic affairs of other states, the doctrine of nonintervention is always subject to small qualifications (such as the inability to protect aliens or prior intervention by another state). Principles of international law, thus, need to be interpreted within the context of specific problems.

One of the important aspects of international law concerns the settlement of disputes. According to international law, states are bound to settle their disputes peacefully. So long as the parties are seeking to resolve the conflict through pacific means, no illegal economic, political, or military force may be used. When a party to a conflict uses illegal force, however, the other state may respond in kind. Such illegal acts that are short of war (reprisal) may include an embargo, a boycott, or a blockade.

The practice of war is also covered by international law. On the one hand, numerous laws and principles have been established on how to fight wars. The Hague Conventions of 1899 and 1907, for example, developed numerous laws covering combatants and noncombatants. Subsequent conventions and protocols have sought to regulate the use of poisonous gases, the protection of museums and historic sites, and the rights of prisoners of war. On the other hand, states have sought not just to regulate war but to eliminate it altogether. This effort was most explicitly made in the Kellogg-Briand Pact of 1928, when the parties to that pact agreed to renounce war as an instrument of national policy. Despite numerous efforts to make war illegal, the status of war is not entirely clear today. ARTICLE 2 (4) of the United Nations Charter provides that "all members shall refrain in their international relations from the threat or use of force against the territorial integrity or political independence of any state." This principle, however, is not entirely absolute since the Charter provides that states can use force individually for self-defense (ARTICLE 51) or collectively through the Security Council when peace is threatened or violated (ARTICLES 41–43).

The Application of International Law to Interstate Conflicts

Adjudication is the process of settling legal disputes through a competent court. In a domestic system, adjudication plays an important role in conflict resolution. In the international system, however, the resolution of disputes through law is far more limited, partly because there may be uncertainty over the law itself and partly because of the unwillingness of states to commit a dispute to an international court. In addition, since the distinction between the political and legal realm is clouded in international relations, the decision of whether an issue is justifiable or not is often difficult and can only be determined by politics.

The major institution for resolving international legal disputes is the International Court of Justice (ICJ). Since the ICJ is a formal part of the United Nations, all U.N. members are automatically party to the court. Other states may become part of the court by signing its statute. The ICJ is composed of fifteen judges, elected by the General Assembly for a term of nine years. The court hears two types of cases—contentious cases, which deal with legal disputes between two or more states, and advisory cases, which deal with questions raised by agencies of the United Nations. Since the Court was established in 1946, it has issued judgments in thirty-eight contentious cases and sixteen advisory opinions on questions concerning U.N. operations. A brief review of one contentious case illustrates the work of the ICJ.

The case involves a dispute over fishing limits between Iceland and the United Kingdom, and more specifically with the legitimacy of Iceland's unilateral claim to a fifty-mile fishing zone. The dispute between the two countries erupted in 1972 when Iceland unilaterally extended its exclusive fishing limits to fifty miles. The United Kingdom who, like Iceland, has historically depended on fishing as a source of foreign exchange, requested that the International Court examine Iceland's action and determine whether it was in accord with international law. Although Iceland never participated in the court's deliberations, the ICJ nonetheless determined that it had jurisdiction in the case and issued a judgment on July 25, 1974. The Court indicated by a vote of ten to four that Iceland was not entitled to unilaterally extend its fishing limits and thereby exclude British fishermen from the waters surrounding Iceland. It therefore called on both parties to resolve their dispute through "negotiations in good faith for the equitable solution of their differences."

This case illustrates some of the weaknesses of adjudication as a means of conflict resolution. Although Iceland and Britain were bound to obey the court, Iceland refused to accept the court's judgment. As a result, both states continued to assert their different positions while fishermen continued their nonmilitary actions in what was known as the "cod war." The conflict subsequently abated largely because customary international law appeared to change as a result of the unilateral extension of fishing zones by many states.

As the United States and other major states increased their fishing waters, the customary international law that appeared to be emerging in the late 1970s was an economic zone of two hundred miles. It is expected that when the Third U.N. Conference on the Law of the Sea concludes its deliberations, a large number of states will ratify a convention recognizing a two hundred-mile fishing limit.

There are two major shortcomings to resolving international conflicts through adjudication. The first is that the content of international law is not always clearly defined. Since international law is not made by an international parliament but derives from a variety of general sources, there often is uncertainty about the rules of the international system. This is particularly the case when the major source of international law is custom and that custom may be in the process of change, as was the case in the United Kingdom-Iceland Fisheries Case.

The second shortcoming is that the ICJ does not have automatic jurisdiction over international legal disputes. The jurisdiction of the ICJ is established only when states voluntarily grant it jurisdiction. One of the ways by which states have attempted to strengthen the international judicial process is by giving the ICJ compulsory jurisdiction before conflicts develop. This is done by the "optional clause" of the Statute of the Court (ARTICLE 36), which declares that states "may at any time declare that they recognize as compulsory *ipso facto* and without special agreement, in relation to any other state accepting the same obligation, the jurisdiction of the Court in all legal disputes." Although some forty-five states have adopted the optional clause, few have done so without reservations. The United States, for example, accepted the court's compulsory jurisdiction in 1946, but in accepting the added jurisdiction it did so with a number of reservations. Fundamentally, the reservations provide that the United States government has the right to determine whether an issue is essentially domestic or international in character. Since the ICJ's compulsory jurisdiction is recognized only for international conflicts, the United States ultimately retains control over the question of jurisdiction.

INTERNATIONAL ORGANIZATIONS AND CONFLICT MANAGEMENT

International institutions play a significant role in the international system by facilitating, coordinating, and regulating the behavior of states. There are at least four functions that international organizations can perform: they can regulate the behavior of states in order to minimize the potential of war; they can facilitate the settlement of disputes through pacific means; they can promote the economic and social well-being of humankind; and they can increase and facilitate the level of interdependence among states. Although public and private institutions have played an important role in caring for the economic, social, and medical needs of people, the fundamental problem in the international system is the continuing of violence and war. Ultimately, the success of international organizations needs to be gauged by their effectiveness in making the international system a safer and more secure environment.

Types of International Organizations

International organizations can be classified into governmental and non-governmental institutions. Governmental institutions are organizations whose members are official government delegations from nation-states. The most important one is the United Nations; other public international organizations include the World Health Organization, the Organization of American States, the International Rice Commission, the Organization of Petroleum Exporting Countries, the International Coffee Organization, the International Telecommunication Union, and the International Labor Organization. As Figure 15.1 indicates, during the twentieth century there has been a dramatic growth in the number of governmental international organizations (from 20 to more than 225 in 1974).

Figure 15.1   The Growth of International Organizations (1875 to 1970)

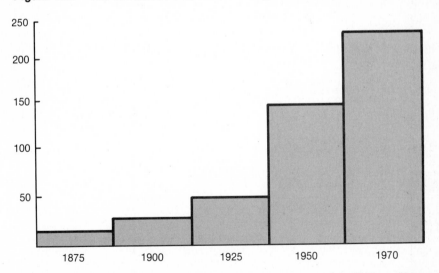

Source: *Union of International Associations,* Yearbook of International Organizations 1974, *vol. 15 (Brussels: UIA, 1974).*

Nongovernmental international organizations are private international associations that seek to facilitate cooperation in areas such as religion, culture, science, and economics. Examples of such organizations include the following: the League of Red Cross Societies, the World Jewish Congress, the World Federation of Trade Unions, the World Alliance of Young Men's Christian Associations, the International Bar Association, Amnesty International, and The Salvation Army. Although nongovernmental associations are much more numerous (in 1975 there were more than twenty-five hundred such organizations), they tend to be much more limited in their scope and to have smaller professional staffs. The size of such organizations is generally less than ten people, and the average yearly budget tends to be less than 1 million dollars. While private international associations do facilitate the growth of interdependency among states, their role is limited in managing and resolving international conflict. We shall therefore be concerned only with governmental organizations and how they contribute to the development of a more orderly and peaceful world.

Governmental international organizations can be classified according to their membership size and scope of purpose. Figure 15.2 illustrates some of the major types of organizations based upon these two criteria. The limited-purpose organizations tend to be concerned primarily with a particular functional area, such as social need, economic trade, military defense, professional and technical cooperation, etc. General-purpose organizations, by contrast, deal with numerous different areas, including the most difficult issues of international aggression and war.

Figure 15.2   Typology of International Governmental Institutions

PURPOSE

	General	Specific
Global	United Nations League of Nations	International Monetary Fund World Health Organization Universal Postal Union
Regional	Organization of American States Organization of African Unity European Economic Community	Inter-American Development Bank Latin American Free Trade Association North Atlantic Treaty Organization

MEMBERSHIP

What is the role of these different types of institutions in building world order? One school assumes that the most effective organizations in building world order are general-purpose institutions, which can deal directly with political incompatibilities among states. Although none of the international governmental organizations has sovereign authority over states, many observers believe that existing global and regional institutions can and do play an important role in creating an international political consensus. Within this school, some emphasize the importance of global organizations like the United Nations; others, on the other hand, believe that regional organizations like the Organization of American States and the European Economic Community can play a limited but significant preliminary role in building regional order.

Another school (which we earlier called functionalism) assumes that the most important role for international organizations is not to manage and resolve political conflict but to facilitate international cooperation in nonpolitical areas. The international organizations most helpful in creating socioeconomic interdependence are the limited-purpose governmental organizations and the private international associations that promote cooperative action along specific functional areas. Organizations strengthening social, economic, cultural, and technical cooperation can play an essential role in building world order by helping establish the foundation on which international peace can be established and maintained.

The United Nations

Background In the twentieth century there have been two major global efforts to institutionalize peace keeping—the League of Nations, established following the First World War, and the United Nations, created in 1945 as a replacement for the League. Established primarily as an effort to promote world peace, the League was based on the theory of collective security, which emphasized an open, public, and collective effort to thwart international aggression. Woodrow Wilson, father of the League, believed that if a general association of states could be formed to preserve the integrity of states and encourage "open covenants, openly arrived at,"[10] the threat of war would decline significantly. Although the League did contribute toward peace-keeping efforts in the immediate postwar period, most students of international organization regard the League as a failure—partly because it was unable to resolve international disputes in the 1930s but ultimately because it was unable to prevent the Second World War. Three reasons are often given for its failure: the United States failed to join the League; the assumptions about peace keeping were unduly optimistic; and the League was tied to the Treaty of Versailles (which ended the War), thus freezing power relations between the victors and the vanquished. Perhaps the major contribution of the League is that it provided an experiment in international organization on which a subsequent, more effective institution could be established.

The Charter of the United Nations was created at the Conference on International Organization in San Francisco in 1945. Previously, statesmen from the major powers had met in Dumbarton Oaks in 1944 and at Yalta in February 1945 to work out preliminary proposals for the new organization. Following two months of deliberations at San Francisco, the U.S. Charter was signed by delegates from 51 nations. The new organization began operating on October 24, 1945. As of 1976, there were 146 member states in the United Nations.

Purposes   ARTICLE 1 of the U.N. Charter lists four goals: to maintain peace and international security; to ensure friendly relations among states on the basis of equal rights and self-determination of peoples; to foster international cooperation on economic, social, humanitarian, and cultural concerns and to promote respect for human rights; and to facilitate international relations to achieve the above political and nonpolitical aims. Although the fundamental purpose of the United Nations is to achieve and facilitate harmonious relations among states, in practice the dominant types of activities have been those relating to the nonpolitical sphere. Of the regular United Nations budget, for example, about 15 percent of the total expenditures are allocated to the maintenance of peace and security.[11] If voluntary contributions to the United Nations operations are included (nearly 60 percent of all U.N. activities are paid for by voluntary contributions rather than assessments on states), the proportion is even less.

Organization   The major organs of the United Nations are the General Assembly, the Security Council, the Economic and Social Council, the Trusteeship Council, the International Court of Justice, and the Secretariat. Figure 15.3 illustrates the major relationships among the various organs.

The major responsibility for peace keeping is in the hands of the *Security Council.* The council is composed of fifteen member states, five permanent and ten nonpermanent. The five permanent members represent the major powers of the world — China, France, the Soviet Union, the United Kingdom, and the United States. The remaining states are elected by the General Assembly for two-year terms. Unlike the League's council, which had limited power, the Security Council has substantial authority to manage and resolve international conflicts — provided the members of the Security Council can agree on what to do. In order for the council to implement any action, it needs the concurrence of nine states. Procedural issues — that is, issues not considered important by the big powers — need nine affirmative votes from any of the states. Substantive issues, however, require nine votes, including those of the

Figure 15.3   Organization of the United Nations

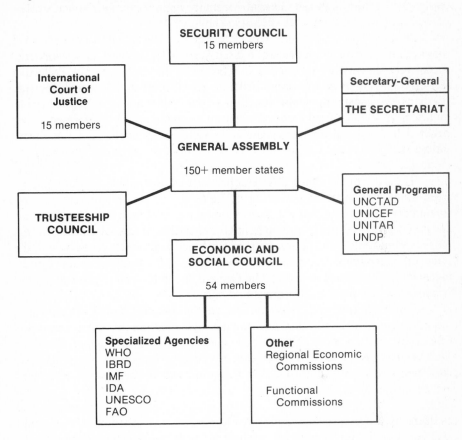

five permanent members. Thus, when any major power opposes (vetoes) a Security Council action, it can effectively prohibit any action. The principal types of actions the Security Council may undertake include: establishing general peace-keeping guidelines (such as Resolution 242 on the Arab-Israeli conflict); recommending political action to preserve peace (such as the establishment of a provisional truce in Cyprus in 1974); involving nonmilitary action against states threatening world peace (such as the economic sanctions invoked against Rhodesia in 1965); and using military force to resolve an international conflict (as was done in the Congo in 1960).

The other primary organ of the United Nations is the *General Assembly*. All member states are represented in this chamber; each state has one vote. Decisions on important issues require a two-thirds majority, while other issues are decided by simple majority. The regular session of the General Assembly begins in September and continues through the end of the year and often into early spring. Although the General Assembly resembles a parliament in that there is much opportunity for discussion and debate, the effective authority of the assembly is quite limited. The U.N. Charter (ARTICLES 10 through 17) provides that its major duties are to discuss, study, and review issues and then make recommendations. It does not have the authority to take collective action to maintain international order or to facilitate conflict management. Perhaps the most important function of the General Assembly is that it provides an international forum for continued dialogue among representatives from all states. Even when the General Assembly is not in session, U.N. diplomats can continue to meet informally to discuss issues of international concern.

The work of the General Assembly is carried out by seven major committees, along with other ad hoc groups. The General Assembly may also create subsidiary organs, such as the U.N. Conference on Trade and Development and the U.N. Industrial Development Organization, to facilitate international cooperation and coordination in specific functional areas. In addition, the General Assembly is responsible for overseeing and coordinating the various agencies of the United Nations. The General Assembly makes the budget and receives reports from U.N. organs and agencies.

The other four organs of the United Nations play a significant role in coordinating and facilitating the international relations of states but a less important role in managing political conflict. The *International Court of Justice,* as noted already, is responsible for settling legal disputes among states who desire to submit cases to it. The *Economic and Social Council,* composed of fifty-four members, is primarily concerned with international socioeconomic concerns, while the *Trusteeship Council* deals with the status and welfare of the non-self-governing territories, such as Namibia (South-West Africa). Finally, the *Secretariat,* headed by the secretary-general, provides the staff support for the various agencies and organs of the United Nations. The staff of the Secretariat comprises an international civil service of some twelve thousand persons, approximately one-half of whom work at the U.S. headquarters in New York City. Besides serving as chief administrative officer of the U.N., the secretary-general can play an important role in peace-keeping activities, as was demonstrated by Dag Hammarskjold, who held the post from 1953 until his death in the Congo in 1961.

Evaluation   In reviewing the role of the United Nations over the past thirty-five years, it is easy to criticize the institution for not being more effective in promoting world harmony. We need to keep in mind, however, that the United Nations is not an international government but a loose association of states that has continued to exist because of the voluntary desires of sovereign states. The United Nations, in other words, does not determine international relations; rather, international relations determine the role and contribution of the United Nations. The only influence the United Nations possesses in world affairs is that which emanates from the cooperative action of states.

One of the strengths of the United Nations is that political actions designed to maintain peace can only be carried out if there is substantial harmony. Since peace-keeping actions of the Security Council require agreeement among the five permanent members, a vigorous role for the Security Council has been possible only when there has been big power harmony. But this strength is also a weakness; since the major powers seldom agree on issues of conflict management, the United Nations is often unable to deal effectively with threats to peace. As a result, the United Nations has been able to carry out significant political action only when there has been substantial political consensus. In short, if the United Nations has been unable to deal effectively with international conflicts, the fundamental reason is not within the organization itself but within the international system it is designed to represent.

An example illustrates the problem. During the 1970s the major tension within the international system focused on economic concerns between the developed, industrial states (North) and the less developed nations (South). This tension is dramatically illustrated over the concern for deep-sea mining — an issue that has been discussed at the ongoing U.N. Conference on the Law of the Sea. The central conflict between the two groups of states focused on whether mining of ocean resources should be governed by an International Seabed Authority or whether states themselves can undertake such mining on their own. The developed states, who possess the technology for deep-sea mining, argued that states should have the right to carry out their own mining efforts. The developing nations, on the other hand, opposed such action because they do not have the means to reap the economic benefits from the ocean floor. Although the deep-sea mining issue has been discussed and debated during the more than seven years of the ongoing Third Law of the Sea Conference, the U.N. discussions have been unable to resolve the dispute. Thus, the inability to resolve the conflict can be interpreted either as a failure or a strength of international organization. It is a failure because the United Nations has been unable to resolve the dispute. On the other hand, it is a strength because the conference deliberations accurately reflect the political tensions between North and South.

But the United Nations has been more than a mere reflection of the political dynamics of the world. Because the United Nations is the only international organization where leaders of all states can exchange views and discuss common concerns, the international organization has served as an important medium for building global community. This is particularly the case in the General Assembly, where representatives from all states have the opportunity of continuing dialogue. In addition, the United Nations has played a significant role in promoting and coordinating common social and economic activities. The peoples of the Third World have benefited enormously from the social, economic, and health programs it has established or supported. Finally, the United Nations has strengthened transnational relations through international programs covering economic, cultural, social, and technical concerns. The United Nations, in short, has helped to facilitate interdependence, although the results of these nonpolitical efforts have yet to be clearly demonstrated in the political realm.

SUMMARY

There are six major approaches to peace keeping: balance of power, collective security, world government, pacific settlement of disputes, functionalism, and disarmament. The first three are primarily concerned with managing power, while the last three attempt to avoid or eliminate power.

Balance of power assumes that peace is a direct outcome of maintaining an equilibrium of power; collective security and world government, by contrast, assume that a preponderance of power is the most effective means of keeping peace.

Pacific settlement seeks to resolve interstate disputes by reducing misperception and misunderstanding between statesmen and, where possible, by applying international law. Functionalism seeks to create world harmony by establishing functional interdependencies among states. Given the intractability of international disputes, the functional approach seeks to create socioeconomic ties that will have a beneficial "spillover" effect into the political arena. Finally, disarmament seeks to encourage world peace by decreasing or eliminating the instruments for waging war. The theory of disarmament is based on the assumption that the arms race is itself a source of interstate tension.

One of the important sources of world order is international law. Although international law does not have the same legitimacy in the world that national law has in states, there is substantial agreement and compliance with the commonly accepted rules, customs, and principles of international law. Since there is no international government to effectively enforce international law, most compliance is the result of voluntary action by states. When disputes over international law arise, states may use the International Court of Justice to adjudicate disputes.

The major international organization for building world harmony is the United Nations. Its major institutions are the General Assembly (the world's parliament) and the Security Council, the fifteen-member agency responsibile for peace keeping.

KEY TERMS

balance of power	functionalism
collective security	EEC
League of Nations	disarmament
world government	international law
pacific settlement	International Court of Justice
mediation	General Assembly
arbitration	Security Council

NOTES

1. A.F.K. Organski *World Politics* (New York: Alfred A. Knopf, 1958), p. 292.
2. For an excellent critique of balance of power see Chapter 3 of Inis L. Claude, Jr., *Power and International Relations* (New York: Random House, 1962).
3. Robert M. Hutchins, "World Government for Now" in ed. Robert A. Goldwin, *Readings in World Politics,* 2nd ed. (New York: Oxford University Press, 1970), p. 523.
4. See Greenville Clark and Louis B. Sohn, *World Peace Through World Law,* 3rd ed. enlarged (Cambridge: Harvard University Press, 1966).
5. See David Mitrany, *A Working Peace System* (Chicago: Quadrangle Books, 1966).
6. See Lewis Richardson, *Arms and Insecurity* (Pittsburgh: Boxwood Press, 1960) and *Statistics of Deadly Quarrels* (Chicago: Quadrangle Books, 1960).
7. Hans Morgenthau, *Politics Among Nations: The Struggle for Power and Peace,* 5th ed. rev. (New York: Random House, 1978), p. 510.
8. Michael Akehurst, *A Modern Introduction to International Law,* 3rd ed. rev. (London: George Allen and Unwin, 1978), p. 30.
9. Roger Fisher, *International Conflict for Beginners* (New York: Harper & Row, 1969), pp. 151–77.
10. This is one of the major points of Woodrow Wilson's "Fourteen Points," which served as a basis for the Treaty of Versailles as well as for the foundation of the League of Nations.
11. See Harold K. Jacobson, *Networks of Interdependence: International Organizations and the Global Political System* (New York: Alfred A. Knopf, 1979), pp. 85–6.

SUGGESTED READING

AKEHURST, MICHAEL. *A Modern Introduction to International Law.* 3rd ed. London: George Allen and Unwin, 1977. A Lucid, up-to-date introduction to international law.

BRIERLY, J. L. *The Law of Nations.* 6th ed. New York: Oxford University Press, 1963. A classic introductory volume on the role of international law in world politics.

CLAUDE, INIS, L., JR. *Power and International Relations.* New York: Random House, 1962. A penetrating analysis of three major modes of managing international power — balance of power, collective security, and world government.

———. *Swords Into Plowshares: The Problems and Progress of International Organization.* 4th ed. New York: Random House, 1971. An analytical introduction to the role of international governmental organizations in the international system. The text focuses on the problems of the League of Nations and the United Nations and examines major approaches of peace keeping through international organizations.

HENKIN, LOUIS. *How Nations Behave: Law and Foreign Policy.* 2nd ed. New York: Columbia University Press, 1979. A distinguished authority on international law explains through examples and cases how international law influences the foreigh-policy process.

JACOBSON, HAROLD K. *Networks of Interdependence: International Organizations and the Global Political System.* New York: Alfred A. Knopf, 1979. An introductory international-organization text focusing on the role of public and private international institutions in world affairs.

NICHOLAS, H. G. *The United Nations as a Political Institution.* 5th ed. New York: Oxford University Press, 1977. An analysis of the evolution and major organs of the United Nations.

NICOLSON, HAROLD. *Diplomacy.* 3rd ed. New York: Oxford University Press, 1973. A concise survey of the evolution, nature, role, and procedures of diplomacy by a noted British statesman.

STOESSINGER, JOHN G. *The United Nations and the Superpowers: China, Russia, and America.* 4th ed. New York: Random House, 1977. An analysis of some of the major great power tensions as they have related to the United Nations.

16 /A CONCLUDING NOTE

In the previous chapters we have suggested that the central issue in political science is the problem of community. This problem involves the search for and the implementation of a desirable balance between the claims of freedom and the claims of social order. Individual freedom is essential in all creative, dynamic existence. At the same time, community harmony and consensus must provide a foundation for individual freedom if life is to be meaningful. Although individuals can maximize their absolute freedom by living in isolation, the only meaningful and desirable freedom is that which is achieved within the context of community norms.

The development and maintenance of peaceful, harmonious, and dynamic communities is not an automatic result of social relations. Indeed, because people misuse their freedom and pursue their particular interests in disregard for, or at the expense of, the interests of others, community life is often conflictual, unstable, and precarious. The fundamental task of politics is thus to build and maintain peaceful and just communities where the legitimate interests of individuals and groups are protected within the context of social order.

THREE CONCLUSIONS ABOUT CONFLICT MANAGEMENT

Our analysis of the problem of community has used the conflict-management perspective. We have suggested that an automatic byproduct of social and political relationships is conflict. The basic task within political communities is not to eradicate social conflict but rather to manage it so that the desirable results of human tensions and incompatibilities can be preserved. Although there are numerous lessons and insights suggested by our examination of conflict management within contemporary nation-states, three general conclusions merit special emphasis.

First, conflict management is a continuous process in all communities. Whether the conflicts are at the interpersonal, intergroup, or intercommunity level, the management and resolution of human incompatibilities is a never-ending process. Since conflicts arise continuously out of the fabric of social relations, there is a constant need to cope with, and when necessary, to manage and resolve human tensions. The need to manage conflicts is greatest when the tensions become violent and destructive. But regardless of the nature and scope of social conflict, all communities must develop and institutionalize processes of conflict management. Indeed, the political maturity of a nation arises not from the suppression or elimination of conflict but rather from the development of institutions to channel and help resolve political and social conflicts.

A second major conclusion is that there are no easy, ready-made solutions in the conflict-management process. Whether the tensions and incompatibilities are between individuals, groups, or states, the management and resolution of conflicts is always a difficult and complex task. Each community must utilize its own resources, abilities, and traditions in dealing with the problem of community building. Moreover, the methods and approaches used in managing and resolving conflict must be based on the interests, orientations, and values of the community. Although the author believes that the participatory-democratic approach to conflict management has decisive advantages over the authoritarian model, it must be recognized that there are no perfect models and ideal approaches that have universal applicability. Many new Third World countries, for example, have been concerned with the development of effective governmental institutions and political processes. The experience to date suggests that the application of Western political practices has not always been possible nor, in some instances, desirable. Rather, Third World political development suggests that the creation of effective governmental institutions requires that the conflict-management processes be based on indigenous customs and values.

A third general conclusion is that the most effective, long-term approach to conflict management involves compromise. The imposition of order through force is certainly possible. But when conflict is resolved through an imposed settlement by either a third party or a participant to the dispute, parties in conflict continue to desire and even pursue their original interests. On the other hand, if incompatible interests are reconciled through compromise — i.e., by the mutual acceptance of a second-best position — then parties tend to view the solution as permanent. Effective conflict resolution requires flexibility and patience. Flexibility is necessary in achieving compromises, while time is essential in generating alternatives acceptable to parties in conflict.

Given the need for flexibility and adaptibility in the conflict-management process, political leaders need to be skeptical of approaches and methods that seek to manage and resolve social and political tensions through quick, ready-made solutions. More significantly, they need to resist the temptation to assume that there are simple, ideal solutions to the complex problems within contemporary states. Jean-Francois Revel in *The Totalitarian Temptation* suggests that in the contemporary world there is a bias or "temptation" in favor of the Marxist totalitarian political solution. This urge for a quick solution for the ills and problems of contemporary democratic states is found, he believes, chiefly in Western European states and is based partly on the people's ignorance of the proposed Marxist-Leninist solutions. Concerned with the need for economic justice and the improvement in human existence, the people accept the Stalinist approach not because of their desire to replicate the conditions and experiences of China and the Soviet Union but to avoid the problems and tensions in their own states.[1] The totalitarian solution is popular because it offers hope — because it provides a quick, ideal solution to the human predicaments of modern democratic states.

Despite the attractiveness of theories and ideologies that purport to "solve" the human predicament, we must recognize that human existence involves tragedy, pain, and loss. The maintenance of harmonious and just communities can never be realized completely. The creation and maintenance of political communities will always be imperfect and incomplete. The task of government is not to "solve" the problem of community (an impossible task) but to seek to refine community life through incremental policies and adjustments in the political order. Reinhold Niebuhr, one of the most perceptive twentieth-century students of human nature, observes that, "A free society requires some confidence in the ability of men to reach tentative and tolerable adjustments between their competing interests and to arrive at some common notions of justice which transcend all partial interests."[2] In approaching the problem of community, however, we must not be too optimistic nor too pessimistic. Man's capacity for community makes authentic freedom possible; yet man's capacity for conflict and disorder makes politics inevitable.

DEVELOPMENTS COMPLICATING CONFLICT MANAGEMENT

Although science and technology have brought the human race much progress, the task of maintaining and strengthening political communities in the contemporary world has not become easier. Indeed, a review of the daily news suggests that the world in which we live is continuously becoming more complex, heterogeneous, and ungovernable. Commentators on the "human prospect" disagree on the future of the human race. Some tend to be optimistic, others pessimistic. But regardless of the basic orientations toward human nature and the impact of modernity, there are a number of developments that have complicated the conflict-management process in contemporary political communities. Some of these changes apply chiefly to local and national concerns, while others relate to the international environment. Of the many social, scientific, and technological developments affecting the governing of modern political societies, the following six changes are particularly significant.

1. Modern states have experienced an increasing breakdown in traditional patterns and values that have historically served as a stabilizing force in society. All communities need common values and norms to preserve social order. The impact of secularization and modernization have threatened and, in many cases, destroyed traditional values and social patterns. The older generation has found it difficult to pass along its customs and orientations to its children. More significantly, not only have young people refused to accept traditional norms but have in many cases been unable to find norms to replace the old ones. As a result, society has become more atomistic — more concerned with the interests of individuals than with general community goals. In the United States the breakdown in traditional values has been particularly evident in the weakening of family ties and in the increasing alienation of young people.

2. Another change is the growth of urbanization. The continued expansion of urban settlements is important because it increases the proportion of society that is politicized, i.e., the number of people who are interested in political decision making and in making claims on those in government authority. Although urbanization is important in both developed and developing nations, it is particularly significant in the Third World, for many of these states are not well-prepared to cope with major population shifts from rural to urban areas. Since urbanization tends to raise the expectations of people, many developing nations find it not only politically destabilizing but costly. While many beneficial developments are associated with urbanization (such as the growing demands placed on literacy, education, the mass media, and social services), the move of large numbers of peoples into cities places enormous economic and social burdens, which, if unmet, can lead to political unrest. Urbanization is thus expected to place heavy conflict-management burdens on many developing nations.

3. Another change acutely felt in the Third World is the population explosion. It has been estimated that by the year 2000 the world population will be between 6 and 6.5 billion persons. While the population of the developed states is expected to grow at less than 1 percent per year, the population of the developing nations is expected to grow by more than 2 percent per year. Since the growth of population will be most extreme in the poorest nations, world hunger will continue to be a major challenge in many Asian, African, and Latin American nations. More generally,

population growth will bring about significant social and educational needs in developing nations, which could result in growing tensions among states over the distribution of economic resources.

4. Another significant change is the proliferation of military arms. The world currently spends more than 450 billion dollars on armaments per year, of which more than one-half is accounted for by the Soviet Union and the United States. Of the various military arms posing a threat to mankind, the most dangerous and destructive are those with nuclear weapons. Both the United States and the Soviet Union possess sufficient nuclear bombs to virtually annihilate each other. (One twenty-megaton bomb has approximately one thousand times the destructive force of the Hiroshima bomb.) Partly because of the increasing threat of nuclear weapons, Richard Falk suggests that future decades will be increasingly grim: the 1980s will be characterized by a Politics of Desperation, the 1990s by a Politics of Catastrophe, and the twenty-first century as an Era of Annihilation.[3]

Despite the potential of nuclear weapons, the violence and destruction in domestic and international wars in postwar years have been carried out through conventional arms. In fact, according to the Brandt Report on International Development (a report by a commission of fifteen distinguished statesmen chaired by former Chancellor of West Germany Willy Brandt), all wars since 1945 have been fought with conventional arms and have resulted in more than 10 million deaths in the Third World.[4] Thus, while nuclear weapons pose the major threat, the immediate challenge is to limit the sale and use of conventional arms.

5. Another significant feature of the modern world is the increasing dependence on scarce raw materials. As nations develop economically, they become more dependent on mineral resources and other primary products. This dependence makes some industrial countries particularly vulnerable to nations that export essential products such as oil, bauxite, and uranium. As the world becomes more industrialized, bringing about a greater demand for scarce economic resources, international competition for such materials inevitably leads to more competition and the potential for international conflicts. While greater economic interdependence may strengthen international political ties among many states, it may also lead to more difficulties in building a peaceful and just world system.

6. A sixth development is the loss of a sense of direction. This lack of direction ironically coincides with the enormous scientific and managerial developments that which have provided increasing control over the activities of people. Some of these developments include the information revolution brought about by the computer (and more recently by the

minicomputer), the increasing speed and facility of travel, the development of new (nuclear and nonnuclear) energy sources, and the ability to influence genetic qualities through DNA manipulation. Although science and technology have brought significant improvements in the quality of life, there have also been unintended negative effects, such as the threat posed by nuclear power plants, the pollution of cars and jets, and the destruction of the natural environment.

More significantly, as modernization improves the ability to care for the needs of people, the increasing choices as to how societies should respond to human needs and wants have resulted in greater uncertainty concerning fundamental goals and directions. In the early part of the century, it was commonly assumed that progress involved economic modernization, by which society could improve levels of living. But as nations achieved higher standards of living, uncertainty has been increasing about the desirability of growth. Whereas in the 1950s and 1960s Americans believed that more possessions would improve the quality of life, by the 1970s many of them had begun to believe that small is beautiful, that less is more. In short, people in industrial states are increasingly less certain about what direction society should take—about what constitutes the *summum bonum* (or highest good). As a result, Western industrial nations are increasingly facing major political disputes over what policies governments should pursue. The expression of these policy difficulties is, of course, based on the more basic, foundational uncertainties about the meaning of social progress.

None of the developments mentioned above poses an insuperable barrier to the maintenance of vigorous, dynamic, and peaceful communities. But these social, technological, and scientific changes do pose significant challenges to the conflict-management process of states and to the world community itself. If people are flexible and open to the challenges posed by these and other related developments, political communities will prosper and grow, as they have in the past. In coping with political challenges of the future, it is less significant that people, groups, and states pursue "correct" policies but far more important that they carry out their actions with an adequate strategy— an approach that facilitates the building and maintenance of mature political systems.

Strategies of Conflict Management

In looking toward the future, there are four fundamental approaches people can adopt in confronting problems and conflicts within their communities. These four strategies are based on different levels of commitment toward two types of interests—those that are general and pertain to the community at large and those that are specific and pertain to individual goals of a person or group. Since conflicts always arise within a social or political context, individuals must decide to what extent they are committed to their particular interests and to those that pertain to the community at large. The different levels of commitment to general and specific interests results in different conflict-management approaches.

Figure 16.1 illustrates four basic approaches to problems and conflicts arising in political communities. The *isolationist strategy* represents a low level of concern for both the particular interests of individuals and groups as well as for the common interests of the community itself. Those who practice this strategy are chiefly concerned with the avoidance of tensions and incompatibilities. They assume that no specific or general policies are worth pursuing, since they may lead to social and political conflict. The best strategy is partial isolation from the tensions and problems of community. Although conducive to social order, this approach leads to a weak, lethargic society. This strategy does not seek to manage and resolve conflict but to avoid it altogether.

Figure 16.1   Strategies of Conflict Management

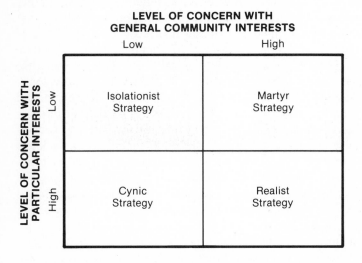

The *martyr strategy* places a much higher value on common community concerns than on specific interests of individuals and groups. The chief concern of this approach involves maximization of the community's general welfare. A key assumption is that common interests must be pursued directly and forcefully and that specific, particular interests must be minimized. This approach has the advantage in that it places a much higher value on the community welfare than does the isolationist strategy. It shares the disadvantage, however, that particular concerns of individuals or interest groups are viewed as contrary to community-building. Although individuals, interest groups, and political parties can and do pursue policies that may be contrary to the general community welfare, the search for and implementation of policies and programs supporting the common good are not found independently of the specific concerns of community members. Indeed, the general interest is found partly out of the competing interests of individuals themselves.

The *cynic strategy* assumes that there is no general community interest — only an aggregate of special interests. The cynic thus believes that the best approach is to maximize particular goals, even at the expense of others. Although this approach has the advantage of creating a highly dynamic environment, it places the community in jeopardy because of the limited concern with the common community concerns. Since the goal is to win at all costs, this strategy does not facilitate conflict management. This strategy is illustrated by the foreign policies of nation-states. The fundamental aim of states is to maximize their national interests, even if the pursuit of those interests further weakens the world community or even leads to war.

The *realist strategy* is characterized by a high commitment to both general and specific interests. Of the four strategies, it is not only the best but also the only one likely to guarantee effective community-building. Rather than seek to suppress or disregard conflict, the realist approach assumes that the expression of competitive and incompatible interests is not only desirable but also essential to the development of a strong community. At the same time it recognizes the importance of social and political order. This strategy thus seeks to balance the claims of the community with the claims of individuals. When parties pursue a realist strategy, they vigorously pursue both general and particular objectives; when conflicts arise, the parties resolve their differences through flexible accommodation. A central feature of this strategy is compromise. Adjustment and flexibility are not viewed as conditions of weakness but as sources of strength in building strong and dynamic political systems. Unlike other approaches, conflict is accepted as a quality of human existence from which social order must be forged. The realist strategy is thus committed to building and strengthening community life by managing and resolving conflicts.

The future is uncertain, and the challenges within and between contemporary states are not likely to become easier. Of the many challenges of the future, creating and maintaining dynamic political communities remains one of the most significant tasks. If people remain sensitive to their own needs and wants and to those of others, the task of community-building will be greatly facilitated. We cannot isolate ourselves from the towns, provinces, and nations of which we are a part. Our task is to proceed tentatively and flexibly as we seek to strengthen our political communities. The realist strategy may not provide solutions but it offers the only reasonable hope.

NOTES

1. Jean-Francois Revel, *The Totalitarian Temptation* (Garden City, N. Y.: Double-day and Co., Inc., 1977), pp. 23–37.
2. Reinhold Niebuhr, *The Children of Light and the Children of Darkness* (New York: Charles Scribner's Sons, 1944), p. xii.
3. Richard Falk, *The Endangered Planet* (New York: Random House, 1971), p. 420.
4. Willy Brandt et al., *North-South: A Programme for Survival; Report of the Independent Commission on International-Development Issues* (Cambridge: MIT Press, 1980), p. 120.

GLOSSARY

adjudication   The resolution of a dispute through the application of relevant statutes and legal principles

agitation   In the Soviet Union, the practice of Communist party officials mobilizing people to action

All-Union Party Congress   The plenary congress of the Soviet Communist party, which meets every five years to approve the general policies and directions to be pursued by party organs

amendment   An alteration or addition to a bill, motion, or constitution

anarchism   A political ideology advocating the abolition of government

anarchy   A disorderly society because of the absence of government authority

arbitration   The use of an outside party to resolve a dispute; once the disputing parties agree to the terms of arbitration, the arbitrator's settlement is binding

autarchy   National self-sufficiency, particularly with reference to the production and distribution of goods

authoritarian   A government or political system where individual rights are not protected and where rulers govern with limited consent

authority   The ability of an institution or person to command compliance

autonomous republic   A provincial government, based significantly on ethnic ties, found within the union republics of the Soviet political system

balance of power   A peace-keeping approach that assumes that world peace is best maintained through an equilibrium of power

bicameral legislature   A legislative assembly consisting of two chambers

bourgeoisie   A commercial, propertied middle class; in Marxist usage, the bourgeoisie represent the owners and managers of the means of production in capitalist society

bureaucracy   A hierarchical and impersonal organization operating with fixed rules and procedures; in a political system, the bureaucracy is the administrative apparatus that supports the application of policies and programs

cabinet   The group of ministers of a government

cabinet government   An executive where power is shared among ministers who are directly and collectively responsible to a parliament

capitalism   An economic system in which the production and distribution of goods and services is largely in private hands

caucus   A closed meeting of party leaders to select candidates or establish policies

Central Committee   The highest official organ of the Soviet Union's Communist party

checks and balances   The notion that the three branches of government should review and balance the work of each other to ensure a limited, constitutional government

chief of state   The symbolic leader of a state; may gain office through election or heredity

442

city-state   A small political system based on a city; as with other types of states, the city-state is an independent, sovereign political system

civil law   The body of law established by states to protect citizen rights; also the tradition of Roman or codified law

civil service   The administrative organization of government designed to implement and apply its policies and programs; excludes military personnel

civil society   A political society where government has sovereign authority

coalition government   A cabinet government where two or more parties share power in order to achieve a parliamentary majority; the distribution of ministerial posts is generally based on the party's parliamentary strength

collective responsibility   A cabinet that is collectively responsible or accountable for the actions of the executive; in practice, this means that ministers must support all major government policies or resign

collective security   An agreement among states that an attack on one member state by another state will result in retaliation by all others

collegial executive   A plural executive, such as a cabinet government

common law   A body of law based on judicial precedents

communism   The Marxist-Leninist ideology that seeks to create a classless society where people work according to their abilities and are rewarded according to their needs

competitive political system   A political system in which political parties openly and freely compete for office and carry out continuing debate and evaluation of government programs

compromise   The reconciliation of incompatible goals by accepting an alternative mutually acceptable goal

conciliation   The efforts to peacefully resolve a dispute through the assistance of a neutral third party

confederal state   A union of political communities for mutual support and common action, with ultimate authority residing in each of the participating units; power is decentralized

conference committee   A U.S. congressional committee composed of members from the Senate and the House to work out a compromise between different versions of a bill passed by each chamber

consensus   Widespread agreement about community principles and issues

consent   Explicit or implicit agreement with aims, goals, policies, and programs

constitution   The written or unwritten rules by which a state is governed; generally, the duties and responsibilities of each branch of government are defined

constitutionalism   The practice of maintaining a limited or constitutional government; the scope of government is effectively circumscribed

Council of Ministers   The cabinet of the Soviet political system; its members are accountable, in theory, to the Soviet Union's legislature, the Supreme Soviet

coup d'etat   A forceful and illegal overthrow of the government

Crown   The symbol of supreme executive authority in parliamentary systems with hereditary monarchs

democracy   A regime where decision-making authority is ultimately in the hands of the people

democratic centralism   The practice in the Soviet Union of making Communist party decisions of higher bodies unconditionally binding on lower-ranking institutions

dependency theory   A neo-Marxist theory explaining world poverty; according to this perspective, the world is divided into centers and peripheries, with gains from international transactions always in favor of the developed center states

deterrence   In international relations, the policy of preventing military aggression by threatening significant military reprisals

devolution   In Britain, the movement to transfer or devolve some government responsibilities from the Parliament to regional assemblies in Scotland and Wales

dictatorship   A government that gains office without consent and rules in disregard for the common aspirations of people

diplomacy   The practice of carrying out foreign policy through negotiation

direct democracy   A political system where decision making is carried out by the people themselves without representation

disarmament   The effort to minimize war by reducing the military potential of states

elite   A small group of privileged individuals who dominate decision making in a community

elitism   Government by a minority group; belief or advocacy of such government

European Economic Community   An economic union of ten Western European states

federal state   A state with two major levels of government, with states and national institutions having final authority in their respective spheres of influence

feudalism   A paternalistic political system prevailing in Europe during the medieval era

Force   The application of coercion in order to influence behavior

foreign policy   The expression of a nation's interests or goals within the international system

freedom   The ability to make choices because of the absence of restraint or coercion

functionalism   A peace-keeping approach that assumes that socioeconomic integration will encourage the development of interstate peace

General Assembly   The legislative assembly of the United Nations, with each member-state having one seat

government   The institution responsible for making binding rules

human rights   The fundamental rights of individuals, derived from the dignity and essential moral worth of persons

idealism   A political tradition emphasizing ideals and norms by which individual and collective action can be directed

ideology   A systematic set of values, beliefs, and assumptions relating to the creation and maintenance of a nation-state

imperialism   The policy or practice of one state seeking to dominate another

indirect democracy   A form of government in which decisions are made by elected officials; also called representative democracy or republican government

individualism   The doctrine that individual interests are supreme and that the common good results from the collective pursuit of individual gain

indoctrination   The process of formally instructing people in the official ideology or creed of a state

influence   The capacity to alter behavior without coercion

inner cabinet   A small group of leading ministers who work with the prime minister in setting the cabinet's agenda and formulating goals and policies

interest aggregation   The process by which the divergent and often conflicting interests in society are drawn together into a harmonious movement or institution

interest articulation   The expression of shared group or party interests in a political system

interest group   A group that seeks to promote a shared interest

International Court of Justice   The fifteen-member court of the international system; located in The Hague, the ICJ is a formal part of the United Nations

international law   A body of principles, customs, and treaties accepted by states as binding in their international relations

judicial review   The process by which courts rule on the constitutionality of governmental laws and policies

junta   A military government where power is shared collectively by different branches of the armed services

Komsomol   The youth organization of the Soviet Communist party

law   A valid and properly enacted binding rule in society

laws of nature   See natural law

League of Nations   An organization created after World War I to inhibit international aggression and facilitate world peace keeping

legitimacy   The voluntary acceptance and approval of the system of government and its rulers by the people

limited government   A government whose scope of authority is limited and effectively protects human rights; a constitutional regime

lobbying   The attempt by interest groups to influence the actions and policies of government

majority rule   The principle of democratic government that decisions should be based on majority support — that is, one vote more than 50 percent of the total

mediation   The effort to resolve a dispute through the offices of a mediator, a neutral third party who seeks to find an acceptable compromise for both parties

military government   A government controlled by the armed forces

multiparty system   A political system where more than two political parties effectively compete for power

nation   A politically organized nationality or group of nationalities

nation-building   The processes involved in the growth and development of nations

national interests   The basic, fundamental interests of a state

nationalism   The conscious exaltation of the culture, heritage, and political goals of a nation

natural law   The moral or legal principles derived by reason, which are assumed to be binding on persons in their interrelationships

natural rights   The rights of individuals derived from the fundamental moral worth of human beings

neofunctionalism   A peace-keeping approach emphasizing creation of transnational political institutions and economic interdependence among states

nonalignment   The effort to remain neutral in the East-West political struggle

noncompetitive political system   A country where electoral competition or opposition to government actions and policies is not tolerated; the only effective political organization is the ruling party

oblast   A regional-level government unit in the Soviet Union

order   A condition of stability and tranquility

pacific settlement of disputes   A peace-keeping approach that assumes that as passion is eliminated and more factual information becomes available, the resolution of disputes will be facilitated

parliamentary system   A political system where executive and legislative responsibilities are fused in a parliament; executive authority is in the hands of a cabinet, which is responsible to the legislature

party discipline   The ability of party legislators to work as a bloc because of strict principles of organization

patriotism   The public expression of approval and support for the political system in which people live

peer   A British lord; a person holding a title of nobility and therefore eligible for membership in the House of Lords

planning   The practice of seeking to guide and direct public or private affairs through the establishment of procedures for setting and implementing goals

pluralism   The existence of numerous different religious, social, and political groups, each of which is accepted as valid and legitimate

plurality   The voting procedure by which electoral victory is gained through an excess, or plurality, of votes over those of opposing candidates

Politburo   The polical bureau of the Central Committee of the Soviet Union's Communist party; it is the highest decision-making organ of the Soviet Union as well as in other Communist countries

political culture   The dominant set of basic political assumptions and values within a political system

political development   The process by which political institutions and processes become more effective and efficient

political equality   The principle that people should be treated equally in the affairs of state, regardless of race, sex, or creed

political participation   The individual or collective effort to seek to influence the selection of government personnel and/or the actions they pursue

political party   A political organization that attempts to promote its values and concerns by electing officials to positions in government

political socialization   The process by which members of a political community learn its political culture—that is, the community's basic political values and orientations

popular sovereignty   The notion that ultimate decision-making authority is in the hands of all members of a political community

political system   A conceptual framework highlighting major governmental institutions and political processes within the state or some other type of community

politics   The actions and activities involved in developing harmonious policies out of the conflicting interests within society; the efforts involved in managing social conflict within the state

poll   A survey to measure public opinion

power   The ability to gain compliance because of the use (or threat of use) of coercion; power is not an entity but a capability

presidential system   A political system where executive, legislative, and judicial responsibilities are in separate branches

primary party organization   The lowest level of Communist party institutions; originally called the party cell, the PPO is the organization that recruits members and communicates party interests to the general public

prime minister   The head of government in a parliamentary system

private sector   The domain in society regulated primarily by the private interests of individuals and groups; refers chiefly to the economic sphere of society that is privately controlled

problem of community   The fundamental problem in all human communities of finding an acceptable balance between individual freedom and community order

proletariat   The lowest economic and social class, composed of laborers who work for the bourgeoisie — that is, people who have part ownership in the means of production

propaganda   The spreading of information, facts, and values to further a cause; in the Soviet Union, it refers to the efforts of Communist party officials to increase people's awareness of the goals and objectives of the Party

proportional representation   A system where legislative representation is based on party strength, with the number of seats for each party proportional to the popular vote

protest campaign   An organized effort to oppose a policy or action

public interest   The assumed general interests of society, as distinct from the particular interests of groups or individuals

public opinion   The collection of peoples' views and opinions about the affairs of state; involves those opinions that government leaders find it prudent to recognize and, at times, follow

quota   A fixed number or proportion of a whole

raion   A city or district government unit in the Soviet Union

realism   The approach to politics that emphasizes practice rather than ideals, consequences rather than motives

referendum   A vote to determine whether the public supports a proposed change in government

republic   A state without a hereditary chief of state; also, used in the United States synonymously with indirect democracy

Russian Soviet Federal Socialist Republic   The largest union republic in the Soviet Union, comprising more than one-half of the nation's population

sample   A group representing significant traits of the whole community

secretariat   The administrative organization that supports political institutions, such as the Secretariat of the Soviet Union's Communist party or the Secretariat of the United Nations

secularization   The process by which the values of society become secular, scientific, and materialistic as a result of modernization

Security Council   A fifteen-member organ of the United Nations charged with interstate peace keeping; the Security Council is the dominant U.N. institution because of the major role played by the five major powers of the world — China, France, the Soviet Union, the United States, and the United Kingdom.

separation of powers   The doctrine that holds that government decision making should be shared by three distinct branches — legislative, executive, and judiciary

social dualism   The existence of both a modern and traditional culture within a transitional or developing nation

socialism   An economic system where government plays a major role in the production and distribution of goods and services

sovereignty   Supreme authority to make binding decisions within a political community

Soviet   A council or legislative assembly in the Soviet political system

Soviet of Nationalities   The upper house of the Supreme Soviet, the bicameral parliament of the Soviet Union

Soviet of Unions   The lower house of the Supreme Soviet, the national legislature of the Soviet Union

stare decisis   A legal practice by which previous court decisions are recognized as binding unless there is a compelling reason not to do so; literally means "let the decision stand"

state   A political community with people, territory, and a sovereign government

state-building   The process of developing the political and governmental institutions of the state

stratified quota sampling   A technique that seeks to duplicate the dominant characteristics of a population within a sample

subsystem autonomy   A political system in which subsidiary institutions such as unions, churches, and business organizations are largely free of government control

Supreme Soviet   The national bicameral parliament of the Soviet Union

surplus value   In Marxist theory, the additional value produced by labor but appropriated by the owners of businesses

territorial representation   A system where legislative representation is based on territorial units, not popular support for a party

totalitarian   A political system in which the government has significant control over all aspects of life

traditional society   A nonmodern society where science, belief in progress, and secular values are largely absent

uneven development   The Marxist theory that the spread of capitalism results in different levels of economic development within nations as well as between them

unicameral legislature   A legislature with only one chamber

union republic   A territorial unit within the Soviet Union; the USSR is comprised of fifteen such provinces or states

unitary government   A type of government where authority is centralized in national institutions; local and provincial governments have no authority except that which is delegated to them by the central government

vote of no confidence   A practice in parliamentary systems by which legislators can determine whether there is continuing "confidence" in the government; if a resolution of "no confidence" is passed, the prime minister and cabinet resign and new parliamentary elections are held.

war   A state of armed hostilities between states

whip   A party leader who ensures that legislators vote in accordance with the wishes of the party leadership

Whitehall   A street in London where most major British government ministries are located and a term used synonymously for the executive of the United Kingdom

world government   An approach to peace keeping that assumes that the transfer of sovereignty from nation-states to a central government leads to international order

INDEX